LEGAL ETHICS IN CHILD CUSTODY AND DEPENDENCY PROCEEDINGS

This book provides the first fully annotated discussion of the ethical universe surrounding state-mandated and private legal disputes involving the custody and best interest of children. It surveys thousands of court cases, statutes, state bar ethics codes, attorney general opinions, and model codes regarding ethical constraints in family and dependency proceedings. The book is unique in several ways. It analyzes ethical rules not only in terms of the chronology of these proceedings but it also surveys those principles for each of the primary participants – children's counsel, parents' counsel, government attorneys, and judges. The book contains chapters on prehearing alternative dispute resolution, motion and trial practice, appellate procedures, and separation of powers. Finally, the book provides a complete child abuse case file with a comprehensive analysis of the inherent ethical issues.

William Wesley Patton received his B.A. from California State University and his M.A. and J.D. from University of California, Los Angeles. He is the founding director of the Center for Children's Rights and Legal Policy Clinic. He is also a professor and the Associate Dean for Clinical Programs at Whittier Law School. He has written many articles and books on the topic of juvenile justice and juvenile law advocacy.

Legal Ethics in Child Custody and Dependency Proceedings

A GUIDE FOR JUDGES AND LAWYERS

William Wesley Patton
Whittier Law School, Costa Mesa, CA

CAMBRIDGE UNIVERSITY PRESS
Cambridge, New York, Melbourne, Madrid, Cape Town,
Singapore, São Paulo, Delhi, Mexico City

Cambridge University Press
The Edinburgh Building, Cambridge CB2 8RU, UK

Published in the United States of America by
Cambridge University Press, New York

www.cambridge.org
Information on this title: www.cambridge.org/9781107407510

© WilliamWesley Patton 2006

This publication is in copyright. Subject to statutory exception
and to the provisions of relevant collective licensing agreements,
no reproduction of any part may take place without the written
permission of Cambridge University Press.

First published 2006
First paperback edition 2012

A catalogue record for this publication is available from the British Library

Library of Congress Cataloguing in Publication data
Patton, William W., 1946–
Legal ethics in child custody and dependency proceedings : a guide for judges
and lawyers / William W. Patton.
  p. cm.
Includes bibliographical references and index.
ISBN-13: 978-0-521-85317-0 (hardback)
ISBN-10: 0-521-85317-6 (hardback)
1. Legal ethics – United States. 2. Attorney and client – United States.
3. Custody of children – Law and legislation – United States. I. Title.
KF306.P38   2006
346.7301'73 – dc22   2006001020

ISBN 978-0-521-85317-0 Hardback
ISBN 978-1-107-40751-0 Paperback

Cambridge University Press has no responsibility for the persistence or
accuracy of URLs for external or third-party internet websites referred to in
this publication, and does not guarantee that any content on such websites is,
or will remain, accurate or appropriate. Information regarding prices, travel
timetables, and other factual information given in this work is correct at
the time of first printing but Cambridge University Press does not guarantee
the accuracy of such information thereafter.

Contents

Foreword, by Martin Guggenheim	*page*	ix
Acknowledgments		xi

Introduction 1

1 **Conflicts of Interest** 7
    I. Children's Attorneys: Potential Divided Loyalties   7
    II. Conflicts of Interest Involving Parents' Attorneys   13
    III. The Department's Attorney: Who Is the Client?   16
    IV. Judges: Limits and Responsibilities of the Neutral and Detached Magistrate   23

2 **Competent and Zealous Representation** 27
    I. Children's Attorneys: Zealous Advocates or Best Interest Storytellers?   28
        A. Children's Competence as a Key in Deciding the Model of Advocacy   30
        B. The Lawyer's Role as the Child's Guardian Ad Litem   33
        C. Hybrid Models of Child Representation   35
    II. Parents' Attorneys   35
        A. Failure to Complete Lawyering Responsibilities   35
        B. Competence and Zealousness   37
    III. The Department's Attorney: Furthering Justice or Zealous Advocate?   44
    IV. Judges: Neutral Magistrates or Children's Defenders?   52
    V. Emerging Issues Regarding Substitution of Counsel and Self-Representation   61
        A. The Right to Substitute Counsel   61
        B. The Right to Self-Representation   65

3	**Confidentiality**	**68**
	I. Children's Attorneys: Safety Versus Secrecy	69
	II. Parents' Attorneys: Duty to Disclose Child Abuse?	74
	III. The Department's Attorney: Disclosure and Trial Tactics	79
	IV. Judges: Parties' Privacy Versus Public Overseer	82
4	**The Ethics of Alternative Dispute Resolution in Child Custody and Dependency Proceedings**	**88**
	Introduction	88
	I. Alternative Dispute Resolution Versus Litigation in Custody Cases	92
	II. Advantages and Disadvantages of Alternative Dispute Resolution in Child Custody and Dependency Proceedings	95
	III. Coming Full Circle: The Evolution of Child Custody Mediation	100
	IV. The Legitimacy of Informal Settlements and the Limits of Mediators' and Arbitrators' Jurisdiction in Child Custody and Dependency Proceedings	101
	A. Finality and Scope of Arbitrated and Mediated Custody and Dependency Settlement Agreements	102
	B. The Duty of Candor: Good Faith, Puffing, and Lies	107
	V. The Scope of Alternative Dispute Resolution Confidentiality	111
	VI. The Role of the Mediator	117
5	**Ethical Considerations and Constraints in Child Custody and Dependency Appeals**	**120**
	I. The History of the Right to Appointed Appellate Counsel in Child Custody and Dependency Proceedings	121
	II. Standing to Appeal	123
	III. The Duty of Competence in Custody and Dependency Appeals	124
	IV. The Duty and Scope of Zealous Appellate Representation	127
	V. The Duty of Candor and Loyalty on Appeal	134
	VI. The Procedural and Substantive Scope of Appeals	141
6	**The Constitutionality of Legislative and Executive Regulation of the Practice of Law and Defining the Attorney-Client Relationship**	**145**
	I. A Short History of the Role of Courts, Legislatures, and the Executive in the Regulation of Attorneys	148

	A. Wisconsin: Separation of Powers in Regulating Attorneys in Child Custody and Dependency Proceedings	151
	B. California: Comity over Independence?	156
II.	Conclusion	163

Appendix A. National Association of Counsel for Children Standards 165

Appendix B. American Bar Association Standards of Practice for Lawyers Who Represent Children in Abuse and Neglect Cases 185

Appendix C. *In re Car* Simulation and Analysis 223

Other Authorities	239
Cases and Ethics Opinions	247
Index	255

Foreword

The United States spends considerable efforts trying to prove to itself and the world that it is as child-friendly and child-centered as the next country. But this is a difficult challenge for a country that remains alone in the world in its refusal to sign the United Nations Convention on the Rights of the Child, and it remains in the company of many significantly poorer nations in its refusal to guarantee a minimum degree of public support or health benefits for children. Even worse, for those who insist on ranking the United States as a nation devoted to the well-being of children, children comprise the largest group of extremely poor Americans. Worse still, the percentage of the population of children who are poor has grown considerably larger over the past generation, even as the United States has all but eliminated extreme poverty for the elderly.

According to the KIDS COUNT Data Book, published annually by the Annie E. Casey Foundation, there were more than 13 million children living in poverty in the United States in 2003, an increase of more than 500,000 since 2000. More than 4 million children currently live in households where no parent has worked within the past year. The Children's Defense Fund reports that more than 9 million children, more than 12 percent of all of America's children, go without any kind of health insurance.

Nonetheless, the United States is able to point with pride to the very large number of legal matters that are litigated on a daily basis in American courts that affect children and their well-being. These cases include a virtual explosion of child custody, visitation, and relocation cases, as well as an ever-growing number of child welfare cases in which parents are charged with inadequately caring for their children, and related foster care review and termination of parental rights and adoption matters. Add all of these matters together, and the United States plainly is the world leader in the extent to which children are the subject of legal proceedings.

But more is owed children than that the significant questions concerning their lives be decided by judges in contested legal proceedings. Even if one were to regard the extraordinarily high number of cases involving children that are contested each day in the courts within the United States as a positive sign, we should rejoice only if it were true that the investment in the judicial system ensured the level of careful, individualized attention that children require if we are to make thoughtful and intelligent decisions about them.

Regrettably, few jurisdictions in the United States commit sufficient resources to these systems. Instead, too often the children are treated as persons without adults who care very much for or about them. In many cities, legislatures and court officials allow judges routinely to handle as many as fifty cases each day on their dockets. Lawyers assigned to represent children sometimes carry caseloads of more than 300 active cases. And other lawyers performing equally crucial roles in custody and child welfare cases are too often vastly underpaid relative to the other available markets for lawyers, and they are undertrained, undermotivated, or overwhelmed with work to give any given case the level of attention it demands and deserves.

In short, too often in too many quarters in the United States, the justice being meted out in cases involving children is a second-class justice that would be unacceptable to judges, legislators, and voters if it affected them and their families. What can be done about all of this?

In addition to complaining about and recognizing the problem, we need to apply the same principles of fairness, ethics, and justice to matters involving children that we insist be made available to the richest corporations that use the justice system when necessary to advance their interests. An important first step toward eliminating the second-class status of courts that address matters involving children is to pay the same degree of attention to them that is paid to our most important institutions. This means more than acknowledging the ways in which we underfund children's court. It also means insisting upon the same requirements for professional standards that are expected in our most important institutions.

This book is especially important because it strives to clarify and establish basic rules of ethical conduct for children's lawyers and other legal representatives of children, as well as for all of the professionals (including the judges) who handle these cases. Beyond explaining the various roles that different jurisdictions expect of professionals in these cases, this book insists that the standards of representation and professional performance improve, if we are to be true to the call for justice for children and if the justice system affecting children is to live up to the basic rules established elsewhere in the legal profession.

This is an important and worthy goal, and those who care about children would do well to insist on raising the bar for everyone associated with legal matters involving children.

Martin Guggenheim
Professor of Clinical Law
New York University School of Law

Acknowledgments

I wish to express my appreciation to the J. Allan Cook and Mary Schalling Cook Trust Fund for assisting me during my research and writing of this book. Their continued support of children's law scholarship has planted many seeds that will, I hope, produce extensive improvements in poor and abused children's legal access.

I also thank Marvin Ventrell and the National Association of Counsel for Children for permission to publish their *Recommendations for Representation of Children in Abuse and Neglect Cases* and the American Bar Association for granting permission to publish its *Standards of Practice for Lawyers Who Represent Children in Abuse and Neglect Cases.*

This book is dedicated to the hundreds of children I have had the opportunity to represent in custody, dependency, delinquency, and educational proceedings. Although the life of a child advocate can be described as the poet Milton characterized Samson after pulling down the temple pillars, "*all passion spent,*" the hope is that, either incrementally or in one blinding revelation, the legal system will stop failing our children.

Introduction

It is known that approximately 43 percent of marriages in America end in divorce.[1] Even though millions of our children's lives are dramatically affected by the family law child custody system, the shifting character of relationships in the United States is having an equally important impact on children's lives. By 1994 approximately 11 percent of children were born out of wedlock, and 40 percent of American children would live with "their unmarried mother and her boyfriend some time before their 16th birthday...."[2] In 1994 of the 18.6 million children living in single-family homes, two-thirds of those children had one parent as a result of divorce or legal separation.[3] Research has also demonstrated a direct correlation between unwed pregnancy or single-parent families and poverty, poor health, child abuse, and juvenile delinquency.[4] It is therefore not surprising that annually there are more than 2.9 million reports of child abuse in this country and that a significant percentage of those reports result in child dependency actions.[5]

---

[1] *Family and Fertility, National Institute of Child Health & Human Development*, at 2 (2003), http://www.nichd.nih.gov/publications/pubs/coundbsb/sub4.htm#divorce. Contemporary divorce data are incomplete because the marriage and divorce national database administered by the National Center for Health Statistics was eliminated in 1995 "because of lack of resources." COUNTING COUPLES: IMPROVING MARRIAGE, DIVORCE, REMARRIAGE, AND COHABITATION DATA IN THE FEDERAL STATISTICAL SYSTEM, at 25–26 (The Data Collection Committee of the Federal Interagency Forum on Child and Family Services, December 13, 2001).

[2] *Increased Cohabitation Changing Children's Family Settings*, 13 Research on Today's Issues, at 1 (September 2002, Demographic and Behavioral Sciences Branch, Center for Population Research, National Institute of Child Health and Human Development, National Institutes of Health).

[3] Richard Kuhn & John Guidubaldi, Child Custody Policies and Divorce Rates in the United States, Paper presented at the 11th Annual Conference of the Children's Rights Council, at 1 (Washington, D.C. 1997).

[4] *Family and Fertility, supra* note 1, at 9.

[5] John E. Myers, *Definition and Origins of the Backlash Against Child Protection*, in EXCELLENCE IN CHILDREN'S LAW, 21, 32 (National Association of Council for Children, 1994).

Family child custody and child dependency proceedings take up a significant portion of states' judicial calendars. For instance, in California in the 1998–9 fiscal year there were 1,594,807 civil filings.[6] Of those civil filings, there were 155,920 family law cases and 41,890 child dependency proceedings, for a cumulative total of 12.5 percent of all civilly litigated disputes. It is no wonder that, in the more than 1 million child custody and juvenile dependency cases litigated annually in the United States, numerous issues involving legal ethics confound, confuse, and capture the tens of thousands of attorneys litigating these emotionally laden disputes.[7]

Child custody and dependency proceedings are unique legal universes that often involve legal issues that defy the ethical categories articulated by the *American Bar Association Model Rules of Professional Conduct*, state ethical rules, and judicial and executive pronouncements upon best practices and minimum standards of representation. And unlike ordinary civil cases, which are usually permanently resolved in a single judgment, custody and dependency proceedings can continue for years in successive court hearings until the child reaches the age of majority.[8] In these quasi-criminal/quasi-civil systems, notions of zealous advocacy collide with the parties' and court's visions of children's best interests. Attorneys representing abusing parents often find themselves at the cusp of ethical violations of client confidentiality as they struggle with their own conscience in not disclosing their clients' future plans or propensity for reabusing their children. And perhaps to a greater extent than in any other legal area, economic necessity tacitly sanctions conflicts of interests among multiple party representation that would never be tolerated in criminal and/or ordinary civil proceedings. Unconscionably underfunded dependency court systems presumptively permit one attorney to represent multiple siblings unless an actual conflict of interest arises. And in civil custody hearings one or more parents, and usually the children who are the subject of the hearing, do not even have legal representation; if they do, it may be no more than a lay guardian ad litem who frequently, unlike a lawyer, has no duty of confidentiality or loyalty to the client.

But on an even more elemental level, a jurisprudential debate has persisted for almost twenty years regarding whether children in child protection and/or family custody proceedings should be represented by counsel and, if so, what the appropriate model of representation should be. "The questions of when and why counsel should be appointed for children lie at the heart of

---

[6] COURT STATISTICS REPORT: STATEWIDE CASELOAD TRENDS 1989–1990 THROUGH 1998–1999, at 46 (Judicial Council of California, Administrative Office of the Courts, 2000).
[7] *Id.* at 46, 56.
[8] *Child Custody Proceedings Reform: High-Conflict Custody Cases: Reforming the System for Children, Conference Report and Action Plan*, at 1 (American Bar Association Family Law Section, September 8, 2000, http://www.abanet.org/child/wingspread.html).

all dialogue about ethical issues in representing children."[9] In 1984, Martin Guggenheim articulated several reasons why attorneys in child family custody cases are not advisable.[10] Whether the child's attorney adopts the role of fact-finder or zealous advocate, Professor Guggenheim argues that such representation (1) is arbitrary because the child's attorney will merely substitute his or her world view in determining the child's best interest; (2) until the state has proven that the parents neglected or abused their children, the presumption should be that the parents speak for the child's best interest; and (3) taking away parents' decision-making power and placing it in a child's attorney before a finding of abuse may be unconstitutional.[11] He further argues that even if the petition is sustained, counsel serves no real purpose until the child is at least 7 years old and has sufficient capacity to assist the attorney. If the child is not competent to assist in the case, the child's attorney is not only "irrelevant; having counsel is also potentially destructive of our legal process" because the attorney as fact-finder supplants the role of judge as fact-finder.[12] Professor Guggenheim further argues that providing counsel for children in family custody cases needlessly "becomes an invitation to pry into the personal affairs of the separating spouses," thus stripping parents of their right to decide what secrets will be publicly revealed. Professor Guggenheim has recently demonstrated that at the heart of the United States Supreme Court opinions regarding children's rights is a core principle that children's rights, vis-à-vis the government, are best protected by focusing on parental rights, not children's autonomy. "Simply stated, the bulk of laws affecting children and the law in the United States are interwoven with the laws of parental authority. One can fully grasp the complete scope of children's rights under American law only by knowing the rights of their parents."[13] He argues that a best interest of the child standard, rather than a parental rights doctrine, leads to unnecessary state intervention into family lives: "Any alternative to the parental rights doctrine empowers state officials to meddle into family affairs and base their decisions on their own values.... A best interests inquiry is not a neutral investigation that leads to an obvious result. It is an intensely value-laden inquiry. And it cannot be otherwise."[14]

John E. B. Myers has gone even further in arguing that parties in child protection cases, including children, meet informally with a judge, without any attorneys, in a form of alternative dispute resolution in which the rules of evidence are suspended, all information disclosed is confidential, and the

---

[9] Catherine J. Ross, *From Vulnerability to Voice: Appointing Counsel for Children in Civil Litigation*, 64 FORDHAM L. REV. 1571, 1618 (1996).
[10] Martin Guggenheim, *The Right To Be Represented but Not Heard: Reflections on Legal Representation For Children*, 59 N. Y. U. L. REV. 76 (1984).
[11] *Id.* at 127.   [12] *Id.* at 102.
[13] Martin Guggenheim, WHAT'S WRONG WITH CHILDREN'S RIGHTS 17 (2005).
[14] *Id.* at 38–39.

"judge decides what is needed to help the family and keep the child safe. The judge discusses her ideas with the others, and comes to a resolution."[15] And Emily Buss articulates a child's attorney role as neutral observer who does not express an opinion regarding the child's best interest, but who rather ensures that the process operates fairly and that the other attorneys perform competently.[16]

But even if a state decides to appoint counsel for children in abuse and neglect proceedings and in family law custody cases, at what age does the child have capacity to determine the goals of the litigation and his or her best interest? The problem is that the child psychological developmental literature does not provide "definitive, fixed information upon which to ground simple, age-based rules."[17] Generalizations regarding the minimum age of competency to make legal decisions and to assist counsel in child abuse and family law proceedings vary from age 7 to 15 before a child can make a reasoned choice among legal alternatives.[18] Other developmental psychologists argue that legal policymakers miss the point when they classify children as merely too young to have capacity or as old enough to make decisions because they ignore the "transitional developmental stage" of adolescence and because "children cross over the line to legal adulthood at different ages for different purposes."[19] Even though legislators persist in using categorical age of majority rules for different social activities, such as driving, drinking, and voting, the use of categorical age limits in defining children's competency to assist in their legal proceedings is not helpful because each child's developmental pace is different; age brackets are at once underinclusive and overinclusive when applied to individual children's developmental capacity for decision making.[20] Elizabeth Scott and Thomas Grisso provide the following assessment of the child developmental literature: "[S]cientific authority indicates that, in general, the cognitive capacity for reasoning and understanding of preadolescents and many younger teens differs substantially in some regards

---

[15] John E. B. Myers, *Session 3: Children's Rights in the Context of Welfare, Dependency, and the Juvenile Court*, 8 U.C. DAVIS J. JUV. L. & POL'Y 267, 285–286 (2004).

[16] Emily Buss, *Confronting Developmental Barriers to the Empowerment of Child Clients*, 84 CORNELL L. REV. 895 (1999).

[17] *Id.* at 919.

[18] *Id.* at 920; Thomas Grisso, *What We Know about Youth's Capacities as Trial Defendants*, in Thomas Grisso & Robert G. Schwartz, YOUTH ON TRIAL: A DEVELOPMENTAL PERSPECTIVE ON JUVENILE JUSTICE 162–163 (2000); Guggenheim, at 86 ["accord children seven years of age and older the power to direct their own counsel in delinquency proceedings"].

[19] Elizabeth S. Scott, *The Legal Construction of Adolesence*, 29 HOFSTRA L. REV. 547, 548, 557–558 (2000).

[20] *Id.* at 560. ["In fact, one likely effect of the categorical approach is that minors will sometimes continue to be treated as legal children when they are competent to make decisions or perform adult functions."]

Introduction

from that of older teens and adults. Tentative authority also supports the conclusion that, by mid-adolescence, youthful capacities for reasoning and understanding approximate those of adults."[21] Therefore, it is clear that the minimal American Bar Association rules for representing child clients provide attorneys with far too little guidance regarding when the child client possesses sufficient capacity to direct the litigation.[22]

Attorneys representing parents and/or children in custody and dependency proceedings are often required to meet standards of representation that are substantially more demanding than those of the average practitioner. For instance, in California, even though the California Supreme Court has held that attorneys, once sworn into office, are presumptively competent to represent any party in any court in the state,[23] dependency attorneys must establish "minimum standards of experience and education" in order to represent a party,[24] including "training and education in the areas of substance abuse and domestic violence... [and] child development...."[25] The dissonance between these elevated standards of competence and the unrealistically high caseloads in these expedited proceedings provides attorneys with a nightmare Catch-22 scenario in which the more competently they represent some clients, the less competently they represent others in this zero-sum legal universe. The excessively large attorney caseloads in these proceedings often lead to a statistically deterministic certainty of incompetent representation in a high percentage of cases.[26]

---

[21] Elizabeth S. Scott & Thomas Grisso, *The Evolution of Adolescence: A Developmental Perspective on Juvenile Justice Reform*, 88 J. CRIM. L. & CRIMINOLOGY 137, 160 (1997).

[22] *American Bar Association Rule MR 1.14* provides: (a) When a client's ability to make adequately considered decisions in connection with the representation is impaired... because of minority... the lawyer shall, as far as reasonably possible, maintain a normal client-lawyer relationship with the client; (b) A lawyer may seek the appointment of a guardian or take other protective action with respect to a client only when the lawyer reasonably believes the client adequately act in the client's own interest."

[23] The California Supreme Court in *Smith v. Superior Court*, 440 P. 2d 65, 73 (Cal. 1968) held that "[t]he admission of an attorney to the bar establishes that the State deems him competent to undertake the practice of law before all our courts, in all types of actions."

[24] *California Welfare & Institutions Code § 317.5*.

[25] *California Rules of Court, Rule 1438*.

[26] For instance, in 1991, the County of Los Angeles, California paid private dependency attorneys $9,839,971.22; however, by 1998 that cost rose to $16,510,750. PACE SYSTEM APPOINTEE EARNINGS SUMMARY REPORT OF THE LOS ANGELES SUPERIOR COURT MP DISTRICT FOR APPOINTEE TYPES, ALL JUVENILE DEPENDENCY CASES 07/02/97 THROUGH 06/29/98, at 15; January 22, 1990, Dependency Court Legal Services Contract, at 1. And in 1998 in Los Angeles County parents' dependency attorneys had caseloads of between 413 and 658 cases. PACE SYSTEM, *supra*, at 1–15. And each of those dependency cases was compensated at a flat rate of just $380 per case. Amy Bentley, *Ventura Defense Attorneys Fear Dependency Court System Unfair*, L. A. DAILY J., Jan. 7, 1999, at 3.

Judges often fare no better because it is sometimes impossible to remain a "neutral and detached magistrate" when the judicial officer sees that incompetent counsel for one or more parties might result in a disposition that is dangerous for the children before the court. But what defines the ethical cusp between the judge ensuring fairness in the hearing and exceeding those ethical bounds by becoming the equivalent to a zealous advocate for the child? How can and should the judge react to media reports that intimate that a specific case before the court resulted in a travesty of injustice? How does the judge meet the ethical duty to educate the public regarding the legal system without commenting on the confidential proceedings or without prejudicing parties before the courts? And what should be the ethical response of judges to the overburdened child dependency system in which precious court resources pressure judges and attorneys to litigate fundamental rights to child custody and termination of parental rights in approximately ten to twenty minutes per case?[27] How do judges resolve the internal conflict of interest between the "whistle-blower" persona that can ensure a more accurate and accountable legal system and the rise up the judicial ladder, which often requires political deftness and understated service?

And finally, how should counsel representing the Department of Family and Children's Services handle the many ethical conundrums that must be resolved on a daily basis? What are the bounds of advocacy for these government lawyers? What data must be disclosed *sua sponte*, who is the client, and what rules apply when a social worker is civilly sued for malpractice and the Department attempts to avoid liability by claiming that the worker's acts were outside the scope of employment?

These are the many issues upon which this book revolves. To provide guidance to judges, government attorneys, and counsel for both parents and children, the following chapters review several sets of ethical standards, judicial cases, attorney general opinions, and state bar ethics opinions. Although many of these terribly complex ethical maelstroms require answers yet to be written, this text provides the foundation for identifying and analyzing attorneys' ethical duties. Although it might be impossible to practice law for an entire career without violating ethical precepts, a judgment tempered through analysis of existing ethical precedent is likely to benefit both attorneys and clients. It is with this goal that I offer the following analyses of the ethical issues involved in representing parties in child custody and dependency proceedings.

---

[27] For instance, in Los Angeles County, dependency judges hear "five to ten new cases and as many as 25 reviews a day of cases already under court jurisdiction." William Wesley Patton, *Forever Torn Asunder: Charting Evidentiary Parameters, The Right to Competent Counsel and the Privilege Against Self-Incrimination in California Child Dependency and Parental Severance Cases*, 27 SANTA CLARA L. REV. 299, 301 (1987).

1 Conflicts of Interest

It might seem unusual for a book on legal ethics to begin with the complicated issue of conflicts of interest. However, if an attorney waits until after the initial client interview to determine whether a conflict exists or is likely to develop during representation, the attorney might prejudice the client by having to conflict off the case at some later time. Conflicting off the case will not only lengthen the litigation time-line by requiring another attorney to prepare the case but also will increase the client's emotional trauma inherent in contested litigation. Therefore, before an attorney considers the detailed facts inherent in any case, engages in an intake or initial client interview, and even reviews all the available evidence, counsel should consider actual and potential conflicts of interest. Furthermore, it is essential for counsel to continually assess conflicts questions until the completion of the client's representation.

I. CHILDREN'S ATTORNEYS: POTENTIAL DIVIDED LOYALTIES

Because of the tremendous expense of representing parties in child dependency cases, one money-saving shortcut is to use a system in which a single legal office represents multiple parties.[1] For instance, a government attorney office, such as a county counsel, district attorney, or public defender office, might represent parents, children, and/or the Department of Child and Family Services in different cases. However, because of the possibility of

---

[1] In recent years Congress and state legislatures have not only limited funds for representing indigents based upon budget concerns but also the types of cases that legal services attorneys can file on behalf of their clients. However, the United States Supreme Court in *Legal Servs. Corp. v. Velazquez,* 531 U.S. 533 (2001) limited the legislature's control over the ambit of attorneys' zealous representation by declaring that such restrictions violate separation of powers and/or First Amendment principles. *See* Laura K. Abel & David S. Udell, *If You Gag the Lawyers, Do You Choke the Courts? Some Implications for Judges When Funding Restrictions Curb Advocacy by Lawyers on Behalf of the Poor,* 29 FORDHAM URB. L. J. 873 (2002).

conflicts of interest, disclosure of confidential data, and breaches of loyalty, such multiparty representation usually violates the canon of ethics. For instance, in *Illinois State Bar Association Opinion No. 91-17*[2] a public defender's office represented both parents and children in child neglect proceedings. The attorneys shared a common office, secretaries, and investigatory services. The Illinois State Bar held that this shared arrangement involved an obvious ethical violation because parents and children are often, if not usually, in conflict in these cases and confidential material may be shared among different public defenders representing adverse parties. The Illinois State Bar Ethics Committee held that if the public defenders did not share secretaries or investigators and had independent law practices sufficiently shielded from one another, then no conflict would exist.[3] It further held that the shared lawyering context was not only unfair to the parent and child clients but also "to attorneys themselves. Public defenders have no immunity from malpractice actions... [and] probably are vulnerable to federal civil rights actions...."[4]

In *Appeal in Yavapai County Juvenile Action No.J-8545*[5] the Arizona Supreme Court held that the trial court erred when it refused to appoint separate counsel for the children, rather than having them represented by parents' or prospective custodians' counsel, because those individuals "would each be pursuing their individual interests at the proceedings and not necessarily the best interest of the children."[6] The Arizona Supreme Court rejected the trial court's logic in refusing to appoint counsel for the children merely because they were currently in custody in another state.

The most frequent type of multiple representation in child dependency cases involves one attorney representing several siblings. Conceptually and economically, such multiple representation seems to be a good policy. A single attorney representative for sibling groups could coordinate all the children's needs, see the total family picture from the perspective of all the children, and save the taxpayers millions of dollars in legal fees as well. However, representation of sibling groups is fraught with numerous actual and probable conflicts.[7]

Consider the following hypothetical:

> An attorney is appointed to represent a sibling group comprising seven children ages 3, 4, 5, 6, 8, 11, and 12 in a child dependency action. The

---

[2] Illinois State Bar Association Opinion No. 91–17 (January, 1992).
[3] *Id.* at 3–4. [4] *Id.* at 4.
[5] *Appeal in Yavapai County Juvenile Action No. J-8545*, 680 P. 2d 146 (Arizona 1984).
[6] *Id.* at 148.
[7] A discussion of the conflicts between the child's stated preference and the attorney's opinion regarding the child's best interest is discussed, *infra*, in Chapter 2, Competent and Zealous Representation.

Department argued that the 8-, 11-, and 12-year-old children should be placed in long-term foster care or guardianship because they were unadoptable; that the 4-, 5-, and 6-year-old children should be placed for adoption; and that the 3-year-old should be placed separately in a placement that could care for the child's special needs.[8]

In the abstract, if the Department's recommendations were accurate and in the children's best interests, and not in opposition to the children's stated preferences, nothing seems to prevent multiple representation in this case. However, during the attorney's initial interviews with the children, he discovered the following information: (1) the 3-year-old was very closely bonded with the 8-, 11-, and 12-year-old children and (2) many of the children in the three placement groups wanted to continue sibling association and visitation even after the termination of parental rights. The court in *Carroll v. Superior Court*[9] determined that there were numerous actual and several probable conflicts of interest inherent in one attorney representing all of the siblings in this case because termination of parental rights and adoption would end the legal relationship among the siblings and make fulfillment of their desire to continue sibling association unlikely. The court noted that zealously arguing for adoption of the 3-year-old child would, in effect, argue against the other children's desires to have continuing postadoption contact with her. The court also noted that some siblings might forgo their right to argue for their best interests in order to assist a permanent placement of a brother or sister that was in that child's best interest but that would result in a severance of sibling association. Because the attorney had interviewed all the children in the case and had established an attorney-client relationship with each child, the only remedy consistent with the requirements of confidentiality and client loyalty was for the attorney to conflict off the representation of all of the siblings: "[T]he attorney must be relieved from representation of any of the minors ... [and] an attorney may not be appointed to represent multiple minors if it is reasonably likely an actual conflict of interest between or among them may arise."[10]

Conflicts of interest in representing multiple siblings also arise in contexts in which one attorney discovers, through interviews, confidential information that will assist one sibling but will harm the others. For instance, assume that an attorney is appointed in a child dependency action to represent three children, ages 14(sister), 11(brother), and (sister) 6. The petition alleges sexual abuse by the mother's boyfriend of the 14-year-old sister and that the 11-year-old brother once saw the mother's boyfriend lying on top of his

---

[8] These facts are based upon *Carroll v. Superior Court*, 124 Cal. Rptr. 2d 891 (Cal. App. Ct. 2002).
[9] *Id.* at 894–897.   [10] *Id.* at 897.

14-year-old sister on the couch. Also assume that the 11-year-old brother informs the attorney that he wants his statements to remain confidential. The 14-year-old sister informs that attorney that she wants to be placed outside the home, but wants continuing contact with her siblings. The 11- and 6-year-old children want to remain in the home. The attorney is thus faced with an actual conflict of interest because he now possesses data that can assist the 14-year-old in proving the sexual abuse case and make her removal from the home more likely. However, if the attorney uses that confidential information, the attorney would violate the duty of loyalty and confidentiality to the 11-year-old brother. In addition, because the use of that confidential data may inform the court that the 6-year-old sister may also be at risk of sexual abuse by the mother's boyfriend, the use of that data would frustrate her desire to stay at home with her mother rather than being placed in relative or foster care.

Although providing siblings with separate counsel in custody and dependency proceedings will undoubtedly increase the cost of legal representation, there is a sound reason why some courts have held that "any doubt about the existence of a conflict [in representing an abused child] should be resolved in favor of disqualification."[11] The American Bar Association has described an adult client's reaction to conflicts of interest in legal representation as a feeling of betrayal and a "fear that the lawyer will pursue that client's case less effectively out of deference to the other client...."[12] But the effect on abused children is substantially greater: "The abused child, already betrayed by a trusted adult, has finally taken a substantial emotional risk by having faith in her attorney. She has relied upon the attorney to protect and argue her case. What must she think when yet another trusted adult abandons her? The jurogenic effects of the legal system re-victimize the child."[13]

It is thus critical for attorneys to determine whether actual or potential conflicts of interest are inherent and probable in the representation of multiple sibling groups. To calculate the potential for conflicts of interest, the attorney should consider the following factors. First, the greater the age gap between the siblings, the higher the risk for a conflict of interest. This is because young siblings are much more likely to be adoptable and to have their parental rights severed than are older children. For instance, even if a 2-year-old and a 15-year-old have psychologically bonded, many courts have determined that the older child will be placed in long-term

---

[11] *In the Matter of H.Children*, 608 N.Y.S. 2d 784, 785 (New York 1994).
[12] Model Rules of Professional Conduct Rule 1.7, comment 6.
[13] William Wesley Patton, *The Interrelationship Between Sibling Custody and Visitation and Conflicts of Interest in the Representation of Multiple Siblings in Dependency Proceedings*, 23 CHILD. LEGAL RTS. J. 18, 29 (2003).

foster or relative care while the younger child will be adopted.[14] Second, if one of more siblings have special needs, it increases exponentially the chances that the children will be ordered into different placements. For example, in *Adoption of Hugo*[15] the court refused to place a 2-year-old boy with special needs in the same adoptive home with his 6-year-old sister because it determined that the paternal aunt had the special training needed to care for the special needs child. Although the Massachusetts Supreme Court found that sibling association is important, it held that the best interest of placing the younger child in a home in which a relative could care for his special needs was more important than continuing the sibling relationship.[16]

Third, the strength of sibling bonds among siblings, as well as between siblings and foster parents, will often determine conflicts of interest that might arise because closely bonded siblings are more likely to argue that they should be placed together. For instance, in *In the Interests of David A*,[17] two siblings who had close psychological bonds with one another were placed into different foster homes. At the termination of parental rights hearing, the court rejected placing both siblings into the same placement because, even though they were bonded to each other, the court found that they were also bonded to their separate foster parents and that separation from the foster parents would cause the children substantial psychological harm.[18]

Fourth, the availability of placements with relatives should be considered. Many jurisdiction have a statutory presumption for relative placement if placement cannot be made in one or both parents' homes.[19] If siblings are placed with the same or with different relatives, association issues are less likely to arise, which decreases the probability of conflicts among the siblings. However, a large percentage of out-of-home custody awards do not involve relatives. For instance, "of California's 98,000 children under court supervision, sixty percent had siblings, but 'forty-one percent were not living in the

---

[14] For an analysis of cases in which psychologically bonded siblings have been placed separately and cases in which the siblings' association rights have been severed, *see* William Wesley Patton & Dr. Sara Latz, *Severing Hansel from Gretel: An Analysis of Siblings' Association Rights*, 48 U. MIAMI L. REV. 745 (1994); William Wesley Patton, *The Status of Siblings' Rights: A View into the New Millennium*, 51 DEPAUL L. REV. 1 (2001).

[15] *Adoption of Hugo*, 700 N. E. 2nd 516 (Mass. 1998), cert. denied, 526 U.S. 1034 (1999).

[16] *Id.* at 524.

[17] *In the Interests of David A.*, 1998 WL 910258 (Conn. Super Ct., Dec. 18, 1998).

[18] *Id.* at 5.

[19] For instance, *California Welfare & Institutions Code* § 361.2 provides a hierarchy or presumptive placements first with both parents, then one parent, then relatives, next with a "nonrelative extended family member," then a foster home, and finally with a licensed community care facility, foster family agency, or a group home.

same foster home ... [and] [f]orty-eight percent of siblings in foster care do not live with relatives.'"[20]

The California Supreme Court in *In re Celine R.*[21] established perhaps the most rigorous standards in the nation regarding conflicts of interest in representing multiple siblings.[22] *Celine R.* is remarkable not only for its heightened tests for conflicts of interests among siblings but also because the Department's attorney attempted to persuade the California Supreme Court that the rules of professional responsibility, and in particular, the prohibition against representation of clients whose interests conflict, should not apply to juvenile clients. The Department's attorney urged that the Supreme Court "hold that the Rules of Professional Responsibility cannot and do not apply strictly to attorneys representing minors in juvenile dependency proceedings...."[23] The California Supreme Court was, needless to say, hostile to that position at oral argument and rejected the reasoning.[24] Instead, the court established a rule that "an attorney may not represent multiple clients if an actual conflict of interest between clients exists and may not accept representation of multiple clients if there is a reasonable likelihood an actual conflict of interest between them may arise."[25] In addition, the court held that, whenever an actual conflict of interest arises, "the court will have to relieve counsel from multiple representation" and the attorney may not represent any of the siblings.[26]

However, the California Supreme Court further held that the standard for reversible error is identical to the standard of error in cases in which children were erroneously denied representation. The children must prove on appeal that it is "reasonably probable the result would have been more favorable to the appealing party [siblings] but for the error."[27] The California Supreme Court in *In re Celine R.* thus created a rigorous standard for determining whether conflicts of interest exist, but created such a demanding standard of prejudice that rarely will such conflict result in a reversal of the dependency trial court judgment.

---

[20] William Wesley Patton, *supra* note 12, at 19; Rod Kodman, *Re–Victimizing Innocent Victims: How California Violates the Constitutional Rights of Its Abused and Neglected Children*, 4 J. L. & POL'Y 67, 87 (2000).

[21] *In re Celine R.*, 1 Cal. Rptr. 3d 432 (2003).

[22] The author orally argued *In re Celine R.* in the California Supreme Court.

[23] Respondent's Answer Brief on the Merits in *In re Celine R.*, filed in the California Supreme Court on April 15, 2003, at page 29 (copy in author's files).

[24] *Id.* at 441.   [25] *Id.* at 442.

[26] *Id.* at 442.

[27] *Id.* at 444. For an extensive analysis of the appropriate standards of appellate review in child dependency proceedings, *see* William Wesley Patton, *Standards of Appellate Review for Denial of Counsel and Ineffective Assistance of Counsel in Child Protection and Parental Severance Cases*, 27 LAY. U. CHI. L. J. 195 (1996).

Whether the children will have a malpractice action against their dependency court attorney will depend upon the malpractice standard adopted in the jurisdiction. If that standard requires that the plaintiff demonstrate that a more favorable outcome would have occurred absent the malpractice, the children may find themselves in the same dilemma as under the *In re Celine R.* remedy.

The Massachusetts Supreme Court in *Care and Protection of Georgette*[28] reached a similar conclusion in a multiple sibling case in which one attorney represented four sisters (Beth, Judith, Georgette, and Lucy) in a termination of parental rights proceeding. The trial court terminated the father's rights to Beth and Judith, but placed Georgette and Lucy in the permanent custody of the Department of Social Services. Georgette and Lucy appealed based upon a claim of ineffective assistance of counsel because the trial counsel who represented all four sisters argued conflicting interests and refused to zealously argue Georgette's and Lucy's desire to remain in their father's home.[29] Although the Massachusetts Supreme Court ratified the siblings' rights against conflicts of interest in their legal representation, the court held that the sisters "failed to demonstrate any prejudice based upon the overwhelming proof of the father's unfitness."[30] However, the court was dissatisfied with the current status of professional rules regarding conflicts of interest in representing children and recommended that the "standing advisory committee on the rules of professional conduct" devise new ethical standards for the representation of abused children.[31]

II. CONFLICTS OF INTEREST INVOLVING PARENTS' ATTORNEYS

Parents' counsel have frequently run into ethical problems when representing both a mother and a father in child custody or dependency proceedings, even if the attorney attempted to secure waivers regarding conflicts of interest. For example, in *Oklahoma Bar Association v. Max M. Berry*[32] an attorney represented a wife in a divorce proceeding, but she discharged him and retained new counsel. After the husband and wife remarried, they again divorced three years later, and this time the attorney represented the husband. Even though the wife informed the attorney that it was inappropriate to represent her husband because he had earlier represented her in the prior divorce, the attorney continued to represent her husband. The Oklahoma

---

[28] *Care and Protection of Georgette*, 785 N. E. 2d 356 (2003).
[29] *Id.* at 358–361.   [30] *Id.* at 361.
[31] *Id.* at 367–368.
[32] *Oklahoma Bar Association v. Max M. Berry*, 969 P. 2d 975 (Oklahoma 1998).

Supreme Court held that the attorney engaged in a conflict of interest that also breached his duty of loyalty to the wife.[33]

In a more egregious conflict of interest case, *Kentucky Bar Association v. Ronald A. Newcomer*,[34] a mother in an initial interview of a contested custody case disclosed confidential data to an attorney. Because the mother lacked sufficient funds to hire the attorney, she proceeded *in propria persona*. However, at the custody hearing the same attorney represented the father and disclosed confidential information gleaned during his initial interview with the mother. The Kentucky Supreme Court suspended the attorney for three years for violating the rule against conflicts of interest and for divulging confidential information obtained during the initial client interview with the mother.[35]

Although conflicts of interests are quite apparent when an attorney represents two clients with conflicting interests in the same proceeding, it is more difficult to determine whether an attorney can represent parties in separate and/or collateral proceedings. For instance, in *In the Matters of the Commitment of the Guardianship and Custody of Destiny D.*,[36] the New York City Legal Aid Society Criminal Division represented a father in a criminal proceeding based upon child abuse. The New York City Legal Aid Society Juvenile Rights Division was also representing the abused children in a termination of parental rights proceeding based, in part, on the facts underlying the father's criminal case. The father informed the Legal Aid Society that it should not represent the children because of a possible conflict of interest and a potential breach of confidentiality. A family court judge denied the father's conflict motion and held that the father must demonstrate (1) a prior attorney-client relationship with the Legal Aid Society, (2) a substantial relationship between the dual representations, and (3) "that the interests of the children in these proceedings are materially adverse to the matters in which the attorney or firm previously represented."[37] The court determined that there was not a sufficient conflict to require withdrawal because the Juvenile Division of the Legal Aid Society never represented the father, because the issues in the criminal trial and the termination hearing were "sufficiently dissimilar," and because there was merely "speculation" that confidential information from the father's criminal representation would be disclosed. The New York court thus set a very high threshold to prove a conflict of

---

[33] *Id.* at 976–977.
[34] *Kentucky Bar Association v. Ronald A. Newcomer*, 977 S. w. 2d 20 (Kentucky 1998).
[35] *Id.* at 21–22. *See also The Florida Bar v. Walter Benton Dunagan*, 731 So. 2d 1237 (Florida 1999).
[36] *In the Matter of Glen L. Houston*, N.Y.S. 2d (Nov. 14, 2002) [not reported; Westlaw Allstates database].
[37] *Id.*

Conflicts of Interest

interest between cases represented by separate divisions of a governmental legal services office. One must wonder whether a narrower test would apply to conflicts of interest within different branches of a private civil or criminal law firm.

In *In the Matter of Glen L. Houston*[38] an attorney was retained by a mother in a divorce action. Subsequently, the mother informed the attorney that the father had sexually molested her daughter, and the attorney advised the mother to file a domestic violence petition. The husband was arrested for sexual abuse and domestic violence. "At the request of the husband, and with the consent of wife," the attorney agreed to represent the husband in the criminal action.[39] The husband was sentenced to three years in prison. The attorney never informed the wife that, if she consented to the representation, she and her daughter might be called as witnesses, and after the conviction the attorney never informed the wife that she could seek a custody modification under the divorce limiting the father's access to the child. Even after the wife said that she did not want the husband to have visitation, the attorney protected the husband's interest to the disadvantage of the wife "by entering a decree containing joint custody and unsupervised visitation" for the husband.[40] The court found that there was a clear conflict of interest even though the attorney represented the two clients in separate proceedings and also held that the wife's consent to the conflict was not valid because the attorney had not properly counseled her regarding the consequences of the conflict waiver.[41] The attorney was suspended for eighteen months.[42]

In a similar case, *Board of Bar Overseers Office of the Bar Counsel Massachusetts Bar Disciplinary Decisions, Admonition 00–68*,[43] a law firm simultaneously represented a mother charged with child abuse and in an unrelated matter also represented the father of the child. Subsequently, a police report made it clear that the father would be an adverse witness against the mother in the child abuse action. The Massachusetts Bar Disciplinary Committee found a clear conflict of interest because the state professional responsibility law treated lawyers within an office identically to a single lawyer representing two clients with conflicts of interest: "Mass. R. Prof. C. 1.10(a) provides that, while lawyers are associated in a firm, none of them shall knowingly represent a client when any one of them practicing alone would be prohibited from doing so by the rules on conflict of interest."[44] The attorney received only a

---

[38] *In the Matter of Glen L. Houston*, 985 P. 2d 752 (New Mexico 1999).
[39] *Id.* at 753.   [40] *Id.* at 754.
[41] *Id.* at 755–756.   [42] *Id.* at 756.
[43] *Board of Bar Overseers Office of the Bar Counsel Massachusetts Bar Disciplinary Decisions, Admonition 00–68*, 2000 WL 34200490 (2000).
[44] *Id.*

private admonition because he "mistakenly believed that since the father did not file the neglect and abuse complaint, he was not adverse" to the mother's interests.[45]

Attorneys should rarely accept dual representation of mothers and fathers in child dependency proceedings in which only one of the parents is alleged to have abused their children because of the high potential for conflicts of interest. It is very common for the nonabusing parent to appear supportive of the abusive parent at an initial client interview based upon (1) a true belief that the abuse allegation is untrue; (2) a sense of duty to one's spouse or lover even if the abuse occurred; (3) fear derived from threats by the abusive spouse; or (4) a fear that cooperation with the Department might lead to loss of the abusing spouse during a period of incarceration in the criminal case, which might reduce the economic vitality of the family. Even if the nonabusing spouse consents to dual representation, the attorney should reluctantly represent both spouses because often, deep into the dependency case, the nonoffending spouse's position may be altered dramatically in two ways. First, the Department may amend the petition to allege that the nonoffending parent knew of the abuse but failed to report it or to protect the children from the abusing parent. And second, the Department may pose a disposition alternative in which the nonoffending parent will have to elect between the marriage relationship and the relationship with her children. One of the most common disposition alternatives is to require the nonabusing parent to elect between allowing an abusing spouse or boyfriend to live in the children's home or to eject him and retain custody of her children. Because of the inherent conflicts in defending the offending and nonoffending parents or lovers, an attorney should rarely, if ever, represent both parties in child dependency and/or child custody proceedings.

III. THE DEPARTMENT'S ATTORNEY: WHO IS THE CLIENT?

Although historically both the legislature and courts have held that the same attorney could represent both the Department and the child abuse victim, contemporary cases have indicated that such dual representation is at the very least a bad policy and at worst an insoluble conflict of interest.[46] A

---

[45] *Id.* For a discussion regarding a conflict of interest in representing adverse parties in separate paternity and guardianship proceedings, *see The Florida Bar v. Jeffrey Evan Cosnow*, 797 So. 2d 1255, 1259 (Florida 2001), in which the Florida Supreme Court issued a sixty-day suspension and a one-year probation sentence.

[46] In 2000 the California legislature deleted county counsel as one of the governmental attorneys available to represent children under *California Welfare & Institutions Code § 317 (c)*. In addition, in *Los Angeles County Dept. Children's Services v. Superior Court*, 7 Cal. 4th 525 (1996), the court rejected county counsel's argument that trial courts could not determine

Department attorney who also represents abused children will be placed in a dilemma of receiving confidential information from the child that the attorney cannot disclose to the Department without the consent of the child. Thus, the attorney will either have to violate his duty of zealousness and competence owed to the Department or violate his duty of confidentiality owed to the child.[47]

Although the Department historically has argued that it represents the best interest of children, internal budgetary pressures often pit the needs of the child against the services available to the Department. "The presence of perverse incentives in the child welfare system is not uncommon. In several areas, the availability of funding, rather than the family's needs, may dictate the service chosen."[48] For instance, in the current era of diminishing public funds and fewer prospective adoptive parents for abused children, the federal government provides states with adoption subsidies that bring in tremendous revenue.[49] The revenue implications of placing a child in an adoptive home with the federal adoption subsidy, rather than placement with a relative or

---

as a matter of policy that county counsel not be appointed to represent children. In addition, Senate Bill 2160 provided that as of July 1, 2001 the social worker, represented by county counsel, can no longer qualify as the child's guardian ad litem and *Welfare and Institutions Code § 326* was repealed.

[47] For instance, the *City of New York Committee on Professional and Judicial Ethics, in Opinion Number 1997-2* (March 1997), at 13–14, concluded, "A lawyer employed by a social services agency generally must preserve confidences and secrets relating to the abuse or mistreatment of a minor client ... [and] [w]ithout client consent, the lawyer may not disclose client confidences or secrets to others employed by the agency unless the lawyer determines that the agency employees would preserve the confidentiality of the disclosures." Another possible problem is that any information shared with the Department might be disclosed to a criminal prosecutor and that evidence might be used against the child or other family members in a criminal prosecution. For instance, in *North Dakota Attorney General Opinion* (December 9, 1999) [1999 WL 1939465] it was held that prosecutors can share data discovered in juvenile proceedings with other prosecutors handling related criminal cases without creating a conflict of interest. And some state child abuse registries mandate disclosure to law enforcement of any data regarding child abuse allegations. *See, e.g., California Penal Code § 11169*: "An agency ... shall forward to the Department of Justice a report in writing of every case it investigates of known or suspected child abuse or severe neglect which is determined not to be unfounded...." Under certain circumstances, mandated child abuse reporters, while working in a different capacity, such as a member of a board of directors of a child abuse prevention program not run by the Department of Child and Family Services, "do not have a reporting duty...." *Oregon Attorney General Opinion Number OP –5543* (June 12, 1984) at 1–2 [1984 WL 192140].

[48] Steven Wilker, *Child Abuse, Substance Abuse, and the Role of the Dependency Court*, 7 HVBLJ 1 (1990) [West Law 7 HARV. BLACKLETTER J. 1 (page reference numbers not available).

[49] "California received $3.9 million last year [1999], the first year of the [adoption] incentive program"; in Los Angeles there was a 65 percent increase in adoptions and in Orange County there were "351 adoptions, a two year increase of 48%." James Rainey, *Foster Child Adoptions Soar in California*, L. A. TIMES, Orange County Edition, May 8, 2000, at A22.

foster parent that is not equally federally subsidized, have a clear and strong influence on the Department's choice of child placement.[50]

Even though California attorneys who represent the Department of Child and Family Services have fought for decades to retain the right to represent both the Department and abused children,[51] an often overlooked comment to *American Bar Association Model Rules of Professional Conduct, Rule 1.7*, which defines conflicts of interest, demonstrates that such dual representation by the Department is ethically problematic. *Comment, paragraph 5* provides the following test to determine whether an attorney should even attempt to obtain clients' consent to dual representation: "[W]hen a disinterested lawyer would conclude that the client should not agree to the representation under the circumstances, the lawyer involved cannot properly ask for such agreement or provide representation on the basis of the client's consent." One might ask whether knowing the potential and actual conflicts of interest inherent in dual representation of the Department and the abused child could lead any "disinterested lawyer" to conclude that that relationship is truly in the child's best interest, especially because other attorneys without such conflicts are available to represent the child.

In *North Carolina State Bar Opinion RPC 14: County Attorney as Guardian Ad Litem*[52] a county attorney who did not represent the Department of Social Services in any proceedings, but who occasionally answered legal questions concerning the Department as counsel for the five-member Board of Commissioners, sought to act as a guardian ad litem in dependency court. The North Carolina Bar Association held that there was a sufficient conflict of interest that prohibited the attorney from acting as a guardian ad litem and also held that due to the children's youth, they could not waive that conflict of interest.[53]

---

[50] *Id.* After the federal adoption subsidy was passed in 1997 the number of adoptions in California rose from 4,021 in 1997 to 5,908 in 1999. *Id.* In "Los Angeles County workers said they felt pressured to increase the number of adoptions, sometimes coercing relatives to adopt."

[51] For a history and discussion of the cases in which county counsel argued that no conflict of interest existed in representing both the Department and the abused child, *see Los Angeles County Department Of Children and Family Services v. Superior Court*, 59 Cal. Rptr. 613 (1997); *In re Zeth S.*, 108 Cal. Rptr. 2d 527 (2001).

[52] North Carolina State Bar Opinion RPC 14 (October 24, 1986).

[53] *Id.* at 1. In *Tennessee Attorney General Opinion No. 93-10* (February 3, 1993), it was held that a juvenile court youth services officer could not also serve as a part-time police officer due to the conflict of interest between the law enforcement duties and the duties of the youth services officer in assisting the juvenile court. In *New Jersey v. Clark*, 735 A. 2d 1, 4–6 (N.J. 1999), the court held that it was a conflict of interest for a criminal defense attorney to also be employed part-time by the municipal prosecutor in the same county where the defense trial took place because of the appearance of impropriety.

In addition to conflicts of interest between the Department and abused children regarding placements, another conflict sometimes develops when the abused child alleges injury while in the custody of the Department or the Department's agent. Although a quick resolution of such legal complaints is clearly in the abused child's best interest, the Department, like most tort defendants, often uses legal strategies that strengthen its case and weaken the child's.[54] For instance, a recent series of newspaper reports have delineated the Los Angeles Department's stalling tactics used against child abuse tort victims. In fact, one study demonstrated that the County Counsel and the county claims adjuster routinely denied every tort claim by abused children in foster care filed against the county.[55] In addition, many attorneys representing foster children suing the Department "accused the county counsel's office of stone-walling court-ordered efforts to investigate the cases," although County Counsel explained that such delays are caused by confidentiality laws.[56] It is uncertain what pressures would develop if County Counsel had dual representation in these cases. If the foster child made any statements to the Department or County Counsel regarding the tort, County Counsel might have to conflict off the case.

In a rather surprising analysis, the South Carolina Bar Ethics Advisory Committee held that an attorney who regularly is hired at $100 per dependency annual review to act as the guardian ad litem for children can, as long as it is not a case in which the attorney represented the child before the court, be hired to represent the Department of Social Services.[57] The Ethics

---

[54] In addition to discovery strategies that county counsel may use in civil litigation in which children are suing the government, there are other more significant trial strategies demonstrating a glaring conflict between the government's interest and the child's interest. For instance, a series of newspaper articles on the government's alleged psychological abuse of child witnesses has pointed out the inherent conflict when the government's goal of criminal conviction or avoidance of a tort judgment clearly conflicts with the emotional health of young child witnesses. For instance, the District Attorney during the penalty phase of their father's trial called to the stand his four children "as witnesses whose testimony help edsecure the death penalty for their father." Caitlin Liu, *Children's Testimony in Case Assailed*, L. A. TIMES, July 26, 2001, at B1. Psychological experts indicated that the children may be emotionally traumatized for the rest of their lives when they recognize that their testimony resulted in their father's death. *Id.* at B11; Jean Guccione, *Jury Urges Execution of Man Who Killed 2 of His Children*, L. A. TIMES, July 26, 2001, at B1. In another case, attorneys representing California in a suit against the state for failing to provide textbooks to schools "came under fire in news reports Thursday for sharply questioning schoolchildren to discredit their testimony that they don't have enough textbooks...." *Late Reports*, L. A. DAILY. J., Sept. 17, 2001, at 1.

[55] Cheryl Romo & Megan Webb, *County Rejects All Claims by Abused Foster Kids, Study Says*, L A. DAILY. J., April 24, 2001, at 1.

[56] Greg Krikorian, *Lawyers for Children Say County Fails to Cooperate*, L. A. TIMES, August 22, 2001, at B1.

[57] South Carolina Bar Ethics Advisory Committee, Advisory Opinion 89-01 (1989), at 1–3.

Committee did not find a conflict of interest because the child would have legal representation that would ameliorate any "propensity for conflict and inadequate representation...."[58] The Ethics Committee did not even discuss the appearance of impropriety or of unfairness that might be created in the minds of parties in the dependency action. The Louisiana Attorney General held that, in the analogous area of criminal law, a district attorney may not serve as a public defender even if the prosecutor has not been involved in the prosecution of defendants in any way because of the appearance of impropriety.[59] One must wonder why in the area of conflicts of interest a similar rule should not apply in child dependency actions that implicate a fundamental right similar to, although not identical to, the liberty interest inherent in criminal trials.

Another common dual representation by County Counsel involves conflicts of interest between the Department and one of its employees. Most ethics codes clearly state that "[i]n representing an organization, a member shall conform his or her representation to the concept that the client is the organization itself...."[60] However, in some jurisdictions that use a "prosecutorial model" of agency representation, the governmental attorney represents "the people" of the state, rather than the agency itself in which the "attorney may override the views of the agency in court."[61] But the American Bar Association recommends against adoption of prosecutorial models of representation because of the many impediments: (1) caseworkers will not have a legal representative in court, (2) the caseworker's expertise may not be adequately considered, (3) the governmental attorney may be a generalist without sufficient training in child protection cases, (4) political issues

---

[58] *Id.* at 3.

[59] Louisiana Attorney General Opinion, No. 00-446 (February 19, 2001). The opinion was based upon state statutory and constitutional grounds, and therefore it did not discuss actual conflicts of interest or due process deprivations by having the district attorney's office represent criminal defendants. And in *New York Attorney General Informal Opinion No. 88-54* (August 17, 1988) it was held that although there is nothing to prevent a government employee from serving in two legal roles, "a person serving as a county social services attorney and as an assistant district attorney may not participate as an assistant district attorney in any cases in which he could potentially be called as a witness." *Id.* at 1–2. The opinion noted that child abuse reporting laws could require the district attorney during the dependency case to inform the district attorney of possible criminal violations by the parents and that the district attorney in the criminal case might call as a witness the assistant district attorney from the dependency case in violation of *Code of Professional Responsibility, DR 5–101.*

[60] *California Rules of Professional Conduct, Rule 3-600.* This rule is subject to *Rule 3-310*, which provides that "[a] member shall not concurrently represent clients whose interests conflict, except with their informed written consent."

[61] *Standards of Practice for Lawyers Representing Child Welfare Agencies, Rule A-3, Commentary* (American Bar Association, August 2004).

may affect the attorney's decision making, (5) the agency may be unaided in its larger policy decisions such as how the case might result in political fallout, and (6) conflicts may arise if the prosecutor also is involved in a child delinquency proceeding involving the children in the child protection case.[62]

However, under the agency-representation model a conflict often arises in that "caseworkers may believe the attorney represents them personally rather than the agency as a whole."[63] Even if the agency attorney knows that the social worker is not his or her client, a lawyer-client relationship between the Department's counsel and a Department employee often develops inadvertently. Consider the following hypothetical:

> The Department's attorney receives a telephone call from one of the Department's caseworkers who says she needs to talk. When they meet outside courtroom number 281 the children's services worker informs counsel that she has been named in a 42 U. S. C. §1983 action for intentionally sexually abusing a foster child and volunteers that, although she did not commit the abuse, she did put her arm around the boy. When counsel returns to the office he informs his supervisor of the facts of the case, and the supervisor tells the attorney to prepare a points and authorities motion to demonstrate that the children's worker acted outside the scope of her employment and that therefore the county is not responsible.[64] What should the Department's counsel do?

First, attorneys can only represent more than one client if they reasonably believe that they can adequately represent both interests simultaneously and if they gain both clients' consent, unless the clients' interests are adverse.[65] In this case who is the Department's client? Generally the client is the Department, not employees of the Department.[66] However, some ethics codes and judicial opinions use a subjective standard in determining whether a lawyer-client relationship has been established. If the client reasonably believed that he or she was consulting an attorney for advice, even if the attorney had no

---

[62] *Id.* at *Rule B–1, Commentary.*   [63] *Id.* at *Rule B–1.*

[64] This hypothetical is loosely based upon an hypothetical illustration contained in Debra Bassett Perschbacher & Rex R. Perschbacher, *Enter at Your Own Risk: The Initial Consultation & Conflicts of Interest*, 3 GEO. J. LEGAL ETHICS 689, 689–690 (1990).

[65] *Id.* at 694–695; *Klemm v. Superior Court*, 142 Cal. Rptr. 509, 512 (1977).

[66] *ABA Model Rules of Professional Conduct, Rule1.13* provides that "[a] lawyer employed or retained by an organization represents the organization...." "California evidentiary and ethical rules view the public entity as the client." Richard C. Solomon, *Wearing Many Hats: Confidentiality and Conflicts of Interest Issues for the California Public Lawyer*, 25 SW. U.L. REV. 265, 272 (1996); *Cal. Evid. Code § 175.*

intention of creating an attorney-client relationship, a legal and ethical relationship probably was created.[67] If it is determined that this was an initial consultation or that the prospective client reasonably believed that it was an initial consultation, then for all intent and purposes an attorney-client relationship was established. The conclusion could "lead to disqualification of the lawyer involved, disqualification of the lawyer's entire law firm, and restricted access to the lawyer's work product by substitute counsel."[68] Therefore, when a Department attorney is faced with a scenario in which an employee of the Department might think that the meeting is an initial consultation, counsel should immediately inform the employee that he or she represents the Department, not the employee, and that counsel potentially may be placed in an adverse relationship with the employee.[69] This, of course, will probably induce the employee into silence, which may in the long run harm the Department because critical data will be lost and the employee will then have to continue operating on the job without perceived necessary legal advice. Thus, the Department's counsel and the Department are caught in a Catch-22. However, the potential for such conflicts of interest to arise can be diminished by explicitly informing the Department's employees in handbooks and training sessions of the role of the Department's attorneys. The American Bar Association Standards suggest that the agency attorney "must clearly communicate that he or she represents the agency as an entity and should use the conflict resolution system [*American Bar Association Model Rule 1.13*] when the caseworker's opinion varies from the agency policy or the attorney has reason to question the caseworker's decision."[70]

---

[67] *State Bar of California Formal Op. 1984–84* (during a meeting in which a client informed attorney of facts underlying her causeof action, an attorney-client relationship was established even though the attorney formally rejected the representation, and the attorney could not take another client in which use of the information gleaned from that prospective client might be used). *ABA Informal Op. 1413*, June 23, 1978, indicates that "[w]e are clear that a Government lawyer assigned to represent a litigant, and who undertakes to do so, has an attorney-client relationship with the litigant, and that the lawyer's status as a Government employee does not exempt him or her from professional obligations, including those to preserve a client's confidences and secrets, that are imposed upon other lawyers."

[68] Perschbacher, *supra* note 46, at 704; *River West, Inc. v. Nickel*, 234 Cal. Rptr. 33, 41 (1987). Richard C. Solomon, *supra* note *48*, at 332–333; *Civil Service Commission of County of San Diego v. Superior Court*, 209 Cal. Rptr. 159 (1984) (county counsel who represented the county in lawsuit with a commission that had been previously advised by county counsel required disqualification of county counsel from the litigation); *ABA Informal Opinion 929, April 6, 1966*.

[69] *ABA Formal Op. 97-405*, April 19, 1997.

[70] *Standards of Practice, supra* note 58, Rule B-1.

IV. JUDGES: LIMITS AND RESPONSIBILITIES OF THE NEUTRAL AND DETACHED MAGISTRATE

Unlike most state rules of professional responsibility for attorneys that delineate specific conflicts of interest that counsel must avoid, such as representing two parties with conflicting interests,[71] most canons of judicial ethics merely rely upon the general prohibitions that judges "[s]hould uphold the integrity and independence of the judiciary" and "[s]hould avoid impropriety and the appearance of impropriety in all his activities."[72] There are very few examples of judicial ethics cases in child dependency and custody law that have illustrated those conflicts of interest.

However, in one case the New York Advisory Committee on Judicial Ethics was asked whether a "part-time Village Justice" could also serve as a caseworker with the County Child Protective Services, which investigates child abuse and neglect allegations.[73] The Committee found that such dual employment did not violate the state judicial code, which provided that a part-time judge "may accept private employment or public employment in a federal, state or municipal department or agency, provided that such employment is not incompatible with judicial office and does not conflict or interfere with the proper performance of the judge's duties."[74] The Committee noted that very few child protection cases ever come before the Village Justice courts and that another judge would be available to hear any case in which the part-time judge had been involved in his capacity as a County Child Protective Service employee.[75] However, the Committee did not analyze this dual role under the traditional standard of whether it created an appearance of impropriety or undermined the independence of the court. It is certainly foreseeable that any witnesses questioned by the judge in his investigation in the child abuse case might have real concerns about the use of their statements should the case be litigated in the part-time judge's courtroom, even if that judge did not preside over the case. One must wonder whether the Committee would come to the same conclusion if the part-time judge worked in the criminal prosecutor's office in investigating criminal allegations. Is the inherent conflict between judge and prosecutor, two jobs

---

[71] *See, e.g., ABA Model Rules of Professional Conduct, Rule 1.7(a)*: "A lawyer shall not represent a client if the representation of that client will be directly adverse to another client. . . ." See also *Rule 1.8(a)*: "A lawyer shall not enter into a business transaction with a client or knowingly acquire an ownership, possessory, security or other pecuniary interest adverse to a client. . . ."

[72] *Iowa State Bar Association Judicial Ethics, Canons 1 & 2.*

[73] *New York Advisory Committeeon Judicial Ethics, Opinion 96-34*, April 25, 1996 (1996 WL 940912).

[74] *Id.* at 1; New York Rules Governing Judicial Conduct, section 100.6(b)(4).

[75] *Id.* at 1.

that are defined as mutually exclusive based upon separation of powers, any different from conflict in the dual role of judge and social worker? Because the social worker is employed by the executive branch, does the judge's intimate relationship with the executive branch raise the appearance of impropriety in his alternative role as judicial officer? Such dual roles in which judges work for both the executive or legislative branches of government should therefore be scrutinized closely for conflicts of interest.

In a more troubling opinion, the New York Advisory Committee on Judicial Ethics held that a judge need not recuse him- or herself merely "because a proceeding comes before the judge in one court which involves basically the same persons and most of the same issues involved in a prior proceeding before the judge in the other court, so long as the judge feels he or she will be impartial in the second proceeding."[76] In that case the judge presided in both the dependency court and in a criminal court trial based upon the same case of child abuse. Unfortunately, the Committee's decision that no conflict existed was based solely upon the judge's conclusion regarding impartiality, not upon several other serious questions inherent in such dual judging. First, the order of the two trials raises significant questions. If the judge heard the dependency case before hearing the criminal case, he or she could become privy to considerable relevant and highly prejudicial evidence that was legally admissible in the dependency case, but that would be inadmissible in the criminal case because of its higher evidentiary standards. The next question is whether the criminal trial is a court hearing or a jury trial. If it is a jury trial, then it might not be prejudicial for the dependency court judge to supervise the guilt phase of the criminal trial because the court would not be the fact-finder. However, if the jury trial is a bench trial, in almost all cases the judge should recuse him- or herself because he or she will have had access to a great deal of evidence not admissible in the criminal cases. In addition, if the criminal case is a court trial, the dependency judge may have sentencing information gleaned from the dependency trial that would be impermissible to consider in the criminal sentencing hearing. If so, the judge should recuse him- or herself as well. If the sentencing hearing is decided by the jury, it is a much closer case because the dependency court judge's role in the criminal case may only be to ensure that the sentence decided by the jury is consistent with justice. However, if the judge must determine any sentence enhancements based upon the culpability of the criminal defendant, then there is a potential that exposure to the dependency court evidence could either consciously or unconsciously affect his or her decision. If the criminal trial takes place first, fewer problems arise because the evidence presented in the criminal

---

[76] New York Advisory Committee on Judicial Ethics, Opinion 89-104 (September 12, 1989).

case will invariably be admissible in the dependency case, and because under most circumstances the criminal verdict and fact determinations will be *res judicata* and *collateral estoppel* in the dependency case, which requires a lower burden of proof than the criminal trial.[77]

Granting a continuance in the child dependency or custody case until the conclusion of the criminal case might appear to be a relatively simple solution to the Fifth Amendment problems inherent in parallel criminal and civil child abuse actions; however, that remedy is replete with problems.[78] First, continuing the dependency case does not provide the child or nonabusive family members with sufficient safety and/or reunification services. Second, unlike expedited dependency and child custody civil proceedings, criminal cases may take years to process before a verdict is rendered. Third, courts have noted that judges have very limited authority in limiting criminal prosecutors' discretion in how and when they will litigate cases because prosecutorial discretion is an executive function that is protected by separation of powers interference from the judicial bench.[79] Another possible accommodation is to permit the civil child dependency or child custody proceeding to be litigated, but to grant use immunity for parents forced to testify prior to the criminal child abuse proceeding. Although this approach works in those states in which an immunity statute exists, other jurisdictions have determined that judges have no inherent authority to provide use immunity, and still others have held that use immunity is an executive decision for prosecutors, not judges.[80]

However, in contrast to cases that have permitted dependency court judges to accept dual roles in different courts or in alternative employment, the New York Advisory Committee on Judicial Ethics found that a surrogate court judge could not serve "on a county task force on child abuse and neglect, which is funded by a charitable organization."[81] Even though the Committee found that the child abuse organization would not be likely to appear before the judge, "its public education function and its name alone might raise a question" and might "reflect adversely upon impartiality or interfere with

---

[77] For cases involving *resjudicata* and/or *collateral estoppel* in criminal and dependency cases, see *In re R.W.B., 241 N.W. 2d 546 (N.D. 1976); In re Robert J. v. Leslie M., 59 Cal. Rptr. 2d 905 (1997); In re Paternity of Amber J.R., 557 N.W. 2d 84 (Wisc. 1996); In re Linda O., 95 Misc. 2d 744, 408 N.Y.S. 2d 308 (Fam. Ct. 1978).*

[78] For a full exploration of the problems inherent in concurrent criminal and civil child abuse trials, *see* William Wesley Patton,*The World Where Parallel Lines Converge: The Privilege Against Self–Incrimination in Concurrent Civil and Criminal Child Abuse Proceedings*, 24 GA. L. REV. 473, 518–524 (1990).

[79] *See, e.g., In re Padget*, 678 P. 2d 870 (Wyo. 1984).

[80] Patton, *supra* note 76, at 510–518.

[81] *New York Advisory Committee on Judicial Ethics, Opinion 88–150, December 8, 1988 (1988 WL 547000).*

the performance of judicial duties."[82] California takes a different approach by not prohibiting judicial membership in organizations, but by placing the burden on the judge to *sua sponte* disclose to parties appearing before him or her; the judge's membership "in an organization [is] relevant to the question of disqualification, even if the judge believes there is no actual basis for disqualification."[83]

The California approach seems to be the wiser one for several reasons. First, permitting dependency and family court judges to associate with organizations that help educate the public regarding child abuse will give them a forum for expressing their views and will assist them in meeting their professional responsibilities of educating the public regarding the juvenile court system. Second, it will permit judges to educate such organizations about the realities of the dependency and family law systems and the realistic need for change. Finally, a vague rule concerning which organizations and under what circumstances judges can join will chill their interest in educating the public. The California scheme fully protects advocates in its judges' courtrooms because they must *sua sponte* disclose the membership and recuse themselves if a potential conflict arises.

---

[82] *Id.* at 1.
[83] *California Rules of Court, California Code of Judicial Ethics, Canon 3, Advisory Committee Commentary, 1996 Amendment.*

2 Competent and Zealous Representation

The requirement of competency is perhaps less controversial than the mandate for zealousness. Media and lay portrayals of the evils of the legal system circle around a mistaken understanding of the meaning and importance of zealousness,[1] which has become synonymous with frivolous causes of action and with grand incivility among those involved in the legal system. It is not surprising, therefore, that the express requirement of Canon 7 of the *ABA Code of Professional Responsibility* that "[a] lawyer should represent a client zealously within the bounds of the law" was eliminated from the *ABA Model Rules of Professional Conduct* except in the Preamble and Comments.[2] And the American Academy of Matrimonial Lawyers has noted that zealous representation "is not always appropriate in family law matters."[3] In contrast, the concept of competence has received a radically different reception by the

---

[1] "Lawyers, especially family and divorce lawyers, have not fared well in the view of the larger society regarding how they tend to handle disputes." Robert D. Benjamin, *The Use of Mediative Strategies in Traditional Legal Practice*, 14 J. AM. ACAD. MATR. LAW. 203, 229 (1997).

[2] *The Bounds of Advocacy*, 9 J. AM. ACAD. MATR. LAW. 1, 2 (1992). For instance, in the *Preamble, section 7* to the *ABA Model Rules of Professional Conduct*, it is noted that "a lawyer can be a zealous advocate on behalf of a client and at the same time assume that justice is being done."

[3] *The Bounds of Advocacy, Preliminary Statement* (American Academy of Matrimonial Lawyers). The *Preliminary Statement* further distinguishes itself from the *ABA Rules of Professional Conduct*, which "perhaps weighed certain principles more heavily in the balancing process than previous codes. While reaffirming the attorney's obligation of competent and zealous representation, the Standards promote greater professionalism, trust, fair dealing, and concern for the opposing parties and counsel, third persons, and the public. In addition, they encourage efforts to reduce costs, delay, and emotional trauma and urge interaction between parties and attorneys on a more reasoned, cooperative level...." The ABA Family Law Section has also noted the sometimes incompatibility of zealousness with the best interests of families. "High-conflict custody cases seriously harm the children involved... [and] drain court, family and mental health resources...." *High-Conflict Custody Cases: Reforming the System for Children: Conference Report and Action Plan 1* (The Johnson Foundation Wingspread Conference Center, Wisconsin, September 8–10, 2000, www.abanet.org/child/wingspread.html).

public and bar, and it is not surprising that it is the first rule in the *ABA Model Rules of Professional Responsibility*.[4]

Rather than disappearing, the requirement of competency has not only survived numerous ethical code iterations but it has also been refined and expanded. For instance, in many jurisdictions competency to represent children in child dependency proceedings now requires knowledge in areas well beyond legal theory. For instance, in California the superior court is required to screen and appoint "competent" counsel with sufficient minimum standards of education in "the law of juvenile dependency" and in "child development, child abuse and neglect, substance abuse, [and] domestic violence...."[5] However, even though the respectability of zealousness and competency may have fluctuated historically, state bar ethics opinions and judicial decisions clearly indicate that both are still essential components of the lawyer-client relationship. The difficulty is not in comprehending definitions of competency and zealousness, but rather in applying them in discrete contexts. The following discussion provides myriad examples and analyses that will help attorneys and judges involved in child custody and child dependency cases decide how to stay on the cusp between zealousness, incivility, and contempt and between general legal knowledge and situational competency.

I. CHILDREN'S ATTORNEYS: ZEALOUS ADVOCATES OR BEST INTEREST STORYTELLERS?

There is no clear consensus among juvenile law scholars, judges, legislators, or children's organizations regarding the best definition of the attorney-child client relationship.[6] However, no matter whether the children's representative

---

[4] *ABA Model Rules of Professional Conduct, Rule 1.1* states that "[a] lawyer shall provide competent representation to a client. Competent representation requires the legal knowledge, skill, thoroughness and preparation reasonably necessary for the representation."

[5] *California Rules of Court, Rule 1438 (c); California Welfare and Institutions Code § 317.6.*

[6] For instance, the *American Bar Association Model Rules, Rule 1.14(a) and (b), and Comment #5* provide that competent minors shall receive the same zealous, loyal, and competent representation as an adult client. The *American Bar Association Institute of Judicial Administration Joint Commission on Juvenile Justice, Standard 3.1(b)(ii)(b)* provides that where a juvenile client is capable of "considered judgment," the child shall determine what is in his or her best interest. Further, *Standard 4.2 and Introduction at 3, 8*, provide, "Where a client's capacity may be affected by extreme youth, mental disability, or other cause . . . such difficulties only underline the attorney's duty to seek to effective communication and consultation with the juvenile and do not justify adoption of a 'guardian' . . . role." In addition, the *American Bar Association Standards for Child Abuse and Neglect Cases, Standard A-1* provides that the child's attorney "owes the same duties of undivided loyalty, confidentiality and competent representation to the child as is due to an adult client." And *Standard B-1* provides for representation of "the child's expressed preferences and follow[ing] the child's directions

is a zealous advocate or a guardian ad litem, that attorney has a duty of competency and zeal.[7] But most jurisdictions fail to sufficiently articulate the role of children's attorneys in child custody and dependency proceedings, and many jurisdictions have created hybrid roles that combine mutually inconsistent aspects of both the zealous lawyer model and the guardian ad litem model. For instance, the following models of child representation exist in different states: (1) the pure zealous advocate model in which the attorney argues the competent child's stated preference even if the attorney does not think that it is in the child's best interest; (2) the pure guardian ad litem model in which the attorney argues what he or she views as the child's best interest even if it conflicts with the child's stated preference; (3) a zealous advocate model unless the attorney thinks that the child's preference is dangerous, and if so, the attorney may request the appointment of a separate guardian

throughout the course of litigation." In 1996 a group of juvenile law advocates, professors, and judges found that the child's lawyer "must presume the child client's capacity." *Fordham Conference on Ethical Issues in the Legal Representation of Children*, XIV FORDHAM L. REV. 1279, at 1339 (1996). Those juvenile law scholars stated that if a child client is competent, the lawyer must act upon and carry out the child client's "well-reasoned . . . rational decision" even when it may threaten the child's life or result in death." *Id.* at 1345. Finally, the *National Association of Counsel For Children Revised Standards of Practice (1999)*, *Standard 4* requires "zealous, loyal, and competent child client representation unless the child's attorney determines that the child's expressed preference would be seriously injurious to the child, in which case the lawyer shall, after unsuccessful use of the attorney's counseling role, request the appointment of a separate guardian *ad litem* and continue to represent the child's expressed preference, unless the child's position is prohibited by law or without any factual foundation. The child's attorney shall not reveal the basis of the request for the appointment of a guardian *ad litem* which would compromise the child's position." However, many state legislatures have set the role of children's attorneys as more of a guardian ad litem than as a zealous advocate. And in California, the legislature has stated that the child's counsel shall not advocate for the return of the minor if, to the best of his or her knowledge, that return conflicts with the protection and safety of the minor. *California Welfare and Institutions Code § 317(e)*. On the other hand, the California Supreme Court, which promulgated and approved the *California Rules on Professional Responsibility*, has not made an exception for attorney-child client relationships that differs from the zealous, loyal, and competent representation owed to adult clients. William Wesley Patton, *Legislative Regulation of Dependency Court Attorneys: Public Relations and Separation of Powers*, 24 NOTRE DAME J. LEGIS. 3 (1998).

[7] "In 1974, by its passage of the Child Abuse Prevention and Treatment Act (CAPTA), Congress established a statutory right to representation, although not necessarily by counsel, for all children who are the subjects of child protection proceedings." Randi Mandelbaum, *Revisiting the Question of Whether Young Children in Child Protection Proceedings Should Be Represented by Lawyers*, 32 LOY. U. CHI. L.J. 1 (2000); David R. Katner, *Coming to Praise, Not to Bury, The New ABA Standards of Practice for Lawyers Who Represent Children in Abuse and Neglect Cases*, 14 GEO. J. LEGAL ETHICS 103 (2000). "The attorney appointed as an attorney for the child . . . owes the same duties of undivided loyalty, confidentiality, and zealous representation of the child's express wishes as he or she would to an adult client, with a few modifications." Marvin R. Ventrell, *The Child's Attorney*, 17 FAM. ADVOC. 73, 73 (1995).

ad litem to argue the child's best interest; and (4) the lawyer as a neutral fact-finder for the court who does not articulate a position regarding the child's stated preference.[8]

A. Children's Competence as a Key in Deciding the Model of Advocacy

Most of the conflicts inherent in selecting the appropriate or required attorney role in representing children center upon the capacity of the child client to make informed decisions. *ABA Model Rule 1.14(a)* provides that

> When a client's ability to make adequately considered decisions in connection with the representation is impaired, whether because of minority, mental disability or for some other reason, the lawyer shall, as far as reasonably possible, maintain a normal client-lawyer relationship with the client. And Rule 1.14(b) provides that if the client lacks sufficient capacity, "[a] lawyer may seek the appointment of a guardian or take other protective action with respect to a client, only when the lawyer reasonably believes the client cannot adequately act in the client's own interest."[9]

Further, *Comment 1 to Rule 1.14* warns that incompetency is not the same as limited or impaired capacity and that children often have competency to make some decisions even if they cannot make other, more sophisticated choices:

> [A] client lacking legal competence often has the ability to understand, deliberate upon, and reach conclusions about matters affecting the client's own well-being. Furthermore, to an increasing extent the law recognizes intermediate degrees of competence. For example, children as young as five or six years of age, and certainly those of ten or twelve, are regarded as having opinions that are entitled to weight in legal proceedings concerning their custody.

Children's attorneys therefore need to understand the distinction between "[c]apacity [which] refers to a client's ability to understand information

---

[8] See Emily Buss, *'You're My What?' The Problem of Children's Misperceptions of Their Lawyers' Roles*, XIV FORDHAM L. REV. 1699, 1700–1703 (1996). For example, the court in *Fox v. Willis*, 822 A. 2d 1289, 1292 (2003) noted that the role of children's representatives might be as "attorney," "[g]uardian *ad litem*," and "investigator" and that there are actually "four different roles: 'waiver, pure representation, pure investigation, or a combination.'"

[9] The *Restatement of the Law Governing Lawyers*, § 35 provides that "[a] lawyer representing a person whom the lawyer reasonably believes to be [incompetent] . . . may seek the appointment of a guardian or take other protective action with respect to a decision on a question within the scope of the representation when doing so is practical and will advance the client's objectives or interests. . . . " And the American Academy of Matrimonial Lawyers, *Bounds of Advocacy*, 1.2 Comment states that if the client is incompetent, the definition of "competent representation" "may require that the attorney recommend that the client consult a mental health professional."

relevant to the case and the ability to appreciate the consequences of decisions ... [from] [c]ompetence [which] is a legal standard, and denotes a specific level of skill, knowledge, or ability."[10]

The American Academy of Matrimonial Lawyers (AAML) has taken a completely different approach from the ABA Model Rules in its standards for representing children in child custody cases. Instead of an age-neutral policy, *AAML Standard 2.2* "provides a rebuttable presumption that children twelve and older are unimpaired and that children younger than twelve are impaired."[11] However, creating a presumption of incompetence based upon age alone is problematic from the child's perspective. First, who has the burden of rebutting the presumption? It certainly should not be the child because children do not have access to the variables underlying a conclusion of legal competency and because they do not have access to someone, other than their own attorney, to argue their own competence. In addition, if a child's attorney comes into the relationship with a presumption of incompetency of children younger than age 12, it is likely that the attorney will not spend sufficient time or resources to attempt to rebut that presumption because of the high caseloads and low pay in child dependency proceedings. In fact, it is likely that the child's attorney will have to determine the child's competency within forty-eight hours of the child being taken into custody and based upon a short initial interview at the detention hearing just before attending that proceeding. The presumption of incompetency can substantially harm children because critical decisions are made at the initial detention hearing. For instance, suppose that a 7-year-old child at the detention hearing informs her attorney that she wants to remain with her 12-year-old sister and wants to be removed from her abusing parents' home. If the child is competent, the child's attorney under *Model Rule 1.14* is required to implement the child's stated preference. However, assume that the attorney thinks that the 7-year-old girl is not at risk and would fare better in her parents' home than in foster care. How will the child's attorney's disagreement with the child's stated preference affect counsel's determination of the minor's competence? If the attorney finds the child incompetent, then counsel may not be required to zealously argue the child's express wish to be removed from her parents' home and be placed with her older sister in foster care.

The Fordham Conference Report (FCR) took a position directly opposite that of the AAML and indicated that "as a starting point of a capacity analysis,

---

[10] Jennifer L. Renne, *Legal Ethics in Child Welfare Cases* 39 (American Bar Association, 2004). "The most critical distinction between the two concepts is that competence is a characteristic that someone either possesses or doesn't. It is an all or nothing principle."

[11] Michael Drews & Pamela Halprin, *Determining the Effective Representation of a Child in Our Legal System: Do Current Standards Accomplish the Goal?*, 13 FAM. CT. REV. 73, 79 (2004). REPRESENTING CHILDREN: STANDARDS FOR ATTORNEYS AND GUARDIAN AD LITEM IN CUSTODY OR VISITATION PROCEEDINGS (1994).

the lawyer must presume the child client's capacity."[12] The FCR places the burden on the attorney to determine competently, based upon the totality of the circumstances, whether the child is competent: "As with adults, lawyers have an ethical obligation to advocate the position of a child unless there is independent evidence that the child is unable to express a reasoned choice. Where such evidence exists, a lawyer must engage in additional fact finding to determine whether the child has or may develop the capacity to direct the lawyer's action."[13]

The child-centered model outlined in the FCR was extensively expanded in the book by Jean Koh Peters, *Representing Children in Child Protective Proceedings: Ethical and Practical Dimensions*.[14] She proposed a model of child advocacy in which the attorney must focus not only on the child's capacity to make reasoned decisions within a "child-in-context" mode but also must look at the child's capacity in relation to the theory of the case.[15] Peters places a heavy burden upon the child's attorney not only to fully investigate all relevant evidence regarding the child's capacity but also to determine whether any bias is inherent in the attorney's conclusion regarding the child's competency. According to Peters, the attorney should consider the following factors:

1. child's development stage (cognitive ability, socialization, and emotional development)
2. child's expression of a relevant position (ability to communicate with lawyer and ability to articulate reasons)
3. child's individual decision-making process (influence, coercion, exploitation, conformity, variability, and consistency)
4. child's ability to understand consequences (risks of harm and finality of decision)[16]

Therefore, under each of the discrete standards and rules of the various professional organizations, once the child is determined sufficiently competent to make a reasoned choice among alternatives, the attorney's

---

[12] *Report of the Working Group on Determining the Child's Capacity to Make Decisions*, 64 FORDHAM L. REV. 1339, 1339–1340 (1996).

[13] *Id.* at 1312–1313. Criticisms of the FCR are that its recommendations "fail to appreciate that a child cannot be neatly categorized and may need an advocate acting primarily as an attorney with regard to one issue, while at other times the child may need an advocate acting primarily as a guardian ad litem." Drews & Halprin, *supra* note 11, at 83.

[14] Jean Koh Peters, REPRESENTING CHILDREN IN CHILD PROTECTION PROCEEDINGS: ETHICAL AND PRACTICAL DIMENSIONS (1997).

[15] Drews & Halprin, *supra* note 11, at 84; Ann M. Haralambie, *In Whose Best Interest?*, 34-June JTLATRIAL 42 (1998).

[16] Peters, *supra* note 14, at 1312–1313.

role is usually to represent the child's stated preference zealously and competently, absent unusual circumstances such as imminent serious danger to the child.

B. *The Lawyer's Role as the Child's Guardian Ad Litem*

A continuing problem with the appointment of advocates for children is the ambiguity inherent in the definition of the advocate's role. When an attorney is appointed to represent a child in a child custody or dependency case, ambiguities arise over whether that appointment is as a zealous advocate or a guardian ad litem or both, because the specific role defines the ambit of zealousness, the child's role in selecting the ultimate resolution, and the confidentiality of the information gleaned by the attorney during the representation.[17]

Because of the inherent consequences to the child of the role of the attorney, the Fordham Conference recommended that lawyers should never function in dual roles in representing a child client:

> When it is uncertain whether a lawyer has been appointed to represent a child as the child's lawyer, to serve as the child's guardian ad litem, to serve in a dual lawyer/guardian ad litem role, or to serve the child in some other role, the lawyer should elect to represent the child as a lawyer.[18] [And] a lawyer should not serve as both a child's lawyer and guardian ad litem. When a lawyer has been appointed to serve in both roles, the lawyer should elect to represent the child as a lawyer and not to serve as guardian ad litem. If that is not permissible, the lawyer should elect to decline the appointment where feasible.[19]

However, assuming that the attorney practices in a jurisdiction in which counsel are appointed as guardians ad litem (GALs), the attorney must recognize the differences between the zealous advocate model and the best interest (GAL) model. "In custody matters, the guardian ad litem has traditionally been viewed as functioning as an agent or arm of the court, to which it owes its principal duty of allegiance, and not strictly as legal counsel to a child client [and] essentially functions as the court's investigative agent...."[20] In

---

[17] Most states now require appointment of a guardian ad litem for children in child dependency proceedings based upon federal mandates for funding under federal child abuse legislation. *See, e.g., Utah Attorney General Opinion No. 77-027*, October 14, 1977; *S. C. Code Ann. Sec. 20-7-110A; South Carolina Attorney General Informal Opinion*, April 2, 1996 (1996 WL 265508).

[18] *Report of the Working Group...*, *supra* note 12, at 1302.

[19] *Id.* at 1302.

[20] *Fox v. Willis*, 822 A. 2d 1289, 1294 (2003). The *Fox* court held that because guardians ad litem perform judicial functions that they were entitled to at least qualified immunity. *Id.* at 1297.

2001 twenty-two states mandated guardians ad litem, twenty-three provided a CASA (court-appointed special advocate), and eleven provided both to assist the court in determining the child's best interest.[21] Guardians ad litem are often called to testify and make representations; however, because the GAL usually does not have a duty of loyalty and confidentiality toward the child, the GAL can give recommendations inconsistent with the express wishes of the child.[22] However, if the child's advocate operates in an attorney role, *American Bar Association Ethics Rule* 3.7 provides that "[a] lawyer shall not act as advocate at a trial in which the lawyer is likely to be a necessary witness except where: (1) the testimony relates to an uncontested issue"; (2) the issue involves a controversy regarding the quality or cost of attorney services; or (3) "disqualification of the lawyer would work substantial hardship on the client."

Although the Child Abuse Prevention and Treatment Act of 1974 required the appointment of guardians ad litem for children in states receiving federal funds, the Act did not specify the role of the GAL. Therefore, states have used GALs for different purposes ranging from zealous advocates to mere judicial fact-finders. Some have argued that if the role of the GAL is identical to the role of a child's attorney, then appointing both is duplicative and a waste of juvenile resources. However, GALs in most jurisdictions need not be attorneys; their roles, even as advocates, are clearly differentiated. To clarify the distinctions between the role of a child's attorney and a child's GAL, the Alaska Bar Association held that GALs, whether they be lay persons or attorneys appointed specifically as a GAL, are "not bound by the normal duty of confidentiality, but rather should act within the context of the proceeding and be responsive to the reason for his appointment, namely the best interest of the child... [however] the attorney must warn the child that any statements made or positions taken by the child may be disclosed to the Court if the attorney deems such disclosure to be in the child's best interest."[23] The Alaska Bar Association noted that children will not intuitively distinguish between the roles of attorneys and GALs, and therefore, the GAL must clearly explain the lack of a duty of loyalty and confidentiality so that the "child's natural trust and perception... not be abused."[24]

---

[21] Michael J. Dale, *Providing Counsel to Children in Dependency Proceedings in Florida*, 25 NOVA L. REV. 769, 795 (2001).

[22] *See* Michelle Johnson-Weider, *Guardians Ad Litem: A Solution without Strength in Helping Protect Dependent Children*, 77 FLA. B. J. 87 (April 2003).

[23] *Alaska State Bar Association, Ethics Opinion No. 854* (November 8, 1985).

[24] *Id.*; *see also* Claudia Wright, *Representation of Children in a Unified Family Court System in Florida*, 14 U. FLA. J. L. PUB. POL'Y 179, 189–191 (2003).

C. Hybrid Models of Child Representation

Unlike Alaska, many states have not sufficiently clarified the role of children's advocates, or that role is defined in ways that appear mutually inconsistent. For example, in California there is a direct conflict between the supreme court's definition of zealous lawyering and the legislature's pared-back advocacy model for children's advocates in *Welfare and Institutions Code § 317*, which holds that children's attorneys may not argue for the return of a child if the attorney reasonably believes that it might endanger the child client.

However, because of the very low pay in representing children in abuse cases, many attorneys carry such a heavy caseload that they can neither zealously present their child client's case nor perform sufficient investigative functions to properly inform the court of the child's best interest. For instance, in Los Angeles, the Children's Law Center, the quasi-public contract firm representing children in dependency court, averaged approximately 240 clients per year per staff attorney.[25]

II. PARENTS' ATTORNEYS

Parents' attorneys, like social workers, judges, and other attorneys involved in the child dependency and custody courts, are poorly paid, seldom lauded publicly, and carry excessively high caseloads.

A. Failure to Complete Lawyering Responsibilities

A heavy caseload is not an excuse, justification, or defense to incompetent representation. For instance, in *Attorney Grievance Commission of Maryland v. Alan C. Drew*,[26] the Maryland court of appeal stated, "This Court has never considered that an attorney's decision to take on more work than the attorney could properly handle was a mitigating factor.... Acceptance of 'workaholism' as an excuse for lack of diligence would effectively 'gut' the duty of diligence."

In addition, lack of adequate preparation time is no defense to a charge of incompetence. In *People v. Barbara J. Felker*[27] the Colorado Supreme Court found that the parents' attorney violated the duty of competence (*ABA Model Rule 1.1*) when the attorney's only preparation for a child support case "was

---

[25] William Wesley Patton, *Searching for the Proper Role of Children's Counsel in California Dependency Cases; Or the Answer to the Riddle of the Dependency Sphinx*, 1 J. CENTER CHILD. FAM. CT. 21, 31 (1999).

[26] *Attorney Grievance Commission of Maryland v. Alan C. Drew*, 669 A. 2d 1344, 1349 (1996).

[27] *People v. Barbara J. Felker*, 770 P. 2d 402, 404 (Colorado 1989).

accomplished in the car on the way to the courthouse...." Fortunately in the *Felker* case, when new counsel was appointed, counsel was able to secure child support until the child reached the age of 18.

The most frequently sustained ethical violation against parents' attorneys is their failure to complete the client's case, often leaving parents without the adoption or custody of their child upon which they had reasonably relied. For instance, in *In the Matter of Anonymous Member of the South Carolina Bar*,[28] an attorney was privately reprimanded for failing to complete a stepfather adoption. The court invalidated a conditional consent to adoption because the biological father had not consented to the stepparent adoption; then, the attorney, even after being notified that the biological father was now willing to consent, failed to refile the adoption papers. In addition to the private reprimand, the court ordered the attorney either to complete the stepparent adoption or to return the $500 fee.[29] And in *In the Matter of Kenneth L. Mitchum*[30] an attorney was publicly reprimanded for failing to complete an adoption and for failing to keep his clients informed regarding the status of the case.[31] Similarly, in *Kentucky Bar Association v. L. M. Tipton Reed*[32] an attorney was disbarred for neglecting to fulfill his promise to a mother to vacate a custody order removing her daughter from her custody.[33] And the Kansas Supreme Court in *In the Matter of Terri Stroh Tweedly*[34] indefinitely suspended an attorney for failing to represent the client in a termination of parental rights action: "Respondent [attorney] failed to keep appointments, failed to return telephone calls, and failed to obtain service on the incarcerated defendant [father]."[35] It is clear that the bar needs to

---

[28] *In the Matter of Anonymous Member of the South Carolina Bar*, 377 S.E. 2nd 572 (South Carolina 1989).

[29] *Id.* at 528529. *See also Grove v. State Bar of California*, 58 Cal. Rptr. 564 (1967).

[30] 501 S.E. 2d 733, 735 (South Carolina 1998).

[31] In *People v. Baird*, 772 P. 2d 110, 111 (Colorado 1989), an attorney was publicly censured for failing to complete a stipulated agreement for a change of custody order. And in *In re Randall B. Kopf*, 767 S.W. 2d 20, an attorney was publicly admonished for failing to complete a stepdaughter adoption within a five-year period.

[32] *Kentucky Bar Association v. L. M. Tipton Reed*, 814 S. W. 2d 927 (Kentucky 1991).

[33] In *In the Matter of Rodney H. Roberts*, 366 S. E. 2d 679, 680 (Georgia 1988), an attorney was disbarred when he lied to his clients that he had filed an adoption proceeding on their behalf and that the adoption was finalized. And the Minnesota Supreme Court in *In the Matter of the Application for the Discipline of Richard W. Curott*, 375 N.W. 2d 472, 473–474 (1985) publicly reprimanded and suspended for two years an attorney who failed "to complete work for a client in a timely manner" in a grandparent visitation action.

[34] *In the Matter of Terri Stroh Tweedly*, 20 P. 3d 1245, 1247 (Kansas 2001).

[35] In *In re Paul L. Wood*, 686 So. 2d 35, 36 (Louisiana 1997) an attorney was suspended for failing to complete an adoption matter and for failing to return the client's files. And in *People v. Paulson*, 930 P. 2d 582, 583 (Colorado 1997) an attorney was suspended for failing to perfect his client's "effort to gain custody of her grandson." In *Broadway v. Kentucky Bar Association*,

provide greater continuing education to counsel representing parents in child custody and dependency proceedings so that counsel can learn not only the substantive law but also case management skills that will enable diligent, as well as zealous and competent, representation in these expedited legal proceedings.

B. *Competence and Zealousness*

Parents' attorneys owe their clients the same duties of competence and zealousness owed to all other clients. Yet, attorneys representing accused parents in dependency court have a difficult job because society rarely provides such counsel with positive feedback because of their "unpopular ... ethical responsibility to zealously represent persons accused of socially abhorrent conduct."[36] However, counsel representing mothers and/or fathers are not shielded by their inexperience or lack of legal expertise in the sometimes very complicated legal proceedings involving child custody.[37] For instance, in *Toledo Bar Association v. Vild*[38] the parents' attorney failed to order a home study in preparation for an adoption proceeding. Although the disciplinary panel found that the attorney's failure to secure the home study was "a result of his complete inexperience and lack of knowledge regarding adoption procedures ... ," the panel publicly reprimanded the attorney for violating *Code of Professional Conduct, DR 6–101(A)(1)*, which provides that "a lawyer shall not undertake a legal matter which he is not competent to handle, unless he associates with a lawyer who is competent to handle it."[39] And in *People v. Aron*[40] an attorney in a child custody matter was suspended from practice for thirty days for failing to adequately "research the issues involved before giving legal advice" and for failing to advise his client that she could be criminally responsible for violating a child custody order. The mother was arrested and the children taken into protective custody and returned to

---

997 S. W. 2d 467 (Kentucky 1999) an attorney voluntarily resigned after the state bar brought charges that he, among other violations, falsely informed a mother that he had adequately represented her in a visitation and custody dispute. The California Supreme Court in *Lester v. State Bar*, 131 Cal. Rptr. 225 (1976) suspended an attorney for willful failure to perform legal services in a paternity case. *See also In Re Complaint of Wesley Scott Bridges*, 728 P. 2d 863 (Oregon 1986), wherein the state supreme court disbarred an attorney for failing to perform work for a parent in a divorce action.

[36] Sandra Anderson Garcia & Robert Batey, *The Roles of Counsel for the Parent in Child Dependency Proceedings*, 22 GA. L. REV. 1079, 1080 (1988).

[37] One study found that "lack of training" was one of the principal factors in the inefficiency of child dependency courts. *Id.* at 1079, 1080.

[38] 702 N.E. 2d 865 (Ohio 1998).

[39] *Id.* at 865-866.

[40] *People v. Aron*, 962 P. 2d 261 (Colorado 1998).

their father in another state. The mother "received a deferred sentence from the court, based in part on her reliance on Aron's [the attorney's] advice regarding keeping her children with her" in another state.[41]

Although many disciplinary cases have involved parents' attorneys' incompetence, perhaps an equal number of cases involve overly zealous attorney behavior in which the attorneys either suggest or facilitate illegal conduct. In *People v. Chappell*[42] the Colorado Supreme Court disbarred an attorney in a child custody case who instructed a mother how to run away with her child after the court ordered a transfer of custody to the father. The attorney explained to the mother "'the underground'... assisted in emptying her bank accounts, and had advised her on how to avoid being caught."[43]

And in a very complicated case, *Harrison v. Mississippi Bar*,[44] the Mississippi Supreme Court disbarred an attorney, in part because he counseled a mother to violate a court order placing the custody of her daughter with her husband. The case was complicated because of the mother's allegations that the father had sexually abused the daughter and because the Department of Social Services in California had intervened in another state for a court order denying the change of custody to the father. However, after medical examinations proved insufficient evidence of sexual abuse, the California dependency court withdrew its jurisdiction and ordered implementation of the Mississippi court order changing the daughter's custody to the father. The Mississippi disciplinary committee found that the mother's attorney "aided Singley [the mother] in hiding Chrissy" from her father.[45]

Courts have also disciplined parents' attorneys for *ex parte* communications and failure to give notice to adverse parties. In both *In the Matter of Carl S. Black*[46] and in *Iowa Supreme Court Board of Professional Ethics and Conduct v. Donna Lesyshen*,[47] the Kansas and Iowa Supreme Courts

---

[41] *Id.* at 262–263. *See also People v. Dowhan*, 951 P. 2d 905, 905–907 (Colorado 1998), in which an attorney was suspended for forty-five days for failing to competently counsel a mother regarding the perils of moving to another jurisdiction before a court modification was made of the custody agreement. As a result, custody of the mother's child was transferred to the father, she was held in contempt of court, fined $1,500 with $1,000 suspended, and granted visitation with her son only every other weekend. *Id.* at 906.

[42] *People v. Chappell*, 927 P. 2d 829 (Colorado 1996).

[43] *Id.* at 830–831.

[44] *Harrison v. Mississippi Bar*, 637 So. 2d 204 (Mississippi 1994).

[45] *See also People v. Mercer*, 35 P. 3d 598 (Colorado 2001), in which the court found that an attorney's return to the noncustodial father of plane tickets sent to the mother to enable the children to travel to visit under a court order with the father was not a violation of ethics because there was insufficient evidence that the mere return of plane tickets "assisted, facilitated or supported the violation of the court visitation order." *Id.* at 607.

[46] *In the Matter of Carl S. Black*, 941 P. 2d 1380 (Kansas 1997).

[47] *Iowa Supreme Court Board of Professional Ethics and Conduct v. Donna Lesyshen*, 585 N. W. 2d 281 (Iowa 1998).

suspended attorneys for representing mothers in *ex parte* child custody proceedings without notifying the fathers of those legal hearings. And the Kansas Supreme Court in *In the Matter of Daniel L. Swagerty*[48] publicly censured an attorney who represented prospective adoptive parents for his failure to notice and obtain consent from the presumed father.

Parents' counsel are sometimes confused over the difference between zealous advocacy and inappropriate fact investigation. For instance, *ABA Model Rule 4.2* states, "In representing a client, a lawyer shall not communicate about the subject of the representation with a party whom the lawyer knows to be represented in the matter by another lawyer, unless the lawyer has the consent of the other lawyer or is authorized by law to do so." What if the parents' attorney wants to speak with the child who is the subject of the petition? Because children in many jurisdictions are represented by the Department's attorney, must parents gain his or her consent before speaking with the allegedly abused child?

The answer to a related question, whether the parents' attorney must seek the consent of the Department's attorney before questioning a social worker, is no. In *Michigan Standing Committee on Professional and Judicial Ethics Opinion RI-316*[49] the Ethics Committee indicated that counsel for a minor may directly contact a social worker because (1) the social worker is a governmental employee; (2) the child's attorney is statutorily obligated to contact government employees involved in the case; and (3) the commentary to *ABA Rule 4.2* provides, "Communications authorized by law include, for example, the right of a party to a controversy with a government agency to speak with government officials about the matter."[50] Because parents, as well as children, are involved as parties with a government agency in the dependency case, it would appear that parents' counsel need not obtain the consent of the Department's attorney before speaking with the social worker. The Ethics Committee further provided that "[i]n order for all parties associated with the case to accomplish the goals of the Child Protection Act, both the guardian ad litem and lawyer for the parents must have access to the government agency that is responsible for the investigation and ultimate recommendation to the court relating to any plan the court may impose should

---

[48] *In the Matter of Daniel L. Swagerty*, 739 P. 2d 937 (Kansas 1987).

[49] *Michigan State Bar Standing Committee on Professional and Judicial Ethics, Opinion RI316* (December 13, 1999).

[50] *Id.* at 2. *See also Alaska Bar Association Ethics Opinions Nos. 71-1* (April 14, 1971) *and 84-11* (Nov. 1, 1984), permitting access to governmental witnesses as long as the attorney "reveals to the employee his identity and representation and the connection between the representation and the communication." *Id.* at *Opinion No. 71-1. See also Alabama State Bar Opinion Number 2003–03.*

jurisdiction be obtained in the case."[51] The practice of giving parties access to the social worker without a formal requirement of consent by the Department's lawyer is consistent with the policy of permitting liberal informal discovery in dependency proceedings in order to expedite permanency.[52]

However, the same informal access to the social worker does not apply when the parents' attorney wishes to question the abused child. Even if the Department's attorney also represents the child, the policy underlying the liberal access rules for social workers does not apply because children are not governmental employees who are mandated to conduct the fact investigation for the government. Thus, in *South Carolina Bar Ethics Advisory Committee Opinion 97-15*[53] the Ethics Committee held that *ABA Rule 4.2* mandated that parents' counsel gain the consent of the child's guardian ad litem before questioning the child.[54] Although the Ethics Committee indicated that *ABA Model Rule 4.2* was not directly applicable because the child was represented by a guardian ad litem and not counsel, it held that, because the child lacks the capacity to represent herself, a guardian ad litem for discovery purposes should be treated as an alternative equivalent of a party represented by counsel. The Ethics Committee noted that even if the child wants to speak with the parents' counsel, consent of the child's representative is still required because the child lacks capacity to waive the consent requirement.[55]

Parents' attorneys have often been disciplined for exceeding the bounds of zealous advocacy by implementing illegal acts and/or violations of court and procedural rules to perfect the parents' wishes. For instance, in *Broadway v. Kentucky Bar Association*[56] a father's attorney forged the judge's signature on a change of custody order, and the father used that order without knowledge of its falsity to regain custody of his child. The Kentucky Supreme Court permanently disbarred the attorney because the forgery "reflects adversely on the

---

[51] *Id.* at 3.
[52] For example, *California Rule of Court, Rule 1420* provides that the dependency discovery rule "shall be liberally construed in favor of informal disclosures, subject to the right of a party to show privilege or other good cause not to disclose specific material or information...."
[53] *South Carolina Bar Ethics Advisory Committee Opinion 97-15* (December 1997).
[54] *Id.* at 1.
[55] *Id.* at 2. The North Carolina State Bar, in *Communication with a Child Represented by GAL and Attorney Advocate*, RPC 249 (April 3, 1997), also held that a parents' counsel must seek consent from either the GAL or child's lawyer in order to interview the abused child. The Ethics Committee also indicated that a prosecutor in the criminal child abuse action and the Department's attorney in the dependency proceeding must also garner consent before interviewing the child. *Id.* at 1. And the Wisconsin Supreme Court in *In the Matter of Disciplinary Proceedings Against Frank X. Kinast*, 530 N.W. 2d 387 (Wisconsin 1995), held that a wife's attorney in a civil custody proceeding must obtain consent from the child's GAL or attorney before questioning the minor.
[56] *Broadway v. Kentucky Bar Association*, 8 S. W. 3d 572 (Kentucky 2000).

lawyer's honesty, trustworthiness or fitness...."[57] In *Ex rel. Nebraska State Bar Association v. Thomas R. Zakrezewski*[58] the Nebraska Supreme Court suspended an attorney for filing a false affidavit alleging that his client's ex-wife's attorney directed her to file a false child abuse claim against his client. The Court merely suspended the offending attorney because the action involved the attorney's brother and because the attorney "was so personally involved that a proper level of objectivity was lost."[59] And in a similar case in Florida, *The Florida Bar v. Charles F. Wishart*,[60] the Florida Supreme Court found that the referee's recommendation for disbarment was excessive and instead issued the attorney a three-year suspension because the ethical violations involved a custody proceeding involving his step-granddaughter. The attorney, in representing the child's father, sent the judge letters "containing information that was beyond the scope of the evidence presented at the prior hearings and potentially damaging to the mother."[61] The dissent argued that disbarment was appropriate because the justice could "think of no more flagrant misconduct by an attorney than deliberately disobeying a series of direct orders by the court ... [and because the attorney] indicated that he would engage in this conduct again not only when his granddaughter was involved but on behalf of clients as well, if he felt it necessary."[62] And in *Disciplinary Action Against Shirley A. Dvorak*,[63] an attorney in a divorce action was suspended from practice for one year after using confidential and privileged statements by a witness in a guardian ad litem questionnaire for the purposes of humiliation and denial of access to witnesses.

In *Colorado v. Karen J. Roose*[64] a mother's counsel in a termination of parental rights proceedings lied to the court regarding material facts, including an assertion that she represented the mother even though another court had relieved her as counsel and forbidden her from filing any more motions for the mother.[65] Because of the attorney's attempted involvement in the case, the mother refused to cooperate and appear at the termination hearing, which resulted in the severance of her parental rights.[66] Based upon

---

[57] *Id.* at 573. In *In the Matter of Disciplinary Proceedings Against Curt M. Weber*, 579 N.W. 2d 229 (Wisconsin 1998) an attorney represented parents in a termination of parental rights case even though his license had previously been revoked. Luckily, the client was not severely prejudiced and was able to secure other counsel to perfect his legal rights. *Id.* at 230.

[58] *Ex rel. Nebraska State Bar Association v. Thomas R. Zakrezewski*, 560 N. W. 2d 150 (Nebraska 1997).

[59] *Id.* at 156.

[60] *The Florida Bar v. Charles F. Wishart*, 543 So. 2d 1250 (Florida 1989).

[61] *Id.* at 1250–1251. [62] *Id.* at 1252–1253.

[63] *Disciplinary Action Against Shirley A. Dvorak*, 611 N.W. 2d 147, 150–151 (North Dakota 2000).

[64] *Colorado v. Karen J. Roose*, 44 P. 2d 266 (Colorado 2002).

[65] *Id.* at 267–268. [66] *Id.* at 268–269.

the misstatements of material facts and the attorney's effect of stripping the mother of a zealous advocate and presence at the termination hearing, the attorney was disbarred.[67]

Parents' attorneys also have been disciplined for breaching rules of civility in highly charged emotional custody proceedings. For instance, in *Cuyahoga County Bar Association v. Stafford*,[68] a case involving a contested visitation schedule, one attorney called the other "a piece of shit," who then responded that the other attorney was "a total asshole."[69] The Ohio supreme court publicly reprimanded both attorneys for engaging in "undignified or discourteous conduct which is degrading to a tribunal" based upon *ABA DR 7-106(C)(6)*.[70] And in *In the Matter of Carl S. Black*[71] the Kansas Supreme Court found that an attorney violated a state rule of professional conduct by using "means that have no substantial purpose other than to embarrass, delay, or burden a third party" when he made "angry outbursts" criticizing a party opposing his client for wearing "the uniform of the United States Army..." in a child custody hearing.[72]

Because parents' attorneys are often solo practitioners without the assistance of other attorneys to help with often unconscionably heavy caseloads and because of the very low pay for dependency court work, often they either rely too much on lay employees or use inexperienced attorneys without providing sufficient supervision. One must question whether court-appointed attorneys who carry a caseload of approximately 658 cases representing parents accused of abusing or neglecting their children can provide all those clients zealous and competent representation.[73] For example, in *Harrison v. Mississippi Bar*[74] the Mississippi Supreme Court disbarred an attorney, in part, for failing to supervise a nonlawyer employee. The attorney used that lay employee to hide his client's daughter from her father, even though the father had a court custody order. The court found that the attorney violated *Rule 5.3(b)*, which provides "that with respect to a nonlawyer employed or retained by or associated with a lawyer: (b) a lawyer having direct supervisory authority over the nonlawyer shall make reasonable efforts to ensure that the person's conduct is compatible with the professional obligations of the lawyer."

And in *In the Matter of Robert C. Yacavino*[75] the New Jersey Supreme Court issued a three-year suspension to an attorney for failing to supervise

---

[67] *Id.* at 73.
[68] *Cuyahoga County Bar Association v. Stafford*, 733 N. E. 2d 587 (Ohio 2000).
[69] *Id.* at 587. [70] *Id.* at 586.
[71] *In the Matter of Carl S. Black*, 941 P. 2d 1380 (Kansas 1997).
[72] *Id.* at 1383–1384. [73] *Id.* at 32.
[74] *Harrison v. Mississippi Bar*, 637 So. 2d 204 (Mississippi 1994).
[75] *In the Matter of Robert C. Yacavino*, 494 A. 2d 801 (New Jersey 1985).

a subordinate attorney in an adoption matter. The court's description of the attorney's satellite office is an ethical horror story: The novice attorney "was left virtually alone and unsupervised in the year that he serviced the firm's Pompton Plains office. The office was lacking in the essential tools of legal practice. Partners rarely attended the office; no member of the firm inquired as to the status of the office matters."[76] The court indicated that a supervising attorney has several ethical obligations regarding new lawyers: (1) collegial support, (2) "a systematic organized routine for periodic review of a newly admitted attorney's files," and (3) assurance that supervised attorneys conform to the rules of professional conduct.[77]

Attorneys who represent parents must be careful not to exploit the mother's or father's vulnerability during the stressful proceedings because doing so might result in the permanent severance of their relationship with their children. The Alaska Bar Association Ethics Committee determined that it is "unethical for a lawyer to become intimately involved with a client of the firm during the course of the firm's representation in a termination of parental rights proceeding."[78] The Ethics Committee noted a number of deleterious effects stemming from such an intimate relationship with a parent: (1) a potential that the attorney will be called as a witness; (2) psychological harm to the parent client; and (3) the possibility that sexual conduct may be "exchanged for legal services, non-consensual, coercive, or illegal."[79] Because of the fragile emotional condition of parents facing termination of their parental rights, the Ethics Committee held that such a sexual relationship "triggers the presumption" of harm to the client, and the firm, not just the attorney having the sexual relationship, must withdraw from representing that client.

The previous examples of parents' attorneys' ethical violations clearly demonstrate the failure of our current professional machinery to sufficiently educate, support, and regulate these attorneys regarding diligence, competence, and zealousness in child dependency and custody proceedings. Parents' counsel often serve on large informal panels of appointed attorneys and work in isolation as solo practitioners without the support and ethical sounding board provided in governmental offices or even in small to medium-sized law offices. If the salary scale or flat-fee rate for parents' attorneys were sufficiently increased to reduce the necessity of such high caseloads, many of the issues involving competency and underzealous advocacy would quickly disappear.

---

[76] *Id.* at 803.   [77] *Id.* at 803–804.
[78] Alaska Bar Association Ethics Committee, Opinion 92-6 (October 30, 1992).
[79] *Id.* at 1–2.

III. THE DEPARTMENT'S ATTORNEY: FURTHERING JUSTICE OR ZEALOUS ADVOCATE?

Because child dependency proceedings are basically civil cases, is the role of the Department's counsel equivalent to that of a private practitioner in ordinary civil litigation, or does the ultimate dispute over the fundamental right to parent ethically elevate the Department's counsel closer to the role of a criminal prosecutor? The history of the treatment of procedural due process in the United States Supreme Court adds to the ambiguous status of the Department's representative, rather than providing clarity. For instance, in *Lassiter v. Department of Social Services*[80] the Supreme Court, in a termination of parental rights case, for the first time indicated that the right to appointed counsel to a party whose personal liberty was not threatened might be required under some circumstances. The Court noted that the loss of a fundamental liberty interest, such as the right to rear one's child, is, like a loss of liberty, sufficient under certain circumstances to trigger the due process clause of the Fourteenth Amendment requiring the appointment of counsel.[81] However, one year later the Supreme Court held that a standard of proof by clear and convincing evidence, rather than the criminal court requirement of beyond a reasonable doubt, was sufficient due process in termination of parental rights cases.[82] Dependency cases are thus quasi-criminal or quasi-civil, depending upon how one characterizes the consequences of losing the fundamental right to associate and rear children.

If one analogizes to the quasi-criminal model in which the Department's counsel functions as a government prosecutor, County Counsel's ethical obligations may be significantly different from that of a quasi-civil private

---

[80] *Lassiter v. Department of Social Services*, 101 S. Ct. 2155 (1981).
[81] *Id.*
[82] *Santosky v. Kramer*, 102 S. Ct. 1388 (1982). The California Supreme Court in *Cynthia D. v. Superior Court*, 19 Cal. Rptr. 2d 608 (1993), determined that because of the unique nature of the California dependency system, which, unlike the New York system analyzed in *Santosky*, has as its main purpose the reunification of the family in an environment in which parents have counsel and the state does not have a decisive advantage over the parents, only a preponderance of the evidence standard was required. However, it is time to rethink *Cynthia D.* because of several changes in the California dependency system. First, in a significant number of cases reunification is no longer the immediate or central goal (*Welf. & Inst. Code* § 361.5). Second, the California system now requires concurrent planning in which reunification services are to be considered at the same time and to the same extent as permanent alternative placement in adoption or long-term guardianship. Therefore, the current California system looks more like the New York system analyzed in *Santosky* because the state has concurrent dual purposes in its treatment of the parents and family. These dual purposes increase exponentially the chances of errors in the fact-finding process and in the state's ability to shape the facts as delineated in *Santosky*. Therefore, the protection of a clear and convincing evidence standard is now needed in California just as it was needed in *Santosky*.

litigator. For example, the *American Bar Association Standards of Practice for Lawyers Representing Child Welfare Agencies* notes that the agency lawyer "should work with the agency to bring only appropriate cases to court" and should counsel the agency regarding the political consequences of its decisions.[83] And in California, the Department's lawyer, like a criminal prosecutor, must *sua sponte* proffer exculpatory evidence.[84] Some might argue that the Department's attorney, like a criminal prosecutor, is entitled to a grant of absolute immunity while acting in the role of a prosecutor during legal advocacy.[85] However, others might argue that the roles of criminal prosecutors and the Department of Children and Family Services counsel are too dissimilar to provide them with absolute immunity.[86] For instance, the criminal prosecutor, unlike the Department's counsel, does not have an identifiable client, but rather represents the public in general.[87]

The absence of an identifiable client places additional ethical burdens on a criminal prosecutor because he or she has greater autonomy and discretion in decision making than most other attorneys.[88] Therefore, *Model*

---

[83] *American Bar Association Standards of Practice for Lawyers Representing Child Welfare Agencies*, Rule C–1(3) (August 2004).

[84] *Brady v. Maryland*, 373 U.S. 83, 87 (1963); ABA Model Code provision DR 7–103(B); Cal. Const. Art. I, § 1. California Rules of Court, Rule 1420(c) provides the "[p]etitioner shall disclose any evidence or information within petitioner's possession or control favorable to the child, parent, or guardian."

[85] Criminal prosecutors are granted absolute immunity from civil damage claims brought under §1983. *Imbler v. Pachtman*, 424 U.S. 409, 428–29 (1976). However, absolute immunity covers those acts that are traditionally considered within the role as advocate in order to protect the judicial process. *Milstein v. County of Los Angeles*, 2001 DJDAR 7514, *7515* (2001). It does not cover such actions as talking to the press outside the courtroom. *Id.* at 7515–17.

[86] In California several courts have held that social workers while conducting quasi-judicial acts, such as filing a child abuse report, act like a prosecutor and are entitled to absolute immunity. *Gensburg v. Miller*, 37 Cal. Rptr. 2d 97 (1994); *Jenkins v. County of Orange*, 260 Cal. Rptr. 645 (1989). However, when the social worker's acts cease being like judicial actions, such as during the long-term supervision of a dependency case during reunification, they may be covered under qualified immunity. *Scott v. County of Los Angeles*, 32 Cal. Rptr. 643 (1994). Because county counsel who represent the Department that supervises social workers receive immunity, one might argue that county counsel's immunity should be coextensive with that of social workers.

[87] Fred Zacharias, *The Professional Discipline of Prosecutors*, 79 N. C. L. REV. 721, 726 (2001). Bruce A. Green states that a criminal prosecutor is different from all other attorneys, including other governmental attorneys, because the prosecutor "is the representative of the sovereignty in two senses: the lawyer is counsel for the government and a government official. In this dual role, prosecutors must serve the government aim of 'seeking justice.'" *Must Government Lawyers "Seek Justice" in Civil Litigation?*, 9 WIDENER J. PUB. L. 235, 238 (2000).

[88] "Prosecutors have significant, often controlling, discretion to determine which constituency of the state should be considered dominant in any particular case. As a result, rules governing conflicts among clients and rules designed to protect the autonomy of decision-making authority of clients rarely apply to them." *Id.*

Rules of Professional Conduct, Rule 3.8 (2000) places many constraints upon prosecutors that might, if imposed upon counsel representing an identifiable client, violate the dictates of zealous, loyal, and confidential representation. For instance, under *Rule 3.8*, a criminal prosecutor must (1) make reasonable efforts to see that the defendant has been advised of his or her rights and an opportunity to obtain counsel, (2) not seek to obtain waivers of rights by an unrepresented client, (3) take care to prevent employees from making prohibited extrajudicial statements, and (4) refrain from making public statements that might be prejudicial to the defendant.[89] None of the codes of professional responsibility places similar burdens upon the Department's attorney if he or she has an identifiable client.

Therefore, are the roles of the prosecutor in a criminal case and that of the Department's counsel in a dependency case really ethically analogous, even though they share many similarities? Perhaps the tie-breaker is the question of whether these attorneys have obligations greater than those of zealous, loyal, and competent representation of an identifiable client. There is a continuing debate over whether all attorneys owe an overarching duty to do justice that transcends client obligations. For instance, in 1908 the American Bar Association required all attorneys to take an oath not to "counsel or maintain[90] any action, proceeding, or defense which shall appear to [us] as unjust."[91] The greatest consensus on whether an attorney must seek justice involves criminal prosecutors who as "ministers of justice" "must not attempt to achieve her ends of justice through unjust means."[92]

However, there is much greater debate over whether other governmental attorneys, like the Department's counsel, must seek justice or just represent their client's interests. For instance, the ABA has determined that "a government lawyer has no greater duty of candor to opposing parties and to the tribunal than a private party's lawyer."[93] Most sources do not extend the prosecutor's duty "to refrain from seeking judicial rulings that they know to be contrary to law, to call the court's attention to its legal or procedural

---

[89] Geoffrey C. Hazard, Jr., *Conflicts of Interest in Representation of Public Agencies in Civil Matters*, 9 WIDENER J. PUB. L. 211 (2000).

[90] Bruce A. Green, *supra* note 58, at 241.

[91] Robert E. Rodes, Jr., *Government Lawyers*, 9 WIDENER J. PUB. L. 281, 281–82 (2000), quoting the Canons of Ethics of the American Bar Association Oath of Admission (1908).

[92] Lesley E. Williams, *The Civil Regulation of Prosecutors*, 67 FORDHAM L. REV. 3441, 3443 (1999); *Model Rule of Professional Responsibility, Rule 3.8*.

[93] Cathleen C. Cavell, *Ethical Lawyering in Massachusetts, Chapter 18, §18.4* (2000). In addition, the ethical standards under the *Model Rules of Professional Conduct for Federal Lawyers, Rule 1.13* "now clearly state that an agency is the client and that, absent illegal or unethical behavior, a DOJ attorney owes loyalty to that agency." James R. Harvey III, *Loyalty in Government Litigation: Department of Justice Representation of Agency Clients*, 37 WM. & MARY L. REV. 1569, 1596 (1996).

mistakes, and to correct the errors and omissions of opposing counsel in certain situations."[94] Determining whether a Department's counsel views his or her role as purely an adversary in representing the Department or as also one of seeking justice as a governmental representative can be delineated by the following hypothetical:

> County counsel [the Department's attorney] in a termination of parental rights case based upon the failure of the parent to visit with the child for a period of six months as a condition of reunification, knows that the foster parents have on several occasions intentionally refused the parent access to visitation with the child.[95] Further assume that the parent's attorney does not raise this issue at the termination hearing.[96]

If the Department's counsel assumes the role of a zealous civil advocate for the Department, he or she will probably be constrained by codes of ethics from *sua sponte* informing the court of this critical fact, which could demonstrate that the parent could not be held accountable for failing to visit with the child. A zealous government counsel might provide several arguments why disclosure of exculpatory evidence within counsel's control was not required. First, it could be argued that requiring disclosure to a parent of exculpatory evidence "within petitioner's possession or control" is inapplicable because the purpose of that section is to provide parents with access to information that a parent might not on his or her own be able to discover. Second, if the Department's legal representative knows that the parent already has that potentially exculpatory evidence, as in this hypothetical, the duty to disclose no longer exists. Therefore, the zealous Department's counsel could confidently remain silent and let the court terminate the parents' rights if that result was consistent with the Department's litigation goal.

However, what if the Department's counsel believes that as a governmental attorney he or she owes loyalty, confidentiality, and zealousness to the Department, as well as a duty to see that justice is served in the individual case? It is critical that governmental attorneys remain vigilant and independent in counseling their clients about the ethical, political, and strategic consequences of their actions. Experts have described the problems that develop

---

[94] Bruce A. Green, *supra* note 58, at 241.

[95] Pursuant to *Welfare & Institutions Code* §366.26(c)(1), if parents have not contacted the child for six months that evidence is a "sufficient basis for terminating parental rights...."

[96] For instance, California Welfare and Institutions Code § 366.26 provides that termination of parental rights shall not proceed if the court finds that "at each and every hearing at which the court was required to consider reasonable efforts or services, the court has found that reasonable efforts were not made or that reasonable services were not offered or provided."

when counsel loses an independent perspective and associates too closely with the client: "Once a lawyer identifies with a client, she now sees things differently from before, directly as a result of that allegiance."[97] The consensus is that a government lawyer, absent a statutory or ethical mandate, may not act on his or her own and disclose the fact of the foster parents' frustration of parental visits because doing so would violate the ethical duties to the client, the Department.[98]

The *American Bar Association Standards of Practice* cast the agency lawyer in a hybrid role as zealous advocate for the agency, but with the added responsibility to see that the child's best interests are also considered by the court. For instance, *Standard D-4* provides that the agency lawyer "[p]lay an active role in deciding whether the child should testify and/or be present in the courtroom during hearings."[99] Although that statement, on its face, might merely refer to the strategic decision whether the child's live testimony would assist the agency's case, the *Comments* to *Standard D-4* indicate that the decision also involves the child's psychological health: "It is important to consider the child's wishes, any possible effects of the testimony and the child's developmental ability to handle cross-examination." But the *Comments* also note that there may be cases in which the agency may not want the child to testify because it might psychologically harm the child, but where the agency attorney needs the child to testify in order to present sufficient evidence of abuse to withstand a motion to dismiss. And the *Comments* recognize the role of the agency and its attorney to propose and/or support prophylactic protections for child witnesses, such as having the child's attorney, rather than the agency's attorney, examine the child or requesting an *in camera* hearing with the child testifying in chambers without the presence of parents.[100]

Often, the role between the attorney and the Department is defined by statute. For instance, in *Mississippi State Attorney General Opinion No. 94-0408*,[101] it was held that the attorney representing the Department acts on behalf of the Department as a client and has no independent status as a governmental prosecutor.[102] In addition, that opinion held that the Department's attorney has no independent judgment to refuse to file a dependency petition against the Department's recommendation or authority to dismiss

---

[97] Robert F. Cochran, Jr. et al., *Symposium: Client Counseling and Moral Responsibility*, 30 PEPP. L. REV. 591, 624 (2003).

[98] *ABA Formal Opinion 94-387* (September 26, 1994).

[99] *Standards of Practice for Lawyers Representing Child Welfare Agencies*, Standard D-4 (American Bar Association, August 2004).

[100] *Id.* Standard D-4, Action and Commentary.

[101] Mississippi State Attorney General Opinion No. 94-0408 (August 17, 1994).

[102] *Id.* at 2.

a petition or enter into a plea agreement with parents without the consent of the Department.[103]

However, a different conclusion was reached in *Kansas Attorney General Opinion No. 90–33*,[104] in which the state statute permits a nongovernmental employee to seek a dependency petition and in which the role of the district attorney is to exercise discretion whether to file that dependency petition. Under that circumstance, the role of the Department social worker is that of fact investigator and witness, not the attorney's client.[105] "As such, the county or district attorney is not required to represent SR [the Department of Social Services] anymore than the county or district attorney is required to represent any other witness."[106]

In addition to zealous representation, the government's attorney also owes the Department a duty of competence. In many jurisdictions criminal prosecutors rotate into assignments in dependency court with little or no training in this specialized area of law. In one study, assistant state attorneys "[expressed] concern that prosecuting attorneys do not have the requisite skills to optimally fulfill their mandate to represent the state in the dependency proceedings."[107] Some states, like California, have specific statutes guaranteeing competent counsel to all parties in dependency proceedings and requiring attorneys to have specific training in such areas as child development before representing a party in court.[108]

In many states the Department's attorney is not treated differently from other attorneys regarding the duty of competence. For instance, the New York State Bar Association Committee on Professional Ethics was questioned whether attorneys who represent the Department of Social Services in dependency, paternity, and family law have a duty of competency, even though they carry excessively large caseloads.[109] The Committee indicated that government attorneys representing the Department are required to meet the ABA competency requirements, as well as those contained in the *American Law*

---

[103] *Id.* at 3–4. And the Department may not turn over its discretion in dependency cases to a nonlawyer professional because that would constitute the practice of law without a license. *See Rozmus v. Rozmus*, 595 N.W. 2d 893 (Nebraska 1999).

[104] *Office of the Attorney General of Kansas, Opinion No. 90-33* (March 19, 1990).

[105] *Id.* at 1.   [106] *Id.* at 3–4.

[107] Sandra Anderson Garcia & Robert Batey, *supra* note 36, 1079, 1090.

[108] *See California Welfare & Institutions Code §§ 317.5 and 317.6*, which provide that "[all parties who are represented by counsel at dependency proceedings shall be entitled to competent counsel" and that the California Judicial Council shall "adopt rules of court regarding the appointment of competent counsel in dependency proceedings...." Arguably, under these statutes, the Department is entitled to competent counsel, but because the Department's counsel is not appointed by the court, the guidelines and/or requirements for training are not applicable to the Department's attorney.

[109] *New York State Bar Association, Committee on Professional Ethics, Opinion 751* (May 6, 2002).

Institute, Restatement Third of the Law Governing Lawyers, § 16(1)(2), which provides that a lawyer must "proceed in a manner reasonably calculated to advance [the] client's lawful objectives," but also must "act with reasonable competence and diligence." The Committee argued by analogy to several ABA and state bar opinions that have held that legal services lawyers have a duty to withdraw from cases if their caseload is so excessive as to lead to incompetent representation.[110] The New York Bar Committee also held that a lawyer may not seek a waiver of the duty of competence from the client because *ABA Model Rule 1.2, Comment* provides that "[an agreement concerning the scope of representation must accord with the Rules of Professional Conduct and other law." Thus, the Committee held that a government lawyer representing the Department may not follow the orders of the Department to provide less than competent lawyering, such as when a Department employee informs the attorney to "just show up" or "just do the best you can do" without sufficient preparation, especially if the government attorney has an ethical obligation to "seek justice."[111]

The recently promulgated *ABA Standards of Practice for Lawyers Representing Child Welfare Agencies* mandate very specific tasks for agency attorneys in defining zealous and competent representation of their clients, including the following: (1) knowledge of applicable laws, rules, and policies; (2) regular communication with the agency; (3) development of a case theory and the petition; (4) sufficient fact investigation; (5) participation in all proceedings, including alternative dispute resolution, such as mediation and negotiation; (6) preparation and presentation of opening arguments, direct and cross-examination of subpoenaed witnesses, and closing arguments; and (7) filing of "necessary post-hearing motions and the notice to appeal."[112]

Because of the negative jurogenic effects of the legal system on children, many jurisdictions have promulgated rules to soften the effects of zealous advocacy on children in child dependency and/or custody cases.[113] And because expediency is essential to reaching permanency as quickly as possible for the abused child, most states have promulgated liberal discovery rules

---

[110] For instance, *ABA Ethics Opinion 399* (1996) held that legal services lawyers must "withdraw from some matters if funding and staff reductions greatly increase these lawyers' workloads, since maintaining an unmanageable case load violates the lawyer's duty...to provide competent representation." ABA Ethics Opinion 347 (1981) earlier had informed legal services lawyers to withdraw from some cases if the caseload might lead to incompetent representation.

[111] NESTA Opinion *751*, at 2.   [112] *Standards, Rule B-1 (1)-(27)*.

[113] For instance, in *In the Matter of the Application for Disciplinary Action Against Shirley A. Dvorak*, 611 N.W. 2d 147 (North Dakota Supreme Court, May 18, 2000), the court in a family law case determined that counsel's obstruction of the parties' access to data and other charges warranted a one-year suspension.

that do not require court intervention. For instance, in California dependency proceedings, "[e]xcept where there is a contested issue of fact or law... [the proceedings] shall be conducted in an informal nonadversary atmosphere with a view to obtaining the maximum cooperation of the minor upon whose behalf the petition is brought and all persons interested in his or her welfare...."[114]

Some jurisdictions not only require liberal discovery but also require counsel, *sua sponte*, to disclose exculpatory information.[115] For instance, the Colorado Ethics Committee publicly censured a deputy district attorney for failing to disclose a "child victim's change in testimony" in a criminal child abuse proceeding.[116] Failure of a criminal prosecutor to disclose exculpatory evidence is a violation not only of due process but also of the *ABA Standards for Criminal Justice, Standard 3.3-11*, which provides, "A prosecutor should not intentionally fail to make timely disclosure to the defense, at the earliest feasible opportunity, of the existence of all evidence or information which tends to negate the guilt of the accused or mitigate the offense charged or which would tend to reduce the punishment of the accused."

For example, in *People v. Rolfe*[117] an attorney was publicly censured by the Colorado Supreme Court for failing to notify the defendant or the court that "a caseworker for the county department of health and human services had found the allegations of abuse 'unsubstantiated.'" Although the United States Supreme Court cases requiring disclosure of exculpatory evidence may not apply in child dependency and custody cases,[118] and even if the state has no rule of court requiring such *sua sponte* disclosure, attorneys who do not reveal that data may violate other ethical constraints. For instance, if the child abuse action in *People v. Rolfe* had been filed in the dependency or family court and if the attorney had presented affirmative evidence of the abuse without disclosing the exculpatory evidence, he or she might be found to have violated the canons prohibiting an attorney knowingly from making a false statement of material fact or law to a court or from engaging in

---

[114] *California Welfare and Institutions Code §350.*

[115] For instance, *California Rules of Court, Rule 1420* provides, "This rule shall be liberally construed in favor of informal disclosures, subject to the party to show privilege or other good cause not to disclose specific material or information...Petitioner [the Department] shall disclose any evidence or information within petitioner's possession or control favorable to the child, parent, or guardian...."

[116] *People v. Mucklow*, No. 00PDJ010 (Colorado, December 16, 2000).

[117] *People v. Rolfe* (Colorado Case No. 98SA114, August 10, 1998).

[118] Of course, a colorable argument can be made for applying the due process duty to disclose exculpatory evidence to child dependency cases because the Supreme Court has compared the loss of liberty with the loss of the fundamental right to rear one's children in both *Santosky v. Kramer*, 455 U.S. 745 (1982), and *Lassiter v. Department of Social Services*, 452 U.S. 18 (1981).

conduct involving dishonesty, fraud, deceit, or misrepresentation.[119] Even if the jurisdiction does not have a rule requiring the disclosure of exculpatory evidence by the Department's attorney, because the Department is, by definition, representing the government's view of the best interest of the child, such disclosure is consistent with the main function of the attorney's representation of the Department. In addition, if the Department's attorney does not disclose exculpatory information, a later determination that the Department, in fact, possessed that data can result either in a continuance or in a reversal of the juvenile court judgment. Therefore, failure to disclose that evidence may place the Department's attorney at risk of violating the ABA standard that requires agency attorneys to "[p]romote timely hearings and reduce case continuances."[120] Furthermore, any appellate reversal based upon a failure to disclose material data might harm the children because permanency will be postponed.

IV. JUDGES: NEUTRAL MAGISTRATES OR CHILDREN'S DEFENDERS?

Just how involved may a judicial officer become in attempting to determine or perfect what he or she sees as the best interest of a child? In *Roberts v. Commission on Judicial Performance*[121] the California Supreme Court set out the parameters of trial court involvement in child dependency cases. In that case, the trial court "improperly acted as an advocate, prejudged issues, abusively curtailed the presentation of evidence, and treated witnesses, litigants and an attorney in a rude, intimidating and demeaning manner."[122] The dependency court judge told both the abused child's mother and one of her witnesses that "[y]ou have no credibility with this court. . . . [s]he would have [the mother], who had abused her own child, babysit hers. Now, I don't have to listen to that kind of evidence."[123] The California Supreme Court noted that a judge's "serious concern for the welfare of the minor . . . " may not be improperly demonstrated through a "nonobjective and nonneutral manner, demonstrating unwarranted impatience, disbelief and hostility toward

---

[119] Even though some courts have found that social workers are absolutely immune from prosecution, even if they fabricate evidence in child abuse cases, the Department's attorney has an obligation to inform the other parties and the court of the social worker's lies. *Doe v. Lebbos* (9th Cir., Nov. 4. 2003; Lexis 22632).

[120] *Standards*, Rule C-1(2), *supra* note 89.

[121] *Roberts v. Commission on Judicial Performance*, 661 P. 2d 1064 (1983).

[122] *Id.* at 1066.

[123] *Id.* at 1066–1067. *See* Alaska Commission on Judicial Conduct Opinion #001 (1994) (judges may not "criticize jurors verbally, directly to them, for their work as jurors"). *See also In re Jesse G.*, 2005 WL 905634 (April 20, 2005); *Gloria M. v. Superior Court*, 21 Cal. Supp. 3d 525, 527 (1971).

counsel, litigant, and witnesses."[124] A judge may not "become an advocate for either party or cast aspersions or ridicule upon a witness."[125] Nor may the judge act as the child's legal counsel.

In *Chrissy v. Ms. Dept. of Public Welfare*[126] the federal district court said that it was an error to rely upon judicial officers to supply legal protection for the minor in a custody dispute between paternal and maternal relatives: "The district court erred in attributing . . . [to judicial officers] the constitutional duty to protect Chrissy F.'s procedural rights beyond appointment of a guardian ad litem. To impose such a duty on a judicial officer in the performance of judicial duties is to circumvent the state appellate procedures and potentially to cast the judge in a role uncomfortably close to that of advocate."[127]

In *In the Matter of Louis Grossman*[128] the New York Commission on Judicial Conduct voted to impose censure on a judge in a custody dispute who turned the trial into "a series of grueling cross-examinations" of the 4-year-old child.[129] The custody battle was "bitterly contested," involved threats from outside sources to manipulate the outcome, and even included bomb threats.[130] The judge strenuously cross-examined the child in chambers regarding allegations of sexual abuse by the father in four successive one-hour sessions.[131] The New York Commission on Judicial Conduct found that the trial judge (1) "called the child a liar . . . more than 200 times," (2) told the minor "approximately 40 times that he had given contradictory testimony," (3) "admonished" the child more than 200 times to tell the truth, (4) asked the child 150 times who had told him to lie about the abuse, (5) told the child four times that "he might go to jail if he did not tell the truth," (6) told the child that "handcuffs worn by the court officer were used for people who did not tell the truth," (7) informed the child more than 50 times that

---

[124] *Id.* at 1068–1069.
[125] *Id.* citing *McCartney v. Commission on Judicial Qualifications*, 116 Cal. Rptr. 260, 268 (1974). Although judges need not all fit into a single mold or style (*Matter of Ross*, 428 A.2d 858 (Maine 1981)), they must avoid hostility and discourtesy toward litigants (*Furey v. Commission On Judicial Performance*, 240 Cal. Rptr. 859 (1987)), gender bias (*Lester v. Lennane*, 101 Cal. Rptr. 2d 86 (2000)), and sexual harassment (53 Cal. Rptr. 2d 788 (1996)). For a discussion of the effects and causes of judges who bully those who appear before them, *see* Stephen Yagman, *Longtime Cycle of Bench Bullying*, L. A. DAILY J., February 12, 2002 at 6.
[126] *Chrissy v. Ms. Dept. of Public Welfare*, 995 F. 2d 595 (District Court, Fifth Circuit, 1993).
[127] *Id.* at 599–600.
[128] *In the Matter of the Proceeding Pursuant to Section 44, Subdivision 4, of the Judiciary Law in Relation to Louis Grossman, A Judge of the Civil Court of the City of New York and Acting Justice of the Supreme Court, First Judicial District*, Commission on Judicial Conduct State of New York, November 20, 1984 (1984 WL 262214).
[129] *Id.* at 2–4. [130] *Id.* at 2–5.
[131] *Id.* at 2.

there would be "serious trouble" or "serious consequences" if he did not tell the truth, (8) and instructed the child that he "would be punished by God" and that his lies would hurt his mother.[132] Also, the judge's questioning was done "roughly and in rapid-fire fashion."[133] In addition, the record reflected that the child cried several times and "protested" fourteen times that he was tired and needed to rest.[134] In finding that the allegations warranted censure, the Commission found that the judge "ignored his obligation to the child" and "lost the sense of detachment required of him."[135] Although the dissent stated that the penalty of "censure" was too severe, the majority might have given a greater sanction had the judge not had a "heretofore unblemished career on the bench."[136]

The *Roberts* and *Luis Grossman* cases make it quite clear that dependency and family court judges have a duty to remain detached and neutral in proceedings to determine the custody of children, even if they are passionate about the dispute before the court and even if their reputation has been impugned. However, because juvenile dependency proceedings often involve serious allegations of child abuse, it is no wonder that judges want to discover as many relevant facts as possible so that a correct decision can be made regarding the child's safety. Most dependency legislative schemes, therefore, provide for the liberal introduction of evidence that would not be admissible in criminal cases or even in other ordinary civil cases. For instance, shaken baby syndrome evidence has been held to be admissible in dependency hearings even though it might not be admissible in criminal court.[137] In addition, hearsay evidence clearly inadmissible in criminal trials is often permitted in dependency proceedings based upon the court's need for that data in determining the child's best interest.[138] The policy of liberally admitting evidence in child dependency cases is succinctly stated in *California Welfare & Institutions Code §355(a)*: "Any legally admissible evidence that is relevant to the circumstances or acts that are alleged to bring the minor within the jurisdiction of the juvenile court is admissible and may be received in evidence."

Most jurisdictions have a presumption that judges are capable of remaining detached and neutral, even in light of the admission of highly inadmissible prejudicial evidence; however, some commentators have questioned the wisdom of that presumption for a legal system based so squarely upon

---

[132] *Id.* at 2–3.
[133] *Id.* at 3.
[134] *Id.* at 2–3.
[135] *Id.* at 3–4.
[136] *Id.* at 4–5.
[137] *In the Interest of A.V.*, 554 N.W. 2d 461 (North Dakota 1996); *State v. Bolin*, 922 S.W. 2d 870, 873 (Tennessee 1996).
[138] *State v. Simmons*, 299 So. 2d 906 (Louisiana 1974); *In re Lucero L.*, 96 Cal Rptr. 2d 56 (2000).

subjective and normative decisions, like child dependency and family law proceedings.[139] In addition, other commentators and courts have demonstrated the judicial and systemic cultural biases inherent in these proceedings.[140] It is therefore problematic when a juvenile court judge presides over both a criminal prosecution and a child dependency action based upon the same predicate child abuse. Because the evidentiary standards in those proceedings are often very different, the juvenile court judge is likely to be affected by inadmissible evidence in one or both proceedings.[141]

The Oregon Supreme Court in *In re Complaint as to the Conduct of the Honorable Ronald D. Schenck*[142] demonstrated the problems that occur when one judge hears both the dependency and criminal trials. In *Schenck* a judge heard the mother's probation violation case in which it was alleged that she had not participated in the required sexual offender treatment program. A few months later, the mother received notice that a hearing regarding her children's custody was scheduled before the same judge in the dependency court. The mother's attorney moved to disqualify the judge in the dependency case based upon her inability to receive a fair trial. However, the judge denied the disqualification motion.[143] Interestingly, the district attorney in the criminal action joined the mother's motion seeking the judge's recusal.[144] In a subsequent telephone conversation between the mother's attorney and the judge, the judge asked, "Who in the hell made you God's gift to the legal

---

[139] *See, e.g.*, Thomas M. Mengler, *The Theory of Discretion in the Federal Rules of Evidence*, 74 IOWA L. REV. 413, 445 (1989) ("A judge cannot keep prejudice to a fair minimum without, in a rough and ready way, tabulating it."); Teri Kathleen Martin, *Developing Disposition Decisonmaking Guidelines for Juvenile Courts* 80 (1985) (unpublished Ph.D. dissertation, University of Illinois at Chicago) ("Emotionalism rather than reason appears to prevail [even in the] legal community charged with decision-making responsibilities for the alleged child molester.") *See also* William Wesley Patton, *Evolution in Child Abuse Litigation: The Theoretical Void Where Evidentiary and Procedural Worlds Collide*, 25 LOY. L. A. L. REV. 1009, 1011–1013 (1992).

[140] Kenneth Cruce Smith, *A Profile of Juvenile Court Judges in the United States*, JUV. JUST., Aug. 1974, at 27–29; Richard Delgado, *Norms and Normal Science: Toward a Critique of Normativity in Legal Thought*, 139 U. PA. L. REV. 933, 943–944 (1991); Frederick Schauer, *The Authority of Legal Scholarship*, 139 U. PA. L. REV. 1003, 1011 (1991); Michael S. Wald, *State Intervention on Behalf of "Neglected" Children: A Search for Realistic Standards*, 27 STAN. L. REV. 985, 1017, n. 168 (1975); *Smith v. Organization of Foster Families*, 431 U.S. 816, 834 (1977); Caramae Richey Mann, *Courtroom Observations of Extra–Legal Factors in the Juvenile Court Dispositions of Runaway Boys: A Field Study*, JUV. & FAM. CT. J., Nov. 1980, at 1, 43.

[141] William Wesley Patton, *The World Where Parallel Lines Converge: The Privilege Against Self-Incrimination in Concurrent Civil and Criminal Child Abuse Proceedings*, 24 GA L. REV. 473 (1990).

[142] *In re Complaint as to the Conduct of the Honorable Ronald D. Schenck*, 870 P. 2d 185 (Oregon 1994).

[143] *Id.* at 190–191.   [144] *Id.* at 192.

profession?"[145] In addition, even though the presiding judge of the judicial district ordered the judge to postpone the dependency hearing, the judge refused and ordered all parties to appear. However, the mother's attorney successfully received a stay of that proceeding from the Oregon Supreme Court.[146] The Oregon Supreme Court found that the juvenile court judge should have recused himself in the dependency case per *Judicial Canon 3 C(1)* based upon either the questioning of the judge's "impartiality" or "actual personal bias or prejudice."[147] However, the judge was not sanctioned because the Oregon Supreme Court held that the trial judge never finally ruled on the recusal motion and because the stay prevented any biased hearing from taking place.[148] One must wonder whether such an "actual prejudice" standard will provide a sufficient deterrent effect from such clearly unwarranted judicial misconduct.

Even if the evidentiary rules in dependency and family court liberally admit evidence, there are limits on the judge's discretion to engage in independent fact investigation. For instance, it violates the canons of judicial ethics for the court to engage in *ex parte* judicial contacts.[149] Thus, in *Guadalupe A. V. Superior Court*,[150] it was held that the juvenile court judge's social conduct with the minor during the trial was judicial misconduct. At a Christmas party hosted by the Department for foster families, the judge spoke with the minor foster child three times and on one occasion picked up the child "and carried her away for five minutes."[151] Even though the dependency judge had a good motive for communicating with the minor and his foster mother, because an issue in the pending case was the extent of the minor's "stranger anxiety," the judge's carrying away the child from her foster mother was the equivalent of an out-of-court experiment, which is an impermissible collateral investigation by the court that "abdicates his or her [judge's] responsibility for deciding the parties' dispute on the pleadings and evidence properly brought before the court."[152]

---

[145] *Id.*
[146] *Id.*
[147] *Id.* at 194.
[148] *Id.*
[149] For instance, *California Canons of Judicial Ethics, Canon 3 (7)* states, "A judge shall not initiate, permit, or consider ex parte communications, or consider other communications made to the judge outside the presence of the parties concerning a pending or impending proceeding...."
[150] *Guadalupe A. v. Superior Court*, 285 Cal. Rptr. 570 (1991).
[151] *Id.* at 574.
[152] *Id.* at 575 citing *Wenger v. Commission on Judicial Performance*, 175 Cal. Rptr. 420 (1981); *Jones v. Sieve*, 281 P. 2d 898 (1986). Of course, not all *ex parte* judicial communications are prohibited. For instance, in jurisdictions that define juvenile probation personnel as officers of the court, the court can entertain *ex parte* requests for juvenile arrest warrants; however, "substantive information that is learned through these communications [with probation officers] should ultimately be provided to the probationer in accordance with the applicable

Whether an *ex parte* communication between a juvenile court judge and the child's guardian ad litem (GAL) is ethically prohibited depends upon the legal status of the GAL. For instance, the Alabama State Bar determined that an *ex parte* communication between the juvenile judge and the GAL violated the *Alabama Rules of Professional Conduct* because the GAL was defined by statute as the child's advocate, rather than as an advisor to the court.[153] Presumably, if the GAL is defined as an investigative arm of the court, rather than as the child's zealous advocate, *ex parte* communications would not violate any ethical constraints.[154]

In a recent case a superior court judge in a criminal child abuse case called the 16-year-old victim "into his chambers but did not inform the defense lawyer. The prosecution declined an invitation to attend the meeting."[155] The in-chambers meeting with the girl lasted twenty minutes, and no court record was made; however, according to the complaint, the judge commended the girl on her testimony, offered to write her a letter of recommendation for college, and told her, "I could be your grandfather."[156] After the in-chambers meeting with the child victim, the judge sentenced the abuser, her uncle, to

---

rules." Utah Ethics Advisory Committee Informal Opinion 97–4, August 28, 1997). *See also* Virginia Judicial Ethics Advisory Committee Opinion 00–4, May 8, 2000 (a judge may not have *ex parte* communication with a probation officer preparing a presentence report). *But see U.S. v. Gonzales*, 765 F. 2d 1393 (9th Cir. 1985) (holding that a probation officer when preparing a presentence report is "acting as an arm of the court and this permits *ex parte* communication."). *Ex parte* communications in criminal cases can be sufficiently prejudicial and can implicate the appearance of impropriety sufficiently to warrant reversal of a conviction. *See, e.g.*, Thomas M. Mengler, *The Theory of Discretion in the Federal Rules of Evidence*, 74 IOWA L. REV. 413, 445 (1989) ("A judge cannot keep prejudice to a fair minimum without, in a rough and ready way, tabulating it."); Teri Kathleen Martin, *supra* note 139, at 80 ("Emotionalism rather than reason appears to prevail [even in the] legal community charged with decision-making responsibilities for the alleged child molester."). *See also* William Wesley Patton, *supra* note 141, 1009, 1011–1013; *In re Hancock*, 136 Cal. Rptr. 901 (1977). And in *In the Matter of Disciplinary Proceedings Against Daniel R. McNamara*, 421 N. W. 2d 513, 367–370 (Wisconsin 1988), an attorney, who also served part-time as a family court commissioner, was given a one-year suspension for, among other violations, *ex parte* communication with an adverse party in the litigation with knowledge that the party was represented by counsel.

[153] Alabama State Bar Opinion No. 2002–02. That opinion cited several jurisdictions that had come to the same conclusion: *See, e.g., Moore v. Moore*, 809 P. 2d 261 (Wyo. 1991); *Veasey v. Veasey*, 560 P. 2d 382 (Alaska 1977); *Riley v. Erie Lackawanna R. Company*, 119 Misc. 2d 619, 463 N.Y.S. 2d 986 (1983); *De Los Santos v. Superior Court of Los Angeles County*, 27 Cal. 3d 677, 613 P. 2d 233 (1980).

[154] For a discussion of the many roles of GALs, *see* Michelle Johnson-Weider, *supra* note 22, at 77; Michael J. Dale, *supra* note 21, at 769.

[155] David Houston, *Judge Faces State Disciplinary Hearings over Alleged Conduct*, L. A. DAILY J., February 20, 2004, p. 1, 5.

[156] *Id.* at 5.

"16 years in state prison." The complaint is being investigated by the Judicial Performance Commission.[157]

Judges are also prohibited from intervening for personal reasons in a child welfare investigation pending in another court. In *In the Matter of Bruce M. Kaplan*,[158] the New York Commission on Judicial Conduct publicly admonished a judge for using the prestige of his office to influence a child abuse investigation.[159] The judge presided over a series of *ex parte* applications between a husband and wife regarding child visitation. The judge became friends with the wife. One night when the daughter was visiting her father, the judge and the wife heard the daughter "yelling" in the husband's apartment. When police officers arrived at the wife's house, the judge intervened, introduced himself as a family court judge and family friend, and accompanied the police, parents, and daughter to the hospital for examination.[160] Because the daughter suffered "abrasions, redness and tenderness about the neck, back and extremities," a report was entered into the Central Child Abuse Registry, which automatically triggered an investigation by a caseworker.[161] The judge once again intervened on behalf of the mother and convinced a unit caseworker and her supervisor to conduct an in-home study of the father's home. The judge described the husband as "violent" and related details from the couple's court case in which the judge had earlier presided. The judge further cajoled the caseworker to forbid visitation between the daughter and the husband.[162] The Commission on Judicial Conduct found that the judge's "advocacy exceeded the limitations placed upon judges" because "he used the influence and prestige of that office to advance the cause of his friend and her daughter."[163] In addition, the Commission found that the court wrongfully gave the appearance of using confidential court data for private purposes.[164] The dissent found that the judge committed "no misconduct" and voted to dismiss the complaint.[165]

In a similar case in North Carolina, *In re Inquiry Harrell*,[166] the North Carolina Supreme Court censured a judge for personally intervening in a child abuse investigation in the juvenile court.[167] The judge "interjected himself at every stage of the matter and at times during the course of proceedings

---

[157] *Id.*
[158] *In the Matter of the Proceeding Pursuant to Section 44, Subdivision 4, of the Judiciary Law in Relation to Bruce M. Kaplan, A Judge of the Family Court*, May 6, 1996 (1996 WL 4418512).
[159] *Id.* at 4.　　　　　　　　　　　[160] *Id.* at 1–3.
[161] *Id.* at 2.　　　　　　　　　　　[162] *Id.* at 2–3.
[163] *Id.* at 3.　　　　　　　　　　　[164] *Id.* at 4.
[165] *Id.*, dissent, at 5–6.
[166] *In re Inquiry Concerning Harrell*, 414 S. E. 2d 36 (1992).
[167] *Id.* at 36–39.

in the matter acted as an advocate" for his friends, who were the adoptive parents of the allegedly abused child.[168] The court found that the judge's active involvement in his friends' child abuse case, including his letter to the State Attorney General seeking a clarification of the term "physical injury," was a clear violation of the canons of judicial ethics.[169]

Finally, even though judges have an interest in the expeditious resolution of proceedings, they may not place expediency above due process. For instance, the California Supreme Court in *McCullough v. Commission on Judicial Performance*[170] removed a judge from office, in part for his proceeding with an action without the presence of the defendant and his attorney. The judge had refused a continuance for the absent attorney based upon a court order requiring the attorney to appear before a judge in another county on the same day. The California Supreme Court held that the trial court's refusal to grant a continuance was "willful misconduct," and even though the trial judge may have wished to punish the absent attorney, he, in effect, punished the lawyer's client.[171]

This same prohibition on punishing clients for their attorney's behavior is applicable in dependency courts as well. In some jurisdictions, legislatures have established that expediency is in children's best interest and that continuances should not be liberally granted if they would be against the children's best interest.[172] However, juvenile court judges must reasonably exercise their discretion on continuance motions. In *In re Michael R.*,[173] the trial court abused its discretion and committed prejudicial error in not considering a mother's motion for a continuance before a permanency planning hearing. And in *In re Julian L.*,[174] the dependency court judge abused his discretion in denying the continuance motion of an attorney representing a parent in a termination of parental rights hearing, even though the attorney was appointed less than two weeks prior to the hearing and had informed the court that he had not yet had an opportunity to fully communicate with this client and determine her wishes regarding the case. The court clearly indicated that dependency court discretion to expedite proceedings is trumped

---

[168] *Id.* at 37.   [169] *Id.* at 38.
[170] *McCullough v. Commission on Judicial Performance*, 260 Cal. Rptr. 557 (1989).
[171] *Id.* at 563.
[172] *See, e.g., California Welfare & Institutions Code* §352(a) provides that the juvenile court judge shall "give substantial weight to a minor's need for prompt resolution of his or her custody status, the need to provide children with stable environments and the damage to a minor of prolonged temporary placements" in deciding whether to grant a continuance in a child dependency proceeding.
[173] *In re Michael R.*, 7 Cal. Rptr. 2d 139 (1992).
[174] *In re Julian L.*, 78 Cal. Rptr. 2d 839 (1998).

by due process requirements, whether they be constitutional or statutory due process rights.[175]

Judges in dependency court are overburdened with extensive caseloads and have too little time either to research the applicable law or hear the full panoply of arguments that attorneys may wish to litigate. For instance, in California in the 1998–9 fiscal year, out of the 8.6 million cases filed, combined domestic cases numbered 645,433, and of those cases 41,890 were child dependency filings.[176] There were only 1,880 authorized judgeships to handle the 8.6 million cases filed, for a per judge caseload of 4,588.[177] In addition, 123 judges specifically designated juvenile, juvenile delinquency, and/or juvenile dependency jurists handled a total of 142,450 dependency and delinquency cases for a per juvenile judge caseload of 1,158 cases per year.[178] Some have argued that juvenile court judges' perceptions of their overcrowded docket lead to three negative results: (1) "'violating parents' due process; (2) 'rubber stamping Human Resource Services,' and (3) being impatient with and verbally abusive to parents."[179] Some critics of the dependency system opine that judges give the Department great deference because of their need "to rush overcrowded dockets...."[180] If it is true that there is a correlation between the size of judges' caseloads and the merit of verdicts, juvenile court judges and attorneys practicing in those courts have a duty to educate the public and legislators on the importance of funding the juvenile courts properly so that the quality of fact-finding can improve and so that the merits, not court management, are outcome determinative.

---

[175] In *Montigny v. Montigny*, 233 N. W. 2d 463, 467 (Wisconsin 1975), the Wisconsin Supreme Court held that judges have a *sua sponte* duty to appoint a guardian ad litem for children in custody decisions and held that the trial court's failure to appoint a GAL was "an abuse of discretion, patently prejudicial . . . to the minor children." The majority disagreed with the concurring opinion that argued that the GAL position is often duplicative of others' arguments and therefore not a cost-efficient way to determine the best custody placement options: "In these instances the investigations and trial participation and opinions of a guardian ad litem can be cumulative and redundant and a source of substantial additional costs and fees that parties can ill afford." *Id.* at 470. For discussions of the importance and role of GAL in representing children's interests in custody and/or dependency proceedings, *see* William A. Kell, *Voices Lost and Found: Training Ethical Lawyers For Children*, 73 IND. L. J. 635 (1998); Cindy Callahan & Vince Willis, *Searching for Answers: About the Role of the Guardian Ad Litem*, 36 MD. B.J. 46 (May/June, 2003).

[176] COURT STATISTICS REPORT: STATEWIDE CASELOAD TRENDS 1989–1990 THROUGH 1998–1999, at viii, x, and 56 (California Judicial Council, Administrative Office of the Court, 2000).

[177] *Id.* at 42.

[178] *Id.* at 56; CALIFORNIA DIRECTORY OF ATTORNEYS (Daily Journal Corporation 2004).

[179] Sandra Anderson Garcia & Robert Batey, *supra* note 36, at 1079, 1092.

[180] *Id.* at 1095.

V. EMERGING ISSUES REGARDING SUBSTITUTION OF COUNSEL AND SELF-REPRESENTATION

It is not surprising that parents' and children's counsel constantly search for precedent to extend parties' rights in child protection proceedings. It is also foreseeable that arguments by analogy to criminal proceedings, the hallmark of procedural due process, would form the basis for expanding due process in dependency proceedings.[181] Therefore, in states that have determined that parents have a constitutional right to counsel in some child protection proceedings pursuant to the Fourteenth Amendment due process clause as elucidated in *Lassister v. Department of Social Services*, or per a state statute, it was only a matter of time before they sought expansion of the right to an attorney to (1) substitute attorneys who parents and/or children determine are either incompetent or with whom the attorney-client relationship has broken down and/or (2) the right to self-representation.

A. *The Right to Substitute Counsel*

Although criminal defendants have a right to court-appointed counsel, they do not have an absolute right to require substitution of appointed counsel. Because the appointment of counsel for criminal defendants is constitutionally mandated, those defendants are entitled to competent representation. If a defendant sufficiently articulates the counsel's incompetence or demonstrates that the attorney-client relationship has deteriorated to a level affecting competent representation, the criminal court has the discretion to order a substitution of court-appointed counsel.[182] Because the substitution of counsel in criminal cases is based upon the constitutional right to competent counsel, extending such a right to dependency cases must be predicated upon a constitutional right to appointment of counsel. But many states have held that appointment of counsel is only required if *Lassiter* applies, such as in a case that involves expert testimony and a possible criminal conviction, and in which the procedural status is termination of parental rights rather than merely a temporary placement of the child outside the home.[183] Therefore,

---

[181] For instance, dependency lawyers analogized to *Gideon v. Wainright*, 372 U.S. 335 in arguing in *Lassiter v. Department of Social Services*, 452 U.S. 18 (1981), that parents have a Fourteenth Amendment due process right to counsel in termination proceedings. They further argued by analogy to criminal cases in *Santosky v. Kramer*, 455 U.S. 745 (1982), that the burden of proof should be beyond a reasonable doubt, rather than clear and convincing or preponderance of the evidence in termination proceedings.

[182] *U.S.v. Anderson*, 189 F. 3d 1201, 1210 (10th Cir. 1999).

[183] *In re Christine P.*, 277 Cal. Rptr. 290 (California 1991); *K. P. B. v. D. C. A.*, 685 So. 2d 750 (Alabama 1996); *Joni B. v. State*, 549 N. W. 411 (Wisconsin 1996).

many states have held that if there is no constitutional mandate to appoint counsel, then there is no right to the substitution of counsel either.

However, some jurisdictions that recognize a right to counsel in dependency cases also recognize a right to substitution of counsel. For example, in California it has been held that "parents must have some mechanism for challenging the representation when they perceive inadeqacy, or the right to counsel is meaningless...."[184] If appointment of counsel was constitutionally required, some courts have held that refusal to substitute counsel is reviewed under the *Chapman v. California*[185] harmless error standard, in which the error will be presumed prejudicial unless the presumption is rebutted beyond a reasonable doubt by demonstrating that failure to substitute counsel did not contribute to the dependency court adjudication or disposition.[186] Other courts have held that parents claiming error in not substituting counsel have the burden of demonstrating that, absent the error, the parent "would have obtained a more favorable result had such a [substitution] motion been granted."[187]

Dependency courts have not favored parents' motions for substitution of counsel. Cases in which recalcitrant parents have requested up to six attorney substitutions have jaded jurists' views toward the legitimacy of many colorable claims of breakdowns in the attorney-client relationship.[188] For instance, in *In re Chevelle D.*,[189] the court described the uncooperativeness of the father: "We are left with the distinct impression father's relationship with *any* attorney would be marred by the same 'communication' problems caused by father's refusal to cooperate." To prevent reversal in a significant number of cases, courts have very strictly construed the requirements that parents articulate their desire specifically and sufficiently and the grounds for the substitution of appointed counsel.[190] First, it is clear that there is no *sua*

---

[184] *In re A. H.*, 2004 WL 1172675 (California, May 27, 2004; not published).

[185] *Chapman v. California*, 386 U.S. 18 (1967).

[186] *People v. Marsden*, 84 Cal. Rptr. 156 (California Supreme Court 1970) [denial of substitution of counsel in an adult criminal action]; *In re Sadie D.*, 2002 WL 1303401 (California, June 14, 2002; unpublished).

[187] *In re A. H.*, 2004 WL 1172675 (California, May 27, 2004; unpublished).

[188] For instance, in *In re Bernard W.*, 2003 WL 22133859 (California, September 16, 2003), the court noted that the "[m]other had a history of asking the dependency court, the presiding judge of the dependency court, and the court administrator to relieve counsel and appoint a new attorney." Upon the mother's seventh substitution motion, the court noted that the motion was based upon evidence that was "patently false."

[189] *In re Chevelle D.*, 2003 WL 141334 (California, January 21, 2003; unpublished). *State v. McDowell*, 681 N. W. 2d 500 (Wisconsin 2004); *State v. Crain*, 84 P. 3d 1092 (Oregon 2004); *People v. Walsh*, 770 N.Y.S. 2d 230 (2003).

[190] On the other hand, dependency court judges who think that an attorney may be providing incompetent representation may not discharge and substitute another attorney without first holding a hearing and determining the wishes of the client. *In re A. H.*, 2004 WL 1172675

sponte obligation on the court to determine whether substitution should take place.[191] Second, ambiguous requests are insufficient to trigger the court's duty to hold an informal hearing regarding the substitution.[192] "Although 'a proper and formal legal motion' is not necessarily required, there must be some clear indication by defendant that he wants a substitute attorney."[193] For instance, a parent's request to retain private counsel and "also . . . a hearing on [her] assigned attorney" was insufficient to require inquiry into substitution of appointed counsel, and the parent's request for the court to instruct her counsel about the scope of competent representation was insufficient to invoke a hearing.[194] And a parent who asserts that her attorney "doesn't represent me in the way I wanted to be represented," without more facts to specifically demonstrate that an "irreconcilable conflict has arisen" between her and her attorney is insufficient to find that failure to grant a hearing was an abuse of discretion.[195]

However, the requirement of expressing the desire to substitute counsel clearly together with sufficient grounds to trigger court inquiry has led to a Catch-22. If the parent details the reasons for wanting substitution of counsel with great detail, the court's refusal to hold a hearing will not be held an abuse of discretion because the court will have denied the hearing based upon the parent's complaints. However, as demonstrated above, if the request is too general or vague, no duty to hold a hearing is triggered. For instance, in *In re Saddie D.*,[196] a father wrote to the dependency judge asking for a substitution of counsel because counsel lacked an interest in his case and did not respond to messages. Even though the trial court did not hold a hearing regarding substitution of counsel, the court of appeal determined that no abuse of discretion occurred because the judge had sufficient facts upon which to decide the substitution motion. The court held that "we cannot say beyond a reasonable doubt that failure to hold a hearing contributed to the result" in the termination of parental rights.[197]

(California, May 27, 2004; unpublished). *Orcutt v. State*, 173 N. W. 2d 66 (Iowa 1969); *In re Christine P.*, 277 Cal. Rptr. 290 (California 1991); *K. P. B. v. D. C. A.*, 685 So. 2d 750 (Alabama 1996); *Joni B. v. State*, 549 N. W. 2d 411, 414 (Wisconsin 1996).

[191] *People v. Leonard*, 93 Cal. Rptr. 2d 180 (2000); *In re Jarred H.*, 2002 WL 1732573 (California, July 25, 2002; unpublished).

[192] *In re B. H.*, 2003 WL 1473563 (California, March 24, 2003; unpublished).

[193] *People v. Lucky*, 115 Cal. Rptr. 2d 828 (California 2002).

[194] *In re Crystal M.*, 2002 WL 387863 (California, March 13, 2002; unpublished).

[195] *In re Jarred H.*, 2002 WL 1732573 (California, July 25, 2002; unpublished).

[196] *In re Sadie D.*, 2002 WL 1303401 (California, June 14, 2002; unpublished).

[197] *See also In re Karen L.*, 2002 WL 31873405 (California, December 20, 2002; unpublished), which held that even though the trial judge erroneously believed that the court lacked jurisdiction to substitute attorneys, failure to hold a hearing or substitute counsel was not prejudicial.

Courts have held that parents' most frequent complaints regarding the quality of their attorneys often do not rise to the level of a significant impairment of the right to competent counsel, and therefore such complaints do not state sufficient evidence to require substitution of counsel. One of the most common complaints about dependency attorneys is that they do not perfect parents' desires about how the litigation should proceed. But several courts have determined that because most "tactical decisions" are the province of the attorney, not the client, substitution motions have usually been denied.[198] In addition, the frequent complaint that dependency court attorneys either do not meet and discuss the case with parents or do not meet until a few hours before a hearing has likewise been held insufficient to support a substitution of counsel.[199] For instance, in *Cardell T.*,[200] the father alleged that "his attorney only spent five minutes with him before the hearing...."[201]

The number of cases in which parents allege that they have either been neglected or mistreated by their attorneys should give the profession cause to futher investigate the quality of dependency court legal services. However, ethical violations, such as not contacting clients, failing to adequately counsel clients, and refusal to engage in requested trial strategies, are often not sufficient to require a substitution of counsel under current standards. The legal response to attorney neglect and incivility toward clients is that "[u]nless the attorney's attitude toward the father's position resulted in her failure to pursue legally cognizable options, the father's right to assistance of counsel was not substantially impaired."[202] This disjunction between parents' negative attitudes toward their attorneys and the lack of judicial remedies other than attorney disciplinary proceedings fosters the poor reputation of parents'

---

[198] In *People v. Washington*, 2002 WL 2017096 (California, August 29, 2002; unpublished), the court held that counsel's refusal to hire an expert to impeach the accuracy and relevance of photographs was merely a tactical decision and did not demonstrate that the "attorney-client relationship had irretrievably broken down." *See also In re Tallie G.*, 2003 WL 21362761 (California, June 12, 2003; unpublished); *In re Hope*, 2004 WL 473979 (California, March 12, 2004; unpublished).

[199] In *In re Justin C.*, 2003 WL 22995273 (California, December 22, 2003; unpublished), the parent alleged that "he had had 'no contact' with counsel and counsel failed to prepare him to testify"; however, because the parent could not demonstrate sufficient prejudice, the refusal to substitute counsel was not an abuse of discretion.

[200] *Cardell T.*, 2004 WL 1588025 (California, July 15, 2004; unpublished). *Id.*; *People v. Cleveland*, 11 Cal. Rptr. 3d 236 (California 2004).

[201] In *In re Ashley A.*, 2001 WL 1497713 (California, November 27, 2001; unpublished), the parent explained that "he did not have a chance to discuss the case with his counsel until a few days prior to the hearing...."

[202] *In re Tallie G.*, 203 WL 21362761 (California, June 12, 2003; unpublished).

counsel. It is clear that greater educational efforts are needed to impress upon this corps of counsel the importance of public relations in relation to client satisfaction.

B. *The Right to Self-Representation*

In 1975 the United States Supreme Court in *Faretta v. California*[203] held that a defendant in a criminal case has a Fourteenth Amendment due process right to self-representation. It is not surprising that parents might argue that they too have a right to self-representation if it is determined that they have a constitutional right to counsel under *Lassiter v. Department of Social Services.*[204] However, no state court has held that parents have a federal constitutional right to self-representation.[205] The court in *In re Angel W.*[206] articulated the rationale for not applying *Faretta's* constitutional mandate to dependency proceedings: "[T]he Sixth Amendment does not apply in dependency proceedings so its structure cannot provide a basis for finding a correlative constitutional right of self-representation." The court noted that *Faretta* was based upon "the history of the right of self-representation since the founding of the United States" and that there was no such history in regard to self-representation in dependency cases. The court further held that, even though the right to self-representation is not mandated by independent state constitutional grounds, parents have a statutory right to self-representation pursuant to *Welfare & Institutions Code § 317 (a) and (b)*, which provide: "When it appears to the court that a parent... of the child desires counsel but is presently financially unable to afford and cannot for that reason employ counsel, the court may appoint counsel... unless the court finds that the parent... has made a knowing and intelligent waiver of counsel...."[207] The court held that parents therefore have a right to waive counsel "in circumstances where appointment of counsel is mandatory" at any time during the proceedings. But unlike the strict admonitions required by the United States Supreme Court for accepting a waiver of counsel, a waiver of the statutory right to counsel does not require "a full *Faretta-type*

---

[203] *Faretta v. California*, 422 U.S. 806 (1975).
[204] *Lassiter v. Department of Social Services*, 452 U.S. 18 (1981).
[205] The closest a court has come to accepting the analogy to *Faretta* is in *In re Brian R.*, 3 Cal. Rptr. 2d 768, 777 (1991), where the court stated that "[e]ven assuming, arguendo, that *Faretta* applies to a parent in a juvenile dependency proceeding, we would have no difficulty, on this record, in determining that appellant's waiver of counsel rose to the standard enunciated in *Faretta*...."
[206] *In re Angel W.*, 113 Cal. Rptr. 2d 659; 93 Cal. App. 4th 1074 (2001).
[207] *Id.* at 1083.

admonition and inquiry...," although a judge should ensure that the parent is competent to make a knowing and intelligent waiver of the statutory right to counsel. The *In re Angel W.* court cautioned against paternalistic decisions denying competent adults the right to self-representation even though the court might conclude that waiver of counsel is against the parent's interest and even though there is "[t]he possibility of disruption and delay" as long as the *pro se* lititgant is not "so disruptive as to significantly delay the proceedings or render them meaningless and negatively impact the rights of the minor in a prompt and fair hearing...." For instance, in *In re K. T.*[208] the trial court's denial of self-representation to the mother was not an abuse of discretion because the mother "had engaged in serious and obstructionist misconduct more than once. The trial court was not required to gamble that [she] could contain herself without the restraining presence of counsel, when faced with the reality that she would lose her child."

In re Angel W. has generated a number of appellate opinions defining the nature and scope of parents' statutory right to self-representation. Courts have consistently held that the request for self-representation must be clear and unambiguous. For instance, a request for substitution of counsel and/or *pro per* status was insufficient where the parent in reality was merely asking for the court to instruct counsel on counsel's ethical responsibilities.[209] In addition, reversal based upon a denial of the statutory right to self-representation is only required if under a harmless error analysis the parent proves that "it appear reasonably probable that a result more favorable to appellant would have been reached had she represented herself."[210] Because it will be the rare case in which a parent can demonstrate that he or she could have litigated the proceeding more competently than counsel, reversal based upon a denial of the statutory right to self-representation is more theoretical than probable.

Although minors in juvenile delinquency proceedings have been held to possess a right to self-representation under *Faretta*,[211] children in California do not have a right to self-representation in child dependency proceedings for two reasons. First, like adults, there is no federal or state constitutional basis for the right to self-representation. Second, unlike adults who have a state statutory right to self-representation, the statute requiring the court to appoint counsel for minors unless such appointment is against their interest

---

[208] *In re K. T.*, 2004 WL 1328273 (California, June 15, 2004; unpublished).

[209] *In re Crystal M.*, 2002 WL 387863 (California, March 13, 2002; unpublished).

[210] *In re Angel W.*, *supra* at 1085; *In re Fabian Z.*, 2003 WL 22120896 (California, September 15, 2003; unpublished).

[211] *In re Shawn F.*, 40 Cal. Rptr. 2d 263 (1995).

Competent and Zealous Representation

does not have a reference to the right to self-representation.[212] Therefore, dependency courts have not been required to determine the level of competence that an abused child must possess in order to validly waive the statutory right to appointment of counsel and to proceed in *pro per.*

---

[212] *California Welfare & Institutions Code § 317(c)* provides, "Where a child is not represented by counsel, the court shall appoint counsel for the child unless the court finds that the child would not benefit from the appointment of counsel."

3 Confidentiality

Attorneys in child custody and child dependency proceedings are much more than mere litigators. One of the central roles in these emotionally charged legal arenas is acting as counselors, not only regarding legal issues but also on nonlegal issues. *ABA Model Rule 2.1* provides that client representation includes reference to "other considerations such as moral, economic, social and political factors...." It is thus not surprising that in these disputes, which involve heightened sensitivity, confidentiality is a central concern of the parties.[1] However, because the best interest of children is central to the child custody and juvenile dependency systems, conflicts with the duty of confidentiality often arise in contexts in which that confidential information demonstrates an admission of past child abuse or threats of future abuse.

This chapter discusses the often differing and sometimes conflicting **balance** between client confidentiality and children's safety. When is a judge permitted to disclose confidential data either to defend the court system or to educate the public, and under what circumstances must or can attorneys disclose confidential client data? Finally, what is the constitutional limit of the court's power to issue contempt citations for violations of confidentiality, and what sanctions are reasonably likely for attorneys who disclose confidential client information that can be both embarrassing and incriminating for parties in concurrent criminal child abuse actions, as, for instance, in *Conduct of the Honorable Ronald D.*?[2]

---

[1] Children's advocates in California dependency actions have a responsibility of determining whether the child has the need for legal assistance in any other disputes: "[C]ounsel shall investigate the interests of the child beyond the scope of the juvenile proceedings and report to the court other interests of the child that may need to be protected by the institution of other administrative or judicial proceedings." *Welfare and Institutions Code § 317(e)*. However, the child's counsel does not have the obligations of a "social worker and is not expected to provide nonlegal services to the child." *Id.*

[2] 870 P. 2d 185 (Oregon 1994). For a discussion of the issues that arise during concurrent criminal and civil child abuse proceedings based upon the same child abuse allegations, see William Wesley Patton, *The World Where Parellel Lines Converge...*, 24 GA. L. REV. 473 (1990).

I. CHILDREN'S ATTORNEYS: SAFETY VERSUS SECRECY

Abused children are extremely emotionally vulnerable. Often, they have been abused by a known adult, and their ability to trust strangers is very compromised. The American Psychological Association has described the abused child's psychological status as "severe emotional distress... [p]ost traumatic stress disorder... stigmatization [guilt and shame] incorporated into the child's self-image...."[3] That assessment has been recently confirmed in a description by the U.S. Department of Justice: "[F]ear, anxiety, posttraumatic stress symptoms, depression... poor self-esteem, stigmatization, difficulty with trust, cognitive distortions, difficulty with affective processing... and peer socialization deficits."[4] Therefore, the concept of confidentiality between the abused child and his or her attorney is a much more complex question than in most legal contexts. If the child's attorney promises the protection of confidentiality and violates that trust, the attorney will not merely create an incentive for the child to withhold potentially relevant data but will also exacerbate the child's fragile mental health and reduce his or her willingness to cooperate with adults in helping seek, as near as possible, emotional equipoise.

The *ABA Model Rules of Professional Responsibility* make no distinction between adult and child clients regarding an attorney's duty of confidentiality. The limited exception provides that "[a] lawyer may reveal such information to the extent the lawyer reasonably believes necessary... to prevent the client from committing a criminal act that the lawyer believes is likely to result in imminent death or substantial bodily harm...."[5] Although that language might provide a lawyer representing an alleged child abuser the discretion to divulge the criminal intent to re-abuse the child, because the child is not the perpetrator of the future criminal act, *ABA Model Rule 1.6 (b)(1)* does not provide the child's attorney with discretion to disclose the threatened abuse. Although most states have adopted language similar to *ABA Model Rule 1.6(b)(1)*, no jurisdiction permits an attorney to disclose that confidential data regarding future criminal action by someone other than the attorney's client, unless some other law mandates such disclosure.[6] And even the more

---

[3] *Amicus curiae* brief filed by the American Psychological Association in *Maryland v. Craig*, 110 S. Ct. 3157 (1990).
[4] CHILD PHYSICAL AND SEXUAL ABUSE: GUIDELINES FOR TREATMENT 25 (U.S. Dept. of Justice, 2003).
[5] *ABA Model Rules of Professional Conduct, Rule 1.6 (b) (1)*.
[6] Each of the evolutionary iterations of *Model Rule 1.6(b)(1)* refer to disclosures of the client's future criminal acts, not acts of others disclosed by the client. *See* 1979 draft, 1980 discussion, 1981 draft, 1982 draft, and 1991 proposal. Stephen Gillers & Roy D. Simon, Jr., REGULATION OF LAWYERS: STATUTES AND STANDARDS 70–74 (1974). For a discussion of each state's peculiar version of *Model Rule 1.6(b)(1), see* Gillers & Simon at 74–78.

"disclosure-friendly" confidentiality rule enacted by the American Academy of Matrimonial Lawyers, *Rule 2.26*, applies only to a client's threat of child abuse: "An attorney should disclose evidence of a substantial risk of physical or sexual abuse of a child by the attorney's client."

This dilemma may have been solved by the proposed changes to current *Model Rule 1.6* by the ABA Ethics 2000 Commission. The proposed modification provides that a lawyer may reveal confidential information "to prevent reasonably certain death or substantial bodily harm."[7] Although the *Reporter's Explanation of Changes* clearly states that the "Commission is proposing substantial expansion of the grounds for permissive disclosure under Rule 1.6" and that "the exception currently recognized for client crimes threatening imminent death or substantial bodily harm be replaced with a broader exception for disclosures to prevent reasonably certain death or substantial bodily harm, with no requirement of client criminality," the proposed rule is still ambiguous.[8] For example, every hypothetical that the Commission provides in its application of Rule 1.6 only permits confidential disclosures involving acts by the client. Therefore, the proposed modification to *Model Rule 1.6* is susceptible to two reasonable interpretations. The first is that the Commission merely intended to expand the nature of the dangerous acts committed or threatened to be committed by the client from those under the current rule, which must be "criminal" and which will cause or threaten "imminent death or substantial bodily harm," to an expansion that includes "non-criminal" acts or threats that will be reasonably certain to cause death or bodily harm. This interpretation would not permit a child's attorney to disclose the child's confidential statement that a parent had threatened the child with future serious bodily harm. However, another reasonable interpretation of the Ethics 2000 Commission's proposed changes to *Model Rule 1.6* is that the omission of the word "client" in relation to threats of reasonably certain death or serious bodily injury was an intentional omission and that therefore the child's attorney could disclose the child's confidential data regarding threats by a third party. Because nothing in the history of the Ethics 2000 Commission's modifications to *Model Rule 1.6* clarifies this ambiguity, we will have to wait for clarification if the ABA adopts these proposed changes.[9]

---

[7] *See Ethics 2000 Rule 1.6*, www.abanet.org/cpr/e2k-rule16h.html). However, *see Utah State Bar Ethics Opinion Number 95-06* (July 28, 1995), in which it was held that "[w]hen an attorney has reason to believe a person who is not a client has abused a child and the information upon which the belief is based derives from the attorney's representation of a client," the attorney may disclose the abuse if required by state law, such as a mandatory child abuse reporting law that requires "any person" to "immediately notify" officials of such abuse.

[8] *Id.* at 1 of *Model Rule 1.6 Reporter's Explanation of Changes.*

[9] Although David L. Walther discusses the changes proposed by the Ethics 2000 Commission and says that "[t]he ABA Commission proposes allowing disclosure of confidences to prevent

However, the *Model Rules* permit disclosure of confidential attorney-client data if disclosure is required by law.[10] Therefore, if an attorney practices in a jurisdiction that has defined attorneys as mandated child abuse reporters, the attorney may be required to disclose the child's confidential data regarding the **past** abuse by another person without violating the code of ethics. Three different types of mandatory child abuse reporting systems exist among the states: (1) statutes that do not mention attorneys; (2) statutes that include attorneys among those obligated to report child abuse; and (3) statutes that include attorneys, but provide certain exemptions from reporting.[11] Currently, "[t]wenty-three states have reporting statutes that provide that anyone 'may' report abuse, but nearly half exempt attorneys in some way. Sixteen states require all individuals to report child abuse, but twelve of those states exempt communications covered by the attorney-client privilege."[12] Alabama, Alaska, Arkansas, California, Colorado, Georgia, Iowa, Kansas, Louisiana, Maryland, Massachusetts, Michigan, Missouri, Montana, North Dakota, South Carolina, South Dakota, Vermont, Virginia, Washington, West Virginia, and Wisconsin all have statutes that specifically exempt attorneys from reporting under certain circumstances.[13] And of the sixteen states that require all persons to report child abuse, twelve recognize the attorney-client privilege as an exception to mandated reporting.[14]

But most mandated child abuse reporting statutes only require disclosure if the observer has reasonable grounds for concluding that the child has been or is being abused, and not subject to threats of future abuse. For example, in California mandated reporting is required only if the reporter "has knowledge of or observes a child whom the mandated reporter knows or reasonably suspects has been the victim of child abuse or neglect."[15] However, in other statutes, like the one in Texas, the duty to report extends not only to observed abuse but also to cases where the child "may be abused or neglected...."[16] Therefore, if a child provides an attorney or other mandated reporter with information about a fear of future abuse at some unspecified time in the

---

death or substantial bodily harm from criminal conduct," he does not address the ambiguity created by deleting the reference in *Model Rule 1.6* to the "client's" acts as opposed to acts by third persons.

[10] ABA *Model Rules of Professional Conduct*, Rule 1.6 (b) (1) Comment 19, titled "Disclosures Otherwise Required or Authorized" states that confidential data can be disclosed if "[t]he lawyer must comply with the final orders of a court or other tribunal of competent jurisdiction requiring the lawyer to give information about the client." Brooke Albrandt, *Turning in the Client: Mandatory Child Abuse Reporting Requirements and the Criminal Defense of Battered Women*, 81 TEX. L. REV. 655, 657 (2002).

[11] *Id.*   [12] *Id.* at 658.

[13] Ellen Marrus, *Please Keep My Secret: Child Abuse Reporting Statutes, Confidentiality, and Juvenile Delinquency*, 11 GEO. J. LEGAL ETHICS 509, 517, fn. 37 (1998).

[14] *Id.* at 517 and fns. 39–40.   [15] California Penal Code § 11166(a).

[16] *Texas Family Code § 261.101(b)*; Marrus, *supra* note 13, at 658.

future, it is unclear whether the mandatory reporting statutes in many states are implicated.

Therefore, what can an attorney do when practicing in a state in which the future crime exception does not apply to the child client's confidential data and in which the child's attorney is not a mandated reporter? The Los Angeles County Bar Association (LACBA) has provided a sophisticated analysis of children's attorneys' options. That opinion is even more interesting because at the time it was written California had not even adopted the discretionary disclosure standard of *Model Rule 1.6(b)(1)*.[17] The LACBA determined that under California rules of professional responsibility an attorney is ethically bound to follow a competent child client's desire to keep attorney-client data confidential, even if the attorney believes that confidentiality is not in the child's best interest and even if the information relates to probable further abuse. The only escape clause for the attorney is the obligation to withdraw from representing the competent child client if "the disagreement between the attorney and client materially impairs the attorney-client relationship such that the attorney cannot competently perform is or her duties."[18] Under the LACBA opinion, if the attorney concludes that the minor client is not sufficiently competent to make a reasoned decision concerning the confidentiality of the future abuse data, the attorney (1) may not disclose the confidential information by merely substituting the attorney's own opinion; (2) may seek appointment of a guardian ad litem without disclosing the confidential data to the court; and (3) if a guardian ad litem is appointed, "the attorney may ethically disclose the minor's confidential information to the guardian ad litem, and should follow the instructions of the guardian ad litem, even if those instructions conflict with those of the minor client."[19] The conclusion that the attorney must follow the guardian ad litem's express orders to violate the incompetent child's directive of confidentiality was based not upon any specific ethics rule but rather upon statutory law, which states that a child must act through a GAL in order to perfect the child's legal rights and that a GAL, as a fiduciary, is empowered to determine the child's best interest, even if that decision conflicts with the child's express wishes.[20]

---

[17] Los Angeles County Bar Association Professional Responsibility and Ethics Committee, Formal Ethics Opinion No. 504, May 15, 2000. Effective on July 1, 2004, *California Business & Professions Code § 6068(e)* will include, for the first time, the future criminal act disclosure discretion of *ABA Model Rule 1.6(b)(1)*. *AALS Professional Responsibility Section Newsletter, Spring 2004*. For a copy of the new California rule, see www.leginfo.ca.gov.

[18] LACBA, Ethics Opinion No. 504, at 6, quoting from *California Rules of Professional Conduct 3–700(C)(1)(a)*.

[19] LACBA, Ethics Opinion No. 504, at 1, http://www.lacba.org/showpage.cfm?pageid=429).

[20] *Id.* at 10, relying on *California Family Code § 6601* and *Moeller v. Superior Court*, 16 Cal. 4th 1124 (1997).

The *LACBA Ethics Opinion Number 504* is problematic for several reasons. First, if the child is competent, the opinion's suggestion that the child's attorney withdraw from the case provides no solution for the ethical dilemma. The attorney's withdrawal from representation will not protect the child client from the threatened child abuse. In fact, even if the attorney is replaced by another, the second attorney will face the same dilemma. In addition, withdrawal will harm the child's best legal interest because the decision regarding legal custody or permanency will be postponed until the new lawyer gets up to speed on the case. But perhaps of equal importance, the abused child will lose another trusted adult, and thus the child's fragile mental health and emotional problems may be exacerbated. How easily will the abused child be able to shift loyalty and trust to a second attorney? Therefore, even though most ethics codes permit an attorney to withdraw when his or her ability to represent the client zealously and competently is compromised by conflicts between the client and the attorney, in cases in which an attorney represents an abused child, withdrawal should be viewed as a drastic remedy that should rarely, if ever, be exercised.

The *LACBA Ethics Opinion Number 504* remedy of appointing a guardian ad litem for abused children who lack capacity to make reasoned choices is equally problematic because of the lack of specificity in the instructions. The broad sweeping language that the "attorney may ethically disclose the minor's confidential information to the guardian ad litem and should follow the instructions of the guardian ad litem, even if those instructions conflict with those of the minor client" requires disclosure well beyond that contemplated by the *ABA Model Rules*, which limit the discretionary disclosure to cases of threatened serious bodily injury. Further, what if the minor was competent when the statement was made and when he or she asserted confidentiality, but later becomes incompetent? It would seem that the moment of substantive importance is the time when the child confidentially discloses the threatened abuse, not when the attorney's conscience is tested by remaining silent. Attorneys who are uncertain about their minor client's competency to make the decision to refuse disclosure of future child abuse must be very careful when deciding whether to seek a mental health competency evaluation of the child. For instance, in Maryland "a mental health provider who learns of an instance of child abuse or neglect must report it, regardless of whether the person revealing the information was referred by an attorney. The only exception is if the attorney's referral occurs after the initiation of a criminal proceeding against a defendant, as part of the attorney's trial preparation."[21]

---

[21] *75 Maryland Attorney General Opinion 76* (February 8, 1990). *See, e.g.,* Ronni K. Burrows & Elaine Buzzinotti, *Legal Therapists and Lawyers Care-Giving Partnerships for the Next Century*, 19 FAM. ADVOC. 33 (1997).

In addition, there is always a problem with a substitute consent justification, which is a phenomenon in which an attorney judges a client's competency by taking into account a decision by the client with which the attorney disagrees. This phenomenon is especially salient when dealing with child clients. It would be simple for the attorneys or the guardians ad litem, once appointed, merely to determine that because they think it is unreasonable to remain silent about the threatened abuse that the child client in asserting confidentiality must be incompetent to make that decision. However, children may make reasonable decisions to suffer physical abuse when the alternative is to be torn from all blood relationships and from all persons with whom the child has bonded psychological relationships. Even adults, after reading the thousands of cases in which children are abused in foster and group homes, might question whether it is better to suffer abuse at home or risk being an orphan in a child dependency system in which the number of children separated from their families exponentially exceeds the number of prospective adoptive homes.

For instance, not a single state has met the federal government permanency planning goals mandated in the Adoption and Safe Families Act of 1997.[22] The federal government review of the California dependency system found that there was noncompliance regarding "the percentage of children achieving reunification within 12 months of entry into foster care..., the percentage of children discharged to finalized adoptions within 24 months of entry into foster care, and that in 19% of cases no diligent efforts had even been made to locate a permanent placement for children already removed from their home."[23] That federal report also found that in California, in "18 percent of applicable cases, the frequency and/or quality of caseworker visits with parents were not sufficient to promote the safety and well-being of the child or promote the attainment of case goals...."[24] Therefore, before a child's attorney concludes that the child's decision to suffer abuse is so unreasonable as to constitute incompetency in decision making, the attorney should factor in the reality of foster care, rather than merely asking what he or she would do were the attorney in the child's shoes.

II. PARENTS' ATTORNEYS: DUTY TO DISCLOSE CHILD ABUSE?

There is often an intimate connection between an attorney's duty of loyalty to a client and the duty to avoid actual or apparent conflicts of interest.

---

[22] Laura Meckler, *States Fail New Test of Child Care System*, at 1 (Associated Press, Aug. 19, 2003).

[23] FINAL REPORT: CALIFORNIA CHILD AND FAMILY SERVICES REVIEW 6–8 (U.S. Department of Health & Human Services, Administration for Children and Families, Administration on Children, Youth and Families Children's Bureau, January 2003).

[24] *Id.* at 10.

Attorneys who represent parents generally have been excluded as mandated child abuse reporters, especially because that information could lead not only to the loss of custody of children but also to their clients' incarceration through criminal prosecution.[25] It would seem axiomatic that an attorney who represents the Department and who is responsible for filing dependency actions against parties could not also defend parents in similar cases filed by the Department.

However, sometimes, because of budget constraints, counties attempt to have attorneys accept such dual roles. For instance, in South Carolina a part-time public defender who represented parents in criminal child abuse actions entered into a contract with the Department of Social Services to also provide attorney services to that agency in dependency court.[26] The South Carolina Ethics Advisory Committee held that "[a]ny attorney who becomes a member of the solicitor's office [representing the Department of Social Services] would be precluded from defending criminal prosecutions in the county. If an attorney can perform those duties without becoming a member of the solicitor's office, the attorney can defend criminal prosecutions in the same county but should first obtain the client's knowledgeable consent."[27] The Ethics Advisory Committee made a distinction between public defenders and all other county attorneys in relation to the dual role. It said that a public defender is absolutely forbidden from working in any capacity for the Department of Social Services because the public defender "could be in the position of representing as public defender a person being prosecuted by the solicitor's office, which is the attorney's other employer"; then, the attorney would clearly have "divided loyalties" and possible access to "files in the Solicitor's Office,"[28] creating an actual or apparent conflict of interest. However, the Ethics Advisory Committee noted that other county attorneys, as long as there is no conflict of interest, may represent the Department of

---

[25] For example, "[w]hen an attorney is representing a battered woman with abused children, the attorney would be prohibited from reporting the suspected abuse to DSS [Department of Social Services]. If the attorney made the report, and DSS substantiated the allegations, the attorney's client could be criminally prosecuted." Christine A. Picker, *The Intersection of Domestic Violence and Child Abuse: Ethical Considerations and Tort Issues for Attorneys Who Represent Battered Women with Abused Children*, 12 ST. LOUIS U. PUB. L. REV. 69, 89 (1993). And in *North Carolina State Bar Revised Opinion Number RPC 120* (July 17, 1992), the state bar held that if an attorney learns of possible child abuse while representing a husband and wife in an unrelated matter and does not report the child abuse, the state bar "will not treat this conduct as unethical" even if failure to report might be deemed a criminal violation. However, on January 13, 1995, in *North Carolina State Bar Opinion Number RPC 175*, it was held that an attorney for a parent has discretion whether or not to report suspected child abuse to the Department of Social Services "even if to do so may result in substantial harm to the interests of the client."

[26] *South Carolina Bar Ethics Advisory Committee, Opinion 85–21* (1985), at 1.
[27] *Id.* at 2.   [28] *Id.* at 3.

Social Services on a part-time basis. But because many county attorneys serve as the child's guardian ad litem in dependency court, they are not permitted to also represent the Department of Social Services.[29]

Parents' attorneys are often faced with cases in which they determine that following the parents' wishes and zealously arguing their case will not, in their view, be in the best interest of the children or may, in fact, place children at risk. *ABA Model Rules of Professional Conduct, Rule 1.16(b)(3)* permits an attorney to withdraw from a case if "a client insists upon pursuing an objective that the lawyer considers repugnant or imprudent" as long as the "withdrawal can be accomplished without material adverse effect on the interests of the client. . . ."[30] However, because the attorney cannot disclose confidential data to the judge in support of the motion to withdraw from representation, in most cases the mere act of seeking to withdraw might prejudice the parent client because the judge will speculate about the reasons underlying the withdrawal request. If the judge thinks that the withdrawal is based upon confidential evidence that is relevant to the children's safety, the judge, in a close case, may be less willing to return the children to their parents. The parents' attorney is thus caught in a Catch-22. If he or she seeks withdrawal it might clue the dependency court judge that facts not in evidence indicate that returning the child to the parents might be dangerous, but zealously arguing the parents' stated preference might facilitate that danger to the children.

What is clear is that the parents' attorney usually may not reveal that confidential data to the court or the Department of Social Services. For instance, in *The Florida Bar v. Susan K. Glant*,[31] an attorney was appointed to represent a parent in her motion to obtain custody of two of her four children who had been removed earlier from the father's custody by the Department of Health and Rehabilitative Services (HRS) based upon allegations of sexual abuse by the father. The mother's attorney knew that she wanted custody of only two of the four children, but the attorney thought that if the other two children were placed in the father's home they would be further sexually abused. In an earlier action the Department did not litigate child sexual abuse allegations against the father due to insufficient evidence.[32] Therefore, the mother's attorney sent a letter to the Department demanding further investigation and "included a copy of an unfiled motion for custody modification which asked that the mother be given custody of all four children," even though

---

[29] *Id.* at 3–4.
[30] Stephen Gillers & Roy D. Simon, Jr., REGULATION OF LAWYERS: STATUTES AND STANDARDS 1996 163 (1996).
[31] *The Florida Bar v. Susan K. Glant*, 645 So. 2d 962 (Florida 1994).
[32] *Id.* at 963.

Confidentiality

the attorney knew that the mother wanted custody of only two of them.[33] The Florida Supreme Court, after noting that the mother's attorney's proper remedy was to have withdrawn in the case, determined that she violated *Florida Rule of Professional Conduct 4 1.2(a)*, which "requires a lawyer to abide by a client's decision regarding the objectives of representation"; the court held that the violation warranted a public reprimand with six months of probation as an appropriate sanction.[34] Although the Florida Supreme Court did not discuss the issue, the mother's attorney also arguably violated her duty of confidentiality and loyalty to the mother because in her motion to withdraw she disclosed confidential information that the mother wanted to remain confidential. In addition, had the court further investigated the case and concluded that the mother actually knew of the father's sexual abuse of the other children, the court might have decided that none of the mother's children should live with her because she was in denial and could not protect them from the father should he visit with them. The mother's attorney would also have violated the requirements of zealous and competent representation under that scenario. In fact, the mother's attorney would have been the strongest state witness against the mother.

The Utah State Bar Ethics Advisory Committee determined that a parent's attorney who discovers evidence that her client has abused her children is more constrained in disclosing that abuse than in a case in which the attorney learns from the parent client that a third party has abused her children.[35] The Ethics Committee held that an attorney can disclose "information leading the attorney to believe a person who is not his client has subjected a child to abuse, even if such information is obtained during the course of representing the attorney's client and even if the client objects to the disclosure."[36] However, if the suspected child abuser is the attorney's client, the attorney's choices are more limited. The Utah Ethics Committee determined that the attorney is not under a mandatory duty to disclose the client's child abuse and that the disclosure, if made, can only relate to past, not to future abuse.[37] The Ethics Committee noted that the Utah ethics standards are in conflict with mandatory child abuse reporting laws and client confidentiality rules. It therefore found that the resolution of the conflicting ethical and statutory duties constituted a legal, not an ethical question, and thus was beyond the committee's jurisdiction.[38] However, the Ethics Committee indicated that due process may trump legal ethics because Utah Constitution, Art. I, § 12

---

[33] *Id.* at 963–964. [34] *Id.* at 963.
[35] *Compare Utah State Bar Ethics Advisory Committee Opinion 97-12* (January 23, 1998) with *Opinion 95-06* (July 28, 1985).
[36] Opinion 97-12, fn. 6 quoting from Opinion 95-06.
[37] Opinion 97-12, at 2. [38] *Id.* at 3.

provides "that a person accused of a criminal offense shall not be compelled to give evidence against himself. Arguably, this extends through the attorney-client relationship to mean the client's attorney cannot be compelled to give such evidence."[39] If the Ethics Committee had reached the opposite conclusion, that a parent's attorney may disclose or can be legally compelled to disclose a parent's confession of child abuse, then certainly attorneys would have a duty to counsel and admonish parents during the formation of the attorney-client relationship about the possibility of disclosure, even if that admonition might chill the parent's willingness to inform the attorney fully of all material facts necessary to ensure competent representation.

The tide is, however, changing to permit more disclosures. For instance, in *McClure v. Thompson*[40] the Ninth Circuit recently held that an attorney was not incompetent based upon his revelation, without client consent, of confidential data he had discovered from his client concerning the location of the two children his client was charged with kidnaping because the disclosure might prevent the resulting death of the children. Of course, the due process question of whether the government can use such a disclosure by a criminal defendant's attorney is far from certain.

For instance, in *Baltimore City Department Of Social Services v. Bouknight*[41] an allegation of physical abuse by the mother was sustained and her child was returned home upon a condition that the mother would participate in therapy, enroll in parenting classes, and refrain from using physical punishment against her child. The mother was uncooperative, refused to bring the child back for a court review hearing, and said that the child had been sent to live with her aunt. After the mother refused to produce her child based upon her Fifth Amendment privilege against self-incrimination, the trial judge held her in contempt of court. The United States Supreme Court found that holding the mother in contempt of court was constitutional, even though the production of the child might provide incriminating evidence that could result in criminal prosecution for child abuse because the mother was the custodian of the child under a court order. However, the Supreme Court was very troubled by the use of any information that might be gleaned had the mother returned her child because of the Fifth Amendment implications. The Court, therefore, noted that even though the mother was required to produce the child even if that production might incriminate her, the government might not be able to use that information in a criminal prosecution:

> [W]e are not called upon to define the precise limitations that may exist upon the State's ability to use the testimonial aspects of Bouknight's act of production in subsequent criminal proceedings. But we note that

---

[39] *Id.* at fn. 3.
[40] *McClure v. Thompson*, 323 F. 3d 1233 (9th Cir. 2003).
[41] *Baltimore City Department of Social Services v. Bouknight*, 493 U.S. 549; 100 S. Ct. 900 (1990).

Confidentiality

imposition of such limitations is not foreclosed. The same custodial role that limited the ability to resist the production order may give rise to corresponding limitations upon the direct and indirect use of that testimony.[42]

Just so, the Supreme Court might hold that, even though a parent's attorney is mandated to report confidential data regarding the parent's child abuse, the Court might declare that the purpose of the disclosure is to protect the child, not to punish the parent. This result, just like that in *Bouknight*, would support society's need to protect children without totally abrogating the critically important rights against self-incrimination under the Fifth Amendment.[43]

III. THE DEPARTMENT'S ATTORNEY: DISCLOSURE AND TRIAL TACTICS

Assume that the Department's attorney receives what appears to be confidential and/or privileged material from the parents' attorney and concludes that the parents' attorney has intentionally disclosed that data. This situation is most likely to occur when parents' counsel uncovers substantial evidence that the parent intends to further abuse his or her children, but ethical rules prohibit the direct disclosure of the probable future child abuse.[44] What are the options for the Department's attorney? *ABA Formal Opinion 92–368 (Inadvertent Disclosure of Confidential Material)* suggests that the attorney may not

---

[42] *Id.*

[43] For an argument against disclosure of confidential client information in cases in which criminal prosecution is possible, *see* Brooke Albrandt, *supra* note 10, at 655, 674, in which the author concludes that "[g]iven the apparently negligible effect of reporting requirements on reducing child abuse, it is the position of this Note that mandatory reporting requirements should not be applied to attorneys."

[44] Whether a parents' attorney is precluded from disclosing confidential information to prevent threatened child abuse depends upon the ethical rules applicable in the jurisdiction. For example, in *Alabama Bar Association Opinion Number 1995-06* an attorney for a father discovered that the father was involved in an ongoing investigation about his sexual abuse of his children. Because the father was so unstable that the attorney could not adequately represent him, the State Bar held that the attorney could disclose the father's condition under two contexts. First, the attorney could disclose "such confidential information as may be required to adequately represent" his client's interests. And second, pursuant to *Alabama Rules of Professional Conduct, Rule 1.6(b)* the attorney could disclose the data if the attorney "reasonably believes disclosure is necessary to prevent the client from committing a criminal act which the lawyer believes is likely to result in imminent death or substantial bodily harm." *Id.* There is a continuing debate among state bar associations regarding the ambit of an attorney's discretion to disclose client's threats of future criminal conduct. *See* Ira L. Shafiroff, *What Evil Lurks: Client Confidentiality Should Not Trump the Life of an Innocent Person*, L. A. DAILY J., January 29, 2003, p. 6, cols. 3–5. And the scope of disclosure of confidential information by government attorneys is broader than the permissible disclosure by private attorneys, especially in criminal proceedings. Thomas Haviena, *Prosecution and Defense Have Different Disclosure Obligations*, L. A. DAILY J., February 2, 2004, p. 7, cols. 1–3.

use confidential materials that are received through inadvertence where the "receiving lawyer was not an unintended recipient of the material."[45] And in *ABA Formal Opinion 94–382* it was suggested that, if a government attorney receives confidential data from "someone other than the opposing party's lawyer," the government attorney should notify "her adversary's lawyer that she has received the documents."[46] However, the ABA Standing Committee questioned the duty to disclose receipt of confidential data or to refrain from using that data because that "could prejudice the legitimate rights of the receiving lawyer's client to employ such materials in the prosecution or defense of a legal action."[47] It held that

> a lawyer receiving such privileged or confidential materials satisfies her professional responsibility by (a) refraining from reviewing materials which are probably privileged or confidential, any further than is necessary to determine how appropriately to proceed; (b) notifying the adverse party or the party's lawyer that the receiving lawyer possesses such documents; (c) following the instructions of the adverse party's lawyer; or (d) in the case of a dispute, refraining from using the materials until a definitive resolution of the proper disposition of the materials is obtained from a court.[48]

The ABA Standing Committee recognizes that these remedies work well when the one who disclosed the data is not the opposing attorney. But in our hypothetical, it was the opposing counsel who released the confidential data. Some states have ruled that zealous advocacy trumps fairness to the opponent's client and permits the use of the confidential data, as long as the receiving governmental attorney did not participate in the garnering of that data:

> An attorney who comes into possession of a document of the opposing party during litigation may use the document at trial provided it is admissible evidence and neither the attorney nor client in any way procured the removal of the document from the possession of the opposing party. An attorney's mere possession of the opposing party's internal and private memorandum does not require the attorney to withdraw from representation of the client.[49]

But what should be the limit of the Department's use of that confidential information? Clearly, a parent's admission of an intention to commit future

---

[45] American Bar Association, *ASK ETHIC Search*, PROF. LAW., V. 8, No. 4 (August 1997) (citing ABA Formal Opinion 92-368).
[46] *Id.*
[47] *Id.*
[48] *Id.*
[49] *Id.*; *Michigan Bar Opinion CI-970* (1983); *Maryland Bar Association Ethics Opinion 89-53* (1989); *Virginia State Bar Opinion 1076* (1988).

child abuse is highly relevant in the dependency case concerning disposition and reunification issues. However, whether that data can be introduced in the dependency proceeding is dependent upon the jurisdiction's hearsay rules and upon the court's determination of whether the parents' attorney's intentional disclosure of the privileged data raises sufficient due process issues to require suppression of that evidence. Although many dependency jurisdictions have held that the Fourth Amendment exclusionary rule is inapplicable in those proceedings because of the necessity of considering all relevant evidence regarding the child's best interest, it is quite a different issue to hold that the intentional violation of client confidentiality, loyalty, competence, and zealousness by the parents' court-appointed attorney does not sufficiently taint the evidence to exclude its introduction.[50] Of course, if the parents' court-appointed attorney is not a state actor, then the exclusionary rule would not be implicated, and the parents' only remedies would be to sue their attorney for malpractice or for invasion of privacy under a theory of public disclosure of embarrassing private facts and to seek state bar sanctions for the attorney's ethical violations.[51]

Whether the Department's attorney can disclose confidential information to the prosecutor in a criminal prosecution based upon identical allegations of child abuse is a detailed statutory question answered differently by the states. For instance, in California, criminal prosecutors, under limited circumstances, have access to the data in the Child Abuse Central Registry.[52]

---

[50] For instance, in *In re Christopher B.*, 147 Cal. Rptr. 390 (Cal. 1978), the court held that the exclusionary rule is inapplicable in dependency proceedings because of the necessity of determining the best interests of the child. Some courts have held that even if a search violates the Fourth Amendment, the exclusionary rule, as opposed to a civil rights action for damages, is inapplicable in dependency proceedings. *See A. R. v. State*, 937 P. 2d 1037 (Utah 1997); *In re Diane*, 494 N. Y. S. 2d 881 (1985); *J. A. R. v. Dept. Health & Rehab. Servs.*, 419 So. 2d 780 (Fla. App. 1982).

[51] Although searches by certain governmental employees, such as teachers, are sufficient state action to implicate the Fourth Amendment and the exclusionary rule, not all searches by governmental employees are treated identically. *New Jersey v. T. L. O.*, 469 U.S. 325 (1985) (school searches conducted by school administrators implicate the Fourth Amendment). However, whether the actor is a sufficient state actor to implicate the Constitution is a question of fact. For instance, courts have reached diametrically opposing judgments on whether social workers are sufficient state actors or independent contractors with no *respondeat superior* relationship with the government. *See Hunte v. Blumenthal*, 680 A. 2d 1231 (1996) [foster parents are state employees]; *Paige Kenal. B. v. Molepske*, 580 N. W. 2d 289 (Wisc. 1998) [children's guardian ad litem immune]; *Tara M. v. City of Philadelphia*, 145 F. 3d 625 (3rd Cir. 1998) [children's guardian ad litem not immune and is responsible for contribution for damages to child placed in foster home]; *DeShaney v. Winnebago*, 489 U.S. 189 (1989) [government not responsible for injuries to child returned to parent while in parents' care].

[52] For instance, California Penal Code Section 11170 (d) provides that the records shall be made available to "out-of-state law enforcement agencies conducting investigations of known or suspected child abuse . . . " as long as that agency makes a sufficient showing of entitlement and need.

However, if a criminal prosecutor represents a party in a child dependency proceeding, all records "are confidential and shall be held separately, and shall not be inspected by members of the district attorney's office not directly involved in the representation of that minor."[53]

Often the Department may want to divulge confidential juvenile court information in order to defend itself against unwarranted allegations of misfeasance or abuses of discretion. Although the American Bar Association *Standards of Practice* require the agency attorney to protect the "positive image of the agency," those standards also hold that the attorney must ensure that the "agency must abide by confidentiality laws, and therefore must keep some information private."[54] The agency lawyer's role involves counseling the agency not only on the confidentiality laws but also on the political and policy consequences of violating those rules and privileges.[55]

IV. JUDGES: PARTIES' PRIVACY VERSUS PUBLIC OVERSEER

Juvenile court judges may not comment publicly upon cases pending in their courtroom that are not yet legally final.[56] In *Schenck*,[57] the Oregon Supreme Court held that a juvenile court judge violated the prohibition against publicly commenting on pending proceedings by writing a letter to the editor explaining his problems with trial counsel: he wrote that "her immaturity led her to view herself as the knight on the white charger and set herself up as the all knowing and righteous in her own position."[58] The Oregon

---

[53] California Penal Code Section 318.

[54] *Standards of Practice for Lawyers Representing Child Welfare Agencies*, Rule B-1(4) (American Bar Association, August 2004). "The agency attorney must thoroughly understand the attorney client confidentiality issue and work diligently to avoid divulging confidential information." *Id.*

[55] *Id.*

[56] In *Broadman v. Commission on Judicial Performance*, 77 Cal. Rptr. 2d 408, 417–418 (1999), the California Supreme Court held that a judge committed judicial misconduct by publicly commenting on a pending case in violation of the California Code of Judicial Ethics, Canon 3B(9), which prohibits jurists from making "public comment about a pending or impending proceeding in any court...." The judge commented upon a case pending in his court and in the Court of Appeal. On the other hand, the court in *In re Hendel*, (Connecticut Judicial Review Counsel, March 6, 1989 [unreported memorandum of decision] WestLaw JDDD database) held that a judge did not violate canons of judicial performance by commenting on two sexual abuse cases that were closed and final. One court held that unauthorized statements by a judge regarding litigants might be outside the protection of absolute judicial immunity and may subject the judge to monetary damages. *Soliz v. Williams III*, 88 Cal. Rptr. 2d 184, 195–196 (1999). In Virginia, judges may not comment upon a pending case even if it is not being litigated within the state of Virginia. *Commonwealth of Virginia Judicial Ethics Advisory Committee Opinion* 99-7, Nov. 17, 1999. *See also In re Hey*, 425 S. E. 2d 221, 222–224 (W.Va., 1992); *In re Inquiry of Broadbelt*, 683 A.2d 543, 546 (N.J., 1996).

[57] *Schenck*, 870 P. 2d 185 (Oregon 1994).   [58] *Id.* at 200.

Confidentiality

Supreme Court found that the judge's editorial demonstrated "maliciousness" toward trial counsel and created the appearance that the judge was not impartial, and the court suspended the judge for forty-five days without pay.[59]

However, judges have an affirmative duty to speak to the public on "the law, the legal system, [and on] the administration of justice and non-legal subjects...."[60] In addition, judicial officers have a duty to publicly comment

---

[59] *Id.* at 209–210.

[60] *American Bar Association Canons of Judicial Conduct, Canon 4(B).* Although ABA rules of professional responsibility are not binding on California attorneys, they "can be looked to as a collateral source, particularly in those instances where there is no direct authority found under applicable California rules...." *California Compendium on Professional Responsibility, Formal Op. No 1983-71, at II A-223* (State Bar of California 1983). Alabama judges are not "prohibited from speaking to groups on the problems of child abuse," but should refrain from addressing the quality of services of any child abuse organization which has invited him to speak, especially if its agents are likely to appear in the judge's court. *Alabama Judicial Inquiry Commission, #87293*, March 2, 1987. Arizona Judicial Canon 3B(12) requires "a judge to participate actively in judicial education programs" and judges may even participate in seminars funded by "businesses, foundations or other non-governmental entities whose interests may come before the judge" as long as no case is pending and the judge does not accept reduced tuition. *Arizona Supreme Court Judicial Ethics Advisory Committee Opinion 00-02*, April 9, 2000. And in Utah judges who hear cases from the Attorney General's Office may participate in a conference administered by that office as long as the judge does not "give legal advice, comment on pending cases, or show improper bias..." and as long as the judge is available to speak to groups who handle cases adverse to the sponsoring organization as well. *Utah Informal Ethics Opinion 99-6*, September 23, 1999. *See also Virginia Judicial Ethics Advisory Committee Opinion 01-04*, March 28, 2001 (judge may lecture to cadets in police training programs regarding expectation of police officers while testifying in court). In Florida judges may serve on a Family Violence Protocol Task Force in the jurisdiction in which they sit if activities are limited to "offering expertise and knowledge; teaching, speaking and presenting information designed to educate the public as to the underlying purposes and efforts of the local task force; and accurately relating the role of judges in the court system...." *Florida Supreme Court Judicial Ethics Advisory Committee Opinion No. 95-84*, July 28, 1995. *See also Utah Informal Opinion No. 88-2*, April 15, 1988 ("Judge may serve on county Child Abuse Coordinating Committee as long as she limits her activities to issues regarding "improvement of the law, the legal system or the administration of justice."); *Virginia Ethics Advisory Committee Opinion 00-3*, March 27, 2000 (judge may not serve on the board of juvenile group home that accepts court referrals); *Wisconsin Judicial Conduct Advisory Committee Opinion 01-1*, January 8, 2002 (judge may serve on a County Community Corrections Advisory Board that develops community resources and community partnerships.); *Arkansas Judicial Ethics Advisory Committee Opinion No. 96-01*, December 29, 1999 (juvenile court judge may serve on Policy and Planning Board of the Division of Youth Services of Department of Human Services because it is a "quasi-governmental agency that is devoted to the administration of justice); *Delaware Judicial Ethics Advisory Committee Opinion 2001-1*, May 15, 2001 (judge may serve as a volunteer judge in the Teen Court Program as long as the judge's role is that "of advisor and not as a participant in the decision-making process" because juveniles who fail the program may appear later before that juvenile court judge). Florida judges may respond to public criticism regarding court philosophy in relation to specific cases once the cases are concluded. *Florida*

upon possible revisions of the juvenile justice system that will contribute to the improvement of the administration of justice.[61] Jurists may speak on issues regarding the improvement of the law and the administration of justice in public hearings before legislative committees, as well as in any other public forum.[62] The United States Supreme Court in *Republican Party of Minnesota v. White*[63] recently struck down as unconstitutional restrictions on judicial candidates from expressing their views on general legal and political questions. And the Michigan Committee on Professional and Judicial Ethics found that a "judge may write an article containing general legal information, provide work project for inclusion in an educational pamphlet or cassette tape sold for profit, and receive compensation therefore, provided that the promotion and sale of the material is not an exploitation of the

---

Advisory Opinion No. 94-8, April 21, 1994 (citing to Illinois Supreme Court Rules 63A(6) and 64(A) that permit judges to make "public statements in the course of their official duties or from explaining for public information the procedures of the court."). Florida has a liberal view of judges' participation in society, which is reflected in Opinion 98-01 by the following quotation from Benjamin Cardozo: "This is no life of cloistered ease to which you dedicated your powers. This is a life that touches your fellow man at every angle of their being, a life that you must live in the crowd, and yet apart from it, man of the world and philosopher by turns." In Nevada, judges may even speak at continuing legal education seminars that also serve as fund-raisers; however, the judge "may not personally engage in fund-raising activities or solicitation of attendance for the event." *Nevada Standing Committee on Judicial Ethics and Election Practices, Opinion JE99-002*, April 5, 1999.

[61] Commentary to *American Bar Association Canons of Judicial Conduct, Canon 4(B)*. However, jurisdictions differ on whether judges may regularly serve as media consultants. For instance, the *Wisconsin Judicial Conduct Advisory Committee in Opinion 99-3*, April 14, 1999 held that a judge may serve on the editorial board of the *Wisconsin Opinions* weekly newspaper only if the judge "serves anonymously after the initial introduction of the editorial board in the newspaper." See also *West Virginia Judicial Investigation Commission Opinion*, November 25, 1997 permitting judges limited participation on radio talk shows discussing the legal system. However, the *Virginia Judicial Ethics Advisory Committee in Opinion 99-7*, November 17, 1999 held that a judge may not "appear on a regular basis on a radio or television interview program or talk show concerning legal issues." But judges are not prohibited from making limited media appearances. To determine whether judicial media appearances are prohibited, the judge should consider "[t]he frequency of his appearance, the audience, the subject matter, and whether the program is commercial or non-commercial."

[62] *American Bar Association Canons of Judicial Conduct, Canon 4(C)*. Judges may speak on pending ballot initiatives that affect juvenile justice reform and "[n]othing in the code prohibits judges from speaking to community groups in support of or in opposition to proposed initiatives to change the judicial system." *Arizona Supreme Court Judicial Ethics Advisory Committee, Opnion 96-8*, August 15, 1996. See also *Arkansas Judicial Ethics Advisory Committee Advisory Opinion No. 94-04*, March 8, 1994 (judges may take public positions regarding the merits of a bond measure to pay for construction of a new courthouse); *Utah Ethics Advisory Committee Informal Opinion 01-1*, January 25, 2001 (Although a judge may voice opinions regarding pending legislation, the judge may not "question the constitutionality of a law, or express an opinion on how a statute might be interpreted by the judge.").

[63] *Minnesota v. White*, 536 U.S. 765 (2002).

author's judicial position and the activity does not interfere with the proper performance of judicial duties."[64] An earlier Michigan case provided that a dependency judge could write a book for judges, lawyers, and the public describing child abuse law that used "materials from actual case histories" because those cases had been finalized.[65]

However, when was the last time that you saw a juvenile court judge on television or heard a judge on the radio correcting false stereotypes, generalizations, or statistics regarding the juvenile justice system? Where has the juvenile law bench been during the irrational juvenile zero tolerance era? From the mid-1980s through the year 2000, juvenile judges hearing juvenile delinquency cases have failed the bench, the public, and children by not speaking out on the punitive statutory changes to the juvenile system.[66] And many of those same juvenile court judges continue to implement hysteria-created punitive juvenile statutes. Why have they failed to correct the record so that the juvenile justice system both fairly and realistically balances the rights of children, families, and citizens? Judges, who are mandated to complete continuing legal education,[67] must have been exposed to the statistics that belie the media-fed juvenile crime hysteria. It is inconceivable that juvenile court judges are ignorant of the most credible and complete juvenile justice statistics that have been published by the U.S. Department of Justice for over a decade. For instance, serious crime in America **decreased** 3 percent from 1999 to 2000;[68] in 1999, 90 percent of murder suspects were adults,

---

[64] *State Bar of Michigan Standing Committee on Professional and Judicial Ethics, Opinion Number JI-76* (December 9, 1993) (1993 WL 566228).

[65] *State Bar of Michigan Standing Committee on Professional and Judicial Ethics, Opinion Number CI–427.* In Oklahoma information in actions filed before the Council on Judicial Complaints is confidential, even as to the identify of the judicial officer being investigated. *Oklahoma Attorney General Opinion No. 00-15* (February 23, 2000), at 2. However, the Attorney General found unconstitutional the provision permitting punishment for contempt for any spectator to the proceedings who discloses truthful information gleaned in that hearing. *Id.* at 9.

[66] In 1997 the California Judicial Council issued the Special Task Force on Court/Community Outreach, which determined that "it is critical for courts to become actively engaged in a wide range of court and community collaboration efforts." Veronica Simmons McBeth & Shelley M. Stump, *Reclaiming the Courts' Historical Role: Judges as Leaders in Their Communities*, 38 JUDGES J. 19, 22 (1999); *California Standards of Judicial Administration § 39* requires judges to "increase public understanding of the court system," and to "increase public understanding and promote public confidence in the integrity of the court system."

[67] *California Standards of Judicial Administration Sections 25.2 and 25.3* require juvenile court judges to attend juvenile law judicial education programs. In addition, *Welfare and Institutions Code § 264* requires the Judicial Council to conduct juvenile law conferences "for the purpose of improving the administration of justice in the juvenile courts."

[68] Press Release, U.S. Dept. of Justice Federal Bureau of Investigation, Crime Index Trends, January through June 2000 (Dec. 18, 2000).

not juveniles;[69] in 1999, juveniles committed only 19 percent of all violent crimes;[70] and juvenile arrests have **dropped** every year since 1995.[71]

Juvenile dependency and family court judges have an equal ethical obligation to speak out on legislation inimical to children served by those court systems. However, how many juvenile law judges have you seen on *60 Minutes, 48 Hours*, PBS, or anywhere in public correcting outrageous allegations about the juvenile dependency system? These judges have failed our children either through ignorance or fear of electorate backlash against judges portrayed as soft on crime and child abuse.[72] It is up to the entire bar and bench to protect judges who meet their ethical obligations of educating the public from hysterical voters' groups or unethical adversaries.

Because of the inherent authority and credibility of judges, should they decide to enter public debate, they must be careful to research the issues presented because decision makers might be lulled into blind acceptance of judicial comments. For example, recently judges were involved in helping design a bill to open California dependency trials to the press and the public for the first time.[73] The bill stated that if reporters are admitted to a hearing,

---

[69] CRIME IN THE UNITED STATES, 1999, U.S. Dept. of Justice Federal Bureau of Investigation, October 15, (2000), at 1–2. Even when the media report on an increase in violent crime, it does so in a way that distorts the increase. For instance, on March 21, 2001, *The Los Angeles Times* published a story by Dolondo Moultre with a large heading in bold type: "*VIOLENT CRIME RISES IN STATE'S LARGE CITIES,*" at A3. However, unless readers read the entire article and go to page 21, they will not learn that a significant factor in the increased reports of some violent crime was that, in cities like Glendale, California, police targeted "cases and got more victims to come forward and file criminal charges...." *Id.* at 21. This most recent report did not delineate changes in the juvenile crime rate.

[70] *Juvenile Arrests 1999*, JUV. JUST. BULL., Dec. 2000, at 1 (Office of Juvenile Justice and Delinquency Prevention, U.S. Dept. of Justice).

[71] *Id.* at 1.

[72] Fear of non-reelection to the bench is not a valid excuse for failing to meet the requirement of educating the public on the administration of justice. Being a judge "means accepting criticism, justified or unjustified, without always being able to respond.... [i]t means accepting the task of explaining the judicial process, which is sometimes hard to understand, and confronting adverse attitudes, which are sometimes hard to impact." Joseph P. Nadeau, *What It Means to Be a Judge*, 39 No. 3 JUDGES J. 34 (2000). Judges have failed our children by failing not only to correct false juvenile crime statistics but also other misperceptions regarding children in the court system. For instance, the public who serves as jurors, believes "the myth that sexual allegations in custody visitation cases are relatively common [even though] the present research strongly suggests that such allegations actually arise in only a small fraction of all contested custody and visitation cases." Nancy Thoennes, *Child Sexual Abuse: Whom Should a Judge Believe? What Should a Judge Believe*, 27 No. 3 JUDGES J. 14 (1988).

[73] I have a great deal of respect for the judges who helped promulgate this open court bill. I am certain that they did not intentionally withhold critical data regarding the effects of the new legislation on children. *California Senate Bill 1391*, 1999–2000 Reg. Sess. (Cal. 2000) sought to amend *Welfare and Institutions Code Section 346*, which holds that all child dependency cases are confidential.

they may not publish the name of the minor who was allegedly abused. However, the judges did not present evidence that such a limitation on the press's First Amendment rights would likely be unconstitutional.[74] Nor did the judges indicate the results in the few jurisdictions that have opened dependency hearings to the press. For instance, in New York the following data on dependency proceedings were permitted to be published by the press. In *Matter of Justin A.*, the *New York Law Journal* published the following facts: (1) the abused child's full name, (2) his mother "had placed his [the child's] penis in her mouth . . . ," and (3) the child engaged in "explicit sexual behavior and language inappropriate to a child of his age . . . [including] acts of exhibitionism and masturbation. . . . "[75] Nor did the judges or any of the judges' associations present evidence of the many other newspaper reports on child dependency proceedings that published (1) the child's full name and the nature of the abuse suffered;[76] (2) the address of the child victim;[77] (3) the name of a murdered child and her siblings and the location of their residence;[78] (4) the name of a 15-year-old mother charged with murdering her infant moments after its birth and the school she attended;[79] and (5) the name of an abused child, the name and location of her school, her physical afflictions, and details of the child abuse gynecological examination, which included "the insertion of a cotton swab in . . . [her] vagina and anus."[80] It is the obligation of juvenile dependency court judges who comment upon proposed legislation to investigate thoroughly the likely results of the statutory modifications on the best interest of children.

---

[74] William Wesley Patton, *Pandora's Box: Opening Child Protection Cases to the Press and Public*, 27 W.S. U. L. REV. 181, 182, fn. 3 (2000). The U.S. Supreme Court has never ruled on the question of whether a court can require the press to waive their rights to publish legally obtained data, such as a minor's name, as a prerequisite for admission to juvenile dependency hearings.

[75] 224 N.Y. L.J. 30 (col. 2) (July 11, 2000).

[76] Sheryl WuDunn, *Japan Confronts Child Abuse*, N.Y. TIMES, Aug. 15, 1999 at 7A.

[77] *5 Arrested on Charges of Child Abuse or Sex*, ORLANDO SENTINEL, Sept. 6, 1999, at 2.

[78] Lenny Savino, *Family Tried to Prevent Little Girl's Violent Death*, ORLANDO SENTINEL, May 26, 1999, at 1.

[79] John Pacenti, *Teen Mom Burdened by Loss of Childhood*, PALM BEACH POST, March 21, 2001, at 1A.

[80] *Tennenbaum v. New York City*, 222 N. Y. L. J. 25, col. 3 (October 15, 1999).

4 The Ethics of Alternative Dispute Resolution in Child Custody and Dependency Proceedings

INTRODUCTION

America's child custody and dependency systems would collapse if most cases were not disposed of through some form of alternative dispute resolution.[1] However, overloaded systems are not merely a recent phenomenon. During the early child reform movements in the 1850s, child welfare systems were laden with children's cases. For instance, in 1879 the New York Children's Aid Society sent 48,000 poor New York children to live with another family, and "after its first fourteen years the New York Society for the Prevention of Cruelty to Children 'investigated nearly 70,000 complaints of ill-treatment of 209,000 children. Prosecutions were pursued in 24,500 of these cases, resulting in almost 24,000 convictions and the removal of 36,300 children.'"[2] So what has changed? What new pressures are forcing an ever-growing percentage of child abuse and child custody cases to settle prior to a formal adjudication?

First, the number of family law custody cases has exploded because of increased divorce rates in America:

> In 1987, the first year divorce statistics were collected, the total number of divorces in the United States was just less than 10,000, about .03 per 1,000 people. By 1967, the divorce rate had jumped 140 times to 4.2 divorces per

---

[1] Charlene Saunders, past Dependency Court Administrator of the Los Angeles Dependency Courts, stated that "[w]ithout an early resolution program like mediation... [o]ur current judicial officers would be unable to respond to the current caseloads without an early resolution program." California Senate Judicial Hearings, Senate Bill 1420, March 24, 1992, contained in APPENDIX: JUVENILE SERVICES REPORT 1991–92 LOS ANGELES COUNTY GRAND JURY, May 30, 1992, at 3–4.

[2] Francis Barry McCarthy, William Wesley Patton, & James G. Carr, JUVENILE LAW AND ITS PROCESSES: CASES AND MATERIALS 30 (3d ed. 2003); Corinne Schiff, *Child Custody and the Ideal of Motherhood in Late Nineteenth Century New York*, 4 GA. J. ON FIGHTING POVERTY 403 (1997).

1,000 people, or about 500,000. By 1981, the number of divorces had more than doubled to 1.21 million, about 5.3 divorces per 1,000. Because modern public policy recognizes divorce as a socially acceptable means of recording family relationships, demographers estimate that approximately forty-five percent of all current marriages will end in divorce.[3]

Family law cases are the fastest growing type of litigation heard in civil courts and have increased by "70% since 1984 . . . ; forty percent of children will participate in the divorce of their parents and half of all children will live with one parent prior to reaching adulthood."[4] However, even though the number of family law cases has exploded, fewer than 2 percent are resolved by a fully litigated court trial, rather than by alternative dispute resolution.[5]

There are three essential pressures to informally resolve family law custody disputes. First, most jurisdictions require or strongly promote some form of alternative dispute resolution, such as negotiation, mediation, or mandatory settlement conferences, prior to trial. "About a tenth of the nation's domestic relations courts have mediation programs, with the vast majority authorizing the courts to compel participation by parties who contest custody or visitation."[6] Second, litigation is expensive; the earlier the case can be informally resolved and the more formal court procedures such as calling expert witnesses that can be avoided, the more able are parties to afford to resolve their custody and visitation disputes. Finally, many parents are unrepresented in child custody cases because there is no constitutional and often no statutory right to counsel. Studies by the American Bar Association found that the percentage of family law cases in which one parent proceeded *pro se* rose from 24 percent of cases in 1980 to 88 percent today, and in 1990 "neither party was represented in 52 percent" of the cases.[7] Considering that the National Center for State Courts found that approximately 37 percent of *pro se* litigants did not understand court procedures, it is not surprising that

---

[3] Dennis P. Saccuzzo, *Controversies in Divorce Mediations*, 79 NOTRE DAME L. REV. 425, 425 (2003).

[4] Nancy Ver Steegh, *Yes, No, and Maybe: Informed Decision Making about Divorce Mediation in the Presence of Domestic Violence*, 9 WM. & MARY J. WOMEN & L. 145, 159–160 (2003).

[5] *Id.* at 161. This 2 percent litigation rate of family law custody cases compares with an overall litigation rate for all civil cases of 5 percent. Richard Birke & Craig R. Fox, *Psychological Principles in Negotiating Civil Settlements*, 4 HARV. NEGOT. L. REV. 1, 1 (1999). "[A]n estimated 50% of custody cases are uncontested and the parents involved in the dissolution report negligible conflict. Most of the remaining custody cases are settled, with less than 2% ultimately resolved by the judge. However, about half of the contested cases involve substantial or intense conflict over custody." Nancy Ver Steegh, *supra* note 4, at 161.

[6] Sarah R. Cole, Nancy H. Rogers, & Craig A. McEwan, MEDIATION: LAW, POLICY, PRACTICE 12-2 (2001).

[7] Nancy Ver Steegh, *supra* note 4, at 165.

those parents would opt for an informal rather than formal court resolution of their custody dispute.[8]

American child dependency courts have experienced a similar explosion in court filings. In 1999 approximately 568,000 children were placed in out-of-home care in the United States, and the estimated cost of this alternative care was $9.4 billion.[9] However, perhaps the single empirical characteristic that distinguishes between family law cases and dependency cases is that litigated dependency cases often require multiple and continuing hearings to manage the family's problems. For instance, the national median time between the disposition and removal of children from foster care after a permanency planning decision in 1999 was 16.5 months.[10] During that 16.5 months, the average litigated dependency case will have resulted in an adjudication hearing, a disposition, and between two and three periodic review hearings and/or a permanency planning hearing. Thus, unlike family court cases, each litigated dependency case results in multiple court hearings. For instance, in 1995, the child dependency courts in Los Angeles heard 77,187 review and permanency planning hearings.[11]

It is therefore no wonder that more than thirty states have instituted alternative dispute resolution procedures in child protection cases.[12] However, mandatory alternative dispute resolution is much more problematic in dependency proceedings than in family law custody cases because many more dependency cases involve charges that can be prosecuted criminally. One must wonder how "voluntary" is a parent's cooperation in informal dispute resolution when one consequence of failing to participate may be the institution of criminal charges, whereas participation may lead to discovery in criminal proceedings:

> Formalized statutory alternative dispute resolution systems have permeated almost all areas of both the civil and criminal law. However, the child dependency system has continued to operate in a secret, informal... mediation

---

[8] *Id.* at 166–167.

[9] U.S. DEPARTMENT OF HEALTH AND HUMAN SERVICES, NATIONAL CLEARINGHOUSE ON CHILD ABUSE AND NEGLECT INFORMATION, FOSTER CARE NATIONAL STATISTICS (April 2001). In 1990, California, alone, had 30,435 children in foster care and another 24,945 in kinship care. LEAGUE OF WOMEN VOTERS OF CALIFORNIA EDUCATION FUND, JUVENILE JUSTICE STUDY COMMITTEE, JUVENILE JUSTICE IN CALIFORNIA PART II: DEPENDENCY SYSTEM, APPENDIX I: NATIONAL AND CALIFORNIA STATISTICS ON CHILD ABUSE AND NEGLECT (July 1998).

[10] U.S. DEPARTMENT OF HEALTH AND HUMAN SERVICES, YOUTH AND FAMILIES CHILDREN'S BUREAU, SAFETY, PERMANENCY, WELL BEING: CHILD WELFARE OUTCOMES, 1999 Annual Report 11, 15.

[11] INTER-AGENCY COUNCIL ON CHILD ABUSE AND NEGLECT, DATA ANALYSIS REPORT FOR 1996: STATUS REPORT ON CHILD ABUSE & NEGLECT IN LOS ANGELES COUNTY, at 142 (1996).

[12] Kelly Browe Olson, *Lessons Learned from a Child Protection Mediation Program: If At First You Succeed and Then You Don't*, 41 FAM. CT. REV. 480, 480–481 (2003).

and plea negotiation environment. Instead of addressing the real needs of the dependency system, legislatures have focused new efforts at criminally prosecuting alleged child abusers. Without fully considering the impact on the best interests of children and families, state statutes have coordinated agency resources in an effort to gain a few more criminal convictions. The result has been an exponential increase in criminal child abuse prosecutions that have substantially increased the risk to parents who cooperate in dependency non-statutory alternative dispute resolution.

The schizophrenic state policies of encouraging parents to admit child abuse in civil dependency cases while increasing criminal prosecutions and district attorneys' access to previously confidential juvenile court reports, files, and statements have a few stark implications. First, fewer parents will plead to civil charges or will plead in a system of secrecy in which they waive constitutional rights without knowing the consequences. Early efforts at family reunification will decrease, thus increasing the likelihood of parental termination that will further needlessly separate family members and burden taxpayers. Second, because parents will refrain from making important confidential statements in dependency mediation for fear of criminal prosecution, fewer prosecutors will gain child abuse admissions for use in the criminal prosecution, thus decreasing the effectiveness and social value of the new emphasis on prosecutorial access to dependency court records. These policies will result in a net social loss both from humanistic and economic perspectives.[13]

Because child abuse allegations can precipitate five distinctively different legal investigations in five different courts, attorneys must be cognizant of the intersystem ramifications of tactical decisions concerning alternative dispute resolution: "In juvenile court, dependency cases focus upon the protection of the abused child; delinquency cases can involve abuse of one child by another; in criminal court, the alleged abuser is prosecuted for his acts; in family court, parents can allege child abuse against each other; and the abused child can bring a civil suit against the alleged abuser for damages and other relief."[14]

Many attorneys have had little formal training in the various modes of alternative dispute resolution; however, the duty of competence requires such knowledge so that clients are not harmed by the process. Thus, this chapter, unlike the previous ones, both surveys the field of dispute resolution and

---

[13] William Wesley Patton, *Child Abuse: The Irreconcilable Differences Between Criminal Prosecution and Informal Dependency Court Mediation*, 31 U. LOUISVILLE J. FAM. L. 37, 38–39 (1993).

[14] Leonard Edwards, *The Relationship of Family and Juvenile Courts in Child Abuse Cases*, 27 SANTA CLARA L. REV. 201, 204 (1987).

delineates its ethical boundaries. This section introduces the debates, tactics, dangers, and ethical questions inherent in child custody and dependency alternative dispute resolution. Because the first formal mediation process in these cases did not occur until between 1981-3 in Los Angeles, the body of law is meager, but is rapidly developing as parties and state bar associations begin to ferret out the minimal ethical standards to be applied.[15]

I. ALTERNATIVE DISPUTE RESOLUTION VERSUS LITIGATION IN CUSTODY CASES

Litigation critics have focused on several aspects of the zealous battle in public tribunals that they assert are antithetical to the purposes of child custody and dependency proceedings. One mediation proponent has identified these essential characteristics of litigation: (1) openness versus privacy; (2) formal due process procedures; (3) objectivity and impartiality; (4) rationality of outcomes; (5) predictability, consistency, and uniformity of results; (6) easy access; and (7) citizen participation.[16] Others have identified these salient characteristics of court litigation: (1) public accountability of judges, (2) public norms, (3) precedent controlling, (4) appealable decisions, (5) public funding, (6) little control over selection of judges, (7) time-consuming, (8) polarizing, (9) noncompromising, (10) limitation on remedies, (11) expensive, and (12) incivility.[17]

Perhaps the strongest criticism of trials in custody cases is that the adversarial model "increases trauma and escalates conflict [and] [c]hildren often suffer the most in the 'tug of war.'"[18] Between 50 to 70 percent of surveyed parents found litigated custody disputes to be "impersonal, intimidating, and intrusive," and 71 percent stated that litigation escalated the level of animosity among parents.[19] Because most child custody and dependency cases involve a continuing relationship between parents and children, the exacerbated tension among the parties that results from litigation makes finding long-term solutions more difficult.

In addition, Carrie Mendel-Meadow, one of the strongest proponents of alternative dispute resolutions, argues that trials and their "binary" solutions

---

[15] Kelly Browe Olson, *supra* note 12, at 481. "California has long been in the vanguard of the public sector march toward mediation. In 1981, it became the first state to mandate child custody mediation." Ellen A. Waldman, *The Challenge of Certification: How to Ensure Mediator Competence while Preserving Diversity*, 30 U.S.F. L. REV. 723, 723 (1996).

[16] Robert A. Creo, *Mediation 2004: The Art and the Artist*, 108 PENN. ST. L. REV. 1017, 1025–1026 (2004).

[17] John W. Cooley, MEDIATION ADVOCACY 8–9 (2d ed. 2002).

[18] Dennis P. Saccuzzo, *supra* note 3, at 425, 426.

[19] Nancy Ver Steegh, *supra* note 4, at 85.

of right/wrong and win/lose are not capable of resolving the complicated issues inherent in many legal disputes: "The inability to reach a binary resolution of these disputes may result because in some cases we cannot determine the facts with any degree of accuracy. In other cases the law may bestow conflicting, though legitimate, legal rights giving some entitlements to both, or all, parties. And, in yet another category of cases, human or emotional equities cannot be divided sharply."[20]

It is not surprising, then, that jurisdictions quickly championed alternatives to trials in custody cases, not only to avoid increased acrimony and to provide more flexibility in the remedies involved but also in an effort to cut court costs. Some jurisdictions have realized savings of as much as 39 percent in child protection cases settled through mediation.[21]

Both negotiation and arbitration have been used in some jurisdictions to help informally resolve custody disputes. Negotiation is the most frequently used alternative dispute resolution mechanism in child custody and protection cases. It has the advantage of being the most flexible, least expensive, and fastest mechanism of party agreement. However, negotiation does not provide mandatory discovery, has no third party to deflect animus among the parties, is subject to severe power imbalances, is not subject to public and/or due process safeguards, and usually is not binding and enforceable without ratification by the court.[22] In addition, many jurisdictions have rejected arbitration as the central dispute resolution methodology in custody and dependency cases, in part because of its formal, often adversarial environment in which parties testify under oath and in which the scope of confidentiality is often within the discretion of the parties, rather than being statutorily defined.[23] Some, however, argue that arbitration is a good vehicle because unlike court trials it (1) is less expensive, (2) provides parties with the ability to define norms, (3) relaxes formal evidentiary standards, (4) eliminates or limits pretrial discovery, and (5) usually

---

[20] Carrie Menkel-Meadow, *The Trouble with the Adversary System in a Postmodern Multicultural World*, 38 WM. & MARY L. REV. 5, 5–7 (1996).

[21] Kelley Browe Olson, *supra* note 12, at 483. Three reasons for settlements are that they are cheaper, avoid all-or-nothing solutions, and permit more creative and individualized dispositions. Brian J. Shoot, *"Don't Come Back without a Reasonable Offer": The Extent of, and Limits on, Court Power to Foster Settlement*, 76 N.Y. ST. B. J. 10, 11 (2004).

[22] "The most notable structured difference between the adversary system ... and most settlement negotiations is the absence of a third-party neutral ... This fact alone may render the adversarial ethic useless as a justification for attorneys' otherwise immoral or unethical conduct in settlement negotiations." Brian C. Haussman, *The ABA Ethical Guidelines for Settlement Negotiations: Exceeding the Limits of the Adversarial Ethic*, 89 CORNELL L. REV. 1218, 1230 (2004).

[23] Carrie Menkel-Meadow, *Ethics in Arbitration and Related Dispute Resolution Processes: What's Happening and What's Not*, 56 U. MIAMI L. REV. 949, 962 (2002).

excludes appellate remedies.[24] One commentator describes the essence of arbitration as

> [A]n adjudicatory process in which a third party neutral simply decides the dispute. It differs substantially [from court trials], however, in that the proceeding is informal rather than formal, and is not bound by traditional rules of evidence or procedure. As decisionmakers, arbitrators wield considerably more unchecked power than their public judicial counterparts.... Moreover, arbitrators generally are free from the constraints of substantive law in either the procedures by which they conduct their hearings, or in the standards they use to resolve disputes. In fact, arbitrators need not and often do not have legal training. Finally, their decisions, called "awards," generally are final, binding, and enforceable by courts, and generally may not be reversed on substantive grounds.[25]

But by far the most universally adopted and often mandated method of dispute resolution in child custody and dependency disputes is mediation. Unlike negotiation, which does not involve a third-party neutral to help the parties brainstorm a mutually acceptable resolution, mediation provides a facilitator who attempts to separate bitter personal battles from the center of the dispute, the best interest of the children. Mediation has been defined as

> a process in which a mediator, an impartial third party, facilitates the resolution of family disputes by promoting the participants' voluntary agreement. The family mediator assists communication, encourages understanding and focuses the participants on their individual and common interests. The family mediator works with the participants to explore options, make decisions and reach their own agreements.[26]

Mediation was quickly adopted because it (1) enhances the voluntary nature of participation in dispute resolution, (2) fosters party cooperation and communication, (3) provides a neutral non-decision maker to facilitate discussion, and (4) gives to the parties responsibility for determining the rules and

---

[24] John W. Cooley, *supra* note 17, at 8–9.

[25] Richard C. Reuben, *Democracy and Dispute Resolution: The Problem of Arbitration*, 67 LAW CONTEMP. PROBS. 279, 296 (2004).

[26] Nancy Ver Steegh, *supra* note 4, at 170 [quoting from the Model Standards of Practice for Family and Divorce Mediation]; *see also* Andrew Schepard, *An Introduction to the Model Standards of Practice for Family and Divorce Mediation*, 35 FAM. L Q. 1, 3 (2001). "Mediation is 'a process by which a neutral mediator... assists the parties in reaching a mutually acceptable agreement as to issues of child custody and visitation.' The role of the mediator is to aid the parties in identifying the issues, reducing misunderstanding, clarifying priorities, exploring areas of compromise, and finding points of agreement." *Carter v. Carter*, 470 S.E. 2d 193, 201, fn. 10 (West Virginia 1996) [quoting Kansas Stat. Ann. § 23–601 (1995).

processes of dispute resolution.[27] Mediation can, under ideal circumstances, provide parties ownership of brainstorming solutions through their participation in the process and decision-making responsibility.[28] Mediation's values of flexibility, reduced trauma to children, instruction to parents on how to informally resolve future disputes, and more cost-effective methods of determining family and children's best interests quickly became evident to legislators and courts.[29]

II. ADVANTAGES AND DISADVANTAGES OF ALTERNATIVE DISPUTE RESOLUTION IN CHILD CUSTODY AND DEPENDENCY PROCEEDINGS

Several studies and surveys have indicated that resolving child custody and protection cases without a trial is beneficial for the parties. Settlement rates in child protection mediation "have ranged from 70% to 89%, mediated plans are produced 1 to 2 months sooner than nonmediated plans and satisfaction rates varied but average between 75% and 90%."[30] An Arkansas study found that "there were 295 days between the initial case filing and permanent placement for mediated cases and 553 days for nonmediated cases."[31] A similar study in California child dependency cases found that 78 percent of the mediated cases reached a full settlement agreement and that the agreements were "reached approximately one month sooner than those in a typical litigation process...."[32] In addition, results in both family custody and child protection cases indicate that the long-term success rate for family harmony and reunification was much higher for mediated than for litigated outcomes.[33] A Wisconsin study of family law mediation found that

> (1) the mediation group was by far more successful in reaching agreements than the control group consisting of persons who participated only in the adversarial process; (2) those who mediated were much more satisfied with the fairness of the final agreements; (3) the parties were less likely to have problems complying with the agreements; (4) relations between ex-spouses with mediated custody/visitation agreements were improved;

---

[27] James R. Coben, Gollem, *Meet Smeagol: A Schizophrenic Rumination on Mediator Values Beyond Self-Determination and Neutrality*, 5 CARDOZO J. CONFLICT RESOL. 65, 68 (2004).
[28] Kelley Brow Olson, *supra* note 12, at 485.
[29] *In re Paternity of Stephanie R. N. v. Wendy L. D.*, 541 N.W. 2d 838; 1995 WL 56300, 56318 (Wisc. 1995; unpublished opinion). For instance, *California Family Code § 3161* has as one of its central goals in mediation to "reduce acrimony" among the parties.
[30] Kelley Browe Olson, *supra* note 12, at 486.   [31] *Id.* at 488–489.
[32] Pamela A. Airey, Comment, *It's a Natural Fit: Expanding Mediation to Alleviate Congestion in the Troubled Juvenile Court System*, 16 J. AM. ACAD. MATR. LAW. 275, 288–289 (1999).
[33] *Id.* at 288–289.

(5) a significantly greater number of mediation couples arrived at joint custody arrangements; and (6) mediation saved time and money.[34]

A New York study of dependency courts found a direct correlation between the empowerment of parents through mediation and the long-term success of mediated settlements: "[By] allowing the parties to take control of their lives [through mediation], compliance with the agreement was higher when all parties concerned participated in the decision making."[35]

If mediation in child custody and dependency cases is cheaper, results in more individualized settlements that are more likely to succeed, reduces trauma to and speeds permanency for children, and promotes family harmony, why would anyone reject the opportunity to engage in alternative dispute resolution in these cases?[36] However, as one scholar has demonstrated, "[t]he very elements that make mediation so appealing compared to the adversarial model also create potential dangers and raise substantial professional, ethical, and legal issues."[37]

Commentators have noted a number of significant problems associated with mandatory mediation of child custody and dependency proceedings. Both the *Model Code of Mediation* and the *Model Family Standards* suggest that as "a central tenet" mediation must be voluntary.[38] Because alternative dispute resolution begins with the premise of providing willing adversaries an opportunity to gain control over formal processes and to experience empowerment, many have acknowledged the inherent disconnect with required mediation: "Mandatory mediations pose ... [a] danger for the weaker spouse precisely because she feels intimidated not only by her husband and the mediator, who is promoting the process, but she is here literally trapped by the requirement that she participate in a process without adversarial safeguards."[39]

Mandatory mediation is more dangerous for two groups of parties – marginalized individuals and victims of domestic violence. Several critics

---

[34] *In re Paternity of Stephanie R.N.*, *supra* note 29, at 18. In other forms of alternative dispute resolution, such as family group conferencing, such procedures "help rebuild family relationships, allow children a sense of community acceptance, and instill feelings of pride and self-importance...." Matthew Kogan, *The Problems and Benefits of Adopting Family Group Conferencing for PINS (CHINS) Children*, 39 FAM. CT. REV. 207, 208 (2002).

[35] Pamela L. Airey, *supra* note 32, at 281.

[36] Mediation "helps families and courts by lowering the amount of time that children spend in foster care and the amount of costs for courts and agencies." Kelly Browe Olson, *supra* note 12, at 480.

[37] Jay Folberg & Alison Taylor, MEDIATION: A COMPREHENSIVE GUIDE TO RESOLVING CONFLICTS WITHOUT LITIGATION 244 (1984).

[38] Nancy Ver Steegh, *supra* note 4, at 190–191.

[39] Marsha B. Freeman, *Divorce Mediation: Sweeping Conflicts under the Rug, Time to Clean House*, 78 U. DET. MERCY L. REV. 67, 87 (2000).

have argued that women and minorities suffer in alternative dispute resolution in which court and legislative due process protections are often absent. As early as 1985 Richard Delgado warned about the dangers of prejudice inherent in confidential informal dispute processes "with resulting adverse impact on minority participants."[40] "In 1991, Trina Grillo wrote eloquently about the risks, particularly for women in divorce mediation, posed by mediators' intentional de-emphasis on principles, blame, and rights and their active discouragement of anger and discussion of past fault."[41] Because mediators attempt to separate parties' animosity from problem solving and long-term relationships, "the mediator is nevertheless invalidating notions of blame and denigrating the weaker spouse's attempts to assert her rights, both of which would actually be more fairly represented in a adversarial setting."[42]

Others have asserted that mediator "neutrality" is a myth because of both internal and external pressures upon the mediator. First, because the alternative dispute resolution system, unlike a court trial, is private, there is little accountability regarding the mediator's performance. Unconscious mediator bias is thus not ameliorated through public exposure and normative evaluation. "In general, people have great difficulty divorcing themselves from their idiosyncratic role sufficiently to take an objective view of disputes in which they are involved...and people generally seek evidence that would confirm initial hypotheses, to a greater extent than they seek 'disconfirming' evidence."[43] In addition, studies have demonstrated that mediators are often fooled by slick ingratiating parties. For instance, a

> California study of mandatory court mediation found that documented pathological liars were able to fool virtually everyone, including the mediator, into believing that they were both the reasonable party in the divorce and the better parent, while making the weaker spouse's fears seem hysterical or irrational. Some women will predictably act defensive from the beginning of the mediation, fearing exactly this result, thereby unwittingly reinforcing this negative view of themselves.[44]

In addition, external pressures of budget deficits and overloaded mediation dockets have led mediators to abandon neutrality in order to achieve more rapid settlement. "A Los Angeles custody mediation program... suggests that caseload pressures will cause the mediator to cut the sessions short if that mediator has authority to issue an influential recommendation to the trier of fact. Shortened mediations, in turn, will discourage the thorough

---

[40] James R. Coben, *supra* note 27, at 65, 72.   [41] *Id.*
[42] Marsha B. Freeman, *supra* note 39, at 86.
[43] Richard Birke & Craig R. Fox, *supra* note 5, at 1, 14, 26.
[44] Marsha B. Freeman, *supra* note 39, at 87.

development of information and the negotiation that will facilitate the settlement of future family disputes."[45] And research demonstrates that the longer the mediation sessions last, the more likely a settlement will be reached.[46] The Society for Professionals in Dispute Resolution warned that "'[c]oercion to settle in the form of reports to the trier of fact and of financial disincentives to trial should not be used in connection with mandatory mediation.'"[47] However, some family court systems permit or require the mediator to make a recommendation to the court regarding child custody if the parties do not settle the dispute in mandatory mediation.[48] In addition, as attorneys have become more involved in mandatory mediations, "the process has become less focused on empowering citizens and more focused on forcing these citizens to confront and become reconciled to the legal, bargaining and transactional norms of the courthouse" rather than developing rules and norms by themselves.[49] And others have argued that forcing parties to contribute to the cost of mandatory mediation is antithetical to the historical impetus of providing parties a voluntary opportunity to participate in alternative dispute resolution. For instance, the court in *Hogoboom v. Superior Court* held that a local court rule in child custody cases requiring a payment of $110 per party for participation in court-annexed mediation was illegal.[50] Because of more aggressive mediators and a restriction on parties' ability to help shape mandatory mediation processes, the percentage of dissatisfied mediation consumers is growing.[51]

Many jurisdictions exclude cases involving domestic violence from participation in mandatory child custody and/or dependency cases.[52] Because

---

[45] Sarah R. Cole, Nancy H. Rogers, & Craig A. McEwen, MEDIATION:LAW, POLICY, PRACTICE 7-28 to 7-29 (2001).

[46] Kelley Browe Olson, *supra* note 12, at 488–489.

[47] Cole et al. at 7–30.

[48] *Id.* at 7–21; *see, e.g., California Civil Code* § 3183.

[49] Nancy A. Welch, *The Place of Court-Connected Mediation in a Democratic Justice System*, 38 WM. & MARY L. REV. 5, 137–138 (2004).

[50] *Hogoboom v. Superior Court*, 59 Cal. Rptr. 2d 254, 267 (California 1997).

[51] Nancy Ver Steegh, *supra* note 4, at 189; Peter H. Thompson, *Enforcing Rights Generated in Court-Connected Mediation – The Tension Between the Aspirations of a Private Facilitative Process and the Reality of Public Adversarial Justice*, 19 OHIO ST. J. DISP. RESOL. 509, 512 (2004).

[52] Although most courts protect domestic violence victims from being revictimized during the custody trial [similar to protection of rape victims under rape shield laws], the court in *Christina L. v. Harry J. L., Jr.*, 1995 WL 788196, at 23 (Delaware Family Court 1995; unpublished) held that a father can raise the mother's domestic violence victimization to demonstrate that she might not be able to protect her children should they be threatened: "Just as there are issues to be considered in the assessment of the abuser's fitness for custody, so are there questions to be asked of the spouse abuse victim... [s]pecifically, what is the likelihood of her entering into another abusive relationship and therefore exposing

approximately 30 percent of women will be assaulted by a partner at some time in their lives, and because domestic violence of some degree occurs in nearly 25 percent of homes in the United States, a high percentage of child custody and dependency cases are potentially unavailable for mandatory mediation.[53] The Minnesota statute is a common form of exclusion: "If the court determines that there is probable cause that one of the parties, or a child of a party, has been physically or sexually abused by the other party, the court shall not require or refer the parties to mediation or any other process that requires parties to meet and confer without counsel, if any, present."[54] Domestic violence cases are excluded from mediation for a number of reasons:

> Critics... argue that victims of domestic violence should not have to negotiate for their physical safety. Moreover, forcing victims to negotiate with their abusers communicates the message that domestic violence is not a crime. Perhaps the most serious criticism of mediation of domestic violence comes from empirical studies that have revealed that battered women are even more likely to be abused after separation if they went through mediation rather than the traditional adversarial process.[55]

A 1995 study indicated that women of domestic violence perceive themselves as having less autonomy and power than nonabused women.[56] Even so, some proponents of mediation in domestic violence cases argue that mediation "actually empowers parties because it involves them both in the resolution process" and provides "an opportunity to end the cycle of violence."[57] Others argue that domestic violence victims should be neither precluded from nor required to engage in mediation, but rather should have the choice regarding participation, which in itself, provides control and empowerment.[58] And some jurisdictions, like California, provide victims of domestic violence with court-paid counselors to accompany them in mandatory mediation of child custody disputes and also provide for separate mediation sessions, if necessary, so that the victim does not have to face the alleged batterer.[59]

---

her children to violence; to what degree has her emotional stability been compromised by the abuse, and, how does she relate to her children and what is her rationale for seeking custody?"

[53] Nancy Ver Steegh, *supra* note 4, at 148.
[54] Minnesota Statute § 518.619 (2003).
[55] Dennis P. Saccuzzo, *supra* note 3, at 425, 435.
[56] Nancy Ver Steegh, *supra* note 4, at 185.
[57] Dennis P. Saccuzzo, *supra* note 3, at 434.
[58] Nancy Ver Steegh, *supra* note 4, at 147.
[59] Sarah R. Cole, *supra* note 45, at 7–11; California Family Code § 3181.

III. COMING FULL CIRCLE: THE EVOLUTION OF CHILD CUSTODY MEDIATION

Initially, alternative dispute resolution was a reaction to the formalized court structures that prohibited parties from designing procedures that were individualized to their specific needs and would promote long-term relationships while empowering them in learning how to resolve future domestic disputes. However, once mandatory mediation became the accepted norm in child custody and dependency proceedings, one set of critics declared that alternative dispute resolution had become no more than an expedited adjunct to formal litigation:

> Once upon a time, people sought to avoid the courts and turned to an alternative to litigation. Third parties selected by the disputants would bring the principals together and urge them to reconcile. The disputants mutually shaped the process and agreed to the ultimate outcome.... Before long, the courts got involved and began using the process to divert cases it couldn't or didn't want to handle.... Observers began to question the fairness of its use. Some lawyers found the alternative threatening because it seemed antithetical to the accepted role of the adversarial system, and others began to view this alternative as an opportunity to gain tactical advantages in litigation. Courts and policy makers began exercising more oversight and control over the process. Eventually, disputants found that the alternative was growing more and more similar to, if not sometimes indistinguishable from, the adjudication for which it was meant to substitute.... Disputants had lost control over the process....[60]

Professor Reuben has identified the following as democratic values inherent in public trials: (1) accountability, (2) transparency of process, (3) rationality, (4) due process, and (5) citizen participation.[61] He alleges that mandatory alternative dispute resolution is undemocratic because it lacks those inherent properties and violates one of the historical aspects of American democracy regarding the "importance to U.S. citizens of having their day in court as a fundamental tenet of the U.S. justice system...."[62] However, other experts respond that those who say that settlements are undemocratic are wrong because "it privileges the group's (or society's) need for public discourse over the needs (dare I say rights) of individuals to seek the most comprehensive and Pareto optimal solution possible to their dispute, by sharing

---

[60] Douglas Yarn, *The Death of ADR: A Cautionary Tale of Isomorphism through Institutionalization*, 108 PENN. ST. L. REV. 929, 929–930 (2004).
[61] Richard C. Reuben, *supra* note 25, at 279, 285.
[62] *Id.* at 310. *See also* Nancy A. Welsh, *supra* note 49, at 5, 137–138, who suggests that "mediation is not infusing the courts with a new manifestation of democracy."

information that is beyond or different from what a court might order them to reveal."[63]

Even many of the leaders of the alternative dispute resolution revolution are beginning to question the advisability of mandatory court-annexed settlement mechanisms. "The Romantic days of alternative dispute resolution appear to be over. To the extent that proponents of ADR, like myself, were attracted to it because of its promise of flexibility, adaptability, and creativity, we now see the need for ethics, standards of practice and rules as potentially limiting and containing the promise of alternatives to rigid adversarial modes of dispute resolution."[64]

IV. THE LEGITIMACY OF INFORMAL SETTLEMENTS AND THE LIMITS OF MEDIATORS' AND ARBITRATORS' JURISDICTION IN CHILD CUSTODY AND DEPENDENCY PROCEEDINGS

It is one thing to determine that alternative dispute resolution is beneficial to parents and/or children, but it is another to determine that the legislature can strip courts of their inherent power to determine the best interest of children through their equitable powers. In England, with the abolition of the Court of Wards, which was concerned primarily with children's property interests, the Court of Chancery asserted authority over the best interest of children through the doctrine of *parens patriae*.[65] English courts' jurisdiction over child custody and visitation in dependency cases was clarified in 1839 with Parliament's passage of the Custody of Infants Act.

The story of court jurisdiction over child custody and dependency took a different path in the United States:

> In America the law respecting the protection of children was not as developed as in England. The colonists focused on two major aspects of English Common law, "the rules" of family government; and the traditions and child-care practices of the Elizabethan Poor Laws of 1601.... Soon, Calvinist theories of poverty as idleness and sin permeated definitions of the best interest of children and children were separated from parents for "neglecting

---

[63] Carrie Menkel-Meadow, *Whose Dispute Is It Anyway?: A Philosophical and Democratic Defense of Settlement (In Some Cases)*, in MEDIATION: THEORY, POLICY AND PRACTICE 39, 61 (Carrie Menkel-Meadow, ed., 2001).

[64] Carrie Menkel-Meadow, *Ethics in Alternative Dispute Resolution: New Issues, No Answers from the Adversary Conception of Lawyers' Responsibilities*, in MEDIATION: THEORY, POLICY AND PRACTICE 429, 430 (Carrie Menkel-Meadow, ed., 2001).

[65] See, T. Pluckett, A CONCISE HISTORY OF THE COMMON LAW 544 (1956); *Corcellis v. Corcellis* No. 1, 23 English Reports 1, Ch. 1673; *Shaftsbury v. Hannam*, 23 English Reports 177, Ch. 1677.

their formal education, not teaching a trade, or [who] were idle, dissolute, unchristian or 'uncapable'"[sic].⁶⁶

By the time of the child reform movement, which occurred between 1820 and 1860, states had started vesting determinations of children's best interests in the courts. And by 1899 Illinois established the first juvenile court in the United States, which supplanted dozens of child welfare organizations as the center of American child welfare law.⁶⁷

Based upon courts' historical jurisdiction over children's welfare, two questions arise in relation to alternative dispute resolution: (1) May a legislature divest courts of such jurisdiction; and (2) may a court delegate child custody decision making to third parties, such as mediators and arbitrators?

A. *Finality and Scope of Arbitrated and Mediated Custody and Dependency Settlement Agreements*

Many jurisdictions have held that binding arbitration in child custody matters is void because it violates public policy. Ohio, South Carolina, and North Carolina are among those states with court opinions prohibiting

> parents from entering into binding arbitration agreements to resolve child support disputes because they are void against public policy... [but] [o]ther jurisdictions [like Pennsylvania, New Jersey, Massachusetts, Maryland, and Texas] permit divorcing parties to submit to binding and non-binding arbitration to resolve child support, custody, and visitation disputes so long as such arbitration awards are subject to judicial review.⁶⁸

In *Kelm v. Kelm*⁶⁹ an Ohio court noted that even though the law "permits parties to voluntarily waive a number of important rights," arbitration of child custody issues violates public policy because binding arbitration would strip courts of their power and duty to determine children's best interests. However, the court held that as long as a court reviews the arbitration award, public

---

⁶⁶ McCarthy, Patton, & Carr, *supra* note 2, at 16–17, relying upon Thomas P. Mason, *Child Abuse and Neglect Part I: Historical Overview, Legal Matrix, and Social Perspectives*, 50 N.C. L. REV. 293 (1972); Douglas R. Rendleman, *Parens Patriae: From Chancery to the Juvenile Court*, 23 S.C. L. REV. 205 (1971).

⁶⁷ *See* Fox, *Juvenile Justice Reform: An Historical Perspective*, 22 STAN. L. REV. 1187 (1970); Thomas Mason, *supra* note 66, at 293; Corinne Schiff, *supra* note 2, at 403: P. A. PLATT, THE CHILD SAVERS 9 (1969).

⁶⁸ *Cohoon v. Cohoon*, 770 N. E. 2d 885 (Indiana Court of Appeal 2002; superceded by *Cohoon v. Cohoon*, 784 N. E. 2d 904, 905 (Indiana Supreme Court 2003) [holding that because of irregularities on appeal "[w]e find it unnecessary in this case to make a judgment on the validity of binding arbitration in domestic relations matters."].

⁶⁹ *Kelm v. Kelm*, 749 N.E. 2d 299, 225–226 (Ohio 2001).

policy is satisfied. Surprisingly, the *Kelm* court held that judges' review is not *de novo* because that would result in expensive and time-consuming procedures that are not "advantageous to the best interests of children" because custody decisions will be postponed.[70]

A majority of states permit wide discretion to those engaged in alternative dispute resolution to fashion child custody and visitation awards as long as courts must or have discretion to review those settlements. For instance, courts in Florida,[71] Indiana,[72] Alaska,[73] California,[74] Michigan,[75] and Missouri[76] have all held that stipulations or settlement agreements between the parties in child abuse and domestic custody cases cannot divest the court of its jurisdiction to review and approve the settlement, nor do the mediator's findings bind the court regarding fact-finding. In addition, many other jurisdictions have gone further in holding that the court may not delegate its ultimate authority of determining children's best interests to any third party, such as an arbitrator, mediator, or special family court master. For instance, in a California case, *In re Marriage of Timothy E. Slayton*,[77] the California court of appeal held that although the trial court may consider the mediator's report and the mediator's interview with the child, the court may not delegate all fact-finding and decision making to the mediator. In a Connecticut case the parents stipulated that future child custody disputes would be subject to the binding decision of an attorney; however, the court held that such a condition could not be approved by the court because it would be an illegal delegation of judicial authority.[78] As a Florida court noted, "[W]hile a trial court can order the parties to mediate the issues of visitation, it cannot delegate its judicial authority to ultimately resolve the issue and settle disputes between the parties."[79] Pennsylvania has taken a medial position, holding that a court can delegate decision making on temporary, but not on permanent custody determinations.[80] Although these jurisdictions favor alternative dispute resolution, they have determined that the court's

---

[70] *Id.* at 225–226.
[71] *Wayno v. Wayno*, 756 So. 2d 1024, 1025 (Florida 2000).
[72] *Marchal v. Craig*, 681 N. E. 2d 1160, 1162 (Indiana 1997).
[73] *Lone Wolf v. Lone Wolf*, 741 P. 2d 1187, 1190 (Alaska 1987).
[74] *In re Christopher S.*, 2002 WL 31033062 (California, September 12, 2002; unpublished).
[75] *Harvey v. Harvey*, 680 N. W. 2d 835 (Michigan Supreme Court 2004).
[76] *Blackburn v. Mackey*, 131 S. W. 3d 392 (Missouri 2004).
[77] *In re Marriage of Timothy E. Slayton*, 103 Cal. Rptr. 2d 545, 549–550 (2001).
[78] *Nashid v. Andrawis*, 847 A. 2d 1908, 1101–1102 (Connecticut 2004).
[79] *Martin v. Martin*, 734 So. 2d 1133, 1136 (1999). *See also In the Marriage of Hanks*, 10 P. 3d 42, 47 (Kansas 2000), in which the court held that in custody disputes judges can appoint "case managers" who are not mediators to assist the court; however, such case managers have "no independent" power to act or bind the parties.
[80] *Littman v. Van Hoek*, 789 A. 2d 280, 281–282 (Pennsylvania 2001).

obligation to determine that the agreement is in the children's best interest trumps budget reduction.[81]

Pennsylvania has taken a very different approach, holding that arbitration awards in custody disputes are not violative of public policy, but that the arbitration award only binds parties who signed the agreement. In addition, any custody arbitration award is "subject to the supervisory power of the court in its *parents patriae* capacity in a proceeding to determine the best interests of the child."[82] Further, the court held that an arbitration agreement between parents does not have *res judicata* effect upon the child unless the child was a party to the proceeding and the terms do not "adversely affect the substantial interest of the child."[83]

Other jurisdictions permit binding arbitration in divorces except for issues involving child custody and visitation.[84] Minnesota has one of the most unusual alternative dispute resolution systems in child custody cases. First, the parties must engage in mandatory mediation; however, if those sessions fail to resolve the disputes, the parties must then engage in binding arbitration. In *In re Coughlan*[85] the court refused to determine what the standard of court review might be on a binding arbitration custody matter. In contrast, in *Kniskern v. Kniskern*[86] a Colorado court determined that, when an arbitration involves child custody, the court "retains jurisdiction to decide all issues relating to the children *de novo* upon the request of either party." However, in *Kniskern*, because the alternative dispute resolution had been conducted by a "parenting coordinator" rather than a formal arbitrator, the court held that there was no right to *de novo* court review.

In a minority of jurisdictions, binding arbitration in custody cases is consistent with public policy as long as the settlement agreement meets statutory or contractual requirements. An Alaska opinion held that "the superior court correctly applied a contractual analysis in interpreting the custody agreement between ... [the parents]; settlement agreements should be interpreted as contracts provided they meet minimal contractual requirements."[87] In addition, most jurisdictions provide that the custody settlement agreement may not exceed the subject matter limitations of the court hearing.[88] In *Byers v.*

---

[81] *L. L. H. v. S. C. H.*, 2002 WL 1943659, at 3 (Alaska 2002; unpublished).

[82] *Miller v. Miller*, 620 A. 2d 1161, 1165 (Pennsylvania 1993).

[83] *Id.* at 1165, fn. 4. *See also Merrill Lynch, Fenner & Smith, Inc. v. Benjamin*, 766 N.Y.S. 2d 1 (2003).

[84] *Cayan v. Cayan*, 38 S. W. 3d 161 (2000).

[85] *In re Coughlan*, 2003 WL 22136814 (Minnesota App. 2003).

[86] *Kniskern v. Kniskern*, 80 P. 3d 939, 941 (Colorado 2003).

[87] *Gaston v. Gaston*, 954 P. 2d 572, 574 (Alaska 1998).

[88] For instance, in *Bauer v. Bauer*, 28 S. W. 3d 877, 885–887 (Missouri 2000), the court held that child custody mediation settlement agreements were limited to custody and visitation

Byers,[89] the Michigan court held that the "parties to a divorce may agree to submit their disputed issues to binding mediation or arbitration... including child custody... [and] absent a showing of fraud, duress or an extension of the mediator's powers, a court is unable to review a mediator's decision." In effect, the court ceded its historic right to review such decisions. The Michigan approach to binding agreements is based upon contract theory. As long as the conditions and terms of the custody settlement are contractually valid, the agreement is not subject to court attack. Texas takes a similar contractual approach to divorce and custody settlement agreements: "Because a mediated settlement agreement is enforceable under contract law, the same procedures used to enforce and enter judgment on other contracts should apply to mediated settlement agreements" and even if one party repudiates the contract, the court can enforce the settlement agreement.[90]

However, the contractual approach raises two critical problems in child custody cases. First, how does a parent demonstrate fraud or duress if the settlement takes place in a confidential alternative dispute resolution setting? Because arbitrators and mediators are often declared incompetent to testify and because few systems provide confidentiality exceptions, it is almost impossible to prove that the settlement agreement was contractually void or voidable. Second, because much of the duress that takes place during confidential alternative dispute resolution is caused by the arbitrator or mediator in an effort to seek a quick resolution, contract principles might not be available to set aside the settlement agreement. In addition, proving contractual duress is difficult, and the source of the duress can be either another party, a mediator, or one of the party's attorneys.[91]

For instance, in *Vogt v. Vogt*,[92] a Minnesota child custody dispute in which there was an allegation of domestic violence and in which the father, but not the mother, was represented by counsel, the court held that a visitation settlement agreement was "forced" upon the mother. Although the court

---

issues and could not decide other marital issues, such as mortgage or medical payments after separation or divorce. *See also* California Family Code § 3178(a): "Where mediation is required to settle a contested issue of custody or visitation, the agreement shall be limited to the resolution of issues relating to parenting plans, custody, visitation, or a combination of these issues."

[89] *Byers v. Byers*, 1996 WL 33348581 (Michigan 1996; unpublished).

[90] *Davis v. Wickham*, 917 S. W. 2d 414, 416 (Texas 1996).

[91] For instance, in *In re Christopher S.*, 2002 WL 31033062 (California, September 12, 2002; unpublished), the court held that the mother in a child dependency case failed to sufficiently "identify any legal duty to reverse a decision already made once a parent suggests the underlying agreement may be suspect." The court refused to set aside the mediated settlement because the mother merely presented her "unsworn and untested surprise statement" about the coercion.

[92] *Vogt v. Vogt*, 455 N. W. 2d 471, 474–475 (Minnesota 1990).

noted that the mere fact that one party is *pro per* is not sufficient to demonstrate duress or coercion, in that case the mediator's actions exceeded the bounds of neutrality and, in effect, strong-armed an agreement from the mother. "The traditional duress defense does not account for the role of the mediator. If the alleged wrongful threat comes from a third-party like a mediator, traditional contract law provides that the agreement is not voidable if the other party to the transaction acted in good faith, had no reason to know of the coercive tactics, and gave value to, or relied materially on, the transaction."[93]

And Peter N. Thompson has described two different ways in which a party's counsel may attempt to convince or cajole a client to settle:

> The context of a mediation creates an atmosphere where parties may be vulnerable to coercive pressures, particularly when the party's attorney wants the client to settle. Attorneys who cannot convince their clients to accept a settlement that they believe is reasonable frequently seek out a mediator to serve as a "reality check" on the client. The attorney and mediator then essentially gang up on the client to "persuade" or "influence" the client to voluntarily accept the settlement.[94]

In Texas custody settlement agreements are not only binding upon the parties but they also preclude court review if all statutory requirements are met. In *In the Interest of J.A.W.-N.*,[95] a Texas court held that because the custody settlement, which included a visitation schedule, met statutory requirements, the trial court was required "to enter judgment." And in *Hirsch v. Hirsch*[96] a New York court held that even though arbitration in domestic disputes did not violate public policy, an agreement requiring the "wife to withdraw a pending criminal complaint against the husband" violated public policy because it "deprives a party of a constitutional right to seek redress or protection in a civil or criminal matter...." Finally, jurisdictions differ on which persons must sign custody/visitation settlements. For instance, in California even though custody mediation agreements must be signed by all the parties, mediation agreements in child dependency cases need be

---

[93] Peter N. Thompson, *Enforcing Rights Generated in Court-Connected Mediation – The Tension Between the Aspirations of a Private Facilitative Process and the Reality of Public Adversarial Justice*, 19 OHIO ST. J. DISP. RESOL. 509, 533 (2004).

[94] *Id.* at 533.

[95] *In the Interest of J.A.W.-N.*, 94 S. W. 3d 119, 121 (Texas 2002).

[96] *Hirsch v. Hirsch*, 774 N.Y.S. 2d 48, 49–50 (New York 2004). *See also Merrill Lynch, Pierce, Fenner & Smith, Inc. v. Benjamin*, 766 N.Y.S. 2d 1, 44 (2003) ["[I]ssues of attorney disqualification involve interpretation and application of the Code of Professional Responsibility ... and cannot be left to the determination of arbitrators selected by the parties...."

signed by the parents, not the children who are also parties in those legal proceedings.[97]

In those jurisdictions that permit judges to merely incorporate custody settlement agreements into the court's order, there is the risk that the settlement will have less legal effect than if the same terms had been reached through an original court hearing. In *In the Matter of D. Keith Jennings*,[98] a Kansas court held that a "mediated custody agreement incorporated into a decree of divorce or other court order does not have the same effect as a court order that is issued after a hearing where evidence is presented and the trial court makes specific findings of fact." The Kansas court held that mediated settlement terms, unlike adjudicated custody issues, do not require the moving party to demonstrate "a material change of circumstances." Therefore, at least under Kansas law, mediated child custody agreements are modified more easily than those reached through court judgments. Depending upon which party is represented, this procedural distinction could be dispositive in determining which mechanism the client should use in a particular case.

Unlike the protean, flexible genesis of custody and dependency alternative dispute resolution in which parties had latitude over the procedures and content of settlement proceedings, the previous discussion demonstrates that those systems have become procedurally narrowed and courts' and parties' discretion and freedom to settle these cases have been pared back significantly.

B. *The Duty of Candor: Good Faith, Puffing, and Lies*

All jurisdictions prescribe an attorney's duty of candor. Most rules apply in court-litigated cases and are based, in part, on an attorney's role as an officer of the court.[99] For instance, California requires attorneys to represent clients "consistent with the truth, and never to seek to mislead the judge or any judicial officer by an artifice or false statement of fact or law."[100] The American Bar Association defines "candor" as not knowingly making "a false statement of material fact or law to a tribunal ... [or] failure to disclose

---

[97] *See Los Angeles County Superior Court Rule 17.22(b)(1)*: "If a settlement is reached ... counsel will prepare a written case plan document, signed by the parties, for submission to the judicial officer for review and approval." And *California Welfare and Dependency Code* § 317.6 provides that "[e]ach minor who is the subject of a dependency proceeding is a party to that proceedings."

[98] *In the Matter of D. Keith Jennings*, 50 P. 3d 506, 506–508 (Kansas 2002).

[99] *See Preamble: A Lawyer's Responsibilities, Rule 1* (American Bar Association Model Rules) stating that a lawyer is "an officer of the legal system...."

[100] California Business and Professions Code § 6068(d).

a material fact to a tribunal when disclosure is necessary to avoid assisting a criminal or fraudulent act by the client."[101] Therefore, it is clear that the duty of candor applies no matter the procedural status of the case heard by a legal tribunal. However, "nowhere do they [the ABA rules] define 'tribunal.'"[102] And what if the official hearing a custody or dependency settlement is not a judge, but rather someone appointed to hear the alternative dispute resolution? In some jurisdictions, like Florida, the mediator is an equivalent official judicial officer: "[the mediator] is, for all intent[s] and purposes, an agent of the court carrying out an official court-ordered function."[103] Because such mediators are court agents, the duty of candor toward judges is arguably applicable. However, what if the judge in a child custody or dependency case refers the parties to some form of family reconciliation dispute resolution? For instance, in Kansas the court can refer parties to a "case manager" who is "not a mediator" and who, unlike the mediator, has the discretion "to take independent action and make recommendations to the court. . . . " One could argue that without some general duty of candor, the rules applicable before the tribunal are not in force.

But most jurisdictions also have promulgated rules of candor applicable to any person with whom an attorney has contact while representing the client. For instance, *American Bar Association Rule 4.1*, "Truthfulness in Statements to Others" provides that an attorney "[i]n the course of representing a client . . . shall not knowingly: (a) make a false statement of material fact or law to a third person; or (b) fail to disclose a material fact to a third person when disclosure is necessary to avoid assisting a criminal or fraudulent act by a client, unless disclosure is prohibited by Rule 1.6 [duty of confidentiality]." However, *Rule 4.1, Comment 2* indicates that this duty of candor refers only to "statements of fact" and that often in negotiation "certain types of statements ordinarily are not taken as statements of material fact."[104] *Rule 4.1* delineates several examples in alternative dispute resolution in which statements do not comprise "material facts," such as "puffing"[105] and in "[e]stimates of price

---

[101] American Bar Association Model Rule 3.3 (a)(1) and (2).

[102] John W. Cooley, *Defining the Ethical Limits of Acceptable Deception in Mediation*, 4 PEPP. DISP. RESOL. L. J. 263, 271.

[103] *Vitakis-Valcine*, 793 So. 2d 1094, 1099 (Florida 2001).

[104] "An attorney cannot encourage or suggest to a client that he or she sign disclosure declarations that the attorney knows are not accurate, nor can the attorney knowingly allow a client to sign a waiver indicating that all information has been disclosed, knowing that it has not. An attorney who attempts to benefit his client through the use of perjured testimony may be subject to criminal prosecution, as well as severe disciplinary action." Stephen James Wagner, *The Ethics of Family Law Disclosure: Have You Suborned Perjury Lately?*, 8 CAL. FAM. L. MONTHLY 197, 198 (August 2004).

[105] The American Bar Association duties of candor "contemplate activities such as puffing, which in the broadest sense are untruthful." James J. White, *Machiavelli and the Bar: Ethical*

or value."[106] Thus, the scope of an attorney's duty of candor is most ambiguous when the attorney is involved in a noncourt tribunal with arbitrators, mediators, and parties in an alternative dispute resolution process.

Many experts have argued that, short of committing fraud, there is no duty of candor in nontribunal proceedings.[107] In fact, many have argued that deception is the essence of successful mediation and negotiation:

> [E]ach party in a mediation is an actual or potential victim of constant deception regarding confidential information – granted, agreed deception – but nonetheless deception. This is the central paradox of the caucused mediation process. The parties, and indeed even the mediator, agree to be deceived as a condition of participating in it in order to find a solution that parties will find "valid" for their purposes.... These competitive bargaining strategies and tactics are layered and interlaced with the mediator's own strategies and tactics to get the best resolution possible for the parties – or at least a resolution that they can accept.... [This]creates an environment rich in gamesmanship and intrigue, naturally conducive to the use of deceptive behaviors by the parties and their counsel, and yes, even the mediators.[108]

Neither the American Bar Association[109] nor the majority of states require candor and/or good faith in mediation. For instance, the American Bar Association *Standards of Practice for Lawyers Represeinting Child Welfare Agencies* require the agency's lawyer to "ensure accurate testimony and correct any misstatements **in the courtroom**," but no such duty of candor is mandated in the *Standards*' definition of the attorney's role in alternative dispute resolution.[110] However, some states have begun to promulgate such requirements. For instance, Indiana, Ohio, and Oklahoma require good faith in mediation, "stating that 'parties and their representatives are required to mediate in good

---

Limitations on Lying in Negotiation, in WHAT'S FAIR: ETHICS IN NEGOTIATION 93 (Carrie Menkel-Meadow & Michael Wheeler, eds., 2001).

[106] American Bar Association section 2.3 Guidelines "which addresses honesty and fair-dealing, allows an attorney to escape the adversarial ethic in settlement negotiations." Brian C. Haussmann, *supra* note 22, at 1218, 1237.

[107] "[W]ith respect of negotiation, the present ethical norms for lawyers do little more than proscribe fraud in negotiation – or, at most, they proscribe only very serious, harmful misrepresentations of material fact made through a lawyer's false verbal or written statement, affirmation, or silence." John W. Cooley, *supra* note 102, at 269–270.

[108] *Id.* at 265.

[109] Under the ABA rules of professional responsibility, "mediators – lawyers and nonlawyers – currently have no specific formal guidance regarding how truthful they must be in conducting mediation." *Id.* at 272.

[110] *Standards of Practice for Lawyers Representing Child Welfare Agencies, Standard C-1(3)and (10)* (American Bar Association, August 2004).

faith', but are not compelled to reach an agreement."[111] Critics of the adversarial mode of litigation have argued that the duty of candor should apply to an even greater extent in alternative dispute resolution where bilateral zealous advocacy is less necessary:

> [O]ne could make a persuasive argument that a heightened standard of truthfulness by advocates in mediation should apply because of the "deception synergy" syndrome resulting from a third-party neutral's involvement. We know from practical experience that the accuracy of communications deteriorates on successive transmissions between and among individuals ... [especially because] mediators tend to embellish information, translate it, and sometimes distort it to meet the momentary needs of their efforts to achieve a settlement.[112]

However, the Uniform Mediation Act[113] and many critics of expanding candor and good faith in alternative dispute resolution have identified a number of reasons why the current rules are a better policy. First, they argue, no jurisdiction has been able to satisfactorily define "good faith" to both provide parties and attorneys notice and to give review courts guidance in implementation. So far, most good faith definitions are too subjective; rely upon a person's mental state, which is difficult to prove; fail "to provide objective grounds for sanctions, and do not give the participants in mandatory-mediation reliable guidelines as to what is appropriate behavior and what is not."[114] In addition, some argue that a formal good faith requirement will make mandatory mediation more formal, reduce parties' willingness to participate because sanctions based upon vague standards are a possibility, reduce the mediator's neutrality because he or she will have to judge the quality of parties' participation, and will weaken confidentiality rules because the facts and circumstances surrounding the mediation must be disclosed to support a court's finding of bad faith without violating due process.[115] "[C]onfidentiality and secrecy, resulting in overlapping privilege rules, makes it difficult for parties to litigate claims of unfairness in the

---

[111] Robert A. Creo, *supra* note 16, at 1017, 1063. *See also* Montgomery Co., Ohio, C.P.R. 2.39 (Anderson 2002); Oklahoma Stat. tit. 12, §1824(3); Indiana Code Ann. Tit. 34, R. 8.5.

[112] John W. Cooley, *supra* note 102, at 270. "The absence of a positive duty to be truthful or candid or to tell an opposing lawyer about a case or fact helpful to that lawyer's matter is based on the principle that each client is entitled only to one zealous representative – his or her own lawyer." Carrie Menkel-Meadows, *Ethics, Morality and Professional Responsibility in Negotiation*, in MEDIATION: A COMPREHENSIVE GUIDE TO RESOLVING CONFLICTS WITHOUT LITIGATION 119, 129 (Jay Folberg & Alison Taylor, eds., 1984).

[113] Sarah R. Cole, Nancy Rogers, et al., *supra* note 6, at 7–7 (2003 Cumulative Supplement).

[114] Dr. Iur Ulrich Boettger, *Efficiency Versus Party Empowerment – Against a Good Faith Requirement in Mandatory Mediation*, 23 REV. LITIG. 1, 20 (2004).

[115] *Id.* at 24–25, 34–35.

mediation process."[116] Many jurisdictions prohibit the introduction of confidential mediation data to demonstrate bad faith, thus rendering all sanctions impossible, except possibly for failure to appear at the mediation.[117]

Certain circumstances enhance the potential for deception and bad faith: (1) an "asymmetry" of information access among parties; (2) contexts in which verification is difficult; (3) the difficulty of proving the intention to deceive; (4) inadequate or unequal assets by the parties to prevent deception or overreaching; (5) "ex post facto" remedies are untimely or too expensive; (6) information about the reputation of the parties or mediator is unavailable; and (7) one party has little to lose and much to gain through deception.[118] In addition, a number of techniques that advocates have termed "deceptive" or "bad faith" alternative dispute resolution tactics are endemic to mediation: (1) last-minute delays, (2) sending representatives without the authority to settle the case, (3) repudiating agreed-upon settlement conditions, (4) interjecting new demands, (5) unwillingness to provide any information even if not confidential, and (6) refusal to sign the settlement agreement.[119] It is important that attorneys representing parties in child custody and dependency proceedings recognize these tactics, even if no action for bad faith is available, so that the tactics can be openly discussed with the mediator at the earliest possible moment. In those jurisdictions that permit the mediator to issue recommendations to the court, discussing bad faith during the mediation may help impeach the credibility of an opponent and may color the mediator's statement of facts even if the mediator has no authority to lodge a complaint based upon the bad faith.

V. THE SCOPE OF ALTERNATIVE DISPUTE RESOLUTION CONFIDENTIALITY

The most complex substantive and strategic topic in alternative dispute resolution is the scope of confidentiality inherent in those voluntary and/or required proceedings. "Presently, there are over 250 mediation confidentiality statutes. Of these statutes, about half contain confidentiality provisions

---

[116] Peter N. Thompson, *supra* note 93, at 514–515.

[117] Perhaps the most famous and stringent court to reject the use of confidential mediation information is the California Supreme Court, which stated that confidentiality is the lynchpin of mediation. *Foxgate Homeowners' Association, Inc. v. Bramalea California, Inc.*, 108 Cal. Rptr. 2d 642 (2001). Alaska has held that a party at least has a good faith obligation to attend a mediation even though the extent of participation is a matter of trial tactics and discretion. *Mackey v. Mackey*, 2001 WL 111267 (Alaska Civil Appeal 2001).

[118] J. Gregory Dees, *Promoting Honesty in Negotiation: An Exercise in Practical Ethics, in* WHAT'S FAIR: ETHICS IN NEGOTIATION 124 (Carrie Mendel-Meadow & Michael Wheeler, eds., 2001).

[119] Dr. Iur Boetger, *supra* note 113, at 18–20.

that are of general application, while the remaining statutes address specific subjects.... Due to the different approaches, lawyers and parties can encounter surprise and uncertainty if the dispute is governed by the law of a different state than where the mediation is conducted."[120] Because most courts and commentators agree that "[o]ne of the fundamental axioms of mediation is the importance of confidentiality," it is not surprising that differences among jurisdictions are reflected in the scope of confidentiality provided in alternative dispute resolution.[121] Congress, state legislators, and federal and state jurists have all concluded that confidentiality is central to providing an incentive for party participation and for ensuring mediator neutrality.[122] Indiana considers mediation confidentiality such an important public policy that not even the parties can agree to waive it.[123] However, jurisdictions disagree regarding the appropriate degree of confidentiality in relation to other important public policies, such as child abuse allegations and confrontation rights. In addition, attorneys must not confuse evidentiary rules, which prohibit the introduction of statements made during compromise negotiations, with privileges, "which usually provide protection against any disclosure rather than merely protection against admission into evidence at a court hearing. Thus, most mediation privileges govern use of the mediation information in all forums, not just those judicial hearings governed by the rules of evidence, as with evidentiary exclusions."[124]

Professor Creo has argued that mediation confidentiality should be controlled by rules analagous to *Federal Rules of Evidence, Rule 408*, which prohibits the use of settlement statements, rather than basing confidentiality rules on analogies to the attorney-client privilege, which is subject to waiver and exceptions.[125] But even the evidentiary exclusion of statements from compromise negotiations is not fully protected because "administrative and

---

[120] Mindy D. Rufenacht, *The Concern over Confidentiality in Mediation – An In-Depth Look at Protection Provided by the Proposed Uniform Mediation Act*, 2000 J. DISP. RESOL. 113, 114 (2000).

[121] Ellen E. Deason, *Enforcing Mediated Settlement Agreements: Contract Law Collides with Confidentiality*, 35 U. CAL. DAVIS L. REV. 33, 35 (2001).

[122] *Id.* at 35. "In the Alternative Dispute Resolution Act of 1998 [28 U.S.C. § 652(d)(1998)], Congress directed all district courts to adopt court-sponsored ADR programs and singled out confidentiality protection as a required element in the programs." *Id.* at 40.

[123] *Marchal v. Craig*, 681 N. E. 2d 1160, 1162 (Indiana 1997).

[124] Sarah R. Cole, *supra* note 6, at 9–10. *See, e.g.,* California Evidence Code § 1119 that "goes beyond an evidentiary privilege, like the attorney-client privilege, by barring communications made in mediation from being disclosed in discovery or trial proceedings." John A. Toker, CALIFORNIA ARBITRATION AND MEDIATION PRACTICE GUIDE: COURT-ORDERED ADR 457 (2003).

[125] Robert A. Creo, *supra* note 16, at 1033.

legislative officers are not required to follow the rules of evidence."[126] It is important to remember that the mediation may involve individuals who follow different ethical codes regarding disclosure of confidential information. Therefore, if mediation involves attorneys, mediators, social workers, and/or therapists, parties' attorneys must be aware of the limits and requirements of disclosure by each of those separate professional canons of ethics.

The question concerning the proper scope of mediation confidentiality must focus both on internal case uses and on uses of that data in other proceedings and contexts. Most jurisdictions provide that the mediator may not disclose any of the parties' statements made during the mediation except for admissions or threats of child abuse.[127] However, even the child abuse reporting exception is subject to variations among and within jurisdictions. For instance, in California each county determines the scope of mediation confidentiality disclosures. Some counties use the American Bar Association approach of permitting disclosure only if it is reasonably necessary to prevent death or serious bodily injury.[128] Other jurisdictions permit mandated reporters to report any mediation statements "that could form the basis of a new [child abuse] petition" or which give rise to a "[r]easonable suspicion of child abuse not previously reported."[129] In contrast, the Uniform Mediation Act suggests a much narrower reporting exception only for future crimes and only if "the actor utilizes the mediation itself to further the commission of a crime."[130]

The following cases illustrate the complexity of determining the scope of confidential privileges in alternative dispute resolution. In an Idaho case, *State v. Trejo*,[131] a husband and wife had a very acrimonious relationship while their divorce and custody proceedings were pending. After two verbal altercations at local bars, the mother and one of her friends went to the

---

[126] Sarah R. Cole, *supra* note 6, at 9–19.

[127] The CPR-Georgetown Commission on Ethics and Standards in ADR, Rule 4.5.2 provides, "A lawyer serving as a third-party neutral shall maintain the confidentiality of all information acquired in the course of serving in that role, unless the third-party neutral is required or permitted by law or agreement of all the parties to disclose or use any otherwise confidential information." 13 WORLD ARB. MEDIATION REP. 331, 334 (2002).

[128] For instance, California Rules of Professional Responsibility, Rule 3-100 (July 1, 2004) provides that "an attorney may, but is not required to, reveal confidential information relating to the representation of a client to the extent that the attorney reasonably believes the disclosure is necessary to prevent a criminal act that the attorney reasonably believes is likely to result in death of, or substantial bodily harm to, an individual."

[129] San Francisco, California, Superior Court Rule 12.47(D)(2); Kern County, California, Superior Court Rule 7.6.3.

[130] *Model Standards of Conduct For Mediators* (American Arbitration Association and American Bar Association, 2002); Uniform Mediation Act, section 2f; Mindy D. Rufenacht, *supra* note 119, at 125–126.

[131] *State v. Trejo*, 979 P. 2d 1230 (Idaho 1999).

father's house to take custody of her child because she believed the father was not properly caring for the baby. The mother's friend confronted the father, who then went into his house, obtained a "9mm semi-automatic pistol," and shot the mother's friend. The father was charged with aggravated battery, and in his criminal trial he sought to introduce testimony given by the mediator in his divorce case. The father stated that the mother had stated that "I want to see him [the father] six feet under" during the mediation, and the father wanted this confidential mediation statement introduced in his criminal case to impeach the mother's credibility in her testimony against him.[132] The state mediation confidentiality statute held that "[a] client has a privilege in any civil or criminal action to which the client is a party to refuse to disclose and to prevent any other person from disclosing confidential communications made in the furtherance of the rendition of mediation services to the client...." The court of appeal reversed the trial court's exclusion of the mother's confidential mediation statement because the mother was merely a witness, not a party, in the father's criminal trial. However, after reviewing the evidence, the court determined that the error in excluding the statement was harmless and did not require reversal.[133] The *Trejo* case is important because it demonstrates the effects of a narrow application of mediation confidentiality statutes, especially when those statements are introduced in collateral proceedings. If the divorce, child custody, or child dependency mediation is based upon facts that might also give rise to criminal prosecution, attorneys must be careful to explain the limited protection of civil mediation confidentiality.

For instance, in *Rinaker v. Superior Court*[134] a minor was charged with vandalism of his neighbor's car. The state filed a juvenile delinquency petition, and the neighbor also filed a civil harassment action. During the harassment action the judge submitted the case to mediation, during which the neighbor allegedly "admitted to all present, including the mediator, that he did not actually see who threw the rocks at his car."[135] The minor subpoenaed the mediator to testify regarding the neighbor's confidential mediation admission, which was strong exculpatory evidence for the child's defense. The court held that the minor's constitutional right to confront and

---

[132] *Id.* at 1234–1236.

[133] *Id.* at 1235–1238. *See also Donnelly v. Donnelly*, 92 P. 3d 298, 302 (Wyoming 2004), in which the mother's attorney in a child custody proceeding asked the father questions about his confidential mediation statements. The court, after reviewing the record, found that the error was not prejudicial because it was a court trial and "we presume that the district court disregarded any improperly admitted evidence unless the record affirmatively demonstrates that the court's decision was influenced by that evidence."

[134] *Rinaker v. Superior Court*, 74 Cal. Rptr. 2d 464 (California 1999).

[135] *Id.* at 467–468.

cross-examination witnesses trumped the state's important public policy of providing confidentiality in mediation proceedings. The court noted that many important public policy privileges, such as the psychotherapist-patient privilege, evidence of plea agreements, subsequent repairs to prove negligence, and evidence of insurance to prove wrongdoing, have to give way when they deny criminal defendants due process.[136] The court further rejected the mediator's argument that the boy waived the right to compel the use of confidential mediation data because the minor signed a confidentiality agreement. However, the court narrowly construed the legal concept of "waiver" and held that when the minor signed the confidentiality agreement, it was prior to the neighbor's inconsistent and exculpatory statement; he therefore did not voluntarily and knowingly waive his right to cross-examination and confrontation.[137] *Rinaker* raises the important concept of waiver in relation to parties' participation in alternative dispute resolution.

Other courts have been willing to apply a broad approach to waiver. For instance, Ohio permits parties to waive any right as long as it is not unconstitutional or against public policy.[138] In *Lamberts v. Lillig*,[139] the Iowa Supreme Court, for instance, held that a father's waiver of parental rights in a dependency mediation was constitutionally defective because there was not a sufficient demonstration that the father "was informed of and knowingly and voluntarily waived his rights."[140] A California court held that parents waived the right to discuss the child's parentage without the presence of the mediator because "they did not object to that condition during the settlement conference."[141] However, the failure of a parent to attend and participate in child abuse mediation does not provide sufficient grounds for holding that the parent waived that right to confront witnesses in the dependency court proceeding because that would violate due process.[142]

Allen v. Leal[143] is one of the most bizarre cases to find that the parties had waived alternative dispute resolution confidentiality. After signing a

---

[136] *Id.* at 470.   [137] *Id.* at 471–472.
[138] *Kelm v. Kelm*, 749 N. E. 2d 299 (Ohio 2001).
[139] *Lamberts v. Lillig*, 670 N. W. 2d 169, 134–135 (Iowa Supreme Court 2003).
[140] *Id.* at 135.
[141] *In re Nicholas H.*, 5 Cal. Rptr. 3d 261, 269 (California 2003).
[142] *In re Dolly D.*, 48 Cal. Rptr. 2d 691, 694–695 (California 1995). *See also Smith v. Smith*, 75 S. W. 3d 815, 826 (Missouri 2002) [father's failure to attend the child custody mediation was not sufficient ground for a change of visitation order because father's act was not purposeful]. But *In re Erik Q.*, 2001 WL 1497742 (California Appellate Second District, November 26, 2001; unpublished) held that the parents' untimely request for mediation services constituted a waiver because of the need for rapid permanency for the child. *See also Ruble v. Ruble*, 2004 WL 1618531 (Florida, July 21, 2004; unpublished); *Kiser v. Kiser*, 595 S. E. 2d 816 (North Carolina 2004; unpublished).
[143] *Allen v. Leal*, 27 F. Supp. 2d 945 (S. D. Texas 1998).

mediated settlement agreement, the parties asked the court to set aside the settlement based upon the mediator's coercive tactics. However, the court held that because the professional credibility of the mediator was being attacked, public policy favored permitting the mediator to testify on the coercion issue, even though the statute held that "[a]ll communications made during ADR procedures are confidential and protected from disclosure...."[144] The court held that the parties waived the confidentiality protection by "'opening the door' by attacking the professionalism and integrity of the mediator...."[145] However, even more interesting than the court's ruling was its reaction to a statement made to the press by the president of the local Association of Attorney-Mediators that "[w]hat some people might consider a little bullying is really just part of how mediation works." The court termed that comment an "egregious statement" that is inconsistent with the Texas law that declares that a mediator "may not compel or coerce the parties to enter into a settlement agreement."[146]

An Oregon court in In the Matter of Marriage of Reich[147] held that "confidential mediation communications may not be offered as evidence in support of a motion to enforce a subsequent settlement agreement." However, because the mother offered the confidential mediation statements not to enforce the mediation agreement, but rather to enforce an agreement entered into by the spouses "long after the mediation failed," the statements were inadmissible.[148] Therefore, even in jurisdictions that permit a limited use of mediation statements to determine the nature of the settlement agreement, the scope of use is limited solely to that agreement in the same proceeding.[149]

The preceding discussion not only demonstrates the complexity of alternative dispute resolution confidentiality laws but also illustrates the traps that await unsuspecting parties who unreasonably rely upon a broad interpretation of that privilege. Even in those jurisdictions that provide almost absolute confidentiality of mediators' statements, due process may trump that confidentiality public policy.[150] Thus, attorneys must be

---

[144] Id. at 947.
[145] Id. at 947, fn. 4.
[146] Id. at 948.
[147] In the Matter of Marriage of Reich, 32 P. 3d 904 (Oregon 2001).
[148] Id. at 908.
[149] For instance, in Few v. Hammack Enterprises, Inc., 511 S. E. 2d 665, 669 (North Carolina 1999), the court held that the confidential mediation statute "does not prohibit the admission of the outcome of a mediation settlement conference before a judge making the determination of whether settlement was reached and of the terms of that settlement" even though specific confidential statements are not admissible for other purposes. See contra Ryan v. Garcia, 33 Cal. Rptr. 2d 158 (California 1994).
[150] For instance, California Evidence Code § 703.5 provides that the mediator is "incompetent" to testify at a subsequent civil proceeding concerning statements made during mediation."

extremely careful in counseling clients regarding confidentiality of child custody and dependency alternative dispute resolution mechanisms.

VI. THE ROLE OF THE MEDIATOR

Commentators, legislators, and judges are almost unanimous in declaring that the preeminent quality of mediators is neutrality and that the method used should be facilitation, not directedness or coercion in assisting parties in resolving disputes. For instance, *The Model Standards for Family and Divorce Mediation* define that alternative dispute resolution genre as "[a] process in which a mediator, an impartial third party, facilitates the resolution of family disputes by promoting the participants' voluntary agreement."[151] And because mediation takes place outside the public's or court's purview, one commentator stated that "'[t]he integrity of mediation... depends largely on the ethics of mediators. To promote the success of the process and protect the rights of the parties, mediators must remain impartial and must preserve the confidentiality of median sessions.'"[152] Even in mediation systems that are evaluative rather than facilitative, neutrality is the central tenet. "In evaluative mediation, the mediator directs the focus of the discussion, including specific issues to be included or, importantly excluded, and sets boundaries about the procedure to be used."[153]

However, parties and their attorneys disagree upon which attributes constitute a good mediator. "According to a 1997 Minnesota study, the most important mediator qualification for attorneys surveyed was 'substantive experience in [the] field of law related to the case.' The next two most highly sought qualifications were 'mediator should be a litigator' and 'mediator should be a lawyer,'" and lawyers prefer evaluative processes, not facilitative.[154] Parties not only prefer facilitative mediation in which they gain a sense of empowerment but they also value most their perception of the "procedural justice and fairness" of the process even if they fail to achieve their mediated goal.[155] In addition, clients, unlike lawyers, are much less interested in "time..., cost, efficiency, or optimal substantive outcomes...."[156] Therefore, attorneys who wish to have satisfied clients, who desire a process that meets clients' expectations, and who wish to reduce the potential for legal malpractice actions must tailor their expectations to those consistent

---

[151] *See* Nancy Ver Steegh, *supra* note 4, at 170.
[152] David A. Ruiz, *Asserting a Comprehensive Approach for Defining Mediation Communication*, 15 OHIO ST. J. DISP. RESOL. 851, 862 (2000).
[153] Marsha B. Freeman, *supra* note 39, at 67, 70.
[154] J. Brad Reich, *Attorney v. Client: Creating a Mechanism to Address Competing Process Interests in Lawyer-Driven Mediation*, 26 S. ILL. U. L. J. 183, 187–188 (2002).
[155] *Id.* at 192–193.   [156] *Id.* at 194–195.

with client interests both in the tenure of the process and the outcome of the settlement.

Researchers have demonstrated that it is very difficult for mediators to maintain neutrality, or at least the appearance of neutrality, in emotionally charged child custody and dependency proceedings. First, the substantive context of mediations often shapes mediator attitudes and tactics regarding "'self-determination' or 'impartiality.'"[157] And additionally, many state mediation statutes place an affirmative duty on the mediator to protect the best interests of children during the settlement negotiations: "The mediator shall use his or her best efforts to effect a settlement of the custody or visitation dispute that is in the best interest of the child...."[158] There is a real question whether a mediator is truly neutral if the interests of one of the parties, the child, are preeminent in what is often a trilateral dispute.

In addition, legislators and ethics codes often place additional affirmative duties upon the mediator:[159] (1) to ensure that one or more parties do not harass or bully other parties,[160] (2) to ensure that parties waiving rights do so with informed consent,[161] and (3) to "inform the participants that they may seek information and advice from a variety of sources during the mediation process."[162] The *Model Standards of Conduct for Mediators* provide that the "mediator may provide information about the process, raise issues, and help parties explore options."[163] However, can mediators remain neutral if they are required to provide parties with factual and legal information, and if so, how can the lay mediator provide such advice without violating state prohibitions against practicing law without a license?[164] In a survey of judges and lawyers, the following settlement tactics were deemed unethical: (1) giving legal advice to the side with the weaker case, (2) speaking personally with a party to encourage a settlement agreement; (3) siding with the stronger party to force an agreement, and (4) giving information to the weaker side.

---

[157] Charles Pou, Jr., *"Embracing Limbo": Thinking About Rethinking Dispute Resolution Ethics*, 108 PENN. ST. L. REV. 199, 203 (2003).

[158] California Family Code § 3180. [159] Charles Pou, Jr., *supra* note 156, at 223.

[160] "The mediation process should ensure that litigants are treated with dignity, respect, and, most critical, fairness." John R. Van Winkle, MEDIATION: A PATH BACK FOR THE LOST LAWYER 23 (2001).

[161] "A mediator shall make all reasonable efforts to assure that all parties understand the mediation process and procedures." National Health Law Association Alternative Dispute Resolution Service Code of Ethics for Mediators, Rule 2.04 (Washington, D.C. 1991).

[162] Model Standards of Practice for Family and Divorce Mediation, Standard 1C.

[163] Model Standards of Conduct for Mediators (American Arbitration Association and American Bar Association 2002) [contained in Abraham P. Ordover & Andrea Doneff, ALTERNATIVES TO LITIGATION: MEDIATION, ARBITRATION, AND THE ART OF DISPUTE RESOLUTION (2d ed. 2002)].

[164] Cynthia E. Nance, *Unrepresented Parties in Mediation*, 15 No. 3 PRAC. LITIG. 47, 49 (2004).

Because many of these tactics are either discretionary or required under various mediator codes of ethics and/or statutes, it is no wonder that there is a disconnect between mediator obligations and attorney and client satisfaction with mediators' services.

Mediation will continue to flourish in child custody and dependency cases because it is faster, cheaper, and better able to fashion individualized family dispute resolution. Because the alternative dispute resolution revolution has already occurred, it is time for law schools to offer and/or require courses in arbitration, negotiation, and mediation as a graduation requirement. Until then, lawyers must assure themselves and clients that they fully understand the substantive, procedural, and strategic necessities of the alternative resolution of children's and parents' legal problems.

5 Ethical Considerations and Constraints in Child Custody and Dependency Appeals

Because many parties in both family custody and in child dependency cases do not have a constitutional or statutory right to appointed counsel on appeal, it should not be surprising that appellate courts have rarely discussed legal ethics in those proceedings. "Historically, family and juvenile courts have been largely *pro se* tribunals in which legal representation was permitted, but not encouraged."[1] And during the last decade of "limited appellate court resources and burgeoning caseloads," some appellate jurists have bemoaned the "general deterioration in the quality of appellate advocacy."[2] State bar association mandatory continuing legal education courses rarely involve appellate advocacy training, and there are few avenues for attorneys, once they graduate from law school, to receive formal training in appellate skills and/or specialized training in the custody and dependency appellate processes.[3] This chapter focuses on those few areas of concentrated ethical decisions in appeals involving child custody and juvenile dependency and attempts to answer some of the following questions: (1) Is there a right to appointed appellate counsel; (2) who has standing to appeal; (3) what is the subject matter jurisdiction of appellate courts in these proceedings; (4) should appellate courts apply a narrow or liberal construction to appellate rules of court; (5) under what circumstances are trial issues waived from consideration on appeal; and (6) what are appellate counsel's ethical duties. Unlike the previous four chapters, this chapter focuses on the complexity of the appellate process, providing attorneys a discussion of existing appellate procedures with the intent of increasing their level of competency in child custody and dependency appeals. Because child custody appeals in

---

[1] Merril Sobie, *The Role of Counsel in Family Court*, 10 N.Y. FAM. CT. PRAC. § 14:1 (November 2004 Update).

[2] Honorable Roger J. Miner, *Professional Responsibility in Appellate Practice: A View from the Bench*, 19 PACE L. REV. 323, 323, 325–326 (1999).

[3] *Id.* at 339–340.

family court are generally controlled by general civil appellate procedures, this chapter focuses more on the unique processes inherent in dependency appeals.

I. THE HISTORY OF THE RIGHT TO APPOINTED APPELLATE COUNSEL IN CHILD CUSTODY AND DEPENDENCY PROCEEDINGS

Historically, expansion of procedural rights in custody and dependency proceedings has been determined by analogy to those rights due criminal defendants. However, the United States Supreme Court has never held that criminal defendants have a right to an appeal in state court in criminal proceedings, but "once established, these avenues (of appellate review) must be kept free of unreasoned distinctions that can only impede open and equal access to the courts."[4] The Supreme Court has held that, if appellate review is granted by the state, the two fundamental procedural necessities are a competent attorney advocate for the criminal defendant and an appellate record that will enable the appellate court a means of reviewing the trial court record.[5] Therefore, the Court has held that in criminal cases in which a state provides convicted criminals "a first appeal of right, the federal constitution guarantees of due process (fair procedure) and equal protection (equality among litigants) require that state to provide appellate counsel for indigent defendants."[6] In addition, if counsel is appointed, the criminal defendant has a right to competent respresentation.[7] But the right to a competent appellate attorney only attaches to the first state right of appeal; neither the due process clause nor the equal protection clause requires states to provide secondary appeals or collateral writs, and even if they do, states need not provide appointed counsel.[8]

Those arguing that the federal constitutional right to competent and zealous counsel applies equally to family law and dependency proceedings have many hurdles to cross. The first problem is that the United States Supreme Court has not clearly stated the constitutional grounds for appellate procedural rights. Justices have relied upon the Sixth Amendment right to counsel, the Fourteenth Amendment due process clause, and the equal protection clause. However, the Court has noted that none of those clauses alone "provides an entirely satisfactory basis for the results reached" on the questions of what

---

[4] *Rinaldi v. Yeager*, 384 U.S. 305, 310 (1966).

[5] *Britt v. North Carolina*, 404 U.S. 226, 227 (1971); *Douglas v. California*, 372 U.S. 353, 355 (1963); *Griffin v. Illinois*, 351 U.S. 12 (1956).

[6] *In re Sanders*, 84 Cal. Rptr. 2d 899, 912 (1999); *Murr v. Giarranton*, 492 U.S. 1, 7 (1989).

[7] *Evitts v. Lucey*, 469 U.S. 387, 396 (1985).

[8] *See Coleman v. Thompson*, 501 U.S. 722, 752–754 (1991); *Pennsylvania v. Finley*, 481 U.S. 551 (1987).

appellate rights are due in criminal cases. If the right to appellate counsel and competent counsel is based upon the Sixth Amendment, then analogy to custody and dependency cases is clearly inapt because the Sixth Amendment applies exclusively to criminal trials. However, the Court has backed off exclusive reliance on the Sixth Amendment as the constitutional ground for the right to appellate counsel.[9] Further, if the right to appellate counsel in custody and/or dependency cases is predicated upon the Fourteenth Amendment due process clause, then one would assume that perfecting the right to appellate counsel would be hampered by the same impediments that convinced the Court in *Lassiter v. Department of Social Services* to hold that counsel in termination of parental rights cases must be decided under the tripartite *Mathews v. Eldridge* balances test, which has usually led to a denial of a federal constitutional right to trial counsel. In addition, because equal protection requires a comparison of two groups who must be sufficiently similarly situated, it is difficult to make a convincing argument that, because criminal defendants have a right to court-appointed appellate counsel, then parents and/or children have an equivalent right in custody and child abuse actions. However, perhaps the strongest argument for a constitutonal right to appointed counsel is based upon an equal protection comparison in states that provide appellate review of child custody and dependency judgments, but only to those who can afford appellate attorneys. The equal protection argument would closely mirror the equal protection argument in criminal cases in which the Supreme Court held that indigent criminal defendants and nonindigent defendants must be treated similarly and that required the states to provide appointment of counsel for indigents as long as appeals were a matter of right.

Few state courts have determined whether parents and/or children who are parties in dependency and/or custody cases have a constituional right to appointment of appellate counsel and, if so, whether there is a concomitant right to competent counsel. A Kansas court[10] held that parents in termination of parental rights proceedings have a right to appointment of appellate counsel in the first appeal under the equal protection clause because

---

[9] "In recognizing the right to effective assistance of counsel on appeal, however, the Court emphasized that the right is a due process right; that is, one based on fundamental fairness secured entirely and directly by the Due Process Clause of the Fourteenth Amendment, rather than through the Equal Protection Clause or by incorporation of the Sixth Amendment." Lissa Griffin, *The Right to Effective Assistance of Appellate Counsel*, 94 W. VA. L. REV. 1, 17–18 (1994) [arguing that the right to effective counsel is not co-extensive under the Sixth Amendment and under the Fourteenth Amendment due process clause].

[10] *In Interest of Brehm*, 3 Kansas App. 2d 325 (1979). For a comprehensive survey of the right to appellate counsel, see Particia C. Kussmann, *Right of Indigent Parent to Appointed Counsel in Proceedings for Involuntary Termination of Parental Rights*, 92 AM. L. REP. 379 (2004).

nonindigent parents can retain such counsel. A Michigan court[11] held that, even though indigent parents had a statutory right to appellate counsel, they were also entitled to counsel pursuant to the equal protection clauses of the U.S. and Michigan Constitutions. And a right to appointed appellate counsel in Florida was predicated upon the due process clause.[12]

However, those few state courts that have held that there is a constitutional right to appointed appellate attorneys have usually limited appointment to the termination of parental rights phase of dependency proceedings.[13] Such a limitation under a due process analysis appears consistent with the United States Supreme Court's analysis of the right to counsel in dependency cases, which it considered only in relation to the termination hearing in *Lassister*. However, if the basis for the right to appointment of counsel is predicated upon the equal protection clause, there is no rationale for limiting such appointment to termination hearings if other appellants can retain counsel in other dependency appeals. In several other states in which there is not a constitutional right to appointment of appellate counsel, appointment is available pursuant to statute.[14]

II. STANDING TO APPEAL

Both family law and dependency cases have expanded the number and classes of individuals permitted either to participate or be present during proceedings to determine the best interest of children. However, mere presence for some classes of participants, such as noncustodial relatives, de facto parents, and/or foster parents, does not necessarily establish standing to appeal. For example, relatives may not only lack party status in dependency proceedings but parties may also lack standing to raise relatives' arguments on appeal.[15] Although a nonrelative, noncustodial guardian may have constitutional grounds for asserting standing, most statutes do not provide such relatives with appellate access. For instance, in a Florida case the maternal aunt argued in the dependency court that she should have standing. However,

---

[11] *Reist v. Bay County Circuit Judge*, 241 N. W. 2d 55 (1976). *See also In re K. S. M.*, 61 S. W. 3d 632 (Texas 2001).

[12] *In re K. W.*, 779 So. 2d 292 (Florida 1998).

[13] *Matter of D. D. F.*, 784 P. 2d 89 (Oklahoma 1989). However, in Washington an indigent parent who has a right to counsel in all dependency proceedings has a right to appointed counsel of appeal as well. *In re Grove*, 897 P. 2d 1252 (1995).

[14] For example, *California Family Code § 7895 and California Rules of Court, rule 1435(b) & (d) (3)* grant indigents the right to counsel on appeal in dependency cases. However, some states have held that even if a parent has a statutory right to counsel at trial, there is no right to appointed appellate counsel. *See Casper v. Huber*, 456 P. 2d 436 (Nevada 1969); *State Department of Human Services v. Harris*, 1992 WL 25928 (Tennessee 1992).

[15] *In re Conn.*, 2003 WL 22290217 (Ohio, October 7, 2003; unpublished opinion).

because the trial court denied the aunt custody of the child, the court held that she lacked standing to appeal that denial order.[16] However, standing is not simply predicated upon child custody and/or relative relationships; rather it can arise from the dependency allegations themselves. For instance, Pennyslvania has granted standing to appeal to mothers' boyfriends when "the adjudication was based on the finding that the paramour sexually abused the child... since the trial court made a direct finding of appellant's complicity in the sexual abuse, since the court ordered that appellant have no contact with the children, and since the court's directives implicitly required appellant to undergo rehabilitation he had a 'substantial and immediate interest in the outcome of the case'."[17]

Even if a prospective appellant can sufficiently assert standing, appellate rules regarding the scope of review and the subject of that review are extremely complex. In fact, because the appeal is often limited by the scope and sufficiency of articulated error in the family and dependency courts, the scope of appellate review is the greatest intersection between the competency of trial and counsel and the competency of appellate counsel. One must wonder how any *pro per* parents could possibly maneuver the rigorous path of appellate and writ rules and procedures.

III. THE DUTY OF COMPETENCE IN CUSTODY AND DEPENDENCY APPEALS

Because neither the *American Bar Association Model Rules* nor state ethics rules differentiate between the responsibilities of attorneys pretrial, during trial, or on appeal, the general rules of ethical competency apply in custody and dependency appeals. Therefore, because "[a]ppellate practice has developed into an increasingly specialized area of the law," trial counsel must first determine whether they possess the full understanding of the procedural and/or substantive appellate legal universe that is necessary to provide their client competent representation.[18] *American Bar Association Model Rule 1.1* states that "[c]ompetent representation requires the legal knowledge, skill, and thoroughness and preparation reasonably necessary for the representation." The *Comments* to *Rule 1.1* indicate that legal competence is affected by the variables of the relative complexity of the case, its specialized requirements, the attorney's training and experience, as well as

---

[16] *In re A. M. V.*, 486 So. 2d 92 (Florida 1986).

[17] *In the Interest of C.L.*, 648 A. 2d 799 (Pennsylvania 1994); *In re M. K.*, 636 A. 2d 198 (Pennsylvania 1994).

[18] Kay Nord Hunt & Eric J. Matgnuson, *Ethical Issues on Appeal*, 19 WM. MITCHELL L. REV. 659, 659–660 (1993).

the necessity of using "methods and procedures meeting the standards of competent practitioners...."[19] The *Model Rules* also indicate that a lawyer may reasonably develop the necessary competence or associate with another attorney who is sufficiently competent to represent the client.[20] This is even as some appellate jurists have bemoaned the level of appellate attorneys' competence and the increasing "number of briefs and oral arguments that appear to be lacking in adequate preparation on the law and on the facts" and that "fail to raise the issue of subject matter jurisdiction."[21]

One of the first decisions that trial counsel must make is whether a trial attorney is as competent as a separate appellate attorney to review the transcripts for appellate error. Trial counsel may determine that they have a better understanding of the facts in the case than a new appellate attorney. However, depending on the potential appellate issues, trial counsel may consciously or unconsciously have a self-interested bias when reviewing their own trial performance. Certainly, if the client or facts indicate that an issue of incompetence of trial counsel might be involved, a neutral appellate specialist is in a better position than the trial counsel to judge the issue of competency. Because ineffective assistance of counsel is one of the most frequently alleged trial court errors in custody and dependency appeals, trial counsel must carefully consider whether they will be sufficiently able to review allegations of their own incompetency.

One court has defined the duty of competence of appellate attorneys as "the duty to prepare a legal brief containing citations to the (appellate record) and appropriate authority, and setting forth all arguable issues, and the further duty not to argue the case against his client."[22] For example, in a child dependency case in which the mother's reunification services were terminated, the mother filed a writ pursuant to the appropriate rule of court, which required the writ to state "the factual basis for the petition." However, because the mother left blank the factual basis section of the statutory form, the court of appeal held that it "must dismiss the petition as factually inadequate."[23]

The most frequent reason for the dismissal of child custody and child dependency appeals is the waiver of trial court errors that were not litigated in the trial court. For example, in *Miller v. Miller*,[24] the husband in a divorce

---

[19] *American Bar Association, Model Rule 1.1, Comments (1)–(6)*.
[20] *Id.*, Comment (4): lk "A lawyer may accept representation where the requisite level of competence can be achieved by reasonable preparation."
[21] Honorable Roger Miner, *supra* note 2, at 331–333.
[22] *People v. Barton*, 146 Cal. Rptr. 727, 730 (California Supreme Court 1978), citing *People v. Lang*, 113 Cal. Rptr. 9, 12 (1974).
[23] *Angela P. v. Superior Court of Madera County*, 2002 WL 31413921 (California, October 28, 2002; not published).
[24] *Miller v. Miller*, 744 A. 2d 778 (Pennsylvania 1999).

action argued in the trial court that a child dependency tax exemption could be awarded to the noncustodial parent. The court dismissed that appellate issue because the father failed to raise the issue in a timely fashion and therefore "acquiesced" in that trial court determination. Many courts have dismissed appeals based upon a failure to raise the issue of incompetence of counsel in the trial court rather than raising it for the first time on appeal. For instance, a Massachussetts court stated that "[a]bsent exceptional circumstances, we [the appellate court] do not review claims of ineffective assistance of counsel for the first time on appeal."[25] However, appellate courts have discretion to entertain the issue of incompetence of counsel under extraordinary circumstances. For instance, in a California case the court noted that incompetency of counsel issues should usually be filed as writs in the appellate court; however, such a claim may be "made as part of the appeal ... [and] asserted even after the order terminating parental rights...."[26] The court found the trial attorney's representation incompetent because he committed a patent error in agreeing that the incarcerated parent lacked the capacity to care for her child, even though the statute required the state to prove that the parent lacked the ability to "*arrange* for the child's care" even if the parent was incarcerated.[27] Appellate courts have held that numerous trial court errors are waived if not properly lodged in the trial court where the judge can determine the prejudicial impact of the alleged error: (1) waiver of review of a dispositional order based upon a nolo contendere plea,[28] (2) waiver of denial of a change of custody,[29] (3) waiver of issues of child placement by Tribe because they were not appealed prior to the current custody decision,[30] (4) waiver of the issue of termination of reunification services because the parent did not meet the statutory period within which to file a writ petition,[31] (5) waiver based upon failure to file an appeal within a reasonable time after the disposition hearing,[32] (6) jurisdictional errors waived if not appealed prior to the disposition hearing,[33] and (7) conflicts of interest waived if not raised in the trial court.[34]

---

[25] *Care and Protection of Oleg & Another*, 776 N. E. 2d 1039, (Massachusetts 2002; unpublished opinion).

[26] *In re S. D.*, 121 Cal. Rptr. 2d 518, 524 (California 2002).

[27] *Id.* at 525. The court stated that "[t]here is not a 'Go to jail, lose your child' rule in California."

[28] *Julie M. v. Orange County Social Services*, 2002 WL 31781145 (California, December 12, 2002; unpublished). *See also In the Matter of the Appeal in Marcopa County, Juvenile Action No. J-74449A*, 511 P. 2d 693 (Arizona 1973) [waiver of incompetency of counsel].

[29] *In re Matthew R.*, 2003 WL 21267213 (California, June 3, 2003; unpublished).

[30] *In re Liliana S.*, 10 Cal. Rptr. 3d 553 (California 2004).

[31] *Christy L.*, 2002 WL 1980689 (California, August 28, 2002; unpublished).

[32] *In re T. T.*, 842 A. 2d 962 (Pennsylvania 2004).

[33] *In re C. H.*, 2003 WL 22966248; (Ohio, December 18, 2003; unpublished).

[34] *In re Sessoms*, 2003 WL 22283495; (Ohio, October 6, 2003; unpublished).

One exception for waiver on appeal of issues not raised in the trial court involve cases in which the parties did not have sufficient notice of the error. For instance, in *Dwayne P.*,[35] the appellate court ruled that Native American parents did not waive dispositional review even though they had not properly appealed those issues because the state failed to follow the proper notice requirements under the Indian Child Welfare Act. Other appellate courts have held that some constitutional errors are never waived and can be litigated even if not raised in the trial court.[36]

IV. THE DUTY AND SCOPE OF ZEALOUS APPELLATE REPRESENTATION

No state bar association, attorney general opinion, ethics code, or court opinion has specifically determined that appellate attorneys representing parties in custody and dependency proceedings have a lower standard of client obligation regarding competence, loyalty, confidentiality, or zealousness than is owed by trial counsel. However, the definition of those duties may differ depending upon whether the attorney's task is one involving the trial or the appeal, or whether more specialized statutory duties of trial counsel may not apply to appellate attorneys. For instance, in a recent case, *In re Zeth S.*,[37] the California Supreme Court had to determine whether specialized statutory attorney duties toward abused children in dependency trial proceedings apply to attorneys representing children in the appeals of dependency findings.[38] In 1994 the California Legislature ordered the California Judicial Council, the court rule-making authority, to draft specialized rules for determining minimal competency of dependency court attorneys.[39] In addition, the California Legislature promulgated minimum competency requirements for children's dependency counsel, including (1) making "any further investigation that he or she deems necessary to ascertain the facts, including the interviewing of witnesses"; (2) "cross-examine witnesses in both the adjudicatory and dispositional hearings"; (3) present necessary witnesses; (4) suggest services

---

[35] *Dwayne P.*, 126 Cal. Rptr. 2d 639 (2003).
[36] *In re Fennell, III*, 2002 WL 194221 (Ohio, January 23, 2002; unpublished). *But see R. G.*, 792 So. 2d 1269 (Florida 2001); *In the interest of W. A.*, 2003 WL 21290900 (Utah, February 6, 2003; unpublished).
[37] *In re Zeth S.*, 2 Cal. Rptr. 3d 683 (California Supreme Court, 2003).
[38] The author orally argued *In re Zeth S.* in the California Supreme Court as *amicus curiae*.
[39] *California Welfare & Institutions Code § 317.6* provides, "On or before January 1, 1996, the Judicial Council shall, after consulting with representatives from the State Bar of California, county counsels, district attorneys, public defenders, county welfare directors, and children's advocacy groups, adopt rules of court regarding the appointment of competent counsel in dependency proceedings...."

needed by the child; and (5) "investigate the interests of the child beyond the scope of the juvenilie proceeding and report to the court other interests of the child that may need to be protected by the institution of other administrative or judicial proceedings."[40]

The issue in *In re Zeth S.* was whether those specialized children's attorney responsibilities in the juvenile dependency trial courts carried over into appeals from dependency court verdicts. The court of appeal appointed a separate appellate attorney for the child. That attorney, relying on the express language of *Welfare & Institutions Code § 317* to "make further investigation," analyzed postjudgment evidence regarding the continuing best interest of the minor. At the termination of parental rights hearing, the court adopted the recommendations of the Department of Child and Family Services and the minor's trial counsel to terminate parental rights and place the child for adoption with the maternal grandfather who was separated from the maternal grandmother, a recovering alcoholic. However, after conducting an independent investigation pursuant to § 317, the child's appellate attorney discovered that the grandfather stated that he had been pressured to adopt his grandchild and instead preferred a legal guardianship.[41] After the child's appellate attorney informed the court of appeal that she was taking a position that was diametrically opposed to the minor's trial counsel based upon this *postjudgment evidence*, the court of appeal ordered further appellate briefing on the appropriate remedy in light of the newly discovered postjudgment evidence. After a supplemental briefing, the court of appeal reversed the termination of parental rights order and remanded the case for a new review hearing.

The California Supreme Court reversed the judgment of the court of appeal by first stating that it was not determining whether children have either a statutory or constitutional right to the appointment of an appellate attorney.[42] The California Supreme Court determined that none of the specialized rules of zealous and competent representation promulgated in *Welfare & Institution Code § 317* were applicable in juvenile dependency appeals

---

[40] *California Welfare & Institutions Code § 317.* In addition, California *Rule of Court, Rule 1438* also requires, as a definition of "competent" counsel in dependency proceedings that the attorney "has participated in training in the law of juvenile dependency, and who demonstrates adequate forensic skills, knowledge and comprehension of the statutory scheme, the purposes and goals of dependency proceedings, the specific statutes, rules of court, and cases relevant to such proceedings, and procedures for filing petitions for extraordinary writs." In addition, competent counsel must also have "a minimum of eight hours of training or education in the area of juvenile dependency, or who have sufficient recent experience in dependency proceedings in which the attorney has demonstrated competency, may be appointed to represent parties."

[41] *In re Zeth S.*, at 688.   [42] *Id.* at fn. 6.

because the statute referred specifically to cases in the "juvenile court," not in all representation arising out of dependency proceedings. The court noted that "[a]lthough a reviewing court is free to appoint separate counsel for a minor in an appeal of an order and judgment terminating parental rights, section 317 does not compel the appellate court to make such an appointment of counsel, nor does that section purport to prescribe or regulate the duties and obligations of appointed counsel in juvenile dependency appeals."[43] The California Supreme Court also held that absent exceptional circumstances, which it found did not exist in the instant case, the consideration of post-judgment evidence cannot be considered in an appeal from a termination of parental rights judgment.[44]

The opinion in *In re Zeth S.* has had a dramatic effect upon children in dependency court appeals. Because the California Supreme Court determined that minor's appellate counsel has no affirmative obligation to investigate postjudgment evidence, and because it did not determine whether children are entitled to separately appointed appellate counsel, the court of appeal, which was the subject of the appeal, has eliminated its procedure of automatically appointing appellate attorneys for children. However, the scope and reach of the *Zeth S.* case are still in doubt. For instance, one appellate court has held that *Zeth S.* is limited to cases of parental termination appeals and that postjudgment evidence is admissible in cases that do not involve the reversal of court judgments, such as changes of custody.[45]

One of the issues inherent in the *In re Zeth S.* case, a conflict between the child's trial counsel and the child's appellate attorney, has resurfaced in another case pending in the California Supreme Court. If both of the minor's attorneys are charged with representing the best interest of the child, what rules should apply when trial counsel determines that an appeal is in the child's best interests, but the minor's appellate counsel thinks that the appeal should be dismissed? In *In re Josiah Z.*,[46] the court of appeal, in a rather facile analysis, concluded that *In re Zeth S.* controlled and that any postjudgment evidence indicating that it would be in the child's best interest to dismiss the appeal was inadmissible in the appellate court. The court further determined that it is "not our role, nor that of appellate counsel, to evaluate the [minor's] best interests. Instead, it is the dependency court judge who is charged with the responsibility of analyzing and determining the best interests of dependent children."[47]

---

[43] *Id.* at 698. [44] *Id.* at 696–697.
[45] *In re Elizabeth C.*, 2003 WL 22100812 (September 11, 2003; unpublished opinion).
[46] *In re Josiah Z.*, 13 Cal. Rptr. 3d 456 (May 19, 2004; hearing granted in the California Supreme Court).
[47] *Id.* at 461.

There are several problems with the analysis in *Josiah Z*. First, unlike the *Zeth S.* case, the minor's appellate counsel was not attempting to use post-judgment evidence to reverse a judgment by the juvenile trial court, but was rather merely arguing that dismissal may be warranted. In fact, in one of her briefs to the California Supreme Court, the minor's appellate attorney stated that she had never requested that the minor's appeal be dismissed, but rather she merely requested funding from the court of appeal to speak with her child client to determine whether or not dismissal would be in the child's best interest.[48] Therefore, the issue in *Josiah Z.* is better defined as whether a child's appellate attorney in a child dependency case has a duty or the discretion to determine whether the appeal is still in the child's best interest, especially if considerable time has elapsed since the trial court's judgment and the trial counsel's decision to file a notice of appeal. Under that scenario, the child's appellate counsel is caught in a Catch-22 regarding the ambit of zealous advocacy. On the one hand, if the appeal is still appropriate, then appellate counsel should file an opening brief. However, on the other hand, if the child's appellate counsel determines that the appeal may harm the child or that trial counsel's original notice of appeal was frivolous, appellate counsel may not be permitted to continue with the appeal. Most jurisdictions provide sanctions and possible awards of appellate court costs for filing a frivolous appeal.[49] For instance, in *Guardianship of Mellissa W.*,[50] the court of appeal awarded $13,004 in sanctions against the grandparents for prosecuting a frivolous appeal because the minor's appeal was moot based upon the child's marriage. In fact, courts have recognized a duty of appellate attorneys to dismiss appeals if postjudgment evidence renders the appeal moot.[51] Therefore, the court of appeal opinion in *Josiah Z.* that the minor's appellate counsel lacked discretion to file a motion to dismiss the child's dependency

---

[48] *Appellant's Answer to Amicus Curiae Brief of Whittier Law School Legal Policy Clinic*, filed in the California Supreme Court on May 19, 2004, at 12.

[49] For proscriptions and sanctions for filing frivolous appeals, *see* Kay Nord Hunt, *supra* note 41, at 655–670; *American Bar Association Model Rule 3.1* ("A lawyer shall not bring or defend a proceeding, or assert or controvert an issue therein, unless there is a basis for doing so that is not frivolous, which includes a good faith argument for an extension, modification or reversal of existing law").

[50] *Guardianship of Mellissa W.*, 118 Cal. Rptr. 2d 42 (2002).

[51] *Hale v. Laden*, 224 Cal. Rptr. 182 (1986); *Wax v. Infante*, 194 Cal. Rptr. 14 (1983); *In re Marriage of Murphy*, 786 N. E. 2d 132 (Illinois 2003) [general discussion of appellate fee awards]; Nancy J. Arnold & Tim Easton, *Illinois Supreme Court Civil Cases: Fees and Family Law, "No" To Immunity, and More*, 92 ILL. B. J. 180 (April, 2004). Because appellate court dockets include "burgeoning caseloads," it is not surprising that sanctions for frivolous appeals would be increasing or that such sanctions will generally be upheld absent an abuse of discretion. Honorable Roger J. Miner, *supra* note 2, at 325–326; *Lockhart v. Grieve*, 834 P. 2d 64 (Wisconsin 1992); *Harrington v. Pailthorp*, 841 P. 2d 1258 (1992).

appeal appears inconsistent both with ethical mandates and general case law if the dismissal was based upon postjudgment evidence demonstrating that the appeal was now moot. In addition, the court of appeal reliance on the *In re Zeth S.* case seems inappropriate because the policy basis for that opinion was not permitting dependency court judgments to be reversed based upon new evidence because a dismissal of the appeal would not affect the juvenile court judgment and would not frustrate the dependency policies of judicial economy or legal finality.

The *Josiah Z.* court suggested that the appropriate remedy for a child's appellate attorney who decides that a "good faith ... argument for reversal can[not] be made" is for the attorney to file a no-merit brief; the court of appeal would then "authorize trial counsel for the child to file a letter brief explaining why he or she believed the juvenile court committed prejudicial error. If trial counsel can show arguable error, we will order supplemental briefing and thereafter review the merits." This, of course, is a variant on the remedy selected by the United States Supreme Court in *Anders v. California*,[52] in which the Court determined that if a criminal defendant's appellate attorney could not discover any nonfrivolous appellate issues, the attorney should attempt to withdraw from the case after filing "a brief referring to anything in the record that might arguably support the appeal" so that the indigent can proceed with the appeal and so that the Court can appoint new appellate counsel should the Court discern a colorable issue.[53]

Although the California Supreme Court, unlike courts in many other states, has rejected a direct application of *Anders* to dependency appeals because *Anders* was based upon the Sixth and Fourteenth Amendments, it has suggested a similar procedure for dependency appeals.[54] The California Supreme Court in *In re Sade C.*[55] determined that the appropriate remedy for appellate attorneys in dependency cases is to file a letter brief "setting

---

[52] *Anders v. California*, 386 U.S. 738 (1967).   [53] *Id.* at 744.

[54] Courts that have applied *Anders* to dependency proceedings include *J. K. v. Lee County*, 668 So. 2d 813 (Alaska 1995); *In re Keller*, 486 N. E. 2d 291 (Illinois 1985); *Morris v. Lucas County Children Serv. Bd.*, 550 N. E. 2d 291 (Ohio 1989); *In re V. E.*, 611 A. 2d 1267 (Pennsylvania 1992); *State v. Balfour*, 814 P. 2d 1069 (Oregon 1991); *In the Interest of D. E. S., et al.*, 135 S. W. 3d 326 (Texas 2004).

[55] *In re Sade C.*, 55 Cal. Rptr. 2d 771 (1996). The California Supreme Court had earlier decided that its pre-*Anders* appellate procedures met the requirements of the due process clause even though they were not identical to those suggested in *Anders*. Under the California approach, and unlike the *Anders* approach, counsel "neither explicitly states that the review has led him or her to conclude that an appeal would be frivolous ... nor request leave to withdraw. Instead, counsel is silent on the merits of the case and expresses availability to brief any issues on which the court might desire briefing.... The appellate court ... must conduct a review of the entire record, regardless of whether the defendant has filed a pro se brief." See *Pullen v. Florida*, 802 So. 2d 1113, fn. 2 (Florida 2001); *People v. Wende*, 25 Cal. 3d 436 (1979).

forth a statement of the case, a summary of the facts, and potential arguable issues"; however, unlike under *Anders*, the appellate court has no duty to conduct an independent review of the record for arguable issues, and if the dependency court party does not file a supplemental appellate brief, the court has discretion to dismiss the appeal.[56] The problem with applying *Sade C.*, the California version of *Anders*, in dependency appeals is that *Josiah Z.* does not involve an attorney who is declaring that there are no colorable appellate issues, but rather that she needs to investigate whether raising such issues, if they exist, is still in the child's best interest. This raises issues that were not implicated in either *Anders* or *Sade C.*, and the policies of those cases are not implicated in *Joziah Z.*

The importance of *Josiah Z.* and *Zeth S.* is that they are perhaps the first comprehensive discussions in American jurisprudence regarding the sometimes conflicting roles of appointed trial and appellate counsel in child abuse proceedings. Although those opinions have begun the debate, the results in those cases raise at least one significant undecided issue. If the child's appointed appellate counsel cannot raise the relevance of postjudgment evidence either on the vitality of the juvenile court's order or on the wisdom of proceeding with the appellate process that was begun months earlier by the child's trial counsel, who is available to represent the child on appeal as the child's guardian ad litem?[57] Section 5106a of the Child Abuse Prevention and Treatment and Adoption Reform Act,[58] hereinafter, CAPTA, provides that any state receiving federal child abuse and foster care funding must adopt "provisions and procedures requiring that in every case involving an abused or neglected child which results in a judicial proceeding, a guardian ad litem, who has received training appropriate to the role, and who may be an attorney or a court appointed special advocate who has received training appropriate to the role (or both), shall be appointed to represent the child in such proceedings."[59]

---

[56] *In re Angbela S.*, 2003 WL 1232583 (California, March 18, 2003; unpublished). However, even though the Supreme Court held in *Sade C.* that the court of appeal need not independently review the record, courts have discretion to do so. *In re Mario C.*, 2002 WL 1608470 (California, July 19, 2002; unpublished opinion).

[57] The author, in his *amicus curiae* brief filed in the California Supreme Court in *In re Josiah Z.*, was the first advocate to articulate the danger of holding that the child's appellate attorney cannot function as the child's GAL in the appeal unless counsel can determine the child's best interest. *See* William Wesley Patton, *Amicus Curiae Brief*, for Whittier Law School Legal Policy Clinic, filed on September 16, 2004, at 7–17.

[58] 42 U.S. C. § 5106a.

[59] The California Legislature has indicated the importance of following the requirements under CAPTA in appointing a GAL for abused children. In fact, during the legislative history of Senate Bill 2160 in 2000, the legislature indicated that failure to follow those statutory dictates

This federal requirement does not make a distinction between trial and appellate court proceedings or among any of the various detention, jurisdictional, disposition, review, or termination of parental rights proceedings inherent in child abuse litigation. Instead, the statute requires a GAL for the abused child in "every case...in such proceedings."[60] Further, it is clear that CAPTA is concerned with providing competent representation not only in trial courts but also on appeal because one of the purposes of the CAPTA grants is "improving legal preparation and representation, including...procedures for appealing and responding to appeals of substantiated reports of abuse and neglect...."[61]

California could meet the CAPTA guardian ad litem (GAL) requirement by appointing a lay GAL for the child on appeal, by continuing the trial counsel as the child's GAL in the appellate court, or by finding that the child's appellate attorney functions in the dual role as counsel/GAL in the appellate courts unless a conflict of interests arises.[62] The first option, of appointing a new lay GAL, is problematic because doing so will introduce yet another adult stranger into the child's already frenetic and emotionally fragile life. Of course, if a lay GAL represented the child in the trial court, then that GAL could continue to represent the child on appeal. However, because the arguments in the court of appeal or in the Supreme Court often require travel away from the local juvenile courts, it may be difficult for the lay guardian to arrange such a travel schedule, especially if the GAL represents other children. In addition, such travel expenses will increase the cost of the appellate process. The second option, retaining the child's trial attorney as the appellate GAL, was adopted by the California Supreme Court.[63] However, that option is equally problematic because doing so would introduce a second attorney's views on appeal regarding the child's best interest, duplicate attorney costs, and cause difficulty with the trial attorney's scheduled cases during the required travel time to the appellate court arguments. The third option is the one rejected by the *Josiah Z.* court, which held that the child's appellate

---

could result in a loss of $5.2 million in federal CAPTA funds. *See* www.leginfo.ca.gov/pub-99-00/bill/sen/sb_2151-2200/sb_2160.

[60] The *Federal Code of Regulations, section 1340.14(g)* also states, "In every case involving an abused or neglected child which results in a judicial proceeding, the State must ensure the appointment of a guardian ad litem or other individual whom the state recognizes as fulfilling the same functions as a guardian ad litem, to represent and protect the rights and best interests of the child."

[61] 42 U.S. C. § 5106a (a) (2) (B) (i); *see also Appellant's Answer, supra* note 70, at 4.

[62] The court in *In re Charles T.*, 102 Cal. App. 4th 869 (2002), found that there was no inherent conflict of interest in having appellate counsel serve as the GAL.

[63] *In re Josiah Z.*, 31 Cal. Rptr. 3d 472, 485 (2005): The California Supreme Court determined that appellate counsel, with the consent of the child or the child's guardian ad litem, can move to dismiss the dependency appeal based upon the best interests of the child. *Id.* at 485.

attorney lacks the discretion to consider the child's best interests based upon postjudgment evidence. However, who is in a better position to consider the child's current interest than the appellate counsel who has represented the minor since the juvenile court judgment? In addition, having the attorney function in the dual role as appellate advocate and as GAL will reduce the administrative cost of dependency court appeals because only one fee and only one travel expense will be involved. It will be interesting to see what other state courts decide regarding the appropriate remedy when children's trial and appellate counsel disagree regarding the child's appellate rights and remedies. In addition, who will ultimately represent children as guardians ad litem during the appellate process?[64]

V. THE DUTY OF CANDOR AND LOYALTY ON APPEAL

The United States Supreme Court has termed the duty of loyalty to a client as "'perhaps the most basic' responsibility of counsel. . . ."[65] No jurisdiction has expressly held that the duty of loyalty of counsel to clients is different in appellate advocacy compared to all other attorney representation. As was discussed in Chapter 1, conflicts of interest implicate the duty of loyalty because a client might presume that if an attorney has conflicting obligations then the attorney's representation might violate both the duty of confidentiality and zealousness.[66] Just so, if an apparently adverse party's attorney, such as counsel for the Department of Children and Family Services or counsel for an abusing parent, represents the child on appeal, there is a real potential for a

---

[64] Appellate Defenders, a group of court-appointed attorneys who represent abused children in appeals in California, suggest that the child's appellate attorney should give great deference to decisions by the child's trial counsel: "In deciding what position to take, the rebuttable presumption is that appellate counsel should defer to trial counsel and take the same position on appeal as was taken at trial, unless appellate counsel believes trial counsel was clearly wrong or unless circumstances have changed significantly." *Guidelines for Minor's Counsel on Appeal*, Appellate Defenders, www.adi-sandiego.com/dependency/guidelines_minors.htm. The Appellate Defender standards also suggest that often only a letter brief, rather than a full appellate brief, should be filed if the child's position is already briefed by another party and that oral argument is not always a necessary component of the child's appellate case. *Id.*

[65] *Burger v. Kemp*, 107 S. Ct. 3114, 3129 (1987).

[66] In addition to addressing conflicts of interests in representing multiple parties in the same appeal, appellate attorneys also have to be cognizant of potential conflicts of interest in representing different clients in separate cases regarding the same appellate issue. These "positional conflicts" by a lawyer or law firm "are more likely to be scrutinized on a comparative basis at the appellate level. When faced with a potential positional conflict, the lawyer must consider the likelihood of the identical issue being raised in each case, the likely impact of a decision in favor of one client on the position of another client, and the significance of the issue." If the issue falls within *ABA Model Rule 1.7* conflicts, then the attorney must "obtain the client's consent after consultation." Hunt, *supra* note 41, at 671.

violation of the duty of loyalty because the Department's and/or the parent's position might conflict with the child's stated preference on appeal. Although *American Bar Association Model Rule 1.7* permits an attorney to represent two or more clients whose interests conflict, such representation can only proceed after "the client consents after consultation. [And] [w]hen representation of multiple clients in a single matter is undertaken, the consultation shall include explanation of the implications of the common representation and the advantages and risks involved." The problem in representing abused children on appeal is that they will seldom have the capacity to make a voluntary and knowing waiver of the conflict of interest. In addition, it will be very difficult, even if the children can legally waive the conflict, to assess whether they are also waiving their right to the duty of loyalty and confidentiality. Therefore, it usually is a bad idea to permit the government's or parents' appellate attorney to represent the interests of the child unless it is extremely clear that no potential conflicts of interest are inherent or will develop during that appellate representation.

So far, states have not determined that abused children have a constitutional right to separately appointed appellate counsel in child abuse appeals. However, in states that have supplied parents and/or the state a right to appeal dependency judgments, children might raise a colorable argument that denying them appellate access violates equal protection. Even though states are not constitutionally required to provide civil appeals, the United States Supreme Court has held that "once established, these avenues must be kept free of unreasoned distinctions that can only impede open and equal access to the courts."[67] For instance, in California a juvenile who had been adjudicated a delinquent argued that he was denied equal protection because he, unlike adult criminal defendants, was not provided with a right to notification of his right to appeal or his right to appointed counsel.[68] The court of appeal found that the minor was denied equal protection because in "cases touching upon fundamental interests of the individual, the state bears the burden of establishing not only that it has a compelling interest which justifies the suspect classification, but also that the distinctions drawn by the regulation are necessary to further its purpose."[69] However, whether state courts will find a child's right to association with parents and/or siblings a sufficient

---

[67] *Rinaldi v. Yeager*, 384 U.S. 305, 310 (1966).
[68] *In the Matter of Arthur N.*, 112 Cal. Rptr. 89 (California 1974).
[69] *Id.* at 91. One California court has held that equal protection was not violated by providing different appellate rules for appealing the denial of suppression motions in criminal and juvenile court because the right to exclude evidence is not a funadamental right and the state need only demonstrate a rational basis supporting the distinction. *In re David. G.*, 155 Cal. Rptr. 500, 502–503 (California 1979).

fundamental right to require a compelling state interest to support different appellate procedural rules for adults and abused children is uncertain.[70]

The California appellate scheme provides two potential equal protection arguments by dependent children. The first is that, although court rules provide the court with discretion to provide both parents and child appellants appointed counsel, in reality, judges routinely appoint counsel for parents, but almost never for children.[71] Children might argue that the failure to exercise discretion to appoint appellate counsel for them is the equivalent of the denial of the right to counsel that is almost always granted to parents.[72] And second, California courts only have discretion to appoint counsel for appellants, not dependency court respondents.[73] Children who want counsel to help them secure the benefits of the dependency court judgment as respondents could argue that they are discriminated against because children seeking to set aside court orders can be provided counsel at the discretion of the appellate court. Whether a state's economic argument that child respondents do not need counsel because other adults, either the Department of Child and Family Services or their parents, will argue the respondent's position will

---

[70] The two principal United States Supreme Court cases concerning equal protection regarding appellate rights both concerned criminal appeals. For instance, in *Griffin v. Illinois*, 76 S. Ct. 585 (1956), the Court determined that once a state established a first right of appeal in criminal cases, equal protection requires similar treatment of indigents and nonindigents. And in *Douglas v. California*, 83 S. Ct. 814 (1963), the Court held that denying indigent criminal defendants appointed appellate counsel denied them equal protection. Because the Supreme Court held in *Lassiter* that due process does not require appointment of counsel to every parent whose parental rights are subject to termination, it is uncertain whether the Court will apply the equal protection clause to dependency appeals. However, because the issue of equal protection does not implicate whether the state must provide appellate remedies as a matter of due process, but rather whether the state can differentiate among different parties in dependency appeals, there is nothing inconsistent in the court finding that equal protection applies to denial of counsel in dependency appeals. There is also a question of whether the Court would require that appointed appellate counsel be competent, even though the Court held that criminal defendants have a right to competent appellate attorneys. *Evitts v. Lucey*, 105 S. Ct. 830 (1985). Pennsylvania has determined that juvenile delinquents also have a right to competent appellate counsel. *In the Interest of A.P.*, 617 A. 2d 764 (1992).

[71] *California Rules of Court, Rule 1435* provides that "[a]ll appellants are entitled to representation by counsel [on appeal] and the reviewing court may appoint counsel to represent an indigent child, parent, or guardian."

[72] The California Supreme Court noted that there "is no uniform statewide requirement or practice that separate counsel be appointed for the minor in an appeal by the parent from an order terminating parental rights.... The parties have not asked us to address that circumstance, nor do the facts of this case present us with an occasion to consider it. It is noteworthy that the Fourth District Court of Appeal is the only Court of Appeal statewide to presently require appointment of counsel for the minor in all dependency appeals coming before that court." *In re Zeth S.*, 2 Cal. Rptr. 3d 683, fn. 6 (California 2003).

[73] *Id. Rule 1435 (d)* provides the "right of an indigent appellant to have counsel appointed by the reviewing court."

Ethical Considerations and Constraints in Child Custody 137

satisfy the equal protection compelling interest standard is uncertain. Those arguments have been articulated for denying children zealous advocates in the trial court on the theory that all other adults will present the relevant law and facts.

Because no state has yet decided that children have a procedural due process or equal protection right to appointment of separate appellate counsel, it is an open question whether the child's trial counsel or the appellate counsel representing the Department of Children and Family Services or the parents on appeal has an obligation to alert the court either of the child's need for separate counsel or of any potential or actual conflicts of interest inherent in dual appellate representation. However, because state professional responsibility conflict rules apply to all proceedings, including appellate proceedings, counsel arguably have a duty to resolve conflicts in the dual representation of children and other clients during the appeal.[74]

But unlike the questions of whether there is a constitutional right to appointed appellate counsel or the scope of conflicts of interest on appeal, it is clear that most ethics codes have held that the duty of candor toward the tribunal trumps the duty of client loyalty in some circumstances. "[A]n appellate attorney's loyalties are divided between the duty of candor owed to the court and the duty of zealous representation owed to the clients. Where these duties conflict, 'the duty to the court is paramount, even to the interests of his client.'"[75] Of course, like most ethics rules, application of the standard to discrete contexts permits creative interpretation.

Lying to the court of appeal, of course, is clearly inappropriate. For instance, in *People v. Roose*[76] an attorney was disbarred for violating Colorado rules of professional responsibility that prohibit an attorney from engaging in "conduct involving dishonesty, fraud, deceit, or misrepresentation" and that prohibit an attorney from knowingly making a false statement of material fact or law to a tribunal."[77] The attorney in *Roose* was appointed by the court to represent a mother in a child dependency proceeding. However, during the second day of the jury trial, the attorney informed the court that she was providing her client incompetent representation because this was her first jury trial and that she did not really know how to proceed. The judge denied the attorney's motion to withdraw, and instead, appointed co-counsel to represent the mother. The attorney informed the judge that she would not proceed with co-counsel and began to walk out of the courtroom, leaving

---

[74] "[T]he appellate lawyer must also conduct a conflicts check." Hunt, *supra* note 41, at 671.

[75] Hunt, *supra* note 41, at 672, quoting from *Steinle v. Warren*, 765 F. 2d 95, 101 (7th Cir. 1985) (*citing VanBerkel v. Fox & Road Mach.*, 581 F. Supp. 1248 (D. Minn. 1984)).

[76] *People v. Roose*, 44 P. 3d 266 (Colorado 2002).

[77] *Id.* at 270–272 (quoting from Colorado RPC 8.4 and 3.3(a)(1)).

her client and co-counsel behind. The judge informed the attorney that if she left the courtroom he would hold her in contempt of court. Co-counsel, after consulting with the mother by telephone, entered the mother's admission to the neglect charges and the jury was dismissed. The court held the first attorney in contempt of court and terminated the attorney's representation of the mother. However, when the attorney learned that the mother had pleaded to the allegations, she filed a motion to set aside the plea. The trial court again informed that attorney that she had been relieved from representing the mother and that she must not file any more court documents for the mother. But the attorney filed a notice of appeal for the mother in which she listed herself as the mother's attorney and did not indicate that she had been removed from the case, with orders by the trial judge not to file any more motions on behalf of the mother. The notice of appeal also included statements that were clearly not true, including that the mother had been excluded from the proceedings at one point.

The court in the attorney disciplinary ethics hearing found the series of false statements and the abandonment of her client when the attorney left the jury trial to be sufficient evidence to warrant disbarment. The court referenced *ABA Standard 6.11*, which provides, "Disbarment is generally appropriate when a lawyer, with the intent to deceive the court, makes a false statement, submits a false document, or improperly withholds material information, and causes serious or potentially serious injury to a party, or causes a significant or potentially significant adverse effect on the legal proceeding." It was clear that the attorney had on multiple occasions made false statements. The prejudice to the mother occurred when the attorney tried to intercede in the case and upset the mother to such a degree that the mother chose not to participate in the termination of parental rights proceeding. "The loss of that opportunity [to personally participate in that hearing] constituted a serious injury to the client."[78] Although the remedy of disbarment is not surprising based upon the seriousness and number of ethical violations in this case, the court's analysis on harm to the client is interesting because it omits a step that is required in an incompetence of counsel claim. To set aside a verdict based upon incompetence of counsel, the parent in a dependency proceeding must not only demonstrate that the attorney performed at a level below the reasonable practitioner in that field of law but also that the client was prejudiced by the attorney's incompetence. Many courts place upon the parent the burden of showing that without counsel's incompetence the parent would have received a more favorable result. However, in determining the level of sanction for ethical violations, the *Roose* court only required a

---

[78] *Id.* at 273.

finding of potential injury to the client, a much lower standard that would not support reversal based upon incompetence of counsel. The irony in *Reese* is that the disciplined attorney attempted to convince the court to permit her to withdraw based upon her incompetency because she did not know how to conduct a jury trial. If the judge had granted her motion to withdraw, the attorney might never have been disciplined; however, if the mother had filed for a reversal of the verdict based upon her attorney's admission of incompetence of counsel, she would likely have lost that motion because she would not have been able to demonstrate the likelihood of a more favorable result.

On the other end of the spectrum from the duty not to deceive the court is the duty to disclose controlling authority even if such disclosure is detrimental to the client's case. For instance, *ABA Model Rule 3.3(a)(3)* requires that "[a] lawyer shall not knowingly ... fail to disclose to the tribunal legal authority in the controlling jurisdiction known to the lawyer to be directly adverse to the position of the client and not disclosed by opposing counsel." Although this mandate clearly states that an atttorney's duty as an officer of the court trumps the duty of client loyalty regarding adverse legal authority, many critics have debated this mandate's efficacy. For example, Monroe Freedman has argued that the adversary system itself is the best assurance that all applicable law will be brought to the court's attention.[79] Because the plaintiff and the defendant often have equal access to legal materials, one might argue that this duel or legal combat should not be tilted by requiring adverse counsel to assist the adversary. However, Judge Roger J. Miner justifies the disclosure rule because the appellate court should provide "a level playing" field in which not all attorneys are of equal ability.[80] He suggests that justice, not a "anything-goes-for-a-client mindset," is the core of the American judicial system and that "[w]e must not lose sight of the fact that the purpose of our enterprise is justice under the law and that anything that moves us away from that purpose, including the non-disclosure of legal precedent, is to be condemned."[81] Judge Miner argues that the rule of disclosure should be expanded to include authority from other jurisdictions.[82]

Of course, even if one agrees with the rule, attorneys have for decades used their creativity to avoid its application by determining that a seemingly controlling case is distinguishable. And a number of appellate opinions have narrowly interpreted the duty to disclose adverse authority in determining that all elements of the mandate must be present before an attorney can be

---

[79] Monroe H. Freedman, *Arguing the Law in an Adversary System*, 16 GA. L. REV. 833 (1982).
[80] Honorable Roger J. Miner, *Professional Responsibility in Appellate Practice: A View from the Bench*, 19 PACE L. REV. 323, 330 (1999).
[81] *Id.* at 329.   [82] *Id.*

found to have violated the duty of disclosure.[83] Thus, the attorney must have "knowingly" failed to disclose authority in the controlling jurisdiction that is "known" by the lawyer to be "directly" adverse to the client's position and "not disclosed" by opposing counsel.

It thus does not take a creative legal genius to see the many ways around being found to have violated this duty of disclosure. First, how will the court determine that an attorney knows the particular legal opinion under consideration? Would it be sufficient to demonstrate that counsel has cited the opinion in other clients' cases? If so, must the ethics panel determine whether the reasonable attorney should remember every case cited in other cases during his or her career? Who is going to disclose the attorney's failure to cite the adverse authority? Because opposing counsel has not cited the authority, it is unlikely that opposing counsel will even know of its existence. If the trial court locates the authority, how would the court prove that the attorney had also found the case unless the attorney admitted such knowledge? And how can the court determine that an attorney who found the authority "knew" that it was controlling if he or she has at least a nonfrivolous argument for why the case is distinguishable and therefore not controlling in the case? Thus, there are few appellate opinions disciplining an attorney for failing to cite adverse authority.[84] However, courts have held that the duty of disclosure applies even after oral argument and exists as long as the court has jurisdiction in the case.[85]

Finally, the duty of candor applies to statements of the case and facts in appellate briefs: "Candor to the court requires fairly portraying the record."[86] For instance, in *CDD Programs, Ltd. v. Leighton*,[87] the court indicated that the duty of candor requires "scrupulous accuracy" to the record because the court "relies on counsel to state clearly, candidly, and accurately the record as it in fact exists." Of course, that does not mean that appellate attorneys in child dependency or child custody proceedings must excise all adjectives and adverbs in zealously providing an accurate statement of the facts. However, if appellate attorneys' statements of facts wax too hyperbolic, there is a risk that the justices will conclude that counsel is attempting to "dupe" the court

---

[83] For a discussion of the cases analyzing violations of the duty to disclose adverse authority in the controlling jurisdiction, *see, e.g.*, Eric J. Magnuson, *Ethical Issues on Appeal*, 19 WM. MITCHELL L. REV. 659, 672–679 (1993); J. Michael Medina, *Ethical Concerns in Civil Appellate Advocacy*, 43 SW. L. J. 677, 704–715 (1989).

[84] For a case holding that an attorney failed to disclose adverse controlling authority, *see Dorso Trailer Sales, Inc. v. American Body & Trailer, Inc.*, 464 N. W. 2d 551, rev. in part at 482 N. W. 2d 771, 773 (Minnesota 1992).

[85] *See, e.g., Board of License Commissioners v. Pastore*, 469 U.S. 238, 240 (1985).

[86] Hunt, *supra* note 41, at 677.

[87] *DCD Programs, Ltd. v. Leighton*, 846 F. 2d 526 (9th Cir. 1988).

and that attitude may influence the justices' attribution of credibility to the remainder of counsel's arguments. In addition, the duty of candor requires counsel to refer only to data that were presented to the trial court. Facts outside the record usually need to be presented through a companion extraordinary writ.[88]

VI. THE PROCEDURAL AND SUBSTANTIVE SCOPE OF APPEALS

Most states apply liberal construction rules to family custody and dependency appeals, in part because of the seriousness of the substantive rights involved and in part because many of these appeals are filed without the assistance of appellate counsel. For example, a father in a Minnesota termination of parental rights appeal alleged that the government's evidence was insufficient to support the termination order; however, "the father failed to challenge specifically the 'neglected and in foster care' basis for terminating parental rights. . . ."[89] Even though the father's appeal was statutorily deficient because it did not expressly attack each of the county's grounds for termination, the appellate court found the notice of appeal sufficient: "We discern no prejudice to the county, the guardian ad litem, or father in treating the issue in this manner and refuse to summarily affirm the termination of father's parental rights."[90] In an Oklahoma case the county moved to dismiss the parents' appeal in a child dependency case because they failed to follow statutory requirements of appeals by failing to "(1) show by affidavit the facts entitling them to an appeal; (2) state in the notice of appeal whether errors were upon questions of law, fact or both, and if upon a question of law the particular ground for appeal relied upon; (3) execute a proper appeal bond executed by two sufficient sureties; (4) file an appeal bond conditioned upon presenting the appeal without delay."[91] The appellate court rejected the county's motion to dismiss the appeal because a statute provided the court with "authority to grant amendments in cases where the appellant, in good faith, gives notice of appeal but inadvertently fails to do other acts necessary to perfect such appeal."[92] The court concluded that "statutes granting a right of appeal are to be construed liberally to effect the ends of justice."[93]

Most appellate courts will not dismiss dependency appeals based upon technical violations of statutory requirements unless prejudice is

---

[88] Hunt, *supra* note 41, at 679.
[89] *In the Matter of the Welfare of J. L. and T. L.*, 1994 WL 34199 (Minn. App., February 8, 1994; unpublished).
[90] *Id.* at 1.
[91] *Livingston v. Graham*, 396 P. 2d 496, 498 (Oklahoma, 1964).
[92] *Id.* at 498–499. [93] *Id.* at 499.

demonstrated. For instance, in *In re Serena M.*[94] the county moved to dismiss the parents' appeal because the notice of appeal was signed by the parents' attorney, but not, as required, by the parents themselves. The appellate court stated that a notice to appeal is to be liberally construed, and that because the parents "attended the contested six-month review hearing, opposed continuation of jurisdiction and received notice of filing of their notices of appeal," it is clear that counsel did not file the notice of appeal without the parents' consent.[95] Further, although many states prohibit appealing errors that occurred prior to the termination of parental rights hearing for the first time in a termination appeal, liberal construction rules have been applied to permit such appeals if the parents were not properly informed of their appellate rights in the pre-termination hearings. As one court noted: "In failing to provide appellant notice of her right to appeal, the juvenile court erred. . . . Under the cirucmstances of this case, and in light of appellant's ineffective assistance of counsel claim, we address each of appellant's contentions on their merits, including those relating to hearings held prior to the . . . [permanency planning hearing"].[96]

In addition to the procedural requirements of appeals, jurisdictions differ regarding which juvenile dependency orders are directly appealable, the timing of those appeals, and the designation of which issues must be brought by a writ rather than a direct appeal. For instance, in Florida dependency appeals receive expedited treatment;[97] however, whether adjudication hearings that do not result in termination of parental rights are sufficiently final judgments that trigger the duty to timely appeal such findings has proven a difficult question of law. Although states differ in their definitions of final orders that are appealable, Arizona's definition is consistent with those in most jurisdictions: "a final order was one 'which ends the proceedings, leaving no question open for further judicial action. . . .'"[98] The Arizona court

---

[94] *In re Serena M.*, 2002 WL 31677059 (California, November 27, 2002; unpublished).

[95] *Id.* at 2. *See also In re Christopher C.*, 2002 WL 31082393 (California, September 17, 2002; unpublished).

[96] *In re Mariah L.*, 2002 WL 31479043, at 7 (California, November 7, 2002; unpublished). And *A. V. v. Morgan County of Department of Human Resources*, 623 So. 2d 331 (Alabama 1993) held that liberal rules relating to the appellate record apply in child dependency cases. That court held that even though there were "some inaudible" portions of the taped transcript of the hearing, because there were over 500 pages available for review, that evidence was sufficient to be certified as the appellate record for review.

[97] *G. L. S. v. Department of Children and Families*, 724 So. 2d 1181, 1186 (Florida 1998): "The district court of appeal shall give an appeal from an order terminating parental rights priority in docketing and shall render a decision on the appeal as expeditiously as possible." Fla. Stat. § 39.473.

[98] *In the Matter of Appeal in Yavapai County Juvenile Action No. J-8545*, 680 P. 2d 146, 150 (1984).

noted that because periodic reviews reaffirming earlier findings of dependency are final decisions, they are therefore appealable.[99] But the timing of the appeal for each dependency proceeding often is determinative of whether appeals have been properly perfected. For instance, in *G. L. S. v. Department of Children and Families*,[100] the court of appeal determined that adjudication orders in which parental rights are terminated are final orders and are appealable. However, the court found that because the parents did not timely file a notice of appeal from that adjudication hearing, the parents' appeal from the termination order must be dismissed because "this Court is without jurisdiction to review it at this juncture." The court of appeal suggested that the parents have a "right to apply to the trial court for a belated appeal pursuant to a petition for writ of habeas corpus."[101] In contrast, California courts have given the term "final order" a much narrower definition than many other states. For instance, in *In re Tomi C.*,[102] the court of appeal held that an order dismissing the dependency proceedings was not appealable because it was not a final order since the proceedings were not dismissed with prejudice and could be filed again by the Department of Family and Children's Services. In contrast, the Florida Supreme Court upheld the court of appeal finding that a termination of parental rights order at the adjudication hearing is appealable; however, it determined that the adjudication termination order could also be appealed from the subsequent dispositional hearing order.[103] Imagine *pro per* parents attempting to maneuver in this procedural appellate morass that the Florida Supreme Court termed an "ambiguous post-disposition statutory framework."[104] In jurisdictions that do not have liberal construction rules on appeal, the parents would be precluded from even gaining appellate review of the decision to sever their fundamental right to rear their children.

There is a dramatic difference among states' scope of dependency appellate review. For instance, in Pennsylvania, the court has asserted the broadest appellate jurisdiction: "Our scope of review ... is of the highest possible nature. It is this Court's responsibility to ensure that the record represents a comprehensive inquiry and that the hearing judge has applied the appropriate legal principles to that record."[105] However, in other jurisdictions, such as Missouri, courts strictly construe the statutory right to appeal because under the common law no appellate rights existed. Thus, in *In the Interest of L.E.C., et al. v. K. C.*,[106] the Missouri court dismissed a mother's appeal of a change

---

[99] *Id.* at 150.
[100] *G. L. S. v. Department of Children and Families*, 700 So. 2d 96, 97, 99 (Florida 1997).
[101] *Id.* at 99.
[102] *In re Tomi C.*, 267 Cal. Rptr. 210, 212–213 (1990).
[103] *Id.* at 1185. [104] *Id.* at 1184.
[105] *In re E. P., et al.*, 841 A. 2d 128, 131 (Pennsylvania, 2004).
[106] *In the Interest of L. E. C., et al. v. K. C.*, 94 S. W. 3d 420 (Missouri, 2003).

in the children's permanency plan because there "is no statutory provision expressly granting the right to appeal" from a change in permanency planning.[107] The Missouri court also rejected policy arguments for providing parents appeals from nonfinal orders because it would "cause inefficiency and lengthen the time needed to address the ultimate issue of parental rights termination."[108]

Finally, some courts strictly construe rules of appellate procedure. For instance, in a California case the mother prematurely filed a notice of appeal on an issue of permanency planning, an issue that under California appellate rules must be brought by a writ, not a direct appeal. The court denied the mother's request to treat the appeal as timely filed and as properly filed under the "constructive filing" doctrine, which provides liberal appellate procedures to prisoners appealing final judgments.[109] The court also refused the mother's request to treat the appeal as the appropriate extraordinary writ because such relief is appropropriate only when the appeal was timely filed.[110]

---

[107] *Id.* at 424.

[108] *Id.* at 425. An Illinois court in *In re Brandon*, 771 N. E. 2d 1117 (Illinois 2002), held that denial of a change of placement motion was not a final order and, therefore, was not appealable. The court defined a "final order" as one that changes the status quo. Because the parents' change of custody motion was denied, it "did not permanently determine the rights of the parties nor definitely resolve any issue in the case. The ultimate issue, the return home of the children, remained to be determined." *Id.* at 1120–1121.

[109] *In re Ricky H. v. Lisa H.*, 12 Cal. Rptr. 2d 578 (California 1992).

[110] *Id.* at 584.

6 The Constitutionality of Legislative and Executive Regulation of the Practice of Law and Defining the Attorney-Client Relationship

Alex de Tocqueville noted that "people in democratic states do not mistrust the members of the legal profession, because it is known that they are interested to serve the popular cause; and the people listen to them without irritation because they do not attribute to them any sinister designs."[1] Times have changed. Today, polls by myriad sources indicate that the public's trust and respect for attorneys have atrophied since de Tocqueville's era. It is not uncommon to confront contemporary descriptions of attorneys as "parasites, hired-guns of large corporations or grasping clients, motivated by greed and neglectful of the public good."[2] The public's principal complaints about lawyers concern (1) perceptions of greed; (2) a minimal commitment to *pro bono publico* obligations; (3) fomenting a system of nastiness, rather than cooperation through alternative dispute resolution; and (4) a failure of attorney self-regulation to control and cure deficiencies in the attorney-client relationship. For instance, a poll by the American Bar Association found that 42 percent favor expanding "alternatives to lawsuits by encouraging use of mediation, arbitration, and other alternative dispute resolution programs."[3] And 56 percent of the public believes that "lawyers tend to recommend more legal work than necessary because it increases their fees."[4]

However, the most critical public attitude is the public's distrust of attorney self-regulation; "lawyer discipline is an oxymoron" according to a majority of

---

[1] Senator Paul Simon, *Foreword: Ethics in Law and Politics*, 28 LOY. U. CHI. L. REV. 221, 225 (1996)(quoting Alexis de Tocqueville, DEMOCRACY IN AMERICA 275–276 (Phillips Bradley, ed., 1987)(1835)). The author presented some of the following analysis in William Wesley Patton, *Legislative Regulation of Dependency Court Attorneys: Public Relations and Separation of Powers*, 24 J.LEGIS. 3 (1998).

[2] Simon, *supra* note 1, at 225.

[3] Gary A. Hengstler, *Vox Populi: The Public Perception of Lawyers: ABA Poll*, ABA J., September 1993, at 62.

[4] Richard Delgado, *Rodrigo's Thirteenth Chronicle: Legal Formalism and Law's Discontents*, 95 MICH. L. REV. 1105, 1116 (1997).

the public.⁵ Because the American Bar Association and state bar associations want to avoid, at all costs, public rather than attorney and judicial control of lawyer regulation and discipline, there has been a renewed emphasis on training law students and lawyers regarding legal ethics. For instance, training in legal ethics usually begins in the second year of law school, is tested on the bar examination, and continues indefinitely through mandatory continuing legal education requirements.⁶ However, the legal profession's renewed emphasis on self-regulation and ethics training has been an insufficient response to the public's concern because "[w]hile many lawyers view ethics as the absence of disciplinary measures and adherence to the profession's own Model Rules of Professional Conduct, the public views ethical conduct on a much broader scope, to include things such as fee disputes, lack of client relations and communication problems."⁷

Because of the public's continuing political action to promote systemic ethical changes in the legal system, pressure has been put on state legislators, administrative agencies, and Congress to step in and provide the perceived needed regulation. The most recent example of legislative regulation of the attorney-client relationship is the Sarbanes-Oxley Act of 2002,⁸ which requires attorneys practicing before the Securities and Exchange Commission to

> report evidence of a material violation of securities law or breach of fiduciary duty or similar violation by the company or any agent thereof, to the chief legal counsel or the chief executive officer of the company ... and if counsel or officer does not appropriately respond to the evidence (adopting, as necessary, appropriate remedial measures or sanctions with respect to the violation), requiring the attorney to report the evidence to the audit committee of the board of directors comprised solely of directors not employed directly or or indirectly by the issuer, or to the board of directors.⁹

Such legislatively mandated ethical rules place attorneys in a Catch-22 dilemma because violating the legislative statute can lead to contempt or civil fines; however, following that statutory ethical precept can lead to discipline

---

⁵ Michael J. Hall & Jean Guccione, *Complaining Consumers Getting Scant Satisfaction: Problems Remain in Bar's "Model" System*, L.A. DAILY J., July 11, 1994, at 1, 10. "[T]he public's distrust of attorneys, and the legal profession in general, is heightened by the imposition of lenient sanctions for attorney misconduct." Blaine Workie, *Chemical Dependency and the Legal Profession: Should Addiction to Drugs and Alcohol Ward Off Heavy Discipline?*, 9 GEO. J. LEGAL ETHICS 1357, 1372 (1996).

⁶ Lorie M. Graham, *Aristotle's Ethics and the Virtuous Lawyer: Part One of a Study on Legal Ethics and Clinical Legal Education*, 20 J. LEGAL PROF. 5 (1995–1996).

⁷ Hengstler, *supra* at 62.   ⁸ Public Law No. 107-204 (2002).

⁹ Section 307 (1) and (2); *Professional Responsibility Section Fall 2002 Newsletter*, at 4 (American Association of Law Schools).

by the state bar, and perhaps even disbarment, if the state bar's ethical rules conflict. For instance, prior to the passage of the Sarbanes-Oxley Act, the California Supreme Court rejected proposed amendments to *California Rules of Professional Responsibility, Rule 3-600*, which would have permitted governmental attorneys to disclose certain client confidentiality in order to report corruption. Because the California confidentiality rules are contained in the Business and Professions Code, the California Supreme Court permitted the legislature to promulgate a whistle-blower act, which appeared to cover attorneys. However, after the passage of the Sarbanes-Oxley Act, the California Bar Association quickly notified its members that the federal act violated several of California's *Rules of Professional Responsibility* and that attorneys were at risk if they blindly followed the requirements of the federal act.[10] The conflict between the federal standard and the California confidentiality standard became a bit murkier after the California Supreme Court modified *Rule 3-100* to permit attorneys to disclose, but not require disclosure, if they "reasonably believe that disclosure is necessary to prevent a criminal act that the attorney reasonably believes is likely to result in death of or substantial bodily harm to an individual."[11]

Although conflicts in legislatively and judicially mandated attorney ethics rules are problematic in every area of legal practice, such conflicts are most troubling in the area of child custody and dependency proceedings for several reasons. Perhaps more than in any other area besides criminal law, high-profile cases of child abuse raise cries by the electorate for immediate legislative fixes. Public outcry in specific cases has led legislators to promulgate expedited cures to perceived weaknesses in the laws and court procedures protecting children. For example, after the killing of 7-year-old Megan Kanka on July 29, 1994, her death became a national symbol of crimes against children and led to the rapid promulgation in forty-five states and Congress of laws requiring notification of the location of child predators. Although such statutes might be wise legislative responses if carefully debated and drafted, because of the tremendous public pressure and the expedited legislative debate concerning those statutes, they were often inartfully crafted. For instance, "Megan's laws in nine states have been challenged,

---

[10] *Attorneys Cautioned on Sarbanes-Oxley Disclosure*, CAL. B.J. (October 2003); *Ethics Alert: The New SEC Attorney Conduct Rules v. California's Duty of Confidentiality* (California Bar Association 2003).

[11] *California Rules of Professional Conduct, Rule 3-100*, effective July 1, 2004, is substantially similar to Assembly Bill Number 1101, which modified the California Business and Profession Code, section 6068 to permit such attorney disclosures. Because the California Supreme Court virtually adopted AB 1101, there was no issue of separation of powers because the California Supreme Court, in effect, approved the legislative draft of the new California confidentiality rules.

stricken or stalled in the courts, in part because they have been applied retroactively."[12]

Although judges are not immune from political pressure, they often are more insulated than legislators. This chapter analyzes the historical and constitutional roles of legislatures, the executive, and courts in promulgating ethical rules that define the role of attorneys and the attorney-client relationship. By studying separation of powers, attorneys working in child custody and dependency proceedings will be better able to resolve conflicts among ethical standards and to fashion legal arguments regarding which set of ethical precepts controls attorneys' conduct.

I. A SHORT HISTORY OF THE ROLE OF COURTS, LEGISLATURES, AND THE EXECUTIVE IN THE REGULATION OF ATTORNEYS

Most legal historians from the turn of the twentieth century until the 1960s characterized the role of courts in regulating attorneys as an absolute and inherent power. It was not uncommon for claims to be made that since the Magna Charta, legislatures "always recognized [that] the admission of attorneys was a matter of judicial discretion."[13] Broad claims of judicial independence were proffered: "[F]or more than six hundred years it has been the practice of the courts to admit attorneys upon their own examination, and ... at the time the Colonies separated from the mother country, the power of examination and admission of attorneys was vested in the courts."[14] It was argued that the admission and regulation of attorneys are so essential to the functioning of the courts that courts' power is "'inherent' or 'implied' in the judicial office itself."[15]

However, as the history of attorney regulation in relation to the separation of powers developed, some scholars began to question the exclusive power of courts to admit and regulate attorneys. During the 1970s and 1980s, articles began to promote a model of "concurrent jurisdiction" over attorney regulation to be shared by the courts and legislature. These analyses set the cusp of exclusive and/or inherent court regulation at the point at which legislative regulation of attorneys would unreasonably hamper the necessary

---

[12] *Problems in "Megan's Laws": Courts Must Bring Order to States' Sex Predator Reporting Rules*, L.A. TIMES, June 8, 1997, at M4; Nicholas Riccardi & Jeff Leeds, *Public Getting Information on 63,900 Sex Offenders*, L.A. TIMES, June 27, 1997, at A1.

[13] *Note, Legislative or Judicial Control of Attorneys*, 8 FORDHAM L. REV. 103, 105 (1939).

[14] Blewett Lee, *The Constitutional Power of the Courts over Admission to the Bar*, 13 HARV. L. REV. 233, 245 (1899).

[15] Charles A. Degnan, *Admission to the Bar and the Separation of Powers*, 7 UTAH L. REV. 82, 86 (1960).

and legitimate functions of the courts.[16] The increasing promotion of the concurrent jurisdiction theory is not surprising because other areas of law that crossed both legislative and judicial turf "[f]or decades... [had]been the subject of a concurrent jurisdiction."[17]

But the tension between a doctrine of concurrent jurisdiction and the often conflicting doctrine of inherent and/or exclusive jurisdiction in the separate branches of government sometimes has created constitutional crises. Often courts avoided such direct conflicts by using notions of comity to prevent direct confrontation with legislators. For instance, the Pennsylvania Supreme Court in *Hoopes v. Bradshaw*[18] recognized that the smooth functioning of the judicial branch requires cooperation between the two branches of government.[19] To avoid continuing constitutional battles between the courts and state legislatures, many states amended state constitutions by vesting most of the power to regulate attorneys in state supreme courts. "Since 1945, Alaska, Florida, Georgia, Missouri, New Jersey and Puerto Rico have adopted new constitutions. In every one but that of Georgia rule-making power is expressly granted to the highest court of the jurisdiction."[20] Vesting state supreme courts with the inherent or express constitutional power to regulate attorneys was proposed by the American Bar Association as early as 1938.[21] And in 1927, Pound and Wigmore recognized that unbridled discretion of attorney regulation in the legislature, as opposed to the courts, is problematic in a number of ways:

> [L]egislatures have neither the immediate familiarity with the day-by-day practice of the courts, which would allow them to isolate the pressing problems of procedural revision nor the experience and expertness necessary to the solution of these problems; legislatures are intolerably slow to act and cause even the slightest and most obviously necessary matter of procedural

---

[16] A 1970s note argued for concurrent jurisdiction unless "the regulation in issue unreasonably hampered the judiciary...." *Note, The Inherent Power of the Judiciary to Regulate the Practice of Law – A Proposed Delineation*, 60 MINN. L. REV. 783, 802 (1976). *See also* Charles W. Wolfram, *Lawyer Turf and Lawyer Regulation – The Role of the Inherent-Powers Doctrine*, 12 U. ARK. LITTLEROCK L. J. 1, 4–6 (1989–1990): (arguing that although courts have an "affirmative" inherent powers doctrine to regulate attorneys without legislative enactment, courts have sometimes exceeded their authority in also arguing that they possess a "negative" inherent powers doctrine that provides the court with exclusive authority to regulate attorneys).

[17] A. Leo Levin & Anthony G. Amsterdam, *Legislative Control over Judicial Rule-Making: A Problem in Constitutional Revision*, 107 U. PA. L. REV. 1, 3 (1958).

[18] *Hoopes v. Bradshaw*, 80 A 1098 (1911).

[19] *See also* John M. Mulcahey, *Separation of Powers in Pennsylvania: The Judiciary's Prevention of Legislative Encroachment*, 32 DUQ. L. REV. 539, 541 (1994).

[20] Levin, *supra* note 17, at 5.

[21] American Bar Association, THE IMPROVEMENT OF THE ADMINISTRATION OF JUSTICE 11–12 (3d ed. 1952).

change to be long delayed; legislatures are subject to the influence of other pressures than those which seek the efficient administration of justice and may often push through some particular and ill-advised pet project of an influential legislator while the comprehensive, long-studied proposal of a bar association molders in committee; and legislatures are not held responsible in the public eye for the efficient administration of the courts and hence do not feel pressed to constant reexamination of procedural methods.[22]

Most states now vest the constitutional power to admit and regulate attorneys in the state supreme court; however, most jurisdictions also reserve concurrent jurisdiction with the state legislature in those areas relevant to the police power and protection of consumers that do not directly hamper the essential role of the courts. "Today, as for the last quarter-century, professional discipline of a lawyer in the United States is conducted pursuant to regulations contained in regulatory codes that have been approved in most states by the highest court in the jurisdiction in which the lawyer has been admitted."[23] However, the battle over which governmental entity will regulate the practice of law has in recent years extended to executive administrative committees as well. Contemporary legal process scholarship has demonstrated that attorney regulation now involves "often-overlapping claims to regulatory authority" including regulatory agencies, such as the Securities and Exchange Commission and the New York Stock Exchange.[24] One legal process scholar has catalogued three different classes of organizations that have some regulatory role over the legal profession:

> One class consists of legal institutions with broad missions that include some incidental regulation of lawyers. Judges and juries regulate lawyers through their decisions in legal malpractice and fee-dispute cases. Congress regulates lawyers, primarily through antitrust and consumer protection laws, through fee caps and fee-shifting statutes, and by imposing conditions on the delivery of subsidized legal services. Trial courts regulate litigators through their powers to disqualify counsel, cite for contempt, impose sanctions for procedural violations, and exclude evidence improperly obtained. To varying degrees, the agencies that administer the federal tax, patent, immigration, banking, and securities laws regulate lawyers who practice before them.[25]

In addition, a second class of institutions, such as law firms, regulates partners and associates. And finally, the third set of attorney regulatory institutions are

---

[22] Levin, *supra* note 17, at 10.
[23] RESTATEMENT 3D THE LAW GOVERNING LAWYERS, Section 1, Comment (b) (2000).
[24] Ted Schneyer, *Legal Process Scholarship and the Regulation of Lawyers*, 65 FORDHAM L. REV. 33, 34 (1996).
[25] *Id.* at 35–36.

bar associations that usually act under the auspices of a state supreme court.[26] In addition to the potentially conflicting attorney standards in these three different sets of regulatory forces, some suggest that regulation is infinitely more complicated because the different roles of attorneys, both contextually and normatively, call out for differing standards, rather than universal rules applicable to all attorneys in all legal and nonlegal situations. "[T]he central premise underlying Who Should Regulate Lawyers? ... is that the traditional claim that a uniform set of ethical rules and enforcement practices governs all lawyers in contexts is both descriptively false and normatively unattractive."[27]

But as this chapter illustrates, the battle between the courts, state legislatures, and administrative agencies over attorney regulation continues to be hotly contested in the area of child custody and dependency proceedings. This chapter uses the experiences in Wisconsin and California to illustrate the many separation of powers dilemmas inherent in every state regarding attorney regulation because those jurisdictions provide the largest published history involving these disputes. As the following analysis demonstrates, the Wisconsin model places a heavy emphasis upon the exclusive powers of the Wisconsin Supreme Court to regulate attorneys. In contrast, the California model places greater emphasis upon comity and concurrent regulatory power among the judiciary, legislature, and executive branches and finds separation of powers violations only when interference by another branch of government frustrates the essential and inherent power of the California Supreme Court to function independently.

A. *Wisconsin: Separation of Powers in Regulating Attorneys in Child Custody and Dependency Proceedings*

The Wisconsin Supreme Court has described the separation of powers in that state as one in which each branch has "exclusive core constitutional powers, into which the other branches may not intrude ... a system of 'separateness but interdependence....'"[28] In addition, to ensure that one branch of government does not take or receive an "overabundance" of power, each branch is also limited in the amount of power that it may delegate to another branch because an excessive delegation of power "will undermine the checks and balances built into our system of government," which leads to unaccountability.[29] However, the Wisconsin Supreme Court often avoids confrontation

---

[26] *Id.* at 36–37.
[27] David B. Wilkins, *How Should We Determine Who Should Regulate Lawyers? – Managing and Context in Professional Regulation*, 65 FORDHAM L. REV. 465, 482–484 (1996).
[28] *Panzer v. Doyle*, 680 N. W. 2d 666, 684–685 (2004).
[29] *Id.* at 684–685.

with another branch if the issue is one outside of its core powers and is one that reasonably may be viewed as of concurrent interest. "Sometimes the court will choose, even in an area where it has considerable power, to defer to either the legislative or the executive branch or both. I would call that a form of interbranch diplomacy."[30]

However, the history of separation of powers battles among the Wisconsin Supreme Court, legislature, and executive in relation to the regulation of the practice of law has been anything but a history of compromises and shared power. In fact, the Wisconsin Supreme Court has adamantly protected its "exclusive authority to regulate the practice of law and to discipline members of the Wisconsin bar for professional misconduct."[31] More than in any other state, the Wisconsin Supreme Court has usually refused to apply comity and instead has declared unconstitutional almost every such intrusion by the legislature and/or executive branches into its central core of exclusive power to regulate. For instance, when the executive branch through its Department of Administration (DOA) proposed making the judiciary's computer system part of the state's general computer system, the Wisconsin Supreme Court "simply refuse[d] to permit the DOA to implement its plan...."[32]

And the Wisconsin Supreme Court has declared unconstitutional almost all attempts by the legislature and the executive branches to regulate the areas of child custody and dependency proceedings. The first legislative encroachment into Wisconsin's child dependency cases occurred in 1987 when the legislature imposed a special legal education requirement for attorneys prior to their appointment by the court as guardians ad litem.[33] The Wisconsin Supreme Court declared the mandatory continuing legal education requirement unconstitutional because the legislation trespassed upon the court's core power to regulate attorneys admitted to the practice of law: "[I]t is the province of the judiciary ultimately to decide the fitness of those who practice before it and to regulate their activities following the admission to practice. A

---

[30] Dianne Molvig, *Is Our Judiciary a Co-Equal Branch of Government?*, 70 WIS. LAW. 14, 16–17 (August 1997).

[31] *Leaf v. Supreme Court of the State of Wisconsin*, 979 F. 2d. 589, 592–593 (1992); *State ex. Rel. Fiedler v. Wisconsin Senate*, 454 N. W. 2d 770, 773 (1990).

[32] David A. Saichek, *Shared Powers: Harmony without Hegemony*, 69 WIS. LAW. 3 (October 1996). Former Chief Justice Nathan S. Heffernan stated that he thought that the executive acted "in good faith. They thought our computer system could be taken over; they didn't realize that this would compromise the integrity of the judiciary, that it's a separation of powers issue. But this is a constant threat. And I think that the main thing that the courts have to be worried about is that they are not treated just as another bureaucracy; that they are independent, and that under the constitution they are independent of both the legislature and the governor...." *Id.* at 3.

[33] Section 757.48(1)(a), Stat., as amended by 1987 Wisc. Act 355.

concomitant of this authority is the power to decide whether special training for a particular area is appropriate."[34]

However, the court found that *before* an attorney is admitted to practice, the legislature and courts have concurrent power and interest in establishing the minimum requirements for admission to the practice of law. The court has the inherent power to require minimum attorney qualifications, just as the legislature has the right to regulate preadmitted attorneys under its "power to promote the general welfare."[35] But, the Wisconsin Supreme Court held that once attorneys are admitted, the court retains exclusive, not concurrent, power to regulate them and that "whenever the court's view of the public interest requires it, the court has the power to make appropriate regulations concerning the practice of law in the interest of the administration of justice, and to modify or declare void any such rule, law, or regulation by whomever promulgated, which appears to the court to interfere with the court's control of such practice for such ends."[36]

The Wisconsin Supreme Court stated that it already regulated attorneys' minimal competence, and should an attorney provide incompetent representation, the attorney can be sued for legal malpractice and is also subject to disciplinary action inherent in the judiciary's regulation of the state bar. It held that the legislature's mandatory legal education requirements for guardians ad litem were unconstitutional because they impose "practical impediments to the court's discharge of its substantive decisionmaking authority, and usurps the uniquely judicial function of determining the qualifications of those seeking to represent a minor litigant's interest."[37]

In another separation of powers battle in 1995, the Wisconsin legislature promulgated a statute taking away trial judges' power to appoint counsel for indigent parents in child dependency proceedings.[38] The Wisconsin Supreme Court established a multivariate test for determining whether legislative encroachment upon judicial discretion violates the separation of powers. First, the analysis must determine whether the Wisconsin Constitution grants power to a particular branch of government to regulate the issue in dispute. The court determined that the statute was a budget-saving measure and involved the legislature's general power to "allocate governmental resources."[39] The second prong of the test is to determine whether the regulated area is also within the judiciary's constitutional power. The court found that it was because "[a]ttorneys are officers of the court and

---

[34] *Fiedler v. Wisconsin Senate*, 454 N. W. 2d 770, 772 (1990).
[35] *Id.* at 773.   [36] *Id.* at 773–774.
[37] *Id.* at 774.
[38] 1995 Wis. Act 27, section 244v, amending Wis. Stat. Section 48.23(3).
[39] *Joni B. v. State*, 549 N. W. 2d 411, 413 (1996).

the duty to furnish representation derives from the constitutional provisions that place the responsibility upon the courts."[40] The third prong of the separation of powers analysis is to determine whether a branch of government has exclusive power to regulate the area or whether the area of regulation is concurrent between or among the three branches of government.[41] However, the Wisconsin Supreme Court determined that it need not decide whether the power to appoint counsel is an exclusive judicial power or a shared power because "the level of [legislative] intrusion here is impermissible under either scenario."[42] The court made an interesting distinction between the right of a parent to counsel and the right of the courts to appoint counsel. Although the legislature, pursuant to its budget power, may abrogate a statutory, rather than a constitutional, right to counsel, it may not take away the court's inherent power to appoint counsel for indigent parents in dependency cases. "A court's inherent power to appoint counsel is not derived from an individual litigant's constitutional right to counsel, 'but rather is inherent to serve the interests of the circuit court.'"[43] The Wisconsin Supreme Court held that because indigent parents pose special problems for judges trying to determine the best interests for children, the court must have the power to appoint counsel to be able to function as a fact-finder and to perfect the interests of justice. It thus held the statute unconstitutional because it abrogated courts' inherent power to appoint counsel for indigents in the interest of justice.[44]

In another budget-cutting measure, the Wisconsin legislature passed a statute that set a fee schedule for paying court-appointed guardians ad litem in child dependency actions.[45] However, the Wisconsin Supreme Court had also promulgated a rule of court that provided that

> [n]otwithstanding any provision of the statutes, in all cases where the statutes fix a fee and provide for the payment of expenses of an attorney to be appointed by the court to perform certain designated duties, the court appointing the attorney, after the services of the attorney have been performed and the disbursements incurred, shall fix the amount of his or her compensation for the services and provide for the repayment of disbursements in such sum as the supreme court has specified....[46]

---

[40] *Id.* at 413.

[41] The Wisconsin Supreme Court, for instance, found that the power to revoke probation was a power shared by both the legislature and the courts and held that a statute shifting such review to an administrative committee was not a violation of separation of powers. *State v. Horn*, 594 N. W. 2nd 772 (1999).

[42] *Id.* at 414.   [43] *Id.* at 414–415.

[44] *Id.* at 415.

[45] Wis. Code Sections 48.235(8); 977.08(4m) (1993–1994).

[46] Wisconsin Supreme Court Rule 81.01 (1994); Rule 81.02 (1994).

The legislature set the attorney fees for court-appointed counsel at "$50 per hour for time in court, $40 per hour for time out of court, and $25 per hour for travel time related to the case."[47] The Wisconsin Supreme Court found that both the legislature and the court have inherent power to regulate the payment of attorneys and that the court "should abide by the statutes when it can retain qualified and effective counsel at the statutory rate for a case before it."[48] However, it held that even though the branches share the regulation of court-appointed attorney fees, the statute was unconstitutional on its face because it totally stripped the court of discretion to pay the rate necessary to appoint competent attorneys in individual cases. "A circuit court should... depart from the statutory fee schedule and order compensation at a rate... set by the Supreme Court... or a higher rate when necessary to secure qualified and effective counsel for a case before it."[49] The Wisconsin Supreme Court further declared that "[a] statute within the area of power shared by the two branches, yet outside of the judiciary's exclusive authority, will be constitutional only if it does not unduly burden or substantially interfere with the judicial branch."[50] The court thus extended its power well beyond powers explicitly stated in the state constitution to "inherent, implied and incidental powers" that involve functions necessary to "enable the judiciary to accomplish its constitutionally or legislatively mandated functions."[51] Because the power to appoint counsel is inherent in the court, that power to appoint includes "the power to compensate," and the judiciary "has the ultimate authority to set compensation."[52] The Wisconsin Supreme Court thus found a way to assert its independent power while at the same time suggesting that courts should, if it is in the interest of justice, follow the legislature's determination of the appropriate compensation. The court thus struck a balance between independence and comity among the branches of government. But it substantially limited the historical effect of judicial comity by noting that its "silence" when the legislature or executive branches exercise discretion in an area of inherent court rights indicates "neither judicial acquiescence in the exercise of that power nor a concession that the legislature's power over the subject matter is paramount."[53]

---

[47] *State v. Bayfield*, 531 N. W. 2d 32, 34 (1995).
[48] *Id.* at 35.   [49] *Id.*
[50] *Id.* at 37.
[51] *Id.*; "Intrinsic to the separation of powers is the doctrine of inherent power of the judiciary. This doctrine is based on the principle of necessity; courts must have certain powers to carry out their functions as courts." Shirley S. Abrahamson, *Remarks of the Hon. Shirley S. Abrahamson Before the American Bar Association Commission on Separation of Powers and Judicial Independence*, 12 ST. JOHN'S J. LEGAL COMMENT. 69, 72 (Fall 1996).
[52] *Id.* at 38.   [53] *Id.* at 39.

The Wisconsin Supreme Court's separation of powers jurisprudence promotes a strong and independent judiciary that stands shoulder to shoulder with the legislature and executive branches. That court, most importantly, possesses inherent, express, implied, exclusive, and plenary jurisdiction to regulate attorneys. However, the court has promoted some interdependency among the branches through an application of comity in areas of concurrent jurisdiction involving the exercise of the police power in protecting consumers.

B. *California: Comity over Independence?*

There is no question that comity among coequal branches of government may lead to a smoother and more friendly political environment; however, when one branch of government either acquiesces or is forced into a subsidiary role, the checks and balances inherent in the separation of powers are weakened. As stated by a Maryland court, although "the separation of powers concept may constitutionally encompass a sensible degree of elasticity . . . [it] cannot be stretched to a point where, in effect, there no longer exists a separation of governmental power. . . ."[54] Until the last two decades, the California Supreme Court had adopted an exclusive power model of court regulation of the legal profession much like that in Wisconsin. For instance, in 1926 *In re Crate*[55] involved a power struggle between the California legislature under its newly created State Bar Act and the California courts regarding whether a disqualified attorney would be readmitted. The California Supreme Court, in no uncertain words, determined that the courts, not the legislature through its State Bar Act, had the exclusive power over the regulation of attorneys. The Supreme Court noted that "it is obvious that they [the courts] can possess no inherent powers prior to their existence, and they owe their existence to the Constitution. Their inherent powers are therefore derived from that paper."[56] The court further opined, "[I]f the courts exercise a constitutional function in making provision for a bar, how can the Legislature *divest* the power through the exercise of an assumed police power? It is too clear for words that the Legislature cannot, under the feeble guise of regulation, destroy a constitutional function of either of the other departments of government."[57]

---

[54] *Attorney General of Maryland v. Waldron*, 426 A. 2d 929, 933 (Maryland 1981) [holding unconstitutional a statute prohibiting retired judges who accept pensions from practicing law for compensation because the regulation of attorneys is an inherent power of the court and the statute was not reasonably related to its legislative goal].

[55] *In re Crate*, 273 P. 617 (1928), rv'd, 279 P. 131 (Cal. 1929).

[56] *Id.* at 620.   [57] *Id.* at 624.

The California Supreme Court jealously guarded its inherent and exclusive power to regulate attorneys in a series of cases through the 1980s. For instance, in 1935 the court determined that the legislature violated separation of powers by reinstating to the practice of law attorneys convicted of felonies, an act that the court described as "tantamount to the vacating of a judicial order by legislative mandate."[58] The court continued its trend of exclusive rights analysis in 1978 when it determined that the legislature violated the separation of powers by promulgating a statute giving nonlawyers the right to appear in municipal court because it infringed upon the judiciary's exclusive right to admit attorneys to the practice of law.[59] And in 1981 the court held that the legislature exceeded its police power by providing in the California Labor Code that workers' compensation judges could suspend attorneys from practicing law in those courts.[60]

But the California Supreme Court's historical assertion regarding its exclusive and plenary power to regulate the practice of law was dramatically pared back by two cases decided in the 1990s and the early twenty-first century. First, in *Santa Clara County Counsel Attorneys Association v. Woodside*[61] the court renewed the concept of concurrent jurisdiction over some areas of attorney regulation because the legislature, through its police power, has an interest in protecting consumers. The case involved governmental county counsel who filed a job action against the county. The California Supreme Court held that a statute that permitted the firing of attorneys at will was unconstitutional. The court noted that the legislature may "'put reasonable restrictions upon the constitutional functions of the courts provided they do not defeat or materially impair the exercise of those functions.'"[62] The California Superior Court delineated a series of questions that must be answered to determine whether legislation unconstitutionally encroaches upon the court's inherent and plenary right to regulate attorneys:

(1) Is the statute "of general application, which does not affect the traditional areas of attorney admission, disbarment and discipline"?
(2) Does the statute "permit an attorney to act in such a way as to seriously violate the integrity of the attorney-client relationship, so as to 'materially impair' the functioning of the courts"?
(3) Does "a direct and fundamental conflict" exist between the statute and "attorneys' settled ethical obligations, as embodied in this state's

---

[58] *In re Lavine*, 41 P. 2d 161, 163 (Cal. 1935).
[59] *Merco Construction Engineers, Inc. v. Municipal Court*, 581 P. 2d 636 (Cal 1978).
[60] *Hustedt v. Worker's Compensation Appeals Board*, 636 P. 2d 1139, 1146 (1981).
[61] *Santa Clara County Counsel Attorneys Association v. Woodside*, 7 Cal. 4th 525; 28 Cal. Rptr. 2d 617 (1994).
[62] *Id.* at 543.

Rules of Professional Conduct or some well-established common law rule"?

And in *Obrien v. Jones*[63] in 2000 the California Supreme Court found that two statutes, which provided that the Governor, the Senate Committee on Rules, and the Speaker of the Assembly shall appoint members of the State Bar court that hears attorney disciplinary actions, did not violate separation of powers because those appointments do not interfere with the court's regulation of attorneys because of the "numerous structural and procedural safeguards ... that exist both within the attorney discipline system and within the State Bar Court appointment process established by this court"; these safeguards include the following: (1) the Supreme Court must review the findings of the State Bar court, (2) the statutory qualifications for State Bar judges are consistent with those established by the Supreme Court, (3) the executive and legislative applicants will be evaluated by the court's Application Evaluation and Nomination Committee, and (4) the appointment of judges to the State Bar court does not involve an "immediate threat to [a] liberty [interest]."[64] The California Supreme Court thus held that executive or legislative decisions that are consistent with Supreme Court standards and that are reviewable by the court do not necessarily violate separation of powers.

In 1998 the California legislature modified *Welfare & Institutions Code Section 317(e)* to strip from abused children in child dependency proceedings the normal attorney-client relationship required for all other competent California citizens. *Section 317(e)* was quickly drafted and passed with little debate after a high-profile child abuse case.[65] The legislature stripped from attorneys the right to argue a child's stated custody preference, even if the attorney found the child competent to make such a decision, if "to the best of his or her [the child's attorney's] knowledge, that return conflicts with the protection and safety of the minor." The statute was thus arguably inconsistent with the decades of Supreme Court opinions and bar opinions requiring attorneys to provide competent clients zealous, competent, and loyal advocacy.[66] Whittier Law School Legal Policy Clinic brought a writ to declare the amendments to *Section 317(e)* unconstitutional based upon the separation

---

[63] *Obrien v. Jones*, 96 Cal. Rptr. 2d 205 (2000).

[64] *Id.* at 208–209; 213, 215–216, 230.

[65] Lance Helms, a 2-year-old, was allegedly killed by the father's girlfriend after he was returned to his father's home. "At a spirited fact-finding hearing on how to prevent such deaths, Sen. Daniel Boatwright (D-Concord) said 'the law failed this child' and criticized those connected to the case, especially ... Lance Helms' court-appointed lawyer." Mark Gladstone, *Child Welfare System Blasted*, L.A. TIMES, January 20, 1996, at B1.

[66] As early as 1902 the court noted the duty of zealous representation. *People v. Puttman*, 61 P. 961, 962 (1902), The California State Bar has also mandated zealous advocacy in both civil

of powers because the California legislature had rewritten the nature of the attorney-client relationship in child dependency cases in a manner that was in direct conflict with the Supreme Court's dictates.[67] The writ argued that none of the standards in *Santa Clara* were met indicating concurrent jurisdiction in defining the attorney-client relationship. First, *Section 317(d)* is not a statute of "general application," but rather focuses exclusively upon a small segment of attorneys representing children in dependency proceedings. Second, forcing the child's attorney to remain silent and not zealously argue the child's case "would permit an attorney to act in such a way as to seriously violate the integrity of the attorney-client relationship. . . ." And finally, *Section 317(e)* creates an absolute conflict with "settled ethical obligations, as embodied in this state's Rules of Professional conduct or some well-established common law rule."[68]

The writ also argued that the amendments to *Section 317(e)* violated the separation of powers test enunciated in *Obrien*. First, unlike in *Obrien*, the legislature in *Section 317(e)* set out a completely different standard of lawyer-client zealousness, competence, and loyalty than the standards set by the California Supreme Court. Attorneys were thus trapped in a Catch-22 because they must either violate the statute and risk contempt or violate the Supreme Court's dictates and risk disbarment. Second, unlike in the *Obrien* case, child dependency proceedings do involve the liberty interest in family association between parents, children, and relatives. And finally, unlike the *Obrien* case in which the court must review all decisions by State Bar court judges, the Supreme Court is not required to review any dependency trial court findings. Thus, it will never see the vast majority of cases in which the legislature stripped abused children of their right to zealous and competent counsel. The writ argued that because amended *Section 317(e)* results in "a material impairment of the court's inherent power over admission and discipline" of attorneys, it violated the state separation of powers clause.

The California Supreme Court did not decide the separation of powers issue because it determined that the issue was not yet ripe and dismissed the writ.[69] However, the writ demonstrates the California legislature's continuing foray into the regulation of attorneys. We will have to wait for another case to determine the constitutionality of *Section 317(3)*.

---

and criminal cases. *In the Matter of Kopinski* (1994) 2 Cal. State Bar Ct. 716, 728. In addition, *California Business & Professions Code Section 6068(e)* mandates attorney loyalty.

[67] *Whittier Law School Legal Policy Clinic v. Attorney General*, Case Number G031321, California Fourth Appellate District, Division 3. The author was also the author of the writ.

[68] Writ, at 16–18.

[69] The writ was denied as unripe on June 10, 2003.

But it is not just the California legislature that is continuously chipping away at the California Supreme Court's inherent power to regulate attorneys. From the 1990s to the present, the court itself, under the leadership of Chief Justice Ronald George, has moved further toward a model of concurrent jurisdiction over attorney regulation and a model that views comity as a central goal of governmental branch interdependence. To understand the genesis of this shift from exclusive court authority, it is necessary to understand the relationship between the Chief Justice of the California Supreme Court and the California Judicial Council.

The California Judicial Council is a constitutional body authorized pursuant to *California Constitution, Article VI, Section 6* "to make recommendations to the courts to improve the administration of justice."[70] Perhaps the most interesting structural element of this constitutional body is that the Chief Justice of the California Supreme Court is a member.[71] Although the Judicial Council is an autonomous body, its power is subsidiary to the other three branches of government because its pronouncements cannot be "inconsistent with statute" and presumably with decisions of the California Supreme Court. Its mandate is to "survey judicial business and make recommendations to the courts, make recommendations annually to the Governor and Legislature, adopt rules for court administration, practice and procedure, and perform other functions prescribed by statute."[72] Historically, few separation of powers conflicts have arisen between the California Judicial Council, the Supreme Court, and the legislature because most Chief Justices of the Supreme Court, as members, have been able to mollify such conflicts. However, when the current Chief Justice of the California Supreme Court, Ronald George, became a member of the Judicial Council, the constitutional picture changed radically. Although the legislature lacks the power to order the California Supreme Court to act within the court's inherent and exclusive jurisdiction in running judicial operations, the legislature can order the Judicial Council to perform certain tasks. If the Chief Justice, as a member of the Judicial Council, does not stand up for judicial independence, then the legislature can do indirectly what it cannot do directly by ordering the Judicial Council to perform functions that would violate separation of powers if conducted directly by the legislature. One author has noted that since the ascension of Chief Justice Ronald George as a member of the Judicial Council, it has assumed "a larger role in the administration and operation of our

---

[70] *Wisniewski v. Clary*, 120 Cal. Rptr. 176, 179 (Cal. Ct. App. 1975).

[71] *California Constitution*, art. VI, section 6 provides that "[t]he Judicial Council consists of the Chief Justice and one other judge of the Supreme Court...."

[72] *California Constitution*, art. VI, section 6.

state courts... [and the Judicial Council] has "taken power away from local courts."[73] The legislature has therefore been able to enact legislative changes in the judiciary indirectly through the Judicial Council that historically would have not been tolerated by the California Supreme Court. It is obvious that having the Chief Justice of the California Supreme Court serve as a member of the Judicial Council adds legitimacy to the Judicial Council's actions and probably reduces the chances that the Supreme Court will actively oppose those pronouncements because doing so would, in effect, allege that the Chief Justice, as well as the other members of the Judicial Council, violated separation of powers. Thus, actions by the Judicial Council, unlike direct actions by the legislature, have a form of de facto Supreme Court comity even though there is no assurance that a majority of the members of the Supreme Court agree with the views of the Chief Justice. Although it is perhaps pragmatically beneficial to have the Chief Justice as a member of the Judicial Council, it nonetheless often creates a constitutional dilemma and dilutes the court's plenary, inherent, and often exclusive power to regulate the legal profession.

One of the most interesting and as of yet unlitigated separation of powers battles among the California legislature, Judicial Council, and the Supreme Court occurred in 1997 when the legislature ordered the Judicial Council to "adopt rules of court regarding the appointment of competent counsel in dependency proceedings."[74] The Judicial Council responded by promulgating *California Rules of Court, Rule 1438* that set the following educational requirements, practical experience, and mandatory legal education as a prerequisite for attorney eligibility to be appointed by trial courts to represent indigent parties in child dependency proceedings:[75]

(1) "Only those attorneys who have completed a minimum of eight hours of training or education in the area of juvenile dependency, or who have sufficient recent experience in dependency proceedings in which the attorney has demonstrated competency, shall be appointed to represent parties."[76]

(2) "'Competent counsel' means an attorney who is a member in good standing of the State Bar of California, who has participated in training

---

[73] Rex S. Heinke, *The Transformation of the Sate Courts: The Association Is Moving to Participate More Fully in the Judicial Council Rule-Making Process*, L.A. LAW., April, 2001.

[74] *California Welfare and Institutions Code Section 317.6(a)(1997)*.

[75] In 1976 the California legislature gave the Judicial Council the power to draft rules regarding practice and procedure for the juvenile courts. Hon. Phil S. Gibson, *Chief Justice Urges Effective Plan to Give Courts Rule-Making* Power, 15 CAL. ST. B.J. 331 (1940); Harry N. Scheiber, *Innovation, Resistance, and Change: A History of Judicial Reform and the California Courts, 1960–1990*, 66 S. CAL. L. REV. 2049, 2086–2087 (1993).

[76] *California Rules of Court, Rule 1438(b)(3)*.

in the law of juvenile dependency, and who demonstrates adequate forensic skills, knowledge and comprehension of the statutory scheme, the purposes and goals of dependency proceedings, and procedures for filing petitions for extraordinary writs."[77]

(3) "Within every three years attorneys are expected to complete at least 8 hours of continuing education related to dependency proceedings."[78]

There is no doubt that had a rule similar to *Rule 1438* been promulgated in Wisconsin that the Wisconsin Supreme Court would have declared it unconstitutional because it would have stripped from the court the power to define attorney competence and to specify minimal educational requirements, and the right to choose whichever attorney the court wanted to represent indigent parties.

It is also clear that the supreme courts in several other jurisdictions also would have declared the rule unconstitutional. For instance, the Oklahoma Supreme Court in *Archer v. Ogden*[79] declared unconstitutional a statute that stripped nonresident attorneys admitted to the Oklahoma bar from practicing in that state because "once admitted to the [Bar] Association, [attorneys] shall be permitted to practice law within all courts of this State. . . ."[80] In *Ball v. Roberts*[81] the Arkansas Supreme Court declared unconstitutional a statute that required attorneys to have recent criminal law experience and education to qualify for appointment as a criminal defense attorney. In *Succession of Wallace*[82] the Louisiana Supreme Court held that it has the exclusive power to define the attorney-client relationship and that a statute that changed the rules for attorney withdrawals in cases violated the separation of powers. The Supreme Court of Illinois in *People v. Finley*[83] struck down a rule requiring greater expertise for attorneys than that required by the court.[84] It is therefore clear that in states that assert exclusive power in the state supreme court to regulate the practice of law, and in California prior to the 1990s, *California Rules of Court, Rule 1438* would be declared unconstitutional as a violation of the separation of powers.

However, it is unclear how the current California Supreme Court will rule once someone challenges the additional attorney requirements under

---

[77] *California Rules of Court, Rule 1438(b)(1).*   [78] *California Rules of Court, Rule 1438(b)(3).*
[79] *Archer v. Ogden*, 600 P. 2d 1223 (Oklahoma 1979).
[80] *Id.* at 1226.
[81] *Ball v. Roberts*, 722 S. W. 2d 829 (Arkansas 1987).
[82] *Succession of Wallace*, 574 So. 2d 348 (Louisiana 1991).
[83] *People v. Finley*, 519 N. E. 2d 898 (Illinois 1988).
[84] And the Maine Supreme Court in *In re Honorable James P. Dunleavy*, 838 A. 2d 338 (Maine 2003), held that even if the legislature creates a new court, it cannot usurp the Supreme Court's inherent authority to regulate the professional conduct of judges.

Rule 1438. The court must first determine whether the Judicial Council is a co-equal branch of government and whether it can order the courts to act. Although *Article VI, Section 6 of the California Constitution* clearly states that the Judicial Council is subordinate to the legislature because its rules may not be inconsistent with statutes, it is silent regarding conflicts between Judicial Council rules and Supreme Court decisions. Some have argued that the Judicial Council is subservient to the court because the California Constitution merely provides that the Council "shall survey judicial business and make recommendations to the courts," not give orders to the courts. Two lower appellate courts have held that the Judicial Council's rules may not conflict with courts' interpretations of the state constitution.[85] But even if the Judicial Council lacks the power to order the courts to accept its new rules defining competent counsel in child dependency proceedings, the court must look to the separation of powers problem in the legislature mandating the Judicial Counsel to promulgate attorney regulations inconsistent with those of the court. If the court decides this issue consistently with its past cases, it will hold *Rule 1348* unconstitutional as a separation of powers violation because it totally strips courts' power to appoint attorneys who do not meet the Judicial Council's standards of attorney competence.

II. CONCLUSION

Although this chapter's discussion of separation of powers in relation to the inherent, plenary, exclusive, and/or concurrent powers of the executive, legislature, courts, and administrative agencies to regulate the practice of law may seem merely academic, in reality, it is an essential body of law for every attorney practicing in child custody and dependency proceedings to understand. As more conflicting ethical obligations are foisted upon them from a variety of powerful sources, attorneys need to understand how to formulate strategies, defenses, and attacks upon unreasonable ethical rules, minimum educational requirements, and mandatory continuing legal education standards. As the previous discussion has illustrated, custody and dependency attorneys not only have a self-interest in the rules that define the attorney-client relationship but they also have an obligation to their clients because those rules might substantially dilute the attorney's obligations and place clients in jeopardy of losing the precious promises of competency, confidentiality, loyalty, and zealousness. It is incumbent upon each of us who practices in these highly visible and emotional proceedings to address

---

[85] *In re Jeanette H.*, 275 Cal. Rptr. 9, 15 (1990); *Cantillon v. Superior Court*, 309 P. 2d 890 (1957).

proposed changes in the rules of ethics and procedure, which form the basis of the law affecting children. Whether it be a letter in response to a state bar association proposal, a supreme court rule change, a proposed legislative enactment, or an amendment to administrative rules, we should individually and collectively provide our expert input at each stage in the process of ethical rules evolution. We owe ourselves and our clients no less.

APPENDIX A

National Association of Counsel for Children Standards

NACC Recommendations for Representation of Children in Abuse and Neglect Cases

National Association of Counsel for Children

*NACC **Recommendations for Representation of Children in Abuse and Neglect Cases*** was produced as part of the NACC's objective to establish the practice of law for children as a legitimate profession and legal specialty. As part of that objective, the NACC periodically produces standards of practice or guidelines for the representation of children.

The document was adopted by a unanimous vote of the NACC Board of Directors on April 28, 2001.

Copyright 2001

CONTENTS

EXECUTIVE SUMMARY

NACC RECOMMENDATIONS FOR REPRESENTATION OF CHILDREN IN ABUSE AND NEGLECT CASES
I. Introduction
II. Children's Legal Representation Policy
   A. Overview
   B. Child Welfare Cases
   C. Private Custody and Adoption Cases
III. Needs Checklist for Children Involved in Abuse and Neglect Cases
   A. Systemic Safeguards
   B. Advocacy Duties
   C. Advocacy Issues
IV. Representation Models
   A. Advocate Directed Representation
      1. The Attorney Guardian *ad Litem* Hybrid

        2. The Lay Guardian *ad Litem* Model
        3. The "Two Distinct Lawyer Roles" Model
    B. Client Directed Representation
        1. Traditional Attorney
        2. Child's Attorney (ABA Standards Model)
        3. Child's Attorney (ABA/NACC Model)
V. Resources

EXECUTIVE SUMMARY

The lack of standards of practice or guidelines for attorneys representing children in child protection proceedings has frequently been cited as a major cause of substandard and ineffective legal representation of children. Unlike more traditional areas of practice where the model of representation and the lawyer code of conduct are essentially uniform from state to state, the practice of law for children has no commonly accepted uniform model or code, and many states provide inadequate guidance for attorneys doing this work. This is the case in part because the practice of law for children is a unique and relatively recent development, and because the evolution has occurred on a state by state basis. Additionally, there has been significant disagreement as to whether representation for children should take a traditional client directed ("expressed wishes"), or an advocate directed ("best interests") form, making it difficult to adopt a model.

Important progress was made toward the creation of a uniform model of representation with the creation of the *ABA Standards of Practice for Lawyers Who Represent Children in Abuse and Neglect Cases* in 1996. Still, jurisdictions struggle to adopt clear and comprehensive guidelines for children's attorneys, frequently because of the long-standing debate over the form of representation.

The *NACC Recommendations for Representation of Children in Abuse and Neglect Cases* is a document designed to assist jurisdictions in the selection and implementation of a model of child representation. Rather than urging jurisdictions to choose a particular model, this document sets out a checklist of children's needs that should be met by whatever representation scheme is chosen. It is the NACC's hope that this approach will allow jurisdictions to focus on what matters, serving the child client, and avoid becoming mired in the debate over best interests and expressed wishes.

The NACC believes that children's legal service needs can be met by both client directed ("expressed wishes") and advocate directed ("best interest") models of representation. In an effort to help jurisdictions understand various models, this document includes a section describing the various models of representation.

Whatever form of representation jurisdictions choose, the NACC believes that every child subject to a child protection proceeding must be provided an independent, competent, and zealous attorney, trained in the law of child protection and the art of trial advocacy, with adequate time and resources to handle the case.

NACC RECOMMENDATIONS FOR REPRESENTATION OF CHILDREN IN ABUSE AND NEGLECT CASES

I. INTRODUCTION

This document is designed to assist children's attorneys, courts, and policy makers working to improve the legal representation of children. The focus is on the representation of children in abuse and neglect proceedings. The document also has application in private custody and adoption matters.

Rather than prescribing one specific model of representation, this document provides a policy framework for the legal representation of children, followed by a checklist of children's needs that representation should meet, whatever form of representation states choose. The document describes various models of representation in an effort to help the reader appreciate the strengths and weaknesses of each.

The NACC is aware of the debate in the child advocacy community over the two primary models of representing children – the attorney guardian *ad litem* (advocate directed "best interests" model) and the traditional attorney (client directed "expressed wishes" model). While this debate can be useful, the NACC suggests that rather than spending time and resources debating the merits of the various models, states should focus on ensuring that the model of representation used meets the children's needs checklist.

II. CHILDREN'S LEGAL REPRESENTATION POLICY

A. OVERVIEW

The NACC believes that each child must be valued as a unique human being, regardless of race, ethnicity, religion, age, social class, physical or mental disability, gender, or sexual orientation. Each child is vested with certain fundamental rights, including a right to physical and emotional health and safety. In order to achieve the physical and emotional well being of children, we must promote legal rights and remedies for children. This includes empowering children by ensuring that courts hear and consider their views in proceedings that affect their lives.

Children's attorneys play a critical role in empowering children and ensuring that children's views are heard in legal proceedings. Outcomes in our adversarial process are directly tied to the quality of legal representation. Additionally, the presence of children's attorneys is critical to ensuring the timeliness of proceedings.

The NACC believes that attorneys representing children should have a combination of knowledge, training, experience, and ability which allows them to effectively discharge their duties to their clients. The NACC supports federal, state, and local programs to enhance the competence of these attorneys.

B. CHILD WELFARE CASES

The NACC believes that in order for justice to be done in child abuse and neglect related court proceedings, all parties, including children, must be represented by independent *legal* counsel.[1] The children who are the subjects of these proceedings are usually the most profoundly affected by the decisions made, and these children are usually the least able to voice their views effectively on their own. In many jurisdictions, however, courts do not appoint independent attorneys for all children in abuse and neglect related proceedings. NACC believes that federal, state, and local law must mandate that independent attorneys be appointed to represent the interests of children in all such proceedings.

C. PRIVATE CUSTODY AND ADOPTION CASES

The NACC believes that while legal representation is not required for every child who is the subject of a child custody determination, the judge *should* appoint an attorney to represent the child in certain cases: when there are certain substantive allegations that make child representation necessary – i.e., when there is an allegation of child neglect or abuse (physical, sexual, or emotional) by a parent or household member, when there is a culture of

---

[1] The U.S. Department of Health and Human Services supports this principle. Adoption 2002: The President's Initiative on Adoption and Foster Care. Guidelines for Public Policy and State Legislation Governing Permanence for Children, U.S. Dept. of HHS ACF ACYF Children's Bureau, 1999.

violence between the parents, when there is an allegation of substance abuse by a parent, when there are allegations of non-paternity, or when there is an allegation of or fear about child snatching – as well as when there are certain procedural situations which make child representation necessary – e.g., when a child will be a witness or when the case develops an extremely adversarial nature. In addition, the judge *should consider* appointing an attorney to represent the child in certain other cases: when there is an allegation of mental illness on the part of a parent, when a custodial parent is relocating geographically, when child representation can reduce undue harm to the child from the litigation itself, when the child has exceptional physical or mental health needs, when the child expresses a strong desire to make his or her opinions known to the judge, when there is *a pro se* parent, when there is a third-party custody action against a parent (e.g., by a grandparent), or when the failure to appoint a representative for the child would otherwise impede the judge's capacity to decide the case properly. (Attorneys can be instrumental in ensuring that judges have the necessary data upon which to make an informed decision.)

III. NEEDS CHECKLIST FOR CHILDREN

The NACC encourages jurisdictions to adopt a system of legal representation of children which satisfies the following checklist. The representation scheme should ensure that each of the following children's rights or needs are satisfied through a combination of systemic safeguards, advocacy duties, and basic advocacy issues.

A. SYSTEMIC SAFEGUARDS

1. Children need competent, independent, and zealous attorneys. The system of representation must require the appointment of competent, independent, zealous attorneys for every child at every stage of the proceedings. The same attorney should represent the child for as long as the child is subject to the court's jurisdiction.

Comment A: Competence is the foundation of all legal representation. The fundamental requirements of competency as defined in each jurisdiction, combined with the ability to function without constraint or obligation to any party other than the child client, are of paramount importance. (See, ABA Model Rules of Professional Conduct (Model Rules): Preamble; 1.14(a); ABA Model Code of Professional Responsibility (Model Code): EC 7-1; EC 7-12; ABA Standards of Practice for Lawyers who Represent Children in Abuse and Neglect Cases (ABA Standards): Preface; A-1.)

Comment B: Competent representation includes knowledge, skill, thoroughness, and preparation. This includes knowledge of placements and services available for the child, and services available to the child's family. (See, Model Rule: 1.1; Model Code DR 6-101(A)(1)(2); ABA Standards B-1; C.) Jurisdictions should provide special initial and periodic training to all attorneys in child welfare proceedings covering substantive law (federal, state, statutory, regulatory, and case law), procedure, trial advocacy, child welfare and child development.

Comment C: Continuity of representation is important to the child. The same lawyer should represent the child for as long as the child is under the jurisdiction of the court. Temporary substitution of counsel, although often unavoidable, should be discouraged. Any substitute counsel must be familiar with the child and the child's case.

2. Children need attorneys with adequate time and resources. The system of representation must include reasonable caseload limits and at the same time provide adequate compensation for attorneys representing children.

Comment A: The NACC recommends that a full time attorney represent no more than 100 individual clients at a time, assuming a caseload that includes clients at various stages of cases, and recognizing that some clients may be part of the same sibling group. This is the same cap recommended by the U.S. Dept. of HHS Children's Bureau and the American Bar Association. One hundred cases averages to 20 hours per case in a 2000-hour year.

Comment B: For the sake of the child client and the interests of the system, attorneys must be provided appropriate and reasonable compensation. The NACC adopts the following position of the Dept. of HHS on this point: "Primary causes of inadequate legal representation of the parties in child welfare cases are low compensation and excessive caseloads. Reasonable compensation of attorneys for this important work is essential. Rather than a flat per case fee, compensate lawyers for time spent. This will help to increase their level of involvement in the case and should help improve the image of attorneys who are engaged in this type of work. When attorneys are paid a set fee for complicated and demanding cases, they cope either by providing less service than the child-client requires or by providing representation on a pro bono or minimum wage basis. Neither of these responses is appropriate. Rates should also reflect the level of seniority and level of experience of the attorneys. In some offices, lawyers handling child welfare cases receive lower pay than other attorneys. This is inappropriate. Compensation of attorneys handling children's cases should be on a par with other lawyers in the office handling legal matters of similar demand and complexity. The need for improved compensation is not for the purpose of benefiting the attorney, but

Appendix A. National Association of Counsel for Children 173

rather to ensure that the child receives the intense and expert legal services required."

3. Children need attorneys who understand their role and duties. The system of representation of children must be well defined by statute, bar standards, administrative guidelines, supreme court directive or other documents such that every attorney appointed for a child can understand his/her precise role and duties, and such that an attorney can be held accountable for performance of those duties.

Comment: It is helpful here to distinguish between role and duties. Role refers to whether, for example, the attorney is client directed (traditional attorney model or child's attorney models) while duties refer to those actions to be taken by the attorney (investigation, calling witnesses, etc.). Although duties are in part dependent on role, most commentators agree that certain fundamental duties should apply regardless of role. See ABA and ABA/NACC Revised Standards C Actions to be Taken.

4. Children need an opportunity to present their positions to the court through counsel. The system of representation must provide the child with an opportunity for his/her needs and wishes to be expressed to the court.

Comment: Children have an independent perspective and may have information and positions to present to the court on a wide range of issues including but extending beyond the issue of placement. Other parties and the court may otherwise be unaware of the child's perspective or of how certain decisions subjectively affect the child.

5. Children need confidential communication with their attorneys. The attorney has a duty to explain the extent of confidentiality in developmentally appropriate language.

Comment A: Every child should have the right to communicate confidentially with the representative. (See, Model Rules: 1.6, 3.7; Model Code: DR 4-101; 5-102; ABA Standards: A-1; Comment B-2(2).)

Comment B: But see Alaska Ethics Op. 854. Some jurisdictions include attorneys as mandatory reporters, and pure confidentiality may be precluded with a GAL – advocate directed representation system.

6. Children need to be involved as litigants in the entire litigation process, including any post disposition, termination of parental rights, and adoption proceedings. The system of representation must recognize the child as a party to the litigation and must include the child in all phases of the litigation, including the opportunity to participate in arguments and jury selection where applicable, offer exhibits, call witnesses, examine and cross examine

witnesses and engage in motions and discovery processes. The child must also be given notice of all proceedings and copies of all pleadings.

Comment: The child should be physically present early in the proceedings, so as to allow all parties and their representatives the opportunity to become acquainted with the child as an individual. Although the child's presence may not be required at every court hearing, it should not be waived by the representative, unless the child has already been introduced to the court and his/her presence is not required by law, custom, or practice in that jurisdiction. Every child should be notified through counsel of every court hearing, every agency meeting, and every case conference or negotiation among the various professionals involved in the case and the child's attorney should be notified concerning any change in the child's welfare, placement, education, or status. Every child should be considered a party to the litigation, and should therefore, be entitled to any and all benefits under the law granted to any other party. Every child should have access to sufficient information to allow his/her representative to provide competent representation including the child's representative having access to social services, psychiatric, psychological, drug and alcohol, medical, law enforcement, school and other records relevant to the case, and opportunity for interviewing child welfare caseworkers, foster parents and other caretakers, school personnel, health professionals, law enforcement, and other persons with relevant information. This access may require the representative to file motions for discovery, subpoenas, subpoenas duces tecum, depositions and interrogatories, according to the discovery mechanisms an opportunity to appeal an adverse ruling. available in the jurisdiction. Every child should have the opportunity to present his/her witnesses in the court proceedings. This requires the representative to investigate facts, identify and communicate with witnesses, and issue subpoenas to ensure that witnesses appear in court.

7. Children need judicial review of adverse decisions. The system of representation must provide an opportunity to appeal an adverse ruling.

Comment: Children need to have access to the court after the adjudication occurs. This may require the representative to forego informal resolution of issues at the review stage of the litigation. See *State ex rel. Jeanette H.*, 529 S.E. 2d 865 (2000).

8. Children need to be able to hold their attorneys accountable. The system of representation must provide recourse for ineffective assistance of counsel.

Comment: Every child should be able to hold the representative accountable for providing less than competent representation.

9. Children need an attorney with a fair opportunity to be effective in the court system. The system of representation must include a court system that devotes adequate time and resources to cases.

Comment: Courts cannot be "rubber stamp" agencies for social service agencies and must be equipped to handle caseloads responsibly. See, *Resource Guidelines, Improving Court Practice in Child Abuse and Neglect Cases*, National Council of Juvenile and Family Court Judges, 1995 NCJFCJ, Reno, NV.

B. ADVOCACY DUTIES

1. Children need attorneys who fully understand their cases. The attorney must perform a full and independent case investigation.

Comment: The child's attorney has a duty of full investigation of the case. (See, Model Rule: 4.2; Model Code: DR 7-104 (A) (1); ABA Standards: C-2(4); C-6.)

2. Children need meaningful communication with their attorneys. The attorney must observe the child, and dependent upon the child's age and capabilities, interview the child. The attorney must engage in regular and meaningful communication with the child. Children need to participate in making decisions that affect their cases. The attorney has a duty to involve the child client in the process, whether under a client directed model or advocate directed model. The attorney has a duty to explain his/her role to the child in developmentally appropriate language.

Comment A: Under a client directed model, the scope of representation by the child's attorney includes the duty to abide by the client's decision concerning the objectives of the representation. (See, Model Rule: 1.2(a); Model Code: DR 7101(A)(1); EC 7-7; EC 7-8; ABA Standards: B-4.)

Comment B: This is a universal need, and it applies whether or not the child is pre-verbal. Visual encounters with children who are represented, even with pre-verbal children, are crucial to the representation. Otherwise, the representative is limited by relying upon the mental impressions of third parties. The child's attorney has a duty of effective, thorough, and developmentally appropriate communication with the client, including the duty to meet with the client. (See, Model Rules: 1.4 (a), (b); Model Code: EC 7-8; 9-2; ABA Standards: C-1; A-3; B-1(5); D-2; E-2; F-4.)

Comment C: Children need education about the law and all options available under the legal system. This need is restricted to developmentally appropriate clients, capable of communication.

Comment D: The child client must be informed about the responsibilities and obligations of the representative, as well as the ability and requirements of the representative to accomplish these things.

3. Children need loyal attorneys. The child's attorney is prohibited from representation that would constitute a conflict of interest.

Comment: Attorneys must be aware of the potential for conflict while representing a sibling group. Additionally, the child's attorney must be sensitive to the age and maturity of the client where waiver is an issue. (See, Model Rules: 1.7; Model Code: DR 5-101 (A); 5-105(A), (C); 5-107 (B); ABA Standards: B-2(2).)

4. Children need the full benefit of legal counsel. The attorney must provide competent, independent and zealous representation for each client. The attorney must have adequate time and resources to devote to the child's case, and to understanding his/her role and duties, insuring confidentiality, and full active participation in all stages of the child's case.

C. ADVOCACY ISSUES

1. Children need permanence. The attorney must advocate for timely resolution and permanent resolution (absent compelling reasons to the contrary) of the case.

Comment: The child's attorney has a duty of diligent and prompt representation, and a duty to expedite litigation, especially where placement of a young child is at issue. (See, Model Rule: 1.3; 3.2; Model Code: DR 6-101(A)(3); EC 6-4; ABA Standards: B-1(4); C-6.)

2. Children need their immediate and basic needs met. The attorney must advocate for food, shelter, clothing, and safety, including a safe temporary placement where necessary and for educational, medical, mental health, and dental needs.

Comment: The child's most immediate physical needs must be addressed and should be the highest priority for the child's representative. After the immediate needs of sustaining life have been addressed, the child's education, mental health, medical, and dental needs must be addressed. Children's attorneys should act as a kind of "watchdog" for the children's needs, insuring that services are provided.

3. Children need family relationships. The attorney must advocate for continuation of appropriate familial relationships and family preservation services where appropriate.

Appendix A. National Association of Counsel for Children

Comment: Without jeopardizing the child's physical or emotional safety, arrangements to maintain familial relationships (including siblings) which are not deemed to be harmful to the child should be established as soon as practicable. Family services may include visitation and services for family members: parenting education, medical and mental health care, drug and alcohol treatment, housing, etc. Such family services may also be appropriate to continue other meaningful relationships and ongoing activities where feasible.

4. Children need to be protected from unnecessary harm that can result from legal proceedings. The attorney must advocate for the utilization of court processes that minimize harm to the child, and make certain that the child is properly prepared and emotionally supported where the child is a witness.

IV. REPRESENTATION MODELS

The following representation models are presented to assist states in evaluating and formulating models of representation. States should consider the requirements of the federal Child Abuse Prevention and Treatment Act (CAPTA) regarding the appointment of representation for the child. The U.S. Department of Health and Human Services, Children's Bureau has indicated that although CAPTA requires a GAL best interests representative, that role may be filled by either an attorney GAL or more traditional client directed attorney.

A. ADVOCATE DIRECTED REPRESENTATION

1. THE ATTORNEY GUARDIAN *AD LITEM* HYBRID 6 MODEL.

This model provides an attorney to represent the child and instructs the attorney to represent the child's "best interests." The attorney GAL advocates for a result which he/she believes (not necessarily what the child believes) is in the child's "best interests." Rather than taking direction from the client, as is the case in traditional attorney representation of adults, the attorney GAL is charged with forming the client's position by using his/her own judgment. Under this model, the attorney GAL's judgment as to the child's "best interests" takes precedence over the client's wishes.

> **Pros:** This model is favored by many as the traditional model of representing children, particularly young children who cannot meaningfully

participate in their litigation. It is also thought to protect older children from the harm of their own bad choices.

Cons: Critics charge that this is an "old fashioned," paternalistic model of representation that treats children as chattel rather than empowering them in the system. Critics charge that advocate directed representation is wrong by definition because: 1) attorneys are not ethically allowed to disregard their clients' directives; 2) attorneys are not qualified to make "best interests" determinations; and 3) the legal system requires that attorneys be zealous advocates for a client's position, not agents of the court. Critics also charge that the system results in "relaxed advocacy" where attorneys appointed as GAL feel, and are treated, as relieved of their traditional lawyering responsibilities. Critics argue that this model has contributed to sub standard representation of children across the country.

Jurisdictions Using a Form of This Model: Approximately 60% of the U/S jurisdictions use a form of this model.

Source: The Colorado version is comprised of the following sources: Colorado Revised Statutes 19-1-103, 19-1-111, 19-3-203; The Colorado Rules of Professional Conduct at CRS, Volume 12 – pages 711–831; Supreme Court of Colorado Chief Justice Directive 97-02; Colorado GAL Standards of Practice.

2. THE LAY GUARDIAN *AD LITEM* MODEL

This advocate directed model provides for a non-attorney to "represent" the child's "best interests." This person, usually a non-professional volunteer, advocates for what he/she believes (not necessarily what the child believes) is in the child's "best interests." The lay GAL "stands" in the proceeding for the presumptively incompetent child. The focus is the protection of the child by an adult who attempts to know and then articulate the child's best interests.

The NACC discourages the use of this as an exclusive model. Children, even more than adults, require trained legal representation and this model, by definition, is not legal representation. While the NACC recognizes the value of non-legal advocacy for children, whether in the form of lay GAL or CASA, we stress that it cannot be a substitute for trained professional attorneys for children. On this point, the NACC and National CASA have agreed. Non-legal advocates play an important role in the process, and jurisdictions should consider implementing such programs *in addition* to appointing attorneys.

Appendix A. National Association of Counsel for Children 179

Due to the substantial shortcomings of this model, states which use this model of representation frequently appoint an attorney to represent the child or the lay GAL.

Pros: The model has value when used in conjunction with legal counsel.

Cons: Assuming this is the only "representation" provided, the child has no legal counsel. Lay GALs are unable to provide "legal" counsel and cannot, for example, present evidence, examine witnesses, appeal adverse decisions, or advise the client of the ramifications of legal matters. Lay GALs attempting to serve in the role of legal counsel are engaging in the unauthorized practice of law. Additionally, lay representatives are less accountable than professionals for their actions because their conduct is not governed by ethical and legal standards.

Ann M. Haralambie identifies and discusses the "hybrid" role in *The Child's Attorney, A Guide to Representing Children in Custody, Adoption and Protection Cases*, ABA 1993 at p. 37.

Child Abuse and Neglect Cases: Representation as a Critical Component of Effective Practice. NCJFCJ Permanency Planning for Children Project, Technical Assistance Bulletin, 1999, page 45.

Jurisdictions Using a Form of this Model Include: Florida, Hawaii, Maine

Sources: Florida uses a lay volunteer Guardian *ad litem* model. Florida's Guardian *Ad Litem* Program includes an attorney who advises volunteers on the protection of children's rights and represents the program in contested court proceedings. Fla. Stat. 39.820 (2000).

In Hawaii, children in dependency cases are generally represented by volunteer lay guardians *ad litem* and CASAs called Volunteer Guardians *Ad Litem* (VGAL). Children *may also* be represented by an Attorney Guardian *Ad Litem*. H.R.S. 587–40.

Maine law calls for a GAL who is usually an attorney but is not required to be by statute. The GAL is considered a party and has the right to call and cross examine witnesses and has access to discovery. Should the GAL be an attorney, he/she essentially functions in the hybrid role of Attorney GAL defined in IV. A. 1. above. It is not clear how such duties can be performed competently or without violating the law against unauthorized practice of law if the appointment is of a lay person. Maine Supreme Judicial Court Rules for Guardians *Ad Litem*; 22 M.R.S. 4005; 4 M.R.S. 1501.

3. THE "TWO DISTINCT LAWYER ROLES" MODEL

A single lawyer model, either advocate directed (best interests) or client directed, may not meet the needs of all children, given their developing and varied capacities from infants to mature and articulate teens. This model would require appointment of a best interest lawyer-guardian *ad litem* or a traditional attorney under certain circumstances as set out in law.

In 1998, Michigan passed a version of this model that creates two separate and distinct roles for the lawyer representing children: attorney and lawyer-guardian *ad litem*. Michigan requires the appointment of a lawyer-GAL in every case and the lawyer-GAL is to represent the best interests of the child. The statute permits the court to appoint an attorney where the mature child and lawyer-GAL are in conflict about identification of the child's interests. The model prescribes aggressive duties for the lawyer-GAL and provides for attorney-client privilege. It requires the lawyer-GAL to tell the court the wishes and preferences of the child even if the lawyer-GAL advocates for a different view and requires the lawyer-GAL to weigh the child's wishes in making the best interests determination according to the age and maturity of the client. When a lawyer is appointed as "attorney," however, the attorney owes the same duties of undivided loyalty, confidentiality and zealous representation of the child's express wishes as the Attorney would to an adult client. Some proponents of the Two Distinct Lawyer Role model urge that the law *require* appointment of an attorney instead of a lawyer-GAL at a certain age (unless the child is mentally handicapped), rather than leave attorney appointment to the discretion of the court.

> **Pros:** Proponents argue that the pure forms of either advocate directed ("best interests") or client directed ("expressed wishes") models are deficient when applied to all children, so that a model which provides clear lawyer duties depending on the age and maturity of the child better serves the child client. This model is also well defined by statute and lessens the tendency toward "relaxed advocacy." This model also reduces the risk inherent in the ABA and NACC models that a lawyer appointed as "attorney" would find an exception to (or water down) the duty of aggressive and client-directed advocacy.
>
> **Cons:** Critics argue that, at its foundation, this is just an attorney directed model with most of the shortcomings of model A. 1. above. The appointment of an attorney GAL is the rule, not the exception, and an attorney is appointed only in rare circumstances. Also, under rare circumstances the child could be represented by both an attorney and a lawyer-guardian *ad litem* which adds to the cost. The test for appointing one or the other lawyer roles remains unsettled.

Appendix A. National Association of Counsel for Children   181

Jurisdictions Using the Model: Michigan

Source: MCL 712A.13a(1)(b) (for definition of "attorney") and MCL 712A.17d (for duties of lawyer-guardian *ad litem*)

B. CLIENT DIRECTED REPRESENTATION

1. TRADITIONAL ATTORNEY

A traditional attorney functions as a client directed advocate. He/she advocates for the expressed wishes of the client and is bound by the client's directives concerning the objectives of representation. The model does not prohibit the attorney from acting in his/her capacity as counselor for the client, and state ethics codes include the counseling function. Attorneys are not required, without first counseling their client as to more appropriate options, to blindly follow directives that are clearly harmful to the client. Further, the model does not require attorneys to advocate positions not supported by facts and the law.

Pros: The model is thought to give voice and autonomy to the client and to empower the child within the system. It allows attorneys to function in a familiar setting. Proponents believe it produces good outcomes for children because it encourages independent, zealous advocacy, and the attorney is not confused by the role or duties.

Cons: Critics charge that the model does not work for young children who cannot meaningfully direct their litigation or for older children who may misdirect their litigation.

Jurisdictions Using a Form of This Model Include: Oregon uses a traditional attorney, but not in all cases. Additionally, a CASA appointment is required in Oregon. Likewise, in many cases a traditional attorney is used in Massachusetts, but in conjunction with a Guardian *ad Litem*.

Sources: Oregon Revised Statutes 419A.170; 419A.012; 419B.195; Ethics provision 3.3. Mass. Gen. Laws ch. 119, 29; Mass. Ethics Opinion 93-6. ABA Model Rules of Professional Conduct (Model Rules): Preamble; 1.14(a); ABA Model Code of Professional Responsibility (Model Code): EC 7-1; EC 7-12.

2. CHILD'S ATTORNEY (ABA STANDARDS MODEL)

The following selected provisions from the *ABA Standards of Practice for Lawyers Who Represent Children in Abuse and Neglect Cases* define the model. "The term 'child's attorney' means a lawyer who provides legal services for a child and who owes the same duties of undivided loyalty, confidentiality, and competent representation to the child as is due an adult client. The child's attorney should elicit the child's preferences in a developmentally appropriate manner, advise the child, and provide guidance. The child's attorney should represent the child's expressed preferences and follow the child's direction throughout the course of litigation. To the extent that a child cannot express a preference, the child's attorney shall make a good faith effort to determine the child's wishes and advocate accordingly or request appointment of a guardian *ad litem*. To the extent that a child does not or will not express a preference about particular issues, the child's attorney should determine and advocate the child's legal interests. If the child's attorney determines that the child's expressed preference would be seriously injurious to the child (as opposed to merely being contrary to the lawyer's opinion of what would be in the child's interests), the lawyer may request appointment of a separate guardian *ad litem* and continue to represent the child's expressed preference, unless the child's position is prohibited by law or without any factual foundation."

Pros: Proponents see the model as the most significant advance in child representation in many years. They see the model as an evolution from the GAL model of the 1970s. The model is a detailed roadmap for representation taking role and duty confusion out of the picture. The model also discourages relaxed advocacy.

Cons: Critics argue the model still does not work well for young children and that the directive to resort to representation of the child's "legal interests" in some cases is not a meaningful directive. Critics complain that focusing on the child's so-called "legal interests" is unsatisfactory because the legal interests of the child may be unclear or contradictory. For example, a child has a legal interest in being protected from abusive or neglectful parents. The ABA Standards are also criticized for including broad exceptions to the client-directed ideal and thus giving the lawyer unfettered and unreviewed discretion identifying the goals of the child – the same sort of unbridled discretion that critics complain about in the best interests substituted judgment model.

Jurisdictions Using a Form of This Model Include: At the time of the preparation of this document, no jurisdiction had adopted the ABA Standards as the exclusive system of representation. A number of jurisdictions have adopted many of the "duties" requirements of the standards (e.g., case investigation, motion practice) as opposed to the "role" requirements. As to "role" of counsel, Oregon uses a traditional attorney similar to this model.

Source: ABA Standards of Practice for Lawyers Who Represent Children in Abuse & Neglect Cases, 1996 American Bar Association, Chicago, IL

3. CHILD'S ATTORNEY (ABA/NACC MODEL)

The *ABA Standards* were adopted by the ABA in 1996. The following year, the NACC adopted the standards with reservation as to Standard B-4. Standard B-4 is the critical client direction language of the standards and some members of the NACC board believed the *ABA Standards* gave too much autonomy to the child client and was unrealistic where young children were concerned. The *ABA Standards (NACC Revised Version)*, is the NACC's attempt to achieve a better balance of client autonomy and protection within standard B-4. This child's attorney model places the attorney in the role of traditional attorney and addresses the needs of the young child through the application of an objective best interests evaluation in limited situations. The model requires that the attorney assume the traditional role of zealous advocate and not GAL to avoid any propensity toward relaxed advocacy. At the same time, it recognizes that some children are not capable of directing their litigation. The model allows for a degree of advocate direction so long as it is the exception to the rule, and based on objective criteria.

The distinction between the *ABA Standards* and the *NACC Revised ABA Standards* is that where the ABA remained consistent with the client directed attorney throughout, the NACC carved out a significant exception where the client cannot meaningfully participate in the formulation of his or her position. In such cases, the NACC's version calls for a GAL type judgment using objective criteria. Additionally, the NACC's version *requires* the attorney to request the appointment of a separate GAL, after unsuccessful attempts at counseling the child, when the child's wishes are considered to be seriously injurious to the child.

> **Pros:** Proponents believe this is the best blending of the traditional attorney and attorney/GAL, providing the best of both options.
>
> **Cons:** One critic has suggested that, by blending the attorney and GAL roles, this model dilutes both. The NACC model is also criticized for giving the lawyer unfettered and unreviewed discretion identifying the goals of the child – the same sort of unbridled discretion that critics complain about in the best interests advocate directed model.

Jurisdictions Using a Form of This Model Include: At the time of the preparation of this document, no jurisdiction had adopted the ABA/NACC Revised Standards as the exclusive system of representation. A number of jurisdictions have adopted many of the "duties" requirements of the model (e.g., case investigation, motion practice) as opposed to the "role" requirements. As to "role" of counsel, Oregon uses a traditional attorney similar to this model.

Source: *ABA Standards of Practice for Lawyers Who Represent Children in Abuse & Neglect Cases*, (NACC Revised Version) NACC Children's Law Manual Series, 1999 Edition, p. 177.

78 *Adoption 2002: The President's Initiative on Adoption and Foster Care. Guidelines for Public Policy and State Legislation Governing Permanence for Children*, U.S. Dept. of HHS ACF ACYF Children's Bureau, 1999, p. VII-21.

APPENDIX B

American Bar Association Standards of Practice for Lawyers Who Represent Children in Abuse and Neglect Cases

Defending Liberty, Pursuing Justice
AMERICAN BAR ASSOCIATION STANDARDS OF PRACTICE FOR
LAWYERS WHO REPRESENT CHILDREN IN ABUSE AND NEGLECT CASES

Approved by the American Bar Association House of Delegates, February 5, 1996

PREFACE

All children subject to court proceedings involving allegations of child abuse and neglect should have legal representation as long as the court jurisdiction continues. These Abuse and Neglect Standards are meant to apply when a lawyer is appointed for a child in any legal action based on: (a) a petition filed for protection of the child; (b) a request to a court to change legal custody, visitation, or guardianship based on allegations of child abuse or neglect based on sufficient cause; or (c) an action to terminate parental rights.

These Standards apply only to lawyers and take the position that although a lawyer *may* accept appointment in the dual capacity of a "lawyer/guardian ad litem," the lawyer's primary duty must still be focused on the protection of the legal rights of the child client. The lawyer/guardian ad litem should therefore perform all the functions of a "child's attorney," except as otherwise noted.

These Standards build upon the ABA-approved JUVENILE JUSTICE STANDARDS RELATING TO COUNSEL FOR PRIVATE PARTIES (1979) which include important directions for lawyers representing children in juvenile court matters generally, but do not contain sufficient guidance to aid lawyers representing children in abuse and neglect cases. These Abuse and Neglect Standards are also intended to help implement a series of ABA-approved policy resolutions (in Appendix) on the importance of legal representation and the improvement of lawyer practice in child protection cases.

In support of having lawyers play an active role in child abuse and neglect cases, in August 1995 the ABA endorsed a set of RESOURCE GUIDELINES: IMPROVING COURT PRACTICE IN CHILD ABUSE & NEGLECT CASES produced by the National Council of Juvenile and Family Court Judges. The RESOURCE GUIDELINES stress the importance of quality representation provided by competent and diligent lawyers by supporting: 1) the approach of vigorous representation of child clients; and 2) the actions that courts should take to help assure such representation.

These Standards contain two parts. Part I addresses the specific roles and responsibilities of a lawyer appointed to represent a child in an abuse and neglect case. Part II provides a set of standards for judicial administrators and trial judges to assure high quality legal representation.

PART I – STANDARDS FOR THE CHILD'S ATTORNEY

A. DEFINITIONS

A-1. The Child's Attorney. The term "child's attorney" means a lawyer who provides legal services for a child and who owes the same duties of undivided loyalty, confidentiality, and competent representation to the child as is due an adult client.

Commentary
These Standards explicitly recognize that the child is a separate individual with potentially discrete and independent views. To ensure that the child's independent voice is heard, the child's attorney must advocate the child's articulated position. Consequently, the child's attorney owes traditional duties to the child as client consistent with ER 1.14(a) of the Model Rules of Professional Conduct. In all but the exceptional case, such as with a preverbal child, the child's attorney will maintain this traditional relationship with the child/client. As with any client, the child's attorney may counsel against the pursuit of a particular position sought by the child. The child's attorney should recognize that the child may be more susceptible to intimidation and manipulation than some adult clients. Therefore, the child's attorney should ensure that the decision the child ultimately makes reflects his or her actual position.

A-2. Lawyer Appointed as Guardian Ad Litem. A lawyer appointed as "guardian ad litem" for a child is an officer of the court appointed to protect the child's interests without being bound by the child's expressed preferences.

Commentary
In some jurisdictions the lawyer may be appointed as guardian ad litem. These Standards, however, express a clear preference for the appointment as the "child's attorney." These Standards address the lawyer's obligations to the child as client.

A lawyer appointed as guardian ad litem is almost inevitably expected to perform legal functions on behalf of the child. Where the local law permits, the lawyer is expected to act in the dual role of guardian ad litem and lawyer of record. The chief distinguishing factor between the roles is the manner and method to be followed in determining the legal position to be advocated. While a guardian ad litem should take the child's point of view into account, the child's preferences are not binding, irrespective of the child's age and the ability or willingness of the child to express preferences. Moreover, in many states, a guardian ad litem may be required by statute or custom to perform specific tasks, such as submitting a report or testifying as a fact or expert witness. These tasks are not part of functioning as a "lawyer."

These Standards do not apply to nonlawyers when such persons are appointed as guardians ad litem or as "court appointed special advocates" (CASA). The nonlawyer guardian ad litem cannot and should not be expected to perform any legal functions on behalf of a child.

A-3. Developmentally Appropriate. "Developmentally appropriate" means that the child's attorney should ensure the child's ability to provide client-based directions by structuring all communications to account for the individual child's age, level of education, cultural context, and degree of language acquisition.

Commentary
The lawyer has an obligation to explain clearly, precisely, and in terms the client can understand the meaning and consequences of action. See DAVID A. BINDER & SUSAN C. PRICE, LEGAL INTERVIEWING AND COUNSELING. A CLIENT-CENTERED APPROACH (1977). A child client may not understand the legal terminology and for a variety of reasons may choose a particular course of action without fully appreciating the implications. With a child the potential for not understanding may be even greater. Therefore, the child's attorney has additional obligations based on the child's age, level of education, and degree of language acquisition. There is also the possibility that because of a particular child's developmental limitations, the lawyer may not completely understand the child's responses. Therefore, the child's attorney must learn how to ask developmentally appropriate questions and how to interpret the child's responses. See ANNE GRAFFAM WALKER, HANDBOOK ON QUESTIONING CHILDREN: A LINGUISTIC PERSPECTIVE (ABA Center on Children and the Law 1994). The child's attorney may work with social workers or other professionals to assess a child's developmental abilities and to facilitate communication.

B. GENERAL AUTHORITY AND DUTIES

B-1. Basic Obligations. The child's attorney should:

(1) Obtain copies of all pleadings and relevant notices;
(2) Participate in depositions, negotiations, discovery, pretrial conferences, and hearings;
(3) Inform other parties and their representatives that he or she is representing the child and expects reasonable notification prior to case conferences, changes of placement, and other changes of circumstances affecting the child and the child's family;
(4) Attempt to reduce case delays and ensure that the court recognizes the need to speedily promote permanency for the child;
(5) Counsel the child concerning the subject matter of the litigation, the child's rights, the court system, the proceedings, the lawyer's role, and what to expect in the legal process;
(6) Develop a theory and strategy of the case to implement at hearings, including factual and legal issues; and
(7) Identify appropriate family and professional resources for the child.

Commentary
The child's attorney should not be merely a fact-finder, but rather, should zealously advocate a position on behalf of the child. (The same is true for the guardian ad litem, although the position to be advocated may be different). In furtherance of that advocacy, the child's attorney must be adequately prepared prior to hearings. The lawyer's presence at and active participation in all hearings is absolutely critical. See, RESOURCE GUIDELINES, *at 23.*

Although the child's position may overlap with the position of one or both parents, third party caretakers, or a state agency, the child's attorney should be prepared to participate fully in any proceedings and not merely defer to the other parties. Any identity of position should be based on the merits of the position, and not a mere endorsement of another party's position.

While subsection (4) recognizes that delays are usually harmful, there may be some circumstances when delay may be beneficial. Section (7) contemplates that the child's attorney will identify counseling, educational and health services, substance abuse programs for the child and other family members, housing and other forms of material assistance for which the child may qualify under law. The lawyer can also identify family members, friends, neighbors, or teachers with whom the child feels it is important to maintain contact; mentoring programs, such as Big Brother/Big Sister; recreational opportunities that develop social skills and self-esteem; educational support programs; and volunteer opportunities which can enhance a child's self-esteem.

B-2. Conflict Situations.

(1) If a lawyer appointed as guardian ad litem determines that there is a conflict caused by performing both roles of guardian ad litem and child's attorney, the lawyer should continue to perform as the child's attorney and withdraw as guardian ad litem. The lawyer should request appointment of a guardian ad litem without revealing the basis for the request.

(2) If a lawyer is appointed as a "child's attorney" for siblings, there may also be a conflict which could require that the lawyer decline representation or withdraw from representing all of the children.

Commentary
The primary conflict that arises between the two roles is when the child's expressed preferences differ from what the lawyer deems to be in the child's best interests. As a practical matter, when the lawyer has established a trusting relationship with the child, most conflicts can be avoided. While the lawyer should be careful not to apply undue pressure to a child, the lawyer's advice and guidance can often persuade the child to change an imprudent position or to identify alternative choices if the child's first choice is denied by the court.

The lawyer-client role involves a confidential relationship with privileged communications, while a guardian ad litem-client role may not be confidential. Compare Alaska Bar Assoc. Ethics Op. *#854 (1985) (lawyer-client privilege does not apply when the lawyer is appointed to be child's guardian ad litem) with Bentley v. Bentley, 448* N.YS. *2d 559 (App. Div. 1982) (communication between minor children and guardian ad litem in divorce custody case is entitled to lawyer-client privilege). Because the child has a right to confidentiality and advocacy of his or her position, the child's attorney can never abandon this role. Once a lawyer has a lawyer-client relationship with a minor, he or she cannot and should not assume any other role for the child, especially as guardian ad litem. When the roles cannot be reconciled, another person must assume the guardian ad litem role. See Arizona State Bar Committee on Rules of Professional Conduct, Opinion No. 86-13 (1986).*

B-3. Client Under Disability. The child's attorney should determine whether the child is "under a disability" pursuant to the Model Rules of Professional Conduct or the Model Code of Professional Responsibility with respect to each issue in which the child is called upon to direct the representation.

Commentary
These Standards do not accept the idea that children of certain ages are "impaired," "disabled," "incompetent," or lack capacity to determine their

position in litigation. Further, these Standards reject the concept that any disability must be globally determined.

Rather, disability is contextual, incremental, and may be intermittent. The child's ability to contribute to a determination of his or her position is functional, depending upon the particular position and the circumstances prevailing at the time the position must be determined. Therefore, a child may be able to determine some positions in the case but not others. Similarly, a child may be able to direct the lawyer with respect to a particular issue at one time but not at another. This Standard relies on empirical knowledge about competencies with respect to both adults and children. See, e.g., ALLENE. BUCHANAN & DAN W. BROCK, DECIDING FOR OTHERS. THE ETHICS OF SURROGATE DECISION MAKING 217 (1989).

B-4. Client Preferences. The child's attorney should elicit the child's preferences in a developmentally appropriate manner, advise the child, and provide guidance. The child's attorney should represent the child's expressed preferences and follow the child's direction throughout the course of litigation.

Commentary
The lawyer has a duty to explain to the child in a developmentally appropriate way such information as will assist the child in having maximum input in determination of the particular position at issue. The lawyer should inform the child of the relevant facts and applicable laws and the ramifications of taking various positions, which may include the impact of such decisions on other family members or on future legal proceedings. The lawyer may express an opinion concerning the likelihood of the court or other parties accepting particular positions. The lawyer may inform the child of an expert's recommendations germane to the issue.

As in any other lawyer/client relationship, the lawyer may express his or her assessment of the case, the best position for the child to take, and the reasons underlying such recommendation. A child, however, may agree with the lawyer for inappropriate reasons. A lawyer must remain aware of the power dynamics inherent in adult/child relationships. Therefore, the lawyer needs to understand what the child knows and what factors are influencing the child's decision. The lawyer should attempt to determine from the child's opinion and reasoning what factors have been most influential or have been confusing or glided over by the child when deciding the best time to express his or her assessment of the case.

Consistent with the rules of confidentiality and with sensitivity to the child's privacy, the lawyer should consult with the child's therapist and other experts and obtain appropriate records. For example, a child's therapist may help the child to understand why an expressed position is dangerous, foolish, or not in the child's best interests. The therapist might also assist the lawyer in understanding the child's perspective, priorities, and individual needs. Similarly, significant persons in the child's life may educate the lawyer about the child's needs, priorities, and previous experiences.

The lawyer for the child has dual fiduciary duties to the child which must be balanced. On one hand, the lawyer has a duty to ensure that the child client is given the information necessary to make an informed decision, including advice and guidance. On the other hand, the lawyer has a duty not to overbear the will of the child. While the lawyer may attempt to persuade the child to accept a particular position, the lawyer may not advocate a position contrary to the child's expressed position except as provided by these Abuse and Neglect Standards or the Code of Professional Responsibility.

While the child is entitled to determine the overall objectives to be pursued, the child's attorney, as any adult's lawyer, may make certain decisions with respect to the manner of achieving those objectives, particularly with respect to procedural matters. These Abuse and Neglect Standards do not require the lawyer to consult with the child on matters which would not require consultation with an adult client. Further, the Standards do not require the child's attorney to discuss with the child issues for which it is not feasible to obtain the child's direction because of the child's developmental limitations, as with an infant or preverbal child.

Commentary
There are circumstances in which a child is unable to express a position, as in the case of a preverbal child, or may not be capable of understanding the legal or factual issues involved. Under such circumstances, the child's attorney should continue to represent the child's legal interests and request appointment of a guardian ad litem. This limitation distinguishes the scope of independent decision making of the child's attorney and a person acting as guardian ad litem.

(1) To the extent that a child cannot express a preference, the child's attorney shall make a good faith effort to determine the child's wishes and advocate accordingly or request appointment of a guardian ad litem.
(2) To the extent that a child does not or will not express a preference about particular issues, the child's attorney should determine and advocate the child's legal interests.

Commentary
The child's failure to express a position is distinguishable from a directive that the lawyer not take a position with respect to certain issues. The child may have no opinion with respect to a particular issue, or may delegate the decision-making authority. For example, the child may not want to assume the responsibility of expressing a position because of loyalty conflicts or the desire not to hurt one of the other parties. The lawyer should clarify with the child whether the child wants the lawyer to take a position or remain silent with respect to that issue

or wants the preference expressed only if the parent or other party is out of the courtroom. The lawyer is then bound by the child's directive. The position taken by the lawyer should not contradict or undermine other issues about which the child has expressed a preference.

Commentary
One of the most difficult ethical issues for lawyers representing children occurs when the child is able to express a position and does so, but the lawyer believes that the position chosen is wholly inappropriate or could result in serious injury to the child. This is particularly likely to happen with respect to an abused child whose home is unsafe, but who desires to remain or return home. A child may desire to live in a dangerous situation because it is all he or she knows, because of a feeling of blame or of responsibility to take care of the parents, or because of threats. The child may choose to deal with a known situation rather than risk the unknown world of a foster home or other out-of-home placement.

(3) If the child's attorney determines that the child's expressed preference would be seriously injurious to the child (as opposed to merely being contrary to the lawyer's opinion of what would be in the child's interests), the lawyer may request appointment of a separate guardian ad litem and continue to represent the child's expressed preference, unless the child's position is prohibited by law or without any factual foundation. The child's attorney shall not reveal the basis of the request for appointment of a guardian ad litem which would compromise the child's position.

In most cases the ethical conflict involved in asserting a position which would seriously endanger the child, especially by disclosure of privileged information, can be resolved through the lawyer's counseling function. If the lawyer has taken the time to establish rapport with the child and gain that child's trust, it is likely that the lawyer will be able to persuade the child to abandon a dangerous position or at least identify an alternate course.

If the child cannot be persuaded, the lawyer has a duty to safeguard the child's interests by requesting appointment of a guardian ad litem, who will be charged with advocating the child's best interests without being bound by the child's direction. As a practical matter, this may not adequately protect the child if the danger to the child was revealed only in a confidential disclosure to the lawyer, because the guardian ad litem may never learn of the disclosed danger.

Confidentiality is abrogated for various professionals by mandatory child abuse reporting laws. Some states abrogate lawyer-client privilege by mandating reports. States which do not abrogate the privilege may permit reports notwithstanding professional privileges. The policy considerations underlying abrogation apply to lawyers where there is a substantial danger of serious injury or death. Under such circumstances, the lawyer must take the minimum steps which would be necessary to ensure the child's safety, respecting and following the child's direction to the greatest extent possible consistent with the child's safety and ethical rules.

The lawyer may never counsel a client or assist a client in conduct the lawyer knows is criminal or fraudulent. See ER *1.2(d), Model Rules of Professional Conduct,* DR *7-102(A)(7), Model Code of Professional Responsibility. Further, existing ethical rules require the lawyer to disclose confidential information to the extent necessary to prevent the client from committing a criminal act likely to result in death or substantial bodily harm, see* ER *1.6(b), Model Rules of Professional Conduct, and permit the lawyer to reveal the intention of the client to commit a crime. See* ER *1.6(c), Model Rules of Professional Conduct,* DR *4-10](C)(3), Model Code of Professional Responsibility. While child abuse, including sexual abuse, are crimes, the child is presumably the victim, rather than the perpetrator of those crimes. Therefore, disclosure of confidences is designed to protect the client, rather than to protect a third party from the client. Where the child is in grave danger of serious injury or death, the child's safety must be the paramount concern.*

The lawyer is not bound to pursue the client's objectives through means not permitted by law and ethical rules. See DR*-7-101(A)(1), Model Code of Professional Responsibility. Further, lawyers may be subject personally to sanctions for taking positions that are not well grounded in fact and warranted by existing law or a good faith argument for the extension, modification, or reversal of existing law.*

B-5. Child's Interests. The determination of the child's legal interests should be based on objective criteria as set forth in the law that are related to the purposes of the proceedings. The criteria should address the child's specific needs and preferences, the goal of expeditious resolution of the case so the child can remain or return home or be placed in a safe, nurturing, and permanent environment, and the use of the least restrictive or detrimental alternatives available.

Commentary
A lawyer who is required to determine the child's interests is functioning in a nontraditional role by determining the position to be advocated independently of the client. The lawyer should base the position, however, on objective criteria concerning the child's needs and interests, and not merely on the lawyer's personal values, philosophies, and experiences. The child's various needs and interests may be in conflict and must be weighed against each other. Even nonverbal children can communicate their needs and interests through their behaviors and developmental levels. See generally JAMES GARBARINO & FRANCES M. STOTT,

WHAT CHILDREN CAN TELL US: ELICITING, INTERPRETING, AND EVALUATING CRITICAL INFORMATION FROM CHILDREN (1992). The lawyer may seek the advice and consultation of experts and other knowledgeable people in both determining and weighing such needs and interests.

A child's legal interests may include basic physical and emotional needs, such as safety, shelter, food, and clothing. Such needs should be assessed in light of the child's vulnerability, dependence upon others, available external resources, and the degree of risk. A child needs family affiliation and stability of placement. The child's developmental level, including his or her sense of time, is relevant to an assessment of need. For example, a very young child may be less able to tolerate separation from a primary caretaker than an older child, and if separation is necessary, more frequent visitation than is ordinarily provided may be necessary.

In general, a child prefers to live with known people, to continue normal activities, and to avoid moving. To that end, the child's attorney should determine whether relatives, friends, neighbors, or other people known to the child are appropriate and available as placement resources. The lawyer must determine the child's feelings about the proposed caretaker, however, because familiarity does not automatically confer positive regard. Further, the lawyer may need to balance competing stability interests, such as living with a relative in another town versus living in a foster home in the same neighborhood. The individual child's needs will influence this balancing task.

In general, a child needs decisions about the custodial environment to be made quickly. Therefore, if the child must be removed from the home, it is generally in the child's best interests to have rehabilitative or reunification services offered to the family quickly. On the other hand, if it appears that reunification will be unlikely, it is generally in the child's best interests to move quickly toward an alternative permanent plan. Delay and indecision are rarely in a child's best interests.

In addition to the general needs and interests of children, individual children have particular needs, and the lawyer must determine the child client's individual needs. There are few rules which apply across the board to all children under all circumstances.

C. ACTIONS TO BE TAKEN

C-1. Meet With Child. Establishing and maintaining a relationship with a child is the foundation of representation. Therefore, irrespective of the child's age, the child's attorney should visit with the child prior to court hearings and when apprised of emergencies or significant events impacting on the child.

Commentary
Meeting with the child is important before court hearings and case reviews. In addition, changes in placement, school suspensions, in-patient hospitalizations, and other similar changes warrant meeting again with the child. Such in person meetings allow the lawyer to explain to the child what is happening, what alternatives might be available, and what will happen next. This also allows the lawyer to assess the child's circumstances, often leading to a greater understanding of the case, which may lead to more creative solutions in the child's interest. A lawyer can learn a great deal from meeting with child clients, including a preverbal child. See, e.g., JAMES GARBARINO, ET AL., WHAT CHILDREN CAN TELL US: ELICITING, INTERPRETING, AND EVALUATING CRITICAL INFORMATION FROM CHILDREN (1992).

C-2. Investigate. To support the client's position, the child's attorney should conduct thorough, continuing, and independent investigations and discovery which may include, but should not be limited to:

Commentary
Thorough, independent investigation of cases, at every stage of the proceedings, is a key aspect of providing competent representation to children. See, RESOURCE GUIDELINES, AT 23. *The lawyer may need to use subpoenas or other discovery or motion procedures to obtain the relevant records, especially those records which pertain to the other parties. In some jurisdictions the statute or the order appointing the lawyer for the child includes provision for obtaining certain records.*

(1) Reviewing the child's social services, psychiatric, psychological, drug and alcohol, medical, law enforcement, school, and other records relevant to the case;
(2) Reviewing the court files of the child and siblings, case-related records of the social service agency and other service providers;

Commentary
Another key aspect of representing children is the review of all documents submitted to the court as well as relevant agency case files and law enforcement reports. See, RESOURCE GUIDELINES, *at 23. Other relevant files that should be reviewed include those concerning child protective services, developmental disabilities, juvenile delinquency, mental health, and educational agencies. These records can provide a more complete context for the current problems of the child and family. Information in the files may suggest additional professionals*

and lay witnesses who should be contacted and may reveal alternate potential placements and services.

(3) Contacting lawyers for other parties and nonlawyer guardians ad litem or court appointed special advocates (CASA) for background information;

Commentary
The other parties' lawyers may have information not included in any of the available records. Further, they can provide information on their respective clients' perspectives. The CASA is typically charged with performing an independent factual investigation, getting to know the child, and speaking up to the court on the child's "best interests." Volunteer CASAs may have more time to perform their functions than the child's attorney and can often provide a great deal of information to assist the child's attorney. Where there appears to be role conflict or confusion over the involvement of both a child's attorney and CASA in the same case, there should be joint efforts to clarify and define mutual responsibilities. See, RESOURCE GUIDELINES, at 24.

(4) Contacting and meeting with the parents/legal guardians/caretakers of the child, with permission of their lawyer;

Commentary
Such contact generally should include visiting the home, which will give the lawyer additional information about the child's custodial circumstances.

(5) Obtaining necessary authorizations for the release of information;

Commentary
If the relevant statute or order appointing the lawyer for the child does not provide explicit authorization for the lawyer's obtaining necessary records, the lawyer should attempt to obtain authorizations for release of information from the agency and from the parents, with their lawyer's consent. Even if it is not required, an older child should be asked to sign authorizations for release of his or her own records, because such a request demonstrates the lawyer's respect for the client's authority over information.

(6) Interviewing individuals involved with the child, including school personnel, child welfare case workers, foster parents and other caretakers, neighbors, relatives, school personnel, coaches, clergy, mental health professionals, physicians, law enforcement officers, and other potential witnesses;

Commentary
In some jurisdictions the child's attorney is permitted free access to agency case workers. In others, contact with the case worker must be arranged through the agency's lawyer.

(7) Reviewing relevant photographs, video or audio tapes and other evidence; and

Commentary
It is essential that the lawyer review the evidence personally, rather than relying on other parties' or counsel's descriptions and characterizations of the evidence.

(8) Attending treatment, placement, administrative hearings, other proceedings involving legal issues, and school case conferences or staffing concerning the child as needed.

Commentary
While some courts will not authorize compensation for the child's attorney to attend such collateral meetings, such attendance is often very important. The child's attorney can present the child's perspective at such meetings, as well as gather information necessary to proper representation. In some cases the child's attorney can be pivotal in achieving a negotiated settlement of all or some issues. The child's attorney may not need to attend collateral meetings if another person involved in the case, such as a social worker who works the lawyer, can get the information or present the child's perspective.

C-3. File Pleadings. The child's attorney should file petitions, motions, responses or objections as necessary to represent the child. Relief requested may include, but is not limited to:

(1) A mental or physical examination of a party or the child;
2(2) A parenting, custody or visitation evaluation;
3(3) An increase, decrease, or termination of contact or visitation;
4(4) Restraining or enjoining a change of placement;
5(5) Contempt for non-compliance with a court order;
6(6) Termination of the parent-child relationship;
7(7) Child support;
8(8) A protective order concerning the child's privileged communications or tangible or intangible property;
9(9) Request services for child or family; and
10(10) Dismissal of petitions or motions.

Commentary
Filing and arguing necessary motions is an essential part of the role of a child's attorney. See, RESOURCE GUIDELINES, *at 23. Unless the lawyer is serving in a role which explicitly precludes the filing of pleadings, the lawyer should file any appropriate pleadings on behalf of the child, including responses to the pleadings of the other parties. The filing of such pleadings can ensure that appropriate issues are properly before the court and can expedite the court's consideration of issues important to the child's interests. In some jurisdictions, guardians ad litem are not permitted to file pleadings, in which case it should be clear to the lawyer that he or she is not the "child's attorney" as defined in these Standards.*

C-4. Request Services. Consistent with the child's wishes, the child's attorney should seek appropriate services (by court order if necessary) to access entitlements, to protect the child's interests and to implement a service plan. These services may include, but not be limited to:

1(1) Family preservation-related prevention or reunification services;
2(2) Sibling and family visitation;
3(3) Child support;
4(4) Domestic violence prevention, intervention, and treatment;
5(5) Medical and mental health care;
6(6) Drug and alcohol treatment;
7(7) Parenting education;
8(8) Semi-independent and independent living services; 9(9) Long-term foster care;
10(10) Termination of parental rights action;
11(11) Adoption services;
12(12) Education;
13(13) Recreational or social services; and
14(14) Housing.

Commentary
The lawyer should request appropriate services even if there is no hearing scheduled. Such requests may be made to the agency or treatment providers, or if such informal methods are unsuccessful, the lawyer should file a motion to bring the matter before the court. In some cases the child's attorney should file collateral actions, such as petitions for termination of parental rights, if such an action would advance the child's interest and is legally permitted and justified. Different resources are available in different localities.

C-5. Child With Special Needs. Consistent with the child's wishes, the child's attorney should assure that a child with special needs receives appropriate

services to address the physical, mental, or developmental disabilities. These services may include, but should not be limited to:
1(1) Special education and related services;
2(2) Supplemental security income (SSI) to help support needed services;
3(3) Therapeutic foster or group home care; and
4(4) Residential/in-patient and out-patient psychiatric treatment.

Commentary
There are many services available from extra judicial, as well as judicial, sources for children with special needs. The child's attorney should be familiar with these other services and how to assure their availability for the client. See generally, THOMAS A. JACOBS, CHILDREN & THE LAW: RIGHTS & OBLIGATIONS (1995); LEGAL RIGHTS OF CHILDREN (2d ed. Donald T. Kramer, ed., 1994).

C-6. Negotiate Settlements. The child's attorney should participate in settlement negotiations to seek expeditious resolution of the case, keeping in mind the effect of continuances and delays on the child. The child's attorney should use suitable mediation resources.

Commentary
Particularly in contentious cases, the child's attorney may effectively assist negotiations of the parties and their lawyers by focusing on the needs of the child. If a parent is legally represented, it is unethical for the child's attorney to negotiate with a parent directly without the consent of the parent's lawyer. Because the court is likely to resolve at least some parts of the dispute in question based on the best interests of the child, the child's attorney is in a pivotal position in negotiation. Settlement frequently obtains at least short term relief for all parties involved and is often the best resolution of a case. The child's attorney, however, should not become merely a facilitator to the parties' reaching a negotiated settlement. As developmentally appropriate, the child's attorney should consult the child prior to any settlement becoming binding.

D. HEARINGS

D-1. Court Appearances. The child's attorney should attend all hearings and participate in all telephone or other conferences with the court unless a particular hearing involves issues completely unrelated to the child.

D-2. Client Explanation. The child's attorney should explain to the client, in a developmentally appropriate manner, what is expected to happen before, during and after each hearing.

D-3. Motions and Objections. The child's attorney should make appropriate motions, including motions *in limine* and evidentiary objections, to advance the child's position at trial or during other hearings. If necessary, the child's attorney should file briefs in support of evidentiary issues. Further, during all hearings, the child's attorney should preserve legal issues for appeal, as appropriate.

D-4. Presentation of Evidence. The child's attorney should present and cross examine witnesses, offer exhibits, and provide independent evidence as necessary.

Commentary
The child's position may overlap with the positions of one or both parents, third-party caretakers, or a child protection agency. Nevertheless, the child's attorney should be prepared to participate fully in every hearing and not merely defer to the other parties. Any identity of position should be based on the merits of the position (consistent with Standard B-6), and not a mere endorsement of another party's position.

D-5. Child at Hearing. In most circumstances, the child should be present at significant court hearings, regardless of whether the child will testify.

Commentary
A child has the right to meaningful participation in the case, which generally includes the child's presence at significant court hearings. Further, the child's presence underscores for the judge that the child is a real party in interest in the case. It may be necessary to obtain a court order or writ of habeas corpus ad testificandum to secure the child's attendance at the hearing.
  A decision to exclude the child from the hearing should be made based on a particularized determination that the child does not want to attend, is too young to sit through the hearing, would be severely traumatized by such attendance, or for other good reason would be better served by nonattendance. There may be other extraordinary reasons for the child's non-attendance. The lawyer should consult the child, therapist, caretaker, or any other knowledgeable person in determining the effect on the child of being present at the hearing. In some jurisdictions the court requires an affirmative waiver of the child's presence if the child will not attend. Even a child who is too young to sit through the hearing may benefit from seeing the courtroom and meeting, or at least seeing, the judge who will be making the decisions. The lawyer should provide the court with any required notice that the child will be present. Concerns about the child being exposed to certain parts of the evidence may be addressed by the child's

temporary exclusion from the court room during the taking of that evidence, rather than by excluding the child from the entire hearing.

The lawyer should ensure that the state/custodian meets its obligation to transport the child to and from the hearing. Similarly, the lawyer should ensure the presence of someone to accompany the child any time the child is temporarily absent from the hearing.

D-6. Whether Child Should Testify. The child's attorney should decide whether to call the child as a witness. The decision should include consideration of the child's need or desire to testify, any repercussions of testifying, the necessity of the child's direct testimony, the availability of other evidence or hearsay exceptions which may substitute for direct testimony by the child, and the child's developmental ability to provide direct testimony and withstand possible cross-examination. Ultimately, the child's attorney is bound by the child's direction concerning testifying.

Commentary
There are no blanket rules regarding a child's testimony. While testifying is undoubtedly traumatic for many children, it is therapeutic and empowering for others. Therefore, the decision about the child's testifying should be made individually, based on the circumstances of the individual child and the individual case. The child's therapist, if any, should be consulted both with respect to the decision itself and assistance with preparation. In the absence of compelling reasons, a child who has a strong desire to testify should be called to do so. See ANNM HARALAMBIE, THE CHILD'S LAWYER: A GUIDE TO REPRESENTING CHILDREN IN CUSTODY, ADOPTION, AND PROTECTION CASES *ch. 4 (1993). If the child should not wish to testify or would be harmed by being forced to testify, the lawyer should seek a stipulation of the parties not to call the child as a witness or seek a protective order from the court. If the child is compelled to testify, the lawyer should seek to minimize the adverse consequences by seeking any appropriate accommodations permitted by local law, such as having the testimony taken informally, in chambers, without presence of the parents. See* JOHN E. B. MYERS, 2 EVIDENCE IN CHILD ABUSE AND NEGLECT CASES *ch. 8 (1992). The child should know whether the in chambers testimony will be shared with others, such as parents who might be excluded from chambers, before agreeing to this forum. The lawyer should also prepare the child for the possibility that the judge may render a decision against the child's wishes which will not be the child's fault.*

D-7. Child Witness. The child's attorney should prepare the child to testify. This should include familiarizing the child with the courtroom, court procedures, and what to expect during direct and cross examination and ensuring that testifying will cause minimum harm to the child.

Commentary
The lawyer's preparation of the child to testify should include attention to the child's developmental needs and abilities as well as to accommodations which should be made by the court and other lawyers. The lawyer should seek any necessary assistance from the court, including location of the testimony (in chambers, at a small table etc.), determination of who will be present, and restrictions on the manner and phrasing of questions posed to the child.

The accuracy of children's testimony is enhanced when they feel comfortable. See, generally, Karen Saywitz, Children in Court: Principles of Child Development for Judicial Application, in A JUDICIAL PRIMER ON CHILD SEXUAL ABUSE 15 (Josephine Bulkley & Claire Sandt, eds., 1994). Courts have permitted support persons to be present in the courtroom, sometimes even with the child sitting on the person's lap to testify. Because child abuse and neglect cases are often closed to the public, special permission may be necessary to enable such persons to be present during hearings. Further, where the rule sequestering witnesses has been invoked, the order of witnesses may need to be changed or an exemption granted where the support person also will be a witness. The child should be asked whether he or she would like someone to be present, and if so, whom the child prefers. Typical support persons include parents, relatives, therapists, Court Appointed Special Advocates (CASA), social workers, victim witness advocates, and members of the clergy. For some, presence of the child's attorney provides sufficient support.

D-8. Questioning the Child. The child's attorney should seek to ensure that questions to the child are phrased in a syntactically and linguistically appropriate manner.

Commentary
The phrasing of questions should take into consideration the law and research regarding children's testimony, memory, and suggestibility. See generally, Karen Saywitz, supra D-7; CHILD VICTIMS, CHILD WITNESSES: UNDERSTANDING AND IMPROVING TESTIMONY (Gail S. Goodman & Bette L. Bottoms, eds. 1993); ANN HARALAMBIE, 2 HANDLING CHILD CUSTODY, ABUSE, AND ADOPTION CASES 24.09v24.22 (2nd ed. 1993); MYERS, supra D-6, at Vol. 1, ch 2; Ellen Matthews & Karen Saywitz, Child Victim Witness Manual, 12/1 C.J.E.R.J. 40 (1992).

The information a child gives in interviews and during testimony is often misleading because the adults have not understood how to ask children developmentally appropriate questions and how to interpret their answers properly. See

Appendix B. Defending Liberty, Pursuing Justice

WALKER, SUPRA, A-3 *Commentary. The child's attorney must become skilled at recognizing the child's developmental limitations. It may be appropriate to present expert testimony on the issue and even to have an expert present during a young child's testimony to point out any developmentally inappropriate phrasing.*

D-9. Challenges to Child's Testimony/Statements. The child's competency to testify, or the reliability of the child's testimony or out-of-court statements, may be called into question. The child's attorney should be familiar with the current law and empirical knowledge about children's competency, memory, and suggestibility and, where appropriate, attempt to establish the competency and reliability of the child.

Commentary
Many jurisdictions have abolished presumptive ages of competency. See HARALAMBIE, SUPRA D-8 AT 24.17. *The jurisdictions which have rejected presumptive ages for testimonial competency have applied more flexible, case-by-case analyses. See Louis I. Parley, Representing Children in Custody Litigation,* 11 J. AM. ACAD. MA TRIM. LAW. *45, 48 (Winter 1993). Competency to testify involves the abilities to perceive and relate.*

If necessary, the child's attorney should present expert testimony to establish competency or reliability or to rehabilitate any impeachment of the child on those bases. See generally, Karen Saywitz, supra D-8 at 15; CHILD VICTIMS, SUPRA D-8; *Haralambie, supra D-8;* J. MYERS, SUPRA D-8; *Matthews & Saywitz, supra D-8.*

D-10. Jury Selection. In those states in which a jury trial is possible, the child's attorney should participate in jury selection and drafting jury instructions.

D-11. Conclusion of Hearing. If appropriate, the child's attorney should make a closing argument, and provide proposed findings of fact and conclusions of law. The child's attorney should ensure that a written order is entered.

Commentary
One of the values of having a trained child's attorney is such a lawyer can often present creative alternative solutions to the court. Further, the child's attorney is able to argue the child's interests from the child's perspective, keeping the case focused on the child's needs and the effect of various dispositions on the child.

D-12. Expanded Scope of Representation. The child's attorney may request authority from the court to pursue issues on behalf of the child, administratively or judicially, even if those issues do not specifically arise from the court appointment. For example:
1(1) Child support;
2(2) Delinquency or status offender matters;
3(3) SSI and other public benefits;
4(4) Custody;
5(5) Guardianship;
6(6) Paternity;
7(7) Personal injury;
8(8) School/education issues, especially for a child with disabilities;
9(9) Mental health proceedings;
10(10) Termination of parental rights; and
11(11) Adoption.

Commentary
The child's interests may be served through proceedings not connected with the case in which the child's attorney is participating. In such cases the lawyer may be able to secure assistance for the child by filing or participating in other actions. See, e.g., In re Appeal in Pima County Juvenile Action No. S-113432, 872 P.2d 1240 (Ariz. Ct. App. 1994). With an older child or a child with involved parents, the child's attorney may not need court authority to pursue other services. For instance, federal law allows the parent to control special education. A Unified Child and Family Court Model would allow for consistency of representation between related court proceedings, such as mental health or juvenile justice.

D-13. Obligations after Disposition. The child's attorney should seek to ensure continued representation of the child at all further hearings, including at administrative or judicial actions that result in changes to the child's placement or services, so long as the court maintains its jurisdiction.

Commentary
Representing a child should reflect the passage of time and the changing needs of the child. The bulk of the child's attorney's work often comes after the initial hearing, including ongoing permanency planning issues, six month reviews, case plan reviews, issues of termination, and so forth. The average length of stay in foster care is over five years in some jurisdictions. Often a child's case workers, therapists, other service providers or even placements change while the case is still pending. Different judges may hear various phases of the case. The child's attorney may be the only source of continuity for the child. Such

Appendix B. Defending Liberty, Pursuing Justice

continuity not only provides the child with a stable point of contact, but also may represent the institutional memory of case facts and procedural history for the agency and court. The child's attorney should stay in touch with the child, third party caretakers, case workers, and service providers throughout the term of appointment to ensure that the child's needs are met and that the case moves quickly to an appropriate resolution.

Generally it is preferable for the lawyer to remain involved so long as the case is pending to enable the child's interest to be addressed from the child's perspective at all stages. Like the JUVENILE JUSTICE STANDARDS, these ABUSE AND NEGLECT STANDARDS require ongoing appointment and active representation as long as the court retains jurisdiction over the child. To the extent that these are separate proceedings in some jurisdictions, the child's attorney should seek reappointment. Where reappointment is not feasible, the child's attorney should provide records and information about the case and cooperate with the successor to ensure continuity of representation.

E. POST HEARING

E-1. Review of Court's Order. The child's attorney should review all written orders to ensure that they conform with the court's verbal orders and statutorily required findings and notices.

E-2. Communicate Order to Child. The child's attorney should discuss the order and its consequences with the child.

Commentary
The child is entitled to understand what the court has done and what that means to the child, at least with respect to those portions of the order that directly affect the child. Children may assume that orders are final and not subject to change. Therefore, the lawyer should explain whether the order may be modified at another hearing, or whether the actions of the parties may affect how the order is carried out. For example, an order may permit the agency to return the child to the parent if certain goals are accomplished.

E-3. Implementation. The child's attorney should monitor the implementation of the court's orders and communicate to the responsible agency and, if necessary, the court, any noncompliance.

Commentary
The lawyer should ensure that services are provided and that the court's orders are implemented in a complete and timely fashion. In order to address problems with implementation, the lawyer should stay in touch with the child, case worker, third

party caretakers, and service providers between review hearings. The lawyer should consider filing any necessary motions, including those for civil or criminal contempt, to compel implementation. See, RESOURCE GUIDELINES, at 23.

F. APPEAL

F-1. Decision to Appeal. The child's attorney should consider and discuss with the child, as developmentally appropriate, the possibility of an appeal. If after such consultation, the child wishes to appeal the order, and the appeal has merit, the lawyer should take all steps necessary to perfect the appeal and seek appropriate temporary orders or extraordinary writs necessary to protect the interests of the child during the pendency of the appeal.

Commentary
The lawyer should explain to the child not only the legal possibility of an appeal, but also the ramifications of filing an appeal, including the potential for delaying implementation of services or placement options. The lawyer should also explain whether the trial court's orders will be stayed pending appeal and what the agency and trial court may do pending a final decision.

F-2. Withdrawal. If the child's attorney determines that an appeal would be frivolous or that he or she lacks the necessary experience or expertise to handle the appeal, the lawyer should notify the court and seek to be discharged or replaced.

F-3. Participation in Appeal. The child's attorney should participate in an appeal filed by another party unless discharged.

Commentary
The child's attorney should take a position in any appeal filed by the parent, agency, or other party. In some jurisdictions, the lawyer's appointment does not include representation on appeal. If the child's interests are affected by the issues raised in the appeal, the lawyer should seek an appointment on appeal or seek appointment of appellate counsel to represent the child's position in the appeal.

F-4. Conclusion of Appeal. When the decision is received, the child's attorney should explain the outcome of the case to the child.

Commentary
As with other court decisions, the lawyer should explain in terms the child can understand the nature and consequences of the appellate decision. In addition,

the lawyer should explain whether there are further appellate remedies and what more, if anything, will be done in the trial court following the decision.

F-5. Cessation of Representation. The child's attorney should discuss the end of the legal representation and determine what contacts, if any, the child's attorney and the child will continue to have.

Commentary
When the representation ends, the child's lawyer should explain in a developmentally appropriate manner why the representation is ending and how the child can obtain assistance in the future should it become necessary. It is important for there to be closure between the child and the lawyer.

PART II – ENHANCING THE JUDICIAL ROLE IN CHILD REPRESENTATION

PREFACE

Enhancing the legal representation provided by court-appointed lawyers for children has long been a special concern of the American Bar Association (*see, e.g.*, JUVENILE JUSTICE STANDARDS RELATING TO COUNSEL FOR PRIVATE PARTIES (1979); ABA Policy Resolutions on Representation of Children (Appendix). Yet, no matter how carefully a bar association, legislature, or court defines the duties of lawyers representing children, practice will only improve if judicial administrators and trial judges play a stronger role in the selection, training, oversight, and prompt payment of court-appointed lawyers in child abuse/neglect and child custody/visitation cases.

The importance of the court's role in helping assure competent representation of children is noted in the JUVENILE JUSTICE STANDARDS RELATING TO COURT ORGANIZATION AND ADMINISTRATION *(1980)* which state in the Commentary to 3.413 that effective representation of parties is "essential" and that the presiding judge of a court "might need to use his or her position to achieve" it. In its RESOURCE GUIDELINES: IMPROVING COURT PRACTICE IN CHILD ABUSE & NEGLECT CASES *(1995)*, the National Council of Juvenile and Family Court Judges stated, "Juvenile and family courts should take active steps to ensure that the parties in child abuse and neglect cases have access to competent representation. . . . " In jurisdictions which engage nonlawyers to represent a child's interests, the court should ensure they have access to legal representation.

These Abuse and Neglect Standards, like the RESOURCE GUIDELINES, recognize that the courts have a great ability to influence positively the quality of counsel through setting judicial prerequisites for lawyer appointments including requirements for experience and training, imposing sanctions for violation of standards (such as terminating a lawyer's appointment to represent a specific child, denying further appointments, or even fines or referrals to the state bar committee for professional responsibility). The following Standards are intended to assist the judiciary in using its authority to accomplish the goal of quality representation for all children before the court in abuse/neglect related proceedings.

G. THE COURT'S ROLE IN STRUCTURING CHILD REPRESENTATION

G-1. Assuring Independence of the Child's Attorney. The child's attorney should be independent from the court, court services, the parties, and the state.

Commentary
To help assure that the child's attorney is not compromised in his or her independent action, these Standards propose that the child's lawyer be independent from other participants in the litigation. "Independence" does not mean that a lawyer may not receive payment from a court, a government entity (e.g., program funding from social services or justice agencies), or even from a parent, relative, or other adult so long as the lawyer retains the full authority for independent action. For ethical conflict reasons, however, lawyers should never accept compensation as retained counsel for the child from a parent accused of abusing or neglecting the child. The child's attorney should not prejudge the case. The concept of independence includes being free from prejudice and other limitations to uncompromised representation.

JUVENILE JUSTICE STANDARD 2.1(d) states that plans for providing counsel for children "must be designed to guarantee the professional independence of counsel and the integrity of the lawyer-client relationship." The Commentary strongly asserts there is "no justification for...judicial preference" to compromise a lawyer's relationship with the child client and notes the "willingness of some judges to direct lawyers' performance and thereby compromise their independence."

G-2. Establishing Uniform Representation Rules. The administrative office for the state trial, family, or juvenile court system should cause to be published and disseminated to all relevant courts a set of uniform, written rules and procedures for court-appointed lawyers for minor children.

Commentary
Although uniform rules of court to govern the processing of various types of child related judicial proceedings have become common, it is still rare for those rules

Appendix B. Defending Liberty, Pursuing Justice

to address comprehensively the manner and scope of representation for children. Many lawyers representing children are unclear as to the court's expectations. Courts in different communities, or even judges within the same court, may have differing views regarding the manner of child representation. These Standards promote statewide uniformity by calling for written publication and distribution of state rules and procedures for the child's attorney.

G-3. Enhancing Lawyer Relationships with Other Court Connected Personnel. Courts that operate or utilize Court Appointed Special Advocate (CASA) and other nonlawyer guardians ad litem, and courts that administer nonjudicial foster care review bodies, should assure that these programs and the individuals performing those roles are trained to understand the role of the child's attorney. There needs to be effective coordination of their efforts with the activities of the child's attorney, and they need to involve the child's attorney in their work. The court should require that reports from agencies be prepared and presented to the parties in a timely fashion.

Commentary
Many courts now regularly involve nonlawyer advocates for children in various capacities. Some courts also operate programs that, outside of the courtroom, review the status of children in foster care or other out-of-home placements. It is critical that these activities are appropriately linked to the work of the child's attorney, and that the court through training, policies, and protocols helps assure that those performing the nonlegal tasks (1) understand the importance and elements of the role of the child's attorney, and (2) work cooperatively with such lawyers. The court should keep abreast of all the different representatives involved with the child, the attorney, social worker for government or private agency, CASA volunteer, guardian ad litem, school mediator, counselors, etc.

H. THE COURT'S ROLE IN APPOINTING THE CHILD'S ATTORNEY

H-1. Timing of Appointments. The child's attorney should be appointed immediately after the earliest of:
1(1) The involuntary removal of the child for placement due to allegations of neglect, abuse, or abandonment;
2(2) The filing of a petition alleging child abuse and neglect, for review of foster care placement, or for termination of parental rights; or
3(3) Allegations of child maltreatment, based upon sufficient cause, are made by a party in the context of proceedings that were not originally initiated by a petition alleging child maltreatment.

Commentary
These ABUSE AND NEGLECT STANDARDS take the position that courts must assure the appointment of a lawyer for a child as soon as practical (ideally, on the day the court first has jurisdiction over the case, and hopefully, no later than the next business day). The three situations are described separately because:

1(1) *A court may authorize, or otherwise learn of, a child's removal from home prior to the time a formal petition is instituted. Lawyer representation of (and, ideally, contact with) the child prior to the initial court hearing following removal (which in some cases may be several days) is important to protect the child's interests;*

2(2) *Once a petition has been filed by a government agency (or, where authorized, by a hospital or other agency with child protection responsibilities), for any reason related to a child's need for protection, the child should have prompt access to a lawyer; and*

3(3) *There are cases (such as custody, visitation, and guardianship disputes and family-related abductions of children) where allegations, with sufficient cause, of serious physical abuse, sexual molestation, or severe neglect of a child are presented to the court not by a government agency (i.e., child protective services) but by a parent, guardian, or other relative. The need of a child for competent, independent representation by a lawyer is just as great in situation (3) as with cases in areas (1) and (2).*

H-2. Entry of Compensation Orders. At the time the court appoints a child's attorney, it should enter a written order addressing compensation and expense costs for that lawyer, unless these are otherwise formally provided for by agreement or contract with the court, or through another government agency.

Commentary
Compensation and expense reimbursement of individual lawyers should be addressed in a specific written court order[, which] is based on a need for all lawyers representing maltreated children to have a uniform understanding of how they will be paid. Commentary to Section 2.1(b) of the JUVENILE JUSTICE STANDARDS observes that it is common for court-appointed lawyers to be confused about the availability of reimbursement of expenses for case-related work.

H-3. Immediate Provision of Access. Unless otherwise provided for, the court should upon appointment of a child's attorney, enter an order authorizing that lawyer access between the child and the lawyer and to all privileged information regarding the child, without the necessity of a further release. The authorization should include, but not be limited to: social services, psychiatric, psychological treatment, drug and alcohol treatment, medical, evaluation, law enforcement, and school records.

Commentary
Because many service providers do not understand or recognize the nature of the role of the lawyer for the child or that person's importance in the court proceeding, these Standards call for the routine use of a written court order that clarifies the lawyers right to contact with their child client and perusal of child related records. Parents, other caretakers, or government social service agencies should not unreasonably interfere with a lawyer's ability to have face-to face contact with the child client nor to obtain relevant information about the child's social services, education, mental health, etc. Such interference disrupts the lawyer's ability to control the representation and undermines his or her independence as the child's legal representative.

H-4. Lawyer Eligibility for and Method of Appointment. Where the court makes individual appointment of counsel, unless impractical, before making the appointment, the court should determine that the lawyer has been trained in representation of children and skilled in litigation (or is working under the supervision of an lawyer who is skilled in litigation). Whenever possible, the trial judge should ensure that the child's attorney has had sufficient training in child advocacy and is familiar with these Standards. The trial judge should also ensure that (unless there is specific reason to appoint a specific lawyer because of their special qualifications related to the case, or where a lawyer's current caseload would prevent them from adequately handling the case) individual lawyers are appointed from the ranks of eligible members of the bar under a fair, systematic, and sequential appointment plan.

Commentary
The JUVENILE JUSTICE STANDARDS 2.2(c) provides that where counsel is assigned by the court, this lawyer should be drawn from "an adequate pool of competent attorneys." In general, such competency can only be gained through relevant continuing legal education and practice-related experience. Those Standards also promote the use of a rational court appointment process drawing from the ranks of qualified lawyers. The Abuse and Neglect Standards reject the concept of ad hoc appointments of counsel that are made without regard to prior training or practice.

H-5. Permitting Child to Retain a Lawyer. The court should permit the child to be represented by a retained private lawyer if it determines that this lawyer is the child's independent choice, and such counsel should be substituted for the appointed lawyer. A person with a legitimate interest in the child's welfare may retain private counsel for the child and/or pay for such representation, and that person should be permitted to serve as the child's attorney, subject to approval of the court. Such approval should not be given if the child opposes the lawyer's representation or if the court determines that there will be a conflict of interest. The court should make it clear that the person paying for the retained lawyer does not have the right to direct the representation of the child or to receive privileged information about the case from the lawyer.

Commentary
Although such representation is rare, there are situations where a child, or someone acting on a child's behalf, seeks out legal representation and wishes that this lawyer, rather than one appointed by the court under the normal appointment process, be recognized as the sole legal representative of the child. Sometimes, judges have refused to accept the formal appearances filed by such retained lawyers. These Standards propose to permit, under carefully scrutinized conditions, the substitution of a court-appointed lawyer with the retained counsel for a child.

I. THE COURT'S ROLE IN LAWYER TRAINING

I-1. Judicial Involvement in Lawyer Training. Trial judges who are regularly involved in child-related matters should participate in training for the child's attorney conducted by the courts, the bar, or any other group.

Commentary
JUVENILE JUSTICE STANDARDS 2.1 indicates that it is the responsibility of the courts (among others) to ensure that competent counsel are available to represent children before the courts. That Standard further suggests that lawyers should "be encouraged" to qualify themselves for participation in child-related cases "through formal training." The Abuse and Neglect Standards go further by suggesting that judges should personally take part in educational programs, whether or not the court conducts them. The National Council of Juvenile and Family Court Judges has suggested that courts can play in important role in training lawyers in child abuse and neglect cases, and that judges and judicial officers can volunteer to provide training and publications for continuing legal education seminars. See, RESOURCE GUIDELINES, at 22.

I-2. Content of Lawyer Training. The appropriate state administrative office of the trial, family, or juvenile courts should provide educational programs, live or on tape, on the role of a child's attorney. At a minimum, the requisite training should include:
1(1) Information about relevant federal and state laws and agency regulations;
2(2) Information about relevant court decisions and court rules;

3(3) Overview of the court process and key personnel in child-related litigation;
4(4) Description of applicable guidelines and standards for representation;
5(5) Focus on child development, needs, and abilities;
6(6) Information on the multidisciplinary input required in child-related cases, including information on local experts who can provide consultation and testimony on the reasonableness and appropriateness of efforts made to safely maintain the child in his or her home;
7(7) Information concerning family dynamics and dysfunction including substance abuse, and the use of kinship care;
8(8) Information on accessible child welfare, family preservation, medical, educational, and mental health resources for child clients and their families, including placement, evaluation/diagnostic, and treatment services; the structure of agencies providing such services as well as provisions and constraints related to agency payment for services; and
9(9) Provision of written material (e.g., representation manuals, checklists, sample forms), including listings of useful material available from other sources.

Commentary
The ABUSE AND NEGLECT STANDARDS *take the position that it is not enough that judges mandate the training of lawyers, or that judges participate in such training. Rather, they call upon the courts to play a key role in training by actually sponsoring (e.g., funding) training opportunities. The pivotal nature of the judiciary's role in educating lawyers means that courts may, on appropriate occasions, stop the hearing of cases on days when training is held so that both lawyers and judges may freely attend without docket conflicts. The required elements of training are based on a review of well-regarded lawyer training offered throughout the country,* RESOURCE GUIDELINES, *and many existing manuals that help guide lawyers in representing children.*

I-3. Continuing Training for Lawyers. The court system should also assure that there are periodic opportunities for lawyers who have taken the "basic" training to receive continuing and "new developments" training.

Commentary
Many courts and judicial organizations recognize that rapid changes occur because of new federal and state legislation, appellate court decisions, systemic reforms, and responses to professional literature. Continuing education opportunities are critical to maintain a high level of performance. These Standards

call for courts to afford these "advanced" or "periodic" training to lawyers who represent children in abuse and neglect related cases.

I-4. Provision of Mentorship Opportunities. Courts should provide individual court appointed lawyers who are new to child representation the opportunity to practice under the guidance of a senior lawyer mentor.

Commentary
In addition to training, particularly for lawyers who work as sole practitioners or in firms that do not specialize in child representation, courts can provide a useful mechanism to help educate new lawyers for children by pairing them with more experienced advocates. One specific thing courts can do is to provide lawyers new to representing children with the opportunity to be assisted by more experienced lawyers in their jurisdiction. Some courts actually require lawyers to "second chair" cases before taking an appointment to a child abuse or neglect case. See, RESOURCE GUIDELINES, *at 22.*

J. THE COURT'S ROLE IN LAWYER COMPENSATION

J-1. Assuring Adequate Compensation. A child's attorney should receive adequate and timely compensation throughout the term of appointment that reflects the complexity of the case and includes both in court and out-of-court preparation, participation in case reviews and postdispositional hearings, and involvement in appeals. To the extent that the court arranges for child representation through contract or agreement with a program in which lawyers represent children, the court should assure that the rate of payment for these legal services is commensurate with the fees paid to equivalently experienced individual court-appointed lawyers who have similar qualifications and responsibilities.

Commentary
JUVENILE JUSTICE STANDARDS *2.1(b) recognize that lawyers for children should be entitled to reasonable compensation for both time and services performed "according to prevailing professional standards", which takes into account the "skill required to perform... properly," and which considers the need for the lawyer to perform both counseling and resource identification/evaluation activities. The* RESOURCE GUIDELINES, *at 22, state that it is necessary to provide reasonable compensation "for improved lawyer representation of children and that where necessary judges should urge state legislatures and local governing bodies to provide sufficient funding" for quality legal representation.*

Because some courts currently compensate lawyers only for time spent in court at the adjudicative or initial disposition stage of cases, these Standards clarify that compensation is to be provided for out-of-court preparation time, as well as for the lawyer's involvement in case reviews and appeals. "Out-of-court preparation" may include, for example, a lawyer's participation in social services or school case conferences relating to the client.

These Standards also call for the level of compensation where lawyers are working under contract with the court to provide child representation to be comparable with what experienced individual counsel would receive from the court. Although courts may, and are encouraged to, seek high quality child representation through enlistment of special children's law offices, law firms, and other programs, the motive should not be a significantly different (i.e., lower) level of financial compensation for the lawyers who provide the representation.

J-2. Supporting Associated Costs. The child's attorney should have access to (or be provided with reimbursement for experts, investigative services, paralegals, research costs, and other services, such as copying medical records, long distance phone calls, service of process, and transcripts of hearings as requested.

Commentary
The ABUSE AND NEGLECT STANDARDS expand upon JUVENILE JUSTICE STANDARDS 2.1(c) which recognizes that a child's attorney should have access to "investigatory, expert and other nonlegal services" as a fundamental part of providing competent representation.

J-3. Reviewing Payment Requests. The trial judge should review requests for compensation for reasonableness based upon the complexity of the case and the hours expended.

Commentary
These Standards implicitly reject the practice of judges arbitrarily "cutting down" the size of lawyer requests for compensation and would limit a judge's ability to reduce the amount of a per/case payment request from a child's attorney unless the request is deemed unreasonable based upon two factors: case complexity and time spent.

J-4. Keeping Compensation Levels Uniform. Each state should set a uniform level of compensation for lawyers appointed by the courts to represent children. Any per/hour level of compensation should be the same for all representation of children in all types of child abuse and neglect-related proceedings.

Commentary
These Standards implicitly reject the concept (and practice) of different courts within a state paying different levels of compensation for lawyers representing children. They call for a uniform approach, established on a statewide basis, towards the setting of payment guidelines.

K. THE COURT'S ROLE IN RECORD ACCESS BY LAWYERS

K-1. Authorizing Lawyer Access. The court should enter an order in child abuse and neglect cases authorizing the child's attorney access to all privileged information regarding the child, without the necessity for a further release.

Commentary
This Standard requires uniform judicial assistance to remove a common barrier to effective representation, i.e., administrative denial of access to significant records concerning the child. The language supports the universal issuance of broadly-worded court orders that grant a child's attorney full access to information (from individuals) or records (from agencies) concerning the child.

K-2. Providing Broad Scope Orders. The authorization order granting the child's attorney access to records should include social services, psychiatric, psychological treatment, drug and alcohol treatment, medical, evaluation, law enforcement, school, and other records relevant to the case.

Commentary
This Standard further elaborates upon the universal application that the court's access order should be given, by listing examples of the most common agency records that should be covered by the court order.

L. THE COURT'S ROLE IN ASSURING REASONABLE LAWYER CASELOADS

L-1. Controlling Lawyer Caseloads. Trial court judges should control the size of court appointed caseloads of individual lawyers representing children, the caseloads of government agency-funded lawyers for children, or court contracts/agreements with lawyers for such representation. Courts should take steps to assure that lawyers appointed to represent children, or lawyers otherwise providing such representation, do not have such a large open number of cases that they are unable to abide by Part I of these Standards.

Commentary
THE ABUSE AND NEGLECT STANDARDS go further than JUVENILE JUSTICE STANDARD 2.2(b) which recognize the "responsibility of every defender office to ensure that its personnel can offer prompt, full, and effective counseling and representation to each (child) client" and that it "should not accept more

assignments than its staff can adequately discharge" by specifically calling upon the courts to help keep lawyer caseloads from getting out of control. The Commentary to 2.2. (b) indicates that: Caseloads must not be exceeded where to do so would "compel lawyers to forego the extensive fact investigation required in both contested and uncontested cases, or to be less than scrupulously careful in preparation for trial, or to forego legal research necessary to develop a theory of representation." We would add: "... or to monitor the implementation of court orders and agency case plans in order to help assure permanency for the child."

L-2. Taking Supportive Caseload Actions. If judges or court administrators become aware that individual lawyers are close to, or exceeding, the levels suggested in these Standards, they should take one or more of the following steps:

1(1) Expand, with the aid of the bar and children's advocacy groups, the size of the list from which appointments are made;
2(2) Alert relevant government or private agency administrators that their lawyers have an excessive caseload problem;
3(3) Recruit law firms or special child advocacy law programs to engage in child representation;
4(4) Review any court contracts/agreements for child representation and amend them accordingly, so that additional lawyers can be compensated for case representation time; and
5(5) Alert state judicial, executive, and legislative branch leaders that excessive caseloads jeopardize the ability of lawyers to competently represent children pursuant to state-approved guidelines, and seek funds for increasing the number of lawyers available to represent children.

Commentary
This Standard provides courts with a range of possible actions when individual lawyer caseloads appear to be inappropriately high.

APPENDIX

Previous American Bar Association Policies Related to Legal Representation of Abused and Neglected Children

GUARDIANS AD LITEM FEBRUARY 1992

BE IT RESOLVED, that the American Bar Association urges:

1(1) Every state and territory to meet the full intent of the Federal Child Abuse Prevention and Treatment Act, whereby every child in the

United States who is the subject of a civil child protection related judicial proceedings will be represented at all stages of these proceedings by a fully-trained, monitored, and evaluated guardian ad litem in addition to appointed legal counsel.

2(2) That state, territory and local bar associations and law schools become involved in setting standards of practice for such guardians ad litem, clarify the ethical responsibilities of these individuals and establish minimum ethical performance requirements for their work, and provide comprehensive multidisciplinary training for all who serve as such guardians ad litem.

3(3) That in every state and territory, where judges are given discretion to appoint a guardian ad litem in private child custody and visitation related proceedings, the bench and bar jointly develop guidelines to aid judges in determining when such an appointment is necessary to protect the best interests of the child.

COURT-APPOINTED SPECIAL ADVOCATES AUGUST 1989

BE IT RESOLVED, that the American Bar Association endorses the concept of utilizing carefully selected, well trained lay volunteers, Court Appointed Special Advocates, in addition to providing attorney representation, in dependency proceedings to assist the court in determining what is in the best interests of abused and neglected children. BE IT FURTHER RESOLVED, that the American Bar Association encourages its members to support the development of CASA programs in their communities.

COUNSEL FOR CHILDREN ENHANCEMENT FEBRUARY 1987

BE IT RESOLVED, that the American Bar Association requests State and local bar associations to determine the extent to which statutory law and court rules in their States guarantee the right to counsel for children in juvenile court proceedings; and BE IT FURTHER RESOLVED, that State and local bar associations are urged to actively participate and support amendments to the statutory law and court rules in their State to bring them into compliance with the *Institute of Judicial Administration/American Bar Association Standards Relating to Counsel for Private Parties*; and BE IT FURTHER RESOLVED, that State and local bar associations are requested to ascertain the extent to which, irrespective of the language in their State statutory laws and court rules, counsel is in fact provided for children in juvenile court proceedings and the extent to which the quality of representation is consistent with the standards and policies of the American Bar Association; and BE IT FURTHER RESOLVED,

Appendix B. Defending Liberty, Pursuing Justice 221

that State and local bar associations are urged to actively support programs of training and education to ensure that lawyers practicing in juvenile court are aware of the American Bar Association's standards relating to representation of children and provide advocacy which meets those standards.

BAR ASSOCIATION AND ATTORNEY ACTION FEBRUARY 1984

BE IT RESOLVED, that the American Bar Association urges the members of the legal profession, as well as state and local bar associations, to respond to the needs of children by directing attention to issues affecting children including, but not limited to: ... (7) establishment of guardian ad litem programs.

BAR AND ATTORNEY INVOLVEMENT IN CHILD PROTECTION CASES AUGUST 1981

BE IT RESOLVED, that the American Bar Association encourages individual attorneys and state and local bar organizations to work more actively to improve the handling of cases involving abused and neglected children as well as children in foster care. Specifically, attorneys should form appropriate committees and groups within the bar to ... work to assure quality legal representation for children....

BE IT RESOLVED, that the American Bar Association adopt (the volume of the) Standards for Juvenile Justice (entitled) Counsel for Private Parties ...

APPENDIX C

In re Car Simulation and Analysis

IN RE CAR

This case involves four family members, Gail Car (mother), William Car (father), Tifini Car (sister), and Ming Car (sister), in a child abuse dependency action alleging that Gail threw hot water on Tifini, causing her severe burns. The petition also alleges that Tifini is an uncontrollable child who needs to be placed in a court-supervised group home where she will learn the importance of being responsible and of following the reasonable demands of her adult custodian. Attached to this set of General Instructions you will find a 12-page dependency court file that contains all pleadings in the instant case.

Your responsibility in this negotiation and/or mediation is to represent your client(s) during a preadjudication (pretrial) negotiation. You should seek to perfect your client's interests while attempting to resolve this dispute without the necessity of a formal trial (the adjudication hearing). It should be noted that the Department's responsibility is to represent the best interests of the children as determined by the Department. Because the Department's views regarding the children's best interests may conflict with the children's expressed desires, the Code of Professional Responsibility may require the appointment of separate counsel for the children. Assume that you represent both children, Tifini and Ming Car.

The dependency petition alleges that Tifini Car sustained second-degree burns to her body that would not have occurred except for the unreasonable neglectful or intentional acts by her mother, Gail Car. The following petition supplies all the relevant facts.

SUPERIOR COURT DEPENDENCY PETITION

TIFINI   AGE: 16   J9480   DPSS REGION 5   COURT DATE: 3-23-00
CAR, MING   AGE: 6   J9480   DPSS REGION 5   COURT DATE: 3-23-00

REASON FOR HEARING:

THIS MATTER IS ON CALENDAR FOR

X   ADJUDICATION
    DISPOSITION SOCIAL STUDY

A PETITION WAS FILED ON BEHALF OF THE MINOR(S) ON <u>1-23-00</u> UNDER SECTION(S) 300, SUBDIVISION(S) <u>601</u> OF THE JUVENILE COURT LAW AT THE REQUEST OF <u>THE LOS ANGELES POLICE DEPARTMENT.</u>

X   THE PETITION HAS NOT BEEN ADJUDICATED. IT ALLEGES MINOR SUFFERED SECOND-DEGREE BURNS TO HER BODY THAT WOULD NOT OCCUR EXCEPT FOR UNREASONABLE NEGLECTFUL ACTS OR OMISSIONS BY MINOR'S PARENTS. ON JANUARY 11, -00, MINOR AND MOTHER WERE INVOLVED IN A VIOLENT ALTERCATION ENDANGERING MINOR'S PHYSICAL AND EMOTIONAL SAFETY. MINOR HAS SPECIAL PROBLEMS AND MINOR'S PARENTS HAVE A LIMITED ABILITY TO DEAL WITH THEM. THEY INCLUDE SCHOOL ABSENTEEISM AND INCORRIGIBLE BEHAVIOR. MINOR HAS BEEN ON PROBATION. THE PETITION WAS SUSTAINED ON BY PLEA EVIDENCE. THE SUSTAINED PETITION ALLEGATIONS FORMED THE BASIS OF THE REUNIFICATION PLAN.

X   IT IS RESPECTFULLY RECOMMENDED THAT THE MINOR(S) <u>TIFINI CAR</u> BE DECLARED A DEPENDENT CHILD OF THE COURT UNDER SECTION 300, SUBDIVISION(S) <u>A & D</u> OF THE JUVENILE COURT LAW;

X   THE MINIOR WAS RELEASED ON 1-23-00 FATHER AS TO MINOR <u>TIFINI</u>

RECOMMENDATION:

IT IS RESPECTFULLY RECOMMENDED THAT THE PETITION FILED ON BEHALF OF THE MINOR(S) <u>MING CAR</u> BE DISMISSED WITHOUT PREJUDICE.

X   THAT THE MINOR(S) <u>TIFINI CAR</u> RESIDE IN THE HOME OF MOTHER/FATHER UNDER THE SUPERVISION OF THE DEPARTMENT OF PUBLIC SOCIAL SERVICES PENDING FURTHER ORDER OF THE COURT;

X THAT THE CUSTODY OF THE MINOR(S) _____ BE TAKEN FROM THE PARENTS AND GUARDIANS, AND THE MINOR(S) BE COMMITTED TO THE CARE, CUSTODY AND CONTROL OF THE DEPARTMENT OF PUBLIC SOCIAL SERVICES FOR SUITABLE PLACEMENT, AS DETAILED IN THE JUVENILE COURT'S DEPENDENCY DISPOSITION MINUTE ORDER FORM;
THAT MINOR _____ BE DETAINED AT PENDING PLACEMENT, EXCEPT FOR PRE-PLACEMENT VISITS;
THAT MINOR _____ BE RELEASED TO PENDING PLACEMENT;
THAT DPSS HAVE DISCRETION TO PLACE THE MINOR(S) _____ IN THE HOME OF THE FOLLOWING RELATIVE _____
THAT MINOR REMAIN AS PLACED UNDER THE SUPERVISION OF THE DEPARTMENT OF SOCIAL SERVICES;

X THAT THE COURT ORDER THE DEPARTMENT OF PUBLIC SOCIAL SERVICES TO PROVIDE

    X FAMILY MAINTENANCE SERVICES
      FAMILY REUNIFICATION SERVICES
      PERMANENT PLACEMENT SERVICES

X THAT THE VISITS TO THE MINOR(S) BE AT THE DISCRETION OF THE DPSS WITH THE EXCEPTION THAT VISITS TO THE MINOR(S) _____ TIFINI CAR BE AS FOLLOWS:

    X NO RESTRICTIONS

    X MONITORED VISITS FOR GAIL CAR _____ AS ARRANGED BY DPSS

    X NO VISITS BY _____ PENDING FURTHER ORDER OF THE COURT;

    X THAT MINOR AND MINOR'S PARENTS_____ BE ORDERED TO PARTICIPATE IN A PROGRAM OF COUNSELING AS APPROVED BY DPSS

X THAT COUNSELING <u>INCLUDE MOTHER-DAUGHTER COUNSELING</u>

X THAT MINOR(S) SCHOOL RECORDS BE DISCLOSED TO DPSS ON REQUEST PURSUANT TO EDUCATION CODE SECTION 49061;

OTHER

X THAT THE MATTER BE CONTINUED TO THE NONAPPEARANCE CALENDAR OF AND TO THE APPEARANCE CALENDAR OF <u>6/1/00</u> IN DEPARTMENT <u>D/C</u> FOR JUDICIAL REVIEW AND REPORT FROM THE DEPARTMENT OF PUBLIC SOCIAL SERVICES CHILDREN'S SERVICES WORKER.

Appendix C. In re Car

FAMILY ASSESSMENT

FAMILY HISTORY

SOCIAL-CULTURAL HISTORY OF EACH PARENT, PARENT FIGURE, MINOR(S), AND OTHER SIGNIFICANT PARTIES

PARENT	MARITAL STATUS	EDUCATION	EMPLMNT	INCOME	CRIMINAL HISTORY
GAIL CAR	SEP.	11TH GRADE	SCREEN EXTRA	$800-$900/MO.	1 ARREST- SHOPLIFTING
WILLIAM CAR	SEP.	HS. GRAD	MGR. LIQUOR STORE		ARREST FOR RESISTING ARREST

MR. CAR WAS BORN IN LOS ANGELES, CALIFORNIA. HE IS ONE OF FIVE CHILDREN AND DESCRIBES HIMSELF AS COMING FROM A FAMILY WHERE THERE WAS LOTS OF LOVE. HE WAS RAISED BY HIS NATURAL PARENTS WITHOUT ANY OUTSTANDING PROBLEMS. HIS MOTHER WAS A HOMEMAKER WHO STAYED HOME AND RAISED ALL FIVE OF HER CHILDREN.

WHEN MR. CAR LEFT HIGH SCHOOL, HE BECAME A HAIR STYLIST AND ULTIMATELY MARRIED MINOR'S MOTHER. THIS IS HIS ONLY MARRIAGE. THE COUPLE HAVE THREE CHILDREN, BRIAN CAR, NOW AGE 18; THE MINOR TIFINI, NOW AGE 16; AND MING, AGE 6. BRIAN CAR LIVES WITH HIS MOTHER AS HAVE THE OTHER CHILDREN SINCE THE COUPLE'S SEPARATION. BRIAN IS EXPERIENCING DIFFICULTIES MAKING THE TRANSITION INTO ADULTHOOD, ACCORDING TO HIS FATHER.

MR. CAR HAS PAID CHILD SUPPORT NOW AND THEN. ACCORDING TO MR CAR, THE COUPLE'S MARRIAGE FAILED BECAUSE HIS WIFE BECAME INVOLVED IN FILM WORK AND THE GLAMOROUS LIFE ASSOCIATED WITH THAT. HE WAS UNCOMFORTABLE WITH THIS CHANGE IN THEIR HOME LIFE AND UNCOMFORTABLE WITH HER NEW FRIENDS.

PRESENTLY, MR. CAR LIVES WITH HIS MOTHER AND AN ADULT SISTER AND HER CHILDREN IN A LARGE NICELY FURNISHED HOME IN A RESIDENTIAL NEIGHBORHOOD IN THE LOS ANGELES AREA. MR. CAR AND HIS MOTHER RESIDE IN HOME AT THE BACK OF THE LOT. THE MINOR TIFINI IS SLEEPING IN THE MAIN HOME. MR. CAR INTENDS TO LOCATE OTHER LIVING QUARTERS IN A MONTH OR SO. THE MINOR TIFINI IS ATTENDING 11TH GRADE AT FAIRFAX HIGH.

GAIL CAR WAS BORN IN DETROIT, MICHIGAN. SHE IS AN ONLY CHILD AND WAS RAISED BY HER PARENTS UNTIL HER FATHER DIED WHEN SHE WAS EIGHT YEARS OLD. HER FATHER WAS A PRIZEFIGHTER AND HER MOTHER A SUNDAY SCHOOL TEACHER. AFTER HER FATHER'S DEATH, THE EXTENDED FAMILY ASSISTED HER MOTHER IN RAISING MS. CAR.

ACCORDING TO MS. CAR, THE DEATH OF HER FATHER WAS DIFFICULT AS THE THREE OF THEM WERE LIVING IN CALIFORNIA AND ALONE WHEN HE DIED WITHOUT FAMILY. HIS DEATH WAS SUDDEN.

MS. CAR STATES SHE OBTAINED GOOD GRADES IN SCHOOL AND DESCRIBED HER RELATIONSHIP WITH HER MOTHER AS ONE OF FRIENDSHIP. HER FATHER AND MOTHER USED CORPORAL PUNISHMENT ON OCCASION UNTIL SHE WAS BELIEVED TO BE TOO OLD FOR THAT, AND THEN OTHER FORMS OF DISCIPLINE WERE USED.

MS. CAR LEFT SCHOOL IN THE 11TH GRADE DESPITE GOOD GRADES FOR A REASON THAT CAN ONLY BE DESCRIBED AS CERTAINLY VAGUE AND BIZARRE. SHE ATTENDED SEVERAL HIGH SCHOOLS AND REQUIRED A BODYGUARD, ACCORDING TO SCHOOL PERSONNEL'S REPORTS TO HER MOTHER. AT HER LAST SCHOOL, SHE ATTENDED ONE DAY AND THEN SHE AND HER MOTHER WERE TOLD THAT SHE WOULD NOT BE ALLOWED TO ATTEND ANY SCHOOL IN THE LOS ANGELES AREA. SHE MAINTAINED THE REASONS FOR THIS WERE NEVER KNOWN.

SHE WAS 16 AND HER MOTHER WANTED TO SEND HER TO SWITZERLAND TO COMPLETE SCHOOL, BUT MS. CAR DID NOT WANT TO LEAVE THE COUNTRY. SHE ENTERED COSMETOLOGY TRAINING AND MET MINOR'S FATHER. MS. CAR REPORTS THEY DATED FOR THREE YEARS AND SHE BECAME PREGNANT WITH THE MINOR BRIAN.

ACCORDING TO MS. CAR, SHE WAS A HOUSEWIFE DURING THE MARRIAGE. SHE FEELS THE MARRIAGE FAILED POSSIBLY BECAUSE SHE NEVER HAD AN OPPORTUNITY TO BE ON HER OWN AND EXPERIENCE ANY FREEDOM AS AN ADULT. THE COUPLE'S SEPARATION TWO YEARS AGO WAS AMIABLE AND THEY GENERALLY SEEMED TO HAVE ACTED IN THE BEST INTERESTS OF THEIR CHILDREN WHERE THEIR OWN RELATIONSHIP IS CONCERNED. THEY STILL SEE EACH OTHER, BUT MS. CAR CONSIDERS THEIR SEPARATION PERMANENT AT THIS TIME.

AT THIS TIME MS. CAR IS LIVING WITH MING AND BRIAN IN A LARGE, ROOMY, NICELY FURNISHED APARTMENT SHE HAS RECENTLY OBTAINED. MING HAS BEEN ENROLLED AT 18TH STREET ELEMENTARY SCHOOL. THERE IS SOME CONCERN OVER THE NUMBER OF TARDIES

Appendix C. In re Car

AND ABSENCES THAT MING HAS EXPERIENCED IN SCHOOL. ACCORDING TO MS. CAR, HER 18-YEAR-OLD SON HAS BEEN RESPONSIBLE FOR GETTING MING TO SCHOOL. THIS ARRANGEMENT DOES NOT APPEAR TO BE WORKING WELL, AND IT WOULD SEEM ADVISABLE THAT MS. CAR MAKE OTHER ARRANGEMENTS BEFORE THE CITY SCHOOL PUPIL SERVICES AND ATTENDANCE BECOMES INVOLVED.

FAMILY FUNCTIONING

THE SPECIFIC PROBLEMS THAT REQUIRE JUVENILE COURT JURISDICTION AND DPSS SUPERVISION ARE:

1. MINOR, TIFINI, RECEIVED 2ND DEGREE BURNS TO HER BACK AS A RESULT OF A VIOLENT ALTERCATION BETWEEN HER AND HER MOTHER. ACCORDING TO A MATERNAL GRANDMOTHER WHO WITNESSED THE INCIDENT, THE ALTERCATION WAS INITIATED BY THE MINOR WHO REPORTEDLY THREW A BOWL OF KNIVES AT HER MOTHER. MINOR'S MOTHER ADMITTEDLY RETALIATED, CLAIMING SELF-DEFENSE, BY THROWING HOT WATER ON THE MINOR.

    THE POTENTIAL FOR VIOLENCE BETWEEN MINOR AND MOTHER IS EVIDENT AND MINOR'S CUSTODY SHOULD NOT BE RETURNED TO HER MOTHER UNTIL THE PARENT AND CHILD HAVE HAD SUFFICIENT EFFECTIVE COUNSELING SO AS TO ENSURE THAT MINOR WILL NOT EXPERIENCE FURTHER ABUSE.

2. MINOR, TIFINI, HAS SPECIAL AND UNIQUE PROBLEMS AND MINOR'S PARENTS HAVE A LIMITED ABILITY TO DEAL WITH SUCH PROBLEMS. THE MINOR TIFINI HAS BEEN ARRESTED TWO TIMES. HER LAST ARREST WAS FOR SHOPLIFTING AND SHE DID NOT COOPERATE WITH THE PROBATION DEPARTMENT'S DIVERSION PROGRAM. HER PROBATION CASE WAS DISMISSED BECAUSE THE FAMILY MOVED AWAY. SHE HAS NOT DONE WELL IN SCHOOL AND SHE HAS BEEN BOTH TRUANT AND SUSPENDED IN THE PAST.

    FOR THE MOST PART, IT WOULD APPEAR THAT THE MINOR'S PROBLEMS WITH HER MOTHER CENTER AROUND DEFIANCE AND HER MOTHER'S STRICTNESS. TIFINI SEEMS TO BE DOING WELL AT HER FATHER'S HOUSE AND HE DESCRIBES HIMSELF AS LENIENT. THUS FAR, THERE IS NO EVIDENCE THAT SHE IS PRESENTING HIM PROBLEMS.

    HOWEVER, WITHOUT COUNSELING, ONE WOULD ANTICIPATE THAT PROBLEMS WILL DEVELOP. ALSO IT IS CLEAR THAT HER FATHER HAS NOT PROVIDED THE KIND OF STRUCTURE TIFINI REQUIRES IN ORDER TO COPE WITH HER PROBLEMS WITH AUTHORITY FIGURES.

FAMILY STRENGTHS THAT COULD AID IN PROBLEM RESOLUTION ARE:

MR. AND MS. CAR, DESPITE THEIR SEPARATION, MAINTAIN AN AMIABLE RELATIONSHIP THAT WORKS IN THE BEST INTEREST OF THEIR CHILDREN. DESPITE SEPARATION, MR. CAR HAS MAINTAINED AN ONGOING RELATIONSHIP WITH HIS CHILDREN AND SEES THEM REGULARLY. MR. CAR, BUT NOT MS. CAR, VERBALIZES A WILLINGNESS FOR COUNSELING.

WHILE MR. CAR HAS EXPRESSED A DESIRE TO GET TIFINI INTO COUNSELING, THUS FAR HE HAS NOT DONE SO. HE WOULD PREFER THE COURT NOT TAKE JURISDICTION OF TIFINI, BUT IT WOULD SEEM INDICATED IN THIS CASE IF THIS MINOR IS TO PROCEED INTO ADULTHOOD IN A HEALTHY MANNER. THERE IS ALSO A QUESTION OF THE AMOUNT OF SUPERVISION MR. CAR IS ABLE TO EXERCISE OVER THE MINOR. SHE FAILED HER APPOINTED INTERVIEW WITH MR. CAR AND THE CSW CONDUCTING THIS INVESTIGATION. SHE ALSO FAILED TO CONTACT THE CSW BY TELEPHONE AS REQUESTED.

THERE IS NO EVIDENCE THAT THE MINOR MING IS IN DANGER OF ABUSE FROM HER MOTHER. WHILE THERE IS SOME CONCERN FOR MING'S ABSENCES AND TARDINESS TO SCHOOL, IT IS FELT THAT MS. CAR WILL CORRECT THESE WITHOUT THE COURT'S JURISDICTION. IT IS ALSO HOPED THAT, THROUGH COUNSELING TO DEAL WITH TIFINI'S PROBLEMS, MS. CAR WILL GAIN THE INSIGHT AND SKILLS NECESSARY TO TAKE MING THROUGH HER TEEN YEARS WITHOUT THE SAME SITUATION DEVELOPING.

PREVIOUS REMEDIAL SERVICES

THIS FAMILY WAS UNKNOWN TO SERVICES AGENCIES PRIOR TO THE PETITION REQUEST

X   THIS FAMILY HAS RECEIVED SOCIAL SERVICES IN THE PAST FROM

PROVIDER	SERVICE	YEAR
LA. COUNTY OF PROBATION	DIVERSION PROGRAM	INCOMPLETED BY MINOR -01

SERVICES WERE FOR CURRENTLY IDENTIFIED PROBLEMS   X YES   NO

AS THE RESULT OF THE PETITION REQUEST, DPSS HAS PROVIDED THE FOLLOWING INITIAL SERVICES BASED ON THE PROBLEMS IDENTIFIED IN THE REQUEST

Appendix C. In re Car

PROBLEM GIVEN/REFERRED	SERVICE/RESOURCE	DATE
CARE/PROTECTION FOR MINOR	SHELTER CARE, PLACEMENT WITH FATHER	1-23-00

PLAN FOR SERVICES:

X THE INITIAL SERVICES OFFERED HAVE BEEN EFFECTIVE AND WILL BE CONTINUED

THE INITIAL SERVICES OFFERED WERE NOT EFFECTIVE FOR THE FOLLOWING REASONS

THE SERVICES PLAN FOR THE FAMILY FOR THE NEXT PERIOD OF SUPERVISION WILL BE:

X FAMILY MAINTENANCE SERVICES
FAMILY REUNIFICATION SERVICES
PERMANENCY PLANNING

OBJECTIVES AND TIMETABLES

TO MAINTAIN THE MINOR TIFINI IN HER FATHER'S HOME DURING THE COMING SIX MONTHS.

1. MINOR'S FATHER TO ENTER TIFINI INTO COUNSELING WITHIN TWO WEEKS OF THIS HEARING.

2. MINOR'S FATHER TO MAINTAIN AN ADEQUATE DEGREE OF SUPERVISION OVER MINOR AND HER WHEREABOUTS.

3. MINOR'S PARENTS TO PARTICIPATE IN COUNSELING WHEN AND AS INDICATED, BY MINOR'S THERAPIST.

4. MINOR TIFINI IS TO REGULARLY ATTEND SCHOOL AND MAINTAIN ATTENDANCE AND GRADES AT AN ACCEPTABLE LEVEL.

During your fact investigation and interviews with all the parties, you have discovered the following information:

A. TIFINI:
  1. Tifini does not want to return to live with her mother, Gail, under any circumstances;
  2. Tifini strongly desires for the court to declare her emancipated pursuant to § 7120;

3. George Johnson, the father of Tifini's best friend, Amy Johnson, has offered Tifini a job working in his restaurant. She would work three nights a week and two nights on weekends from 4:00–8:00 p.m. She would earn approximately $250.00 a week. The job would not interfere with her attending school;
4. Although she really wants to be emancipated, she will consider moving in with her father;
5. If she lives with her father, she would also like Ming to live there too so that she will not have to see her mother, Gail, every time she visits Ming;
6. She wants the § 601 petition dismissed because she will obey the reasonable conditions her dad sets up and will no longer need to deal with her mother's overreaching control of her life.

B. MING:
7. Ming is in a unique position because the Department is willing to dismiss the petitions alleging that she should be declared a ward of the court;
8. Ming is willing to live anywhere and with anyone as long as she is able to stay with Tifini;
9. Ming has indicated that she considers Tifini her real mother because Tifini, not Gail, provides her with most of her daily physical and emotional care;
10. However, if she can't live with Tifini, she would rather live with her mother, Gail, than her father, William;
11. Ming was in the next room during the altercation between Gail and Tifini. However, after hearing the argument, she thinks that the burns were caused by an accident and that her mother never intended to hurt Tifini.

C. GAIL:
12. Gail does not want Tifini to live with her father because she feels that Tifini's problems with self-control and her attitude toward authority figures will be exacerbated;
13. Gail does not want Tifini to return home until she is willing to listen to Gail's reasonable demands;
14. Gail is willing to agree to Tifini's proposed emancipation upon the condition that the court order Tifini to attend psychological counseling to help her with her anger and resentment of authority figures;
15. Only if the Department threatens to permanently sever Gail's parental rights will she agree to attend counseling;
16. Gail is unwilling to voluntarily permit Ming to live with William, even if the court grants William custody of Tifini.

D. WILLIAM:

17. William Car is adamantly opposed to Tifini's proposed emancipation and would only consent if the court will agree to continue periodically monitoring her welfare;
18. William does not think that Tifini should return to Gail's home;
19. If Tifini cannot be placed with him, he thinks that the best alternative placement is with a foster family, as long as the court grants him reasonable unmonitored visitation with Tifini;
20. He would like Ming to live with him even if he does not become Tifini's custodial parent.

E. THE DEPARTMENT:

21. The Department's two main interests are the protection of Tifini Car and placing Tifini Car in a custodial arrangement that will help her learn personal responsibility and the importance of complying with reasonable demands of her custodial parent or guardian;
22. Because the Department has no plans at the present time to seek a severance of the parental bond between Gail Car and Tifini Car, the Department wants Gail to participate in either individual or family counseling;
23. If the Department can be convinced that emancipation is in the best interest of Tifini Car, it will probably not oppose such a motion;
24. If this case proceeds to trial the Department will argue against placing Tifini Car in her father's home because he does not appear to have the capacity to provide Tifini the disciplined upbringing she needs;
25. Depending on how the parents participate and react in this negotiation and/or mediation, the Department may reconsider its intent to dismiss the petition regarding Ming Car. If the parents appear unreasonable, the Department will seek to have Ming Car placed in foster care.

ETHICAL ANALYSIS OF *IN RE CAR*

In re Car provides an opportunity to negotiate or mediate an out-of-court settlement in a dependency child abuse case. The procedural context is very simple. The Department of Social Services has filed a petition alleging that Gail Car, the divorced custodial mother of 16-year-old Tifini Car and 6-year-old Ming Car, intentionally threw a pan of hot water on Tifini Car during a heated verbal confrontation with Tifini, causing her to suffer second-degree burns. The negotiation takes place after the state met its burden of demonstrating a prima facie case at the detention hearing (the rough equivalent of an arraignment in criminal court), but before the trial on the merits (the adjudication hearing). During this negotiation five parties will be represented by four separate counsel:

> Gail Car (custodial mother of Tifini and Ming Car);
> William Car (noncustodial father of Tifini and Ming Car);
> Tifini and Ming are represented by you; and
> The Department of Social Services.

One of the issues that the attorneys need to raise, especially in relation to Gail Car, is the scope of confidentiality and/or immunity during the mediation. Because the charges of intentional child abuse could also be filed against Gail Car in a criminal case, she will obviously be unwilling to participate in the mediation without some assurance of confidentiality and/or immunity. For a discussion of confidentiality and immunity in child abuse mediations, *see* William Wesley Patton, *Child Abuse: The Irreconcilable Differences between Criminal Prosecution and Informal Dependency Court Mediation*, 31 U. LOUISVILLE J. OF FAMILY L. 37 (1992–93).

A. LEGAL ISSUES.

A. THE PLEADINGS.

One of the central procedural issues in this negotiation is whether the case will proceed only in the child dependency court or whether actions will be brought against Tifini as a status offender or against Gail in criminal court.

II. EVIDENTIARY ISSUES.

It is likely that during the negotiation the various parties will use the admissibility and weight of various evidence as leverage. The following discussion lists some of the major evidentiary debates in which the parties may engage:

1. Tifini Car.

The FAMILY ASSESSMENT lists two of Tifini's prior arrests. In many jurisdictions prior arrests, as opposed to convictions, are inadmissible evidence. However, pursuant to *Federal Rules of Evidence, Rule 404(b)*, if the proponent can demonstrate a relevant use, other than to demonstrate the character of a person to show that he or she acted in conformity with the prior bad act, the evidence may be admissible. Although Tifini's attorney will argue that the prior arrests are not admissible at the dependency or status abuse adjudications, the Department will probably argue that they are admissible to demonstrate that Tifini "did not follow through on the requirement of community service work." The Department will argue that the prior arrests and failure to meet diversion requirements demonstrate a lack of control by the parents and a refusal by Tifini to follow express orders by a government official. This evidence is relevant to illustrate the need for declaring Tifini a ward of the court so that it can closely monitor Tifini and her parents.

2. Ming Car.

Because Ming is only 6 years old, there may be questions whether, if the case goes to trial, she is sufficiently competent to testify. Many evidence codes, including the *Federal Rules of Evidence, Rule 601*, provide that all witnesses are presumptively competent. However, *Rule 602* still requires that the witness have personal knowledge of the facts to which they testify. Ming's confidential instructions indicate that she was in the next room when Gail and Tifini argued and when Gail allegedly threw the pan of hot water at Tifini. Based upon the verbal fight, Ming thinks that the burning was just an accident. The Department will probably argue that, because Ming did not see the confrontation, but merely heard the fight out of context, she lacks personal knowledge. They will also argue that Ming's conclusion that the injury was accidental is pure speculation.

3. Gail Car.

The mother, Gail Car, will argue that her family history as a child is inadmissible. She will probably argue that her parents' use of corporal punishment on her as a child is also inadmissible. Further, she will argue that her need for a bodyguard at school is inadmissible. The Department will argue that that evidence is relevant to demonstrate that Gail was reared in a family environment that saw violence (corporal punishment) as one means of controlling children and that the need for a bodyguard further reflects on Gail being surrounded by violence. The Department may argue that the psychological literature has established a nexus between the manner in which a child is reared and the child-rearing methods that child will use as an adult while rearing her own child. In addition to the specific instances of bad acts, there is a great deal of data regarding Gail's relationship with her parents that she may argue should be inadmissible because the probative value is substantially outweighed by its prejudicial impact. However, because most dependency child abuse cases are court trials, not jury trials, it is unlikely that the evidence will be excluded under Fed. R. Evid. 403.

4. William Car.

The father, William Car, will probably make arguments similar to Gail's regarding the data describing his past. However, because much of this information casts William in a positive light, his attorney will have a difficult strategic decision whether or not to object were the case to proceed to the adjudication hearing [trial].

C. NEGOTIATION STRATEGIES.

1. Tifini Car.

Tifini Car wants to be emancipated pursuant to § 7120. Her best friend's father, George Johnson, has offered Tifini a job from 4:00–8:00 p.m. at his restaurant and she will earn approximately $250.00 dollars a week. That job will enable her to continue attending school and work three nights a week and two nights on the weekend. Her confidential instructions indicate that under no circumstances does she want to move back home to live with her mother, Gail Car. Although she might consider moving in with her father, William Car, she really prefers emancipation. Further, she will argue that if she is emancipated the court should dismiss both the dependency and status offenses cases because emancipation will prevent further violence between her and her mother.

2. Ming Car.

Ming Car is willing to live in any arrangement in which she and Tifini will remain together. She relies more heavily on Tifini to help rear her than on her mother or father. She does not care whether they live with their mother, father, or with foster parents. One of the most interesting VII-21 aspects of Ming's case is that the Department is recommending that the petition regarding her be dismissed. Her attorney is thus placed in a difficult position. If he or she cooperates with the Department regarding the relationship among Tifini, Gail, and William, it is likely that the Department will make its recommendation of dismissal to the court, which has the ultimate authority to accept or reject the Department's motion to dismiss. However, if the attorney represents Ming's position that she wants to stay with her sister no matter where Tifini is ultimately placed, he or she risks alienating the Department, which might result in the Department deciding to proceed with its petition regarding Ming. Because Ming is only 6 years old, her attorney will have a difficult time explaining to her the legal consequences of her negotiation and/or mediation strategy.

Thus, it appears to be a violation of the duty of loyalty, zealousness, and competence to represent both Tifini and Ming because a zealous argument for emancipating Tifini will frustrate Ming's goal of remaining with her in any custodial arrangement. Further, the more that an attorney zealously argues that the mother, Gail, is dangerous, the more likely the dependency court will find that Ming is also in danger. As a result, Ming may not only be placed

Appendix C. In re Car 237

without Tifini but may also be taken away from her only other emotional bond, her mother.

3. *Gail Car.*

Gail's case is extremely complex. On the one hand she appears not to accept any responsibility for her relationship with her daughter Tifini. In fact, she might serve as the Department's strongest witness against Tifini if the case proceeds under a status offense [which focuses on Tifini's recalcitrance] rather than under dependency [which focuses on the weaknesses of Gail's parenting skills]. However, her attorney must counsel her regarding her refusal to accept any responsibility for Tifini's burns because the issue in the dependency case will focus as much on her ability to reasonably parent Tifini as on her moral culpability in causing the burns. In addition, Gail needs to be counseled regarding her almost flippant desire to have Tifini placed almost anywhere except with her or with William. There is always the possibility that the court could eventually sever her parental rights if the court takes jurisdiction over Tifini and if Gail continues to refuse to cooperate with the family reunification plan. Gail's attitude toward William's caring for Tifini substantially increases the chances that the Department will go forward with the hearing and place Tifini with a nonrelative caretaker. Finally, unless Gail agrees to participate in court-ordered counseling, it is unlikely that the Department will ever reunite Tifini and her, and it is likely that the Department will argue that even their visits should be monitored by the Department.

4. *William Car.*

William's confidential instructions indicate that he would strongly resist Tifini's desire for emancipation. Because emancipation requires the consent of both parents, William holds veto power over this option. But what if the Department during the negotiation rejects both Gail and William as the proper custodial parent? Does William prefer that Tifini be placed with a foster parent or in the Department's suggested group home, rather than becoming emancipated, an option that would permit her to visit with William at any time that they found mutually agreeable? Remember, William is adamantly opposed to any state intervention.

5. *The Department.*

The Department is in the driver's seat in this negotiation because it controls the ambit of the petition and the direction that this litigation will take. Will the Department focus on the weaknesses of the Car family structure in a dependency proceeding or proceed under a status petition in treating Tifini as an uncontrollable teenager? The Department has significant leverage in this case and may demand certain conditions from the parents in exchange for dismissing the petition. First, the Department may require the parents to agree to attend family counseling, something that Gail has so far been unwilling to try. Eventually, if Gail refuses to follow court-ordered counseling, the Department could seek to sever her parental rights. Is it ethically permissible for the Department to threaten the removal of Ming if the mother, Gail, refuses treatment? The attorney representing the Department must always keep in mind that it is charged with representing the best interests of the children and thus should not transform this negotiation into a bitter power struggle for positional bargaining.

In re Car is a very realistic simulation because it weaves the highly emotional family members' interrelationships within the legal fabric of child dependency law. Each of the possible negotiated family plans (placing Tifini with her father, in a group home, or with foster parents or freeing her to live alone through emancipation) creates incentives and problems for each family member. One of the serious issues that complicates the resolution is Ming's dependence upon Tifini as one of her primary child caretakers. How the parties and the Department will balance the seemingly conflicting needs of these two children within the obviously dysfunctional dynamic of the Car family is an interesting legal dynamic replete with ethical issues.

Other Authorities

Abel, Laura K., & David S. Udell, *If You Gag the Lawyers, Do You Choke the Courts? Some Implications for Judges When Funding Restrictions Curb Advocacy by Lawyers on Behalf of the Poor*, 29 FORDHAM URB. L.J. 873 (2002). 7
Abrahamson, Shirley S., *Remarks of the Hon. Shirley S. Abrahamson before the American Bar Association Commission on Separation of Powers and Judicial Independence*, 12 ST. JOHN'S J. LEGAL COMMENT. 69, 72 (Fall 1996). 155
Airey, Pamela A., Comment, *It's a Natural Fit: Expanding Mediation to Alleviate Congestion in the Troubled Juvenile Court System*, 16 J. AM. ACAD. MATR. LAW. 275, 288–289 (1999). 95
Albrandt, Brooke, *Turning in the Client: Mandatory Child Abuse Reporting Requirements and the Criminal Defense of Battered Women*, 81 TEX. L. REV. 655, 657, 674 (2002). 71, 79
American Bar Association, ASK ETHICSearch, PROF. LAW., V. 8, No. 4 (August 1997) (citing ABA Formal Op. 92–368). 80
American Bar Association, THE IMPROVEMENT OF THE ADMINISTRATION OF JUSTICE 11–12 (3d ed. 1952). 149
Anderson Garcia, Sandra & Robert Batey, *The Roles of Counsel for the Parent in Child Dependency Proceedings*, 22 GA. L. REV. 1079, 1080, 1090, 1092 (1988). 37, 57, 60
Benjamin, Robert D., *The Use of Mediative Strategies in Traditional Legal Practice*, 14 J. AM. ACAD. MATR. LAW. 203, 229 (1997). 27
Bentley, Amy, *Ventura Defense Attorneys Fear Dependency Court System Unfair*, L. A. DAILY J., Jan. 7, 1999, at 3. 5
Birke, Richard & Craig R. Fox, *Psychological Principles in Negotiating Civil Settlements*, 4 HARV. NEGOT. L. REV. 1, 1, 14, 26 (1999). 89, 97
Boettger, Dr. Iur Ulrich, *Efficiency Versus Party Empowerment – Against a Good Faith Requirement in Mandatory Mediation*, 23 REV. LITIG. 1, 20 (2004). 110
Burrows, Ronni K. & Elaine Buzzinotti, *Legal Therapists and Lawyers Care-Giving Partnerships for the Next Century*, 19 FAM. ADVOC. 33 (1997). 73
Buss, Emily, *Confronting Developmental Barriers to the Empowerment of Child Clients*, Family and Fertility, National Institute of Child Health & Human Development, at 2 (2003). http://www.nichd.nih.gov/publications/pubs/coundbsb/sub4.htm#divorce. 1, 4
———, *"You're My What?" The Problem of Children's Misperceptions of Their Lawyers' Roles*, LXIV FORDHAM L. REV. 1699, 1700–1703 (1996). 30
Callahan, Cindy, & Vince Willis, *Searching for Answers: About the Role of the Guardian Ad Litem*, 36 MD. B.J. 46 (May/June, 2003). 60
Cavell, Cathleen C., *Ethical Lawyering in Massachusetts*, Chapter 18, §18.4 (2000). 46

Child Custody Proceedings Reform: High-Conflict Custody Cases: Reforming the System for Children, Conference Report and Action Plan, at 1 (American Bar Association Family Law Section, September 8, 2000), http://www.abanet.org/child/wingspread.html. 2

CHILD PHYSICAL AND SEXUAL ABUSE: GUIDELINES FOR TREATMENT 25 (U.S. Dept. of Justice, 2003). 69

Coben, James R., *Gollum, Meet Smeagol: A Schizophrenic Rumination on Mediator Values beyond Self-Determination and Neutrality*, 5 CARDOZO J. CONFLICT RESOL. 65, 68 (2004). 95

Cochran, Robert F., Jr., et al., *Symposium: Client Counseling and Moral Responsibility*, 30 PEPP. L. REV. 591, 624 (2003). 48

Cole, Sarah R., Nancy H. Rogers, & Craig A. McEwan, MEDIATION: LAW, POLICY, PRACTICE, 7–28 to 7–29, 12–2 (2001). 89, 98

Cooley, John W., *Defining the Ethical Limits of Acceptable Deception in Mediation*, 4 PEPP. DISP. RESOL. L.J. 263, 271 (2004). 108

_____, MEDIATION ADVOCACY, 8, 9 (2d ed. 2002). 92

COUNTING COUPLES: IMPROVING MARRIAGE, DIVORCE, REMARRIAGE, AND COHABITATION DATA IN THE FEDERAL STATISTICAL SYSTEM, at 25–26 (The Data Collection Committee of the Federal Interagency Forum on Child and Family Services, December 13, 2001). 1

COURT STATISTICS REPORT: STATEWIDE CASELOAD TRENDS 1989–1990 THROUGH 1998–1999, at vii, x, 46, 56 (Judicial Council of California, Administrative Office of the Courts, 2000). 2, 60

Creo, Robert A., *Mediation 2004: The Art and the Artist*, 108 PENN. ST. L. REV. 1017, 1025–1026, 1063 (2004). 92, 110

Crime in the United States, 1999, U.S. Dept. of Justice Federal Bureau of Investigation, October 15 (2000). 85, 86

Dale, Michael J., *Providing Counsel to Children in Dependency Proceedings in Florida*, 25 NOVA L. REV. 769, 795 (2001). 34, 57

Deason, Ellen E., *Enforcing Mediated Settlement Agreements: Contract Law Collides with Confidentiality*, 35 U. C. Davis L. Rev. 33 (2001). 112

Dees, J. Gregory, *Promoting Honesty in Negotiation: An Exercise in Practical Ethics, in* WHAT'S FAIR: ETHICS IN NEGOTIATION 124 (Carrie Mendel-Meadow & Michael Wheeler, eds., 2001). 111

Degnan, Charles A., *Admission to the Bar and the Separation of Powers*, 7 UTAH L. REV. 82, 86 (1960). 148

Delgado, Richard, *Norms and Normal Science: Toward a Critique of Normativity in Legal Thought*, 139 U. PA. L. REV. 933, 943–44 (1991). 55

_____, *Rodrigo's Thirteenth Chronicle: Legal Formalism and Law's Discontents*, 95 MICH. L. REV. 1105, 1116 (1997). 145

Drews & Halprin, *Determining the Effective Representation of a Child in Our Legal System: Do Current Standards Accomplish the Goal?*, 13 FAM. CT. REV. 73 (2004). 32

Drews, Michael & Pamela Halprin, *Determining the Effective Representation of a Child in Our Legal System: Do Current Standards Accomplish the Goal?*, 13 FAM. CT. REV. 73, 79 (2004). 31

Edwards, Leonard, *The Relationship of Family and Juvenile Courts in Child Abuse Cases*, 27 SANTA CLARA L. REV. 201, 204 (1987). 91

FINAL REPORT: CALIFORNIA CHILD AND FAMILY SERVICES REVIEW 6–8 (U.S. Department of Health & Human Services, Administration for Children and Families, Administration on Children, Youth and Families Children's Bureau, January 2003). 74

Folberg, Jay & Alison Taylor, MEDIATION: A COMPREHENSIVE GUIDE TO RESOLVING
   CONFLICTS WITHOUT LITIGATION 244 (1984). 96
Fordham Conference on Ethical Issues in the Legal Representation of Children, LXIV
   FORDHAM L. REV. 1279, at 1339 (1996). 29
Fox, Sanford, *Juvenile Justice Reform: An Historical Perspective*, 22 STAN. L. REV. 1187
   (1970). 102
Freeman, Marsha B., *Divorce Mediation: Sweeping Conflicts under the Rug, Time to
   Clean House*, 73 U. DET. MERCY L. REV. 67 (2000). 96
Gibson, Hon. Phil S., *Chief Justice Urges Effective Plan to Give Courts Rule-Making
   Power*, 15 CAL. ST. B. J. 331 (1940) 161
Gillers, Stephen & Roy D. Simon, Jr., REGULATION OF LAWYERS: STATUTES
   AND STANDARDS 70–74, 163 (1974). 69, 76
Graham, Lorie M., *Aristotle's Ethics and the Virtuous Lawyer: Part One of a Study on
   Legal Ethics and Clinical Legal Education*, 20 J. LEGAL PROF. 5 (1995–1996). 146
Grisso, Thomas, *What We Know about Youth's Capacities as Trial Defendants*, in
   Thomas Grisso & Robert G. Schwartz, YOUTH ON TRIAL: A DEVELOPMENTAL
   PERSPECTIVE ON JUVENILE JUSTICE 162–163 (2000). 4
Guccione, Jean, *Jury Urges Execution of Man Who Killed 2 of His Children*, L.A. TIMES,
   July 26, 2001, at B1. 19
Guggenheim, Martin, *The Right to Be Represented but Not Heard: Reflections on
   Legal Representation for Children*, 59 N. Y. U. L. REV. 76 (1984). 3
———, *What's Wrong with Children's Rights*, 17 HARV. L. REV. 162 (2005). 3
Hall, Michael J. & Jean Guccione, *Complaining Consumers Getting Scant Satisfaction:
   Problems Remain in Bar's "Model" System*, L.A. DAILY J., July 11, 1994, at 1, 10. 146
Harvey III, James R., *Loyalty in Government Litigation: Department of Justice
   Representation of Agency Clients*, 37 WM. & MARY L. REV. 1569, 1596 (1996). 46
Haussmann, Brian C., *The ABA Ethical Guidelines for Settlement Negotiations:
   Exceeding the Limits of the Adversarial Ethic*, 89 CORNELL L. REV. 1218, 1230, 1237
   (2004). 93, 109
Haviena, Thomas, *Prosecution and Defense Have Different Disclosure Obligations*,
   L.A. DAILY J., February 2, 2004, p. 7, cols. 1–3. 79
Hazard, Geoffrey C., Jr., *Conflicts of Interest in Representation of Public Agencies in
   Civil Matters*, 9 WIDENER J. PUB. L. 211 (2000). 46
Heinke, Rex S., *The Transformation of the State Courts: The Association Is Moving to
   Participate More Fully in the Judicial Council Rule-Making Process*, L.A. LAW.,
   April, 2001. 161
Hengstler, Gary A., *Vox Populi: The Public Perception of Lawyers: ABA Poll*, A.B.A.J.,
   September 1993, at 62. 145
*High-Conflict Custody Cases: Reforming the System for Children: Conference Report
   and Action Plan 1* (The Johnson Foundation Wingspread Conference
   Center, Wisconsin, September 8–10, 2000). 27
*In the Matter of the Proceeding Pursuant to Section 44, Subdivision 4, of the Judiciary
   Law in Relation to Bruce M. Kaplan, A Judge of the Family Court*, May 6, 1996
   (1996 WL 4418512). 58
INTER-AGENCY COUNCIL ON CHILD ABUSE AND NEGLECT, DATA ANALYSIS REPORT
   FOR 1996: STATUS REPORT ON CHILD ABUSE & NEGLECT IN LOS ANGELES
   COUNTY, at 142 (1996). 90
Johnson-Weider, Michelle, *Guardians Ad Litem: A Solution without Strength in
   Helping Protect Dependent Children*, 77, 87 FLA. B.J. 87 (2003). 34, 57
Joseph P. Nadeau, *What It Means to Be a Judge*, 39 No. 3 JUDGES J. 34 (2000). 86
Judge Faces State Disciplinary Hearings over Alleged Conduct, L.A. DAILY J., February
   20, 2004, at 1, 5. 57

Juvenile Arrests 1999, JUV. JUST. BULL., Dec. 2000, at 1 (Office of Juvenile Justice and
   Delinquency Prevention, U.S. Dept. of Justice). 86
Katner, David R., *Coming to Praise, Not to Bury, The New ABA Standards Of Practice
   For Lawyers Who Represent Children in Abuse and Neglect Cases*, 14 GEO. J. LEGAL
   ETHICS 103 (2000). 29
Kell, William A., *Voices Lost and Found: Training Ethical Lawyers for Children*, 73
   IND. L.J. 635 (1998). 60
Kodman, Rod, *Re-Victimizing Innocent Victims: How California Violates the
   Constitutional Rights of its Abused and Neglected Children*, 4 J.L. & POL'Y 67, 87
   (2000). 12
Kogan, Matthew, *The Problems and Benefits of Adopting Family Group Conferencing
   for PINS (CHINS) Children*, 39 FAM. CT. REV. 207, 208 (2002). 96
Krikorian, Greg, *Lawyers for Children Say County Fails to Cooperate*, L.A. TIMES,
   August 22, 2001, at B1. 19
Kuhn, Richard, and John Guidubaldi, *Child Custody Policies and Divorce Rates in
   the United States* (Paper presented at the 11th Annual Conference of the Children's
   Rights Council, at 1 (Washington, D.C., 1997)). 1
Late Reports, L.A. DAILY J., Sept. 17, 2001, at 1. 19
LEAGUE OF WOMEN VOTERS OF CALIFORNIA EDUCATION FUND, JUVENILE JUSTICE
   STUDY COMMITTEE, JUVENILE JUSTICE IN CALIFORNIA PART II: DEPENDENCY
   SYSTEM, APPENDIX I: NATIONAL AND CALIFORNIA STATISTICS ON CHILD ABUSE
   AND NEGLECT (July 1998). 90
Lee, Blewett, *The Constitutional Power of the Courts over Admission to the Bar*, 13
   HARV. L. REV. 233, 245 (1899). 148
Levin, A. Leo and Anthony G. Amsterdam, *Legislative Control over Judicial
   Rule-Making: A Problem in Constitutional Revision*, 107 U. PA. L. REV. 1, 3 (1958). . . 149
Liu, Caitlin, *Children's Testimony in Case Assailed*, L.A. TIMES, July 26, 2001, at B1. 19
Mandelbaum, Randi, *Revisiting the Question of Whether Young Children in
   Child Protection Proceedings Should Be Represented by Lawyers*, 32 LOY. U. CHI. L J. 1
   (2000). 29
Mann, Caramae Richey, *Courtroom Observations of Extra-Legal Factors in the Juvenile
   Court Dispositions of Runaway Boys: A Field Study*, JUV. FAM. CT. J., Nov. 1980, at 1,
   43. 55
Marrus, Ellen, *Please Keep My Secret: Child Abuse Reporting Statutes, Confidentiality,
   and Juvenile Delinquency*, 11 GEO. J. LEGAL ETHICS 509, 517, fn. 37 (1998). 71
Martin, Teri Kathleen, *Developing Disposition Decisonmaking Guidelines for Juvenile
   Courts* 80 (1985), 129 (unpublished Ph.D. dissertation, University of
   Illinois at Chicago). 55
Mason, Thomas P., *Child Abuse and Neglect Part I: Historical Overview, Legal Matrix,
   and Social Perspectives*, 50 N.C. L. REV. 293 (1972). 102
McBeth, Veronica Simmons & Shelley M. Stump, *Reclaiming the Courts' Historical
   Role: Judges as Leaders in Their Communities*, 38 JUDGES J. 19, 22 (1999). 85
McCarthy, Francis Barry, William Wesley Patton, & James G. Carr, JUVENILE LAW
   AND ITS PROCESSES: CASES AND MATERIALS 30 (3d. 2003). 88
Mengler, Thomas M., *The Theory of Discretion in the Federal Rules of Evidence*, 74
   IOWA L. REV. 129, 413, 445 (1989). 55
Menkel-Meadow, Carrie, *Ethics in Alternative Dispute Resolution: New Issues, No
   Answers from the Adversary Conception of Lawyers' Responsibilities*, *in* MEDIATION:
   THEORY, POLICY AND PRACTICE 429, 430 (Carrie Menkel-Meadow, ed., 2001). 101
——, *Ethics in Arbitration and Related Dispute Resolution Processes: What's
   Happening and What's Not*, 56 U. MIAMI L. REV. 949, 962 (2002). 93

―――, *Ethics, Morality and Professional Responsibility in Negotiation, in*
MEDIATION: A COMPREHENSIVE GUIDE TO RESOLVING CONFLICTS WITHOUT
LITIGATION 119, 129 (Jay Folberg & Alison Taylor, eds. 1984). 110
―――, *The Trouble with the Adversary System in a Postmodern*
Multicultural World, 38 WM. & MARY L. REV. 5, 5–7 (1996). 93
―――, *Whose Dispute Is It Anyway?: A Philosophical and Democratic Defense*
of Settlement (In Some Cases), in MEDIATION: THEORY, POLICY AND PRACTICE
39, 61 (Carrie Menkel-Meadow, ed. 2001). 101
Molvig, Dianne, *Is Our Judiciary a Co-Equal Branch of Government?*, 70 WIS. LAW.
14, 16–17 (August 1997). 152
Mulcahey, John M., *Separation of Powers in Pennsylvania: The Judiciary's Prevention*
of Legislative Encroachment, 32 DUQ. L. REV. 539, 541 (1994). 149
Must Government Lawyers "Seek Justice" in Civil Litigation?, 9 WIDENER J. PUB. L.
235, 238 (2000). 45
Myers, John E. B., *Session 3: Children's Rights in the Context of Welfare, Dependency,*
and the Juvenile Court, 8 U. C. DAVIS J. JUV. L. & POL'Y 267 (2004). 4
Myers, John E., *Definition and Origins of the Backlash Against Child Protection, in*
EXCELLENCE IN CHILDREN'S LAW, 21, 32 (1994). 1
Note, Legislative or Judicial Control of Attorneys, 8 FORDHAM L. REV. 103, 105 (1939). . . 148
Note, The Inherent Power of the Judiciary to Regulate the Practice of Law – A Proposed
Delineation, 60 MINN. L. REV. 783, 802 (1976). 149
Olson, Kelly Browe, *Lessons Learned from a Child Protection Mediation Program: If at*
First You Succeed and Then You Don't, 41 FAM. CT. REV. 480, 480–481 (2003). 90
PACE SYSTEM APPOINTEE EARNINGS SUMMARY REPORT OF THE LOS ANGELES SUPERIOR
COURT MP DISTRICT FOR APPOINTEE TYPES, ALL JUVENILE DEPENDENCY CASES
07/02/97 THROUGH 06/29/98, at 15; January 22, 1990, Dependency Court Legal
Services Contract, at 1. 5
Patton, William Wesley & Dr. Sara Latz, *Severing Hansel from Gretel: An Analysis*
of Siblings' Association Rights, 48 U. MIAMI L. REV. 745 (1994). 11
Patton, William Wesley, *Child Abuse: The Irreconcilable Differences between Criminal Pros-*
ecution and Informal Dependency Court Mediation, 31 U. LOUISVILLE J. FAM. L. 37,
38–39 (1993). 91
―――, *Evolution in Child Abuse Litigation: The Theoretical Void*
Where Evidentiary and Procedural Worlds Collide, 25 LOY. L.A.L. REV. 1009,
1011–1013 (1992) 129. 55
―――, *Forever Torn Asunder: Charting Evidentiary Parameters, The*
Right to Competent Counsel and the Privilege against Self-Incrimination in
California Child Dependency and Parental Severance Cases, 27 SANTA CLARA
L. REV. 299, 301 (1987). 6
―――, *Legislative Regulation of Dependency Court Attorneys:*
Public Relations and Separation of Powers, 24 NOTRE DAME J. LEGIS. 3 (1998). . . . 29, 145
―――, *Pandora's Box: Opening Child Protection Cases to the Press and Public,*
27 W.S. U. L. REV. 181, 182, fn. 3 (2000). 87
―――, *Searching for the Proper Role of Children's Counsel in California Dependency*
Cases; Or the Answer to the Riddle of the Dependency Sphinx, 1 J (1999). 35
―――, *Standards of Appellate Review for Denial of Counsel and*
Ineffective Assistance of Counsel In Child Protection and Parental Severance
Cases, 27 LOYLA UNIV. CHICAGO L. J. 195 (1996). 12
―――, *The Interrelationship between Sibling Custody and Visitation and Conflicts*
of Interest in the Representation of Multiple Siblings in Dependency Proceedings,
23 CHILD. LEGAL RTS. J. 18, 29 (2003). 10

_____, *The World Where Parallel Lines Converge: The Privilege against Self-Incrimination in Concurrent Civil and Criminal Child Abuse Proceedings*, 24 GA L.REV. 473, 518–524 (1990). 25, 55

Perschbacher, Rex R., *Enter at Your Own Risk: The Initial Consultation & Conflicts of Interest*, 3 GEO. J. LEGAL ETHICS 689, 689–690 (1990). 21

Peters, Jean Koh, *Representing Children in Child Protection Proceedings: Ethical and Practical Dimensions* (LexisNexis, 1997). 32

Picker, Christine A., *The Intersection of Domestic Violence and Child Abuse: Ethical Considerations and Tort Issues for Attorneys Who Represent Battered Women with Abused Children*, 12 ST. LOUIS U. PUB. L. REV. 69, 89 (1993). 75

A. Platt, THE CHILD SAVERS 9 (1969). 102

Pluckett, T., A CONCISE HISTORY OF THE COMMON LAW 544 (1956). 101

Press Release, U.S. Dept. of Justice Federal Bureau of Investigation, Crime Index Trends, January through June 2000 (Dec. 18, 2000).

Rainey, James, *Foster Child Adoptions Soar in California*, L.A. TIMES, Orange County ed., May 8, 2000, at A22. 17

Rendleman, Douglas R., *Parens Patriae: From Chancery to the Juvenile Court*, 23 S.C.L. REV. 205 (1971). 102

Report of the Working Group on Determining the Child's Capacity to Make Decisions, 64 FORDHAM L. REV. 1339, 1339–1340 (1996). 32

REPRESENTING CHILDREN: STANDARDS FOR ATTORNEYS AND GUARDIAN AD LITEM IN CUSTODY OR VISITATION PROCEEDINGS (1994). 31

Reuben, Richard C., *Democracy and Dispute Resolution: The Problem of Arbitration*, 67 LAW & CONTEMP. PROBS. 279, 285 (2004). 94, 100

Rodes, Robert E., Jr., *Government Lawyers*, 9 WIDENER J. PUB. L. 281, 28–182 (2000). . . . 46

Ross, Catherine J., *From Vulnerability to Voice: Appointing Counsel for Children in Civil Litigation*, 64 FORDHAM L. REV. 1571 (1996). 3

Rufenacht, Mindy D., *The Concern over Confidentiality in Mediation – An In-Depth Look at the Protection Provided by the Proposed Uniform Mediation Act*, 2000 J. DISP. RESOL. 113 (2000). 112

Saccuzzo, Dennis P., *Controversies in Divorce Mediations*, 79 NOTRE DAME L. REV. 425, 426, 435 (2003). 89, 92, 99

Saichek, David A., *Shared Powers: Harmony without Hegemony*, 69 WIS. LAW. 3 (October 1996). 152

Schauer, Frederich, *The Authority of Legal Scholarship*, 139 U. PA. L. REV. 1003, 1011 (1991). 55

Scheiber, Harry N., *Innovation, Resistance, and Change: A History of Judicial Reform and the California Courts, 1960–1990*, 66 S. CAL. L. REV. 2049, 2086–2087 (1993). 161

Schepard, Andrew, *An Introduction to the Model Standards of Practice for Family and Divorce Mediation*, 35 FAM L.Q. 1, 3 (2001). 94

Schiff, Corinne, *Child Custody and the Ideal of Motherhood in Late Nineteenth Century New York*, 4 GEO. J. ON FIGHTING POVERTY 403 (1997). 88, 102

Schneyer, Ted, *Legal Process Scholarship and the Regulation of Lawyers*, 65 FORDHAM L. REV. 33, 34 (1996). 150

Scott, Elizabeth S., *The Legal Construction of Adolescence*, 29 HOFSTRA L. REV. 547 (2000). 4

Scott, Elizabeth S. & Thomas Grisso, *The Evolution of Adolescence: A Developmental Perspective On Juvenile Justice Reform*, 88 J. CRIM. L. & CRIMINOLOGY 137(1977). 5

Shafiroff, Ira L., *What Evil Lurks: Client Confidentiality Should Not Trump the Life of an Innocent Person*, L.A. DAILY J., January 29, 2003, p. 6, cols. 3–5. 79

Other Authorities 245

Shoot, Brian J., *"Don't Come Back Without A Reasonable Offer": The Extent of, and Limits on, Court Power to Foster Settlement*, 76 N.Y. ST. B.J. 10, 11 (2004). 93
Simon, Paul, *Foreword: Ethics in Law and Politics*, 28 LOY. U. CHI. L. REV. 221, 225 (1996). 145
Smith, Kenneth Cruce, *A Profile of Juvenile Court Judges in the United States*, JUV. JUST., Aug. 1974, at 27–29 55
Solomon, Richard C., *Wearing Many Hats: Confidentiality and Conflicts of Interest Issues for the California Public Lawyer*, 25 SW. U. L. REV. 265, 272 (1996); CAL. EVID. CODE §175. 21
The Bounds of Advocacy, 9 J. AM. ACAD. MATR. LAW. 1, 2 (1992). 27
The Bounds of Advocacy, Preliminary Statement (American Academy of Matrimonial Lawyers). 27
Thoennes, Nancy, *Child Sexual Abuse: Whom Should a Judge Believe? What Should a Judge Believe*, 27 NO. 3 JUDGES J. 14 (1988). 86
Thompson, Peter H., *Enforcing Rights Generated in Court-Connected Mediation – The Tension between the Aspirations of a Private Facilitative Process and the Reality of Public Adversarial Justice*, 19 OHIO ST. J. DISP. RESOL. 509, 512, 533 (2004). 98, 106
Tocqueville, Alexis de, DEMOCRACY IN AMERICA 275–276 (Phillips Bradley, ed., 1987) (1835). 145
Toker, John A., CALIFORNIA ARBITRATION AND MEDIATION PRACTICE GUIDE: COURT-ORDERED ADR 457 (Lawpress 2003). 112
U.S. DEPARTMENT OF HEALTH AND HUMAN SERVICES, ADMINISTRATION FOR CHILDREN AND FAMILIES, ADMINISTRATION ON CHILDREN, YOUTH AND FAMILIES CHILDREN'S BUREAU (JANUARY 2003). 90
U.S. DEPARTMENT OF HEALTH AND HUMAN SERVICES, NATIONAL CLEARINGHOUSE ON CHILD ABUSE AND NEGLECT INFORMATION, FOSTER CARE NATIONAL STATISTICS (April 2001). 90
Ventrell, Marvin R., *The Child's Attorney*, 17 FAM. ADVOC. 73, 73 (1995). 29
Ver Steegh, Nancy, *Yes, No, and Maybe: Informed Decision Making about Divorce Mediation in the Presence of Domestic Violence*, 9 WM. & MARY J. WOMEN & L. 145, 159–160 (2003). 89
Wagner, Stephen James, *The Ethics of Family Law Disclosure: Have You Suborned Perjury Lately?*, 8 CAL. FAM. L. MONTHLY 197, 198 (August 2004). 108
Wald, Michael S., *State Intervention on Behalf of 'Neglected' Children: A Search for Realistic Standards*, 27 STAN. L. REV. 985, 1017, n. 168 (1975). 55
Waldman, Ellen A., *The Challenge of Certification: How to Ensure Mediator Competence while Preserving Diversity*, 30 U.S.F.L. REV. 723, 723 (1996). 92
Welch, Nancy A., *The Place of Court-Connected Mediation in a Democratic Justice System*, 38 WM. & MARY L. REV. 5, 137–138 (2004). 98
White, James J., *Machiavelli and the Bar: Ethical Limitations on Lying in Negotiation*, in WHAT'S FAIR: ETHICS IN NEGOTIATION 93 (Carrie Mendel-Meadow & Michael Wheeler eds. 2001). 109
Wilker, Steven, *Child Abuse, Substance Abuse, and the Role of the Dependency Court*, 7 1 WEST LAW 7 HARV. BLACKLETTER J. 1 (1990). 17
Wilkins, David B., *How Should We Determine Who Should Regulate Lawyers? – Managing and Context in Professional Regulation*, 65 FORDHAM L. REV. 465, 482–484 (1996). 151
Williams, Lesley E., *The Civil Regulation of Prosecutors*, 67 FORDHAM L. REV. 3441, 3443 (1999). 46
Wolfram, Charles W., *Lawyer Turf and Lawyer Regulation – The Role of the Inherent-Powers Doctrine*, 12 U. ARK. LITTLE-ROCK L. REV. 1, 4–6 (1989–1990). 149

Workie, Blaine, *Chemical Dependency and the Legal Profession: Should Addiction to Drugs and Alcohol Ward off Heavy Discipline?*, 9 GEO. J. LEGAL ETHICS 1357, 1372 (1996)..146
Wright, Claudia, *Representation of Children in a Unified Family Court System in Florida*, 14 U. FLA. J. L. & PUB. POL'Y 179, 189–191 (2003)....................34
WuDunn, Sheryl, *Japan Confronts Child Abuse*, N.Y. TIMES, Aug. 15, 1999 at 7A......87
Yagman, Stephen, *Longtime Cycle of Bench Bullying*, L.A. DAILY J., February 12, 2002 at 6..53
Yarn, Douglas, *The Death of ADR: A Cautionary Tale of Isomorphism through Institutionalization*, 108 PENN. ST. L. REV. 929, 929–930 (2004)..............100
Zacharias, Fred, *The Professional Discipline of Prosecutors*, 79 N.C.L. REV. 721, 726 (2001)..45

Cases and Ethics Opinions

A. R. v. State, 937 P. 2d 1037 (Utah 1997). 81
ABA Ethics Opinion 347 (1981). 50
ABA Ethics Opinion 399 (1996). 50
ABA Formal Op. 97-405, April 19, 1997. 22
ABA Formal Opinion 94-387. 48
ABA Formal Opinion 94-387 (September 26, 1994). 48
ABA Informal Op. 1413, June 23, 1978. 22
ABA Informal Opinion 929. 22
Adoption of Hugo, 700 N. E. 2nd 516 (Mass. 1998), cert. denied, 526 U. S.
　1034 (1999). 11
Alabama Bar Association Opinion Number 1995-06. 79
Alabama Judicial Inquiry Commission, #87293, March 2, 1987. 83
Alabama State Bar Opinion No. 2002-02. 57
Alabama State Bar Opinion Number 2003-03. 39
Alaska Bar Association Ethics Committee, Opinion 92-6 (October 30, 1992). 43
Alaska Bar Association Ethics Opinions Nos. 71-1 (April 14, 1971). 39
Alaska Commission on Judicial Conduct Opinion #001 (1994). 52
Alaska State Bar Association, Ethics Opinion No. 85-4 (November 8, 1985). 34
Archer v. Ogden, 600 P. 2d 1223 (Oklahoma 1979). 162
Arizona Supreme Court Judicial Ethics Advisory Committee Opinion 00-02,
　April 9, 2000. 83
Arizona Supreme Court Judicial Ethics Advisory Committee, Opinion 96-8,
　August 15, 1996. 84
Arkansas Judicial Ethics Advisory Committee Advisory Opinion No. 94-04,
　March 8, 1994. 84
Arkansas Judicial Ethics Advisory Committee Opinion No. 96-01,
　December 29, 1999. 83
Attorney General of Maryland v. Waldron, 426 A. 2d 929, 933 (Maryland 1981). . . . 156
Attorney Grievance Commission of Maryland v. Alan C. Drew, 669 A. 2d 1344,
　1349 (1996). 35
Ball v. Roberts, 722 S. W. 2d 829 (Arkansas 1987). 162
Baltimore City Department of Social Services v. Bouknight, 493 U.S. 549; 100
　S. Ct. 900 (1990). 79
Bauer v. Bauer, 28 S. W. 3d 877, 885–887 (Missouri 2000). 104
Blackburn v. Mackey, 131 S. W. 3d 392 (Missouri 2004). 103

Board of Bar Overseers Office of the Bar Counsel Massachusetts Bar Disciplinary Decisions, Admonition 00-68, 2000 WL 34200490 (2000). 15
Brady v. Maryland, 373 U.S. 83, 87 (1963). 45
Broadman v. Commission On Judicial Performance, 77 Cal. Rptr. 2d 408, 417–418 (1999). 82
Broadway v. Kentucky Bar Association, 8 S. W. 3d 572 (Kentucky 2000). 40
Broadway v. Kentucky Bar Association, 997 S. W. 2d 467 (Kentucky 1999). 37
Byers v. Byers, 1996 WL 33348581 (Michigan 1996; unpublished). 105
California Compendium on Professional Responsibility, Formal Op. No 1983-71, at II A-223 (State Bar of California 1983). 83
Cantillon v. Superior Court, 309 P. 2d 890 (1957). 163
Care and Protection of Georgette, 785 N. E. 2d 356 (2003). 13
Carroll v. Superior Court, 124 Cal. Rptr. 2d 891 (Cal. App. Ct. 2002). 9
Carter v. Carter, 470 S. E. 2d 193, 201, fn. 10 (West Virginia 1996). 94
Cayan v. Cayan, 38 S. W. 3d 161 (2000). 104
Chrissy v. Ms. Dept. of Public Welfare, 995 F. 2d 595 (District Court, Fifth Circuit, 1993). 53
Christina L. v. Harry J. L., Jr., 1995 WL 788196, at 23 (Delaware Family Court 1995; unpublished). 98
City of New York Committee on Professional and Judicial Ethics, in Opinion Number 1997-2 (March 1997). 17
Civil Service Commission Of County. 22
Cohoon v. Cohoon, 770 N. E. 2d 885. 102
Cohoon v. Cohoon, 784 N. E. 2d 904, 905. 102
Colorado v. Karen J. Roose, 44 P. 2d 266 (Colorado 2002). 41
Commonwealth of Virginia Judicial Ethics Advisory Committee Opinion 99-7, Nov. 17, 1999. 82
Cuyahoga County Bar Association v. Stafford, 733 N. E. 2d 587 (Ohio 2000). 42
Cynthia D. v. Superior Court, 19 Cal. Rptr. 2d 608 (1993). 44
Davis v. Wickham, 917 S. W. 2d 414, 416 (Texas 1996). 105
De Los Santos v. Superior Court of Los Angeles County, 27 Cal. 3d 677, 613 P. 2d 233 (1980). 57
Delaware Judicial Ethics Advisory Committee Opinion 2001-1, May 15, 2001. 83
DeShaney v. Winnebago, 489 U.S. 189 (1989). 81
Disciplinary Action Against Shirley A. Dvorak, 611 N. W. 2d 147, 150–151 (North Dakota 2000). 41
Doe V. Lebbos (9th Cir., Nov. 4. 2003; Lexis 22632). 52
Ex Rel. Nebraska State Bar Association v. Thomas R. Zakrezewski, 560 N. W. 2d 150 (Nebraska 1997). 41
Fiedler v. Wisconsin Senate, 454 N. W. 2d 770, 772 (1990). 153
Florida Advisory Opinion No. 94-8, April 21, 1994. 84
Florida Supreme Court Judicial Ethics Advisory Committee Opinion No. 95-84, July 28, 1995. 83
Fox v. Willis, 822 A. 2d 1289 (2003). 30
Foxgate Homeowners' Association, Inc. v. Bramalea California, Inc., 108 Cal. Rptr. 2d 642 (2001). 111
Furey v. Commission On Judicial Performance, 240 Cal. Rptr. 859 (1987). 53
Gaston v. Gaston, 954 P. 2d 572, 574 (Alaska 1998). 104
Gensburg v. Miller, 37 Cal. Rptr. 2d 97 (1994). 45
Grove v. State Bar of California, 58 Cal. Rptr. 564 (1967). 36

Cases and Ethics Opinions 249

Guadalupe A. v. Superior Court, 285 Cal. Rptr. 570 (1991). 56
Harrison v. Mississippi Bar, 637 So. 2d 204 (Mississippi 1994). 38, 42
Harvey v. Harvey, 680 N. W. 2d 835 (Michigan Supreme Court 2004). 103
Hirsch v. Hirsch, 774 N.Y.S. 2d 48, 49–50 (New York 2004). 106
Hogoboom v. Superior Court, 59 Cal. Rptr. 2d 254, 267 (California 1997). 98
Hoopes v. Bradshaw, 80 A 1098 (1911). 149
Hunte v. Blumenthal, 680 A. 2d 1231 (1996). 81
Hustedt v. Worker's Compensation Appeals Board, 636 P. 2d 1139, 1146 (1981). 157
Imbler v. Pachtman, 424 U.S. 409, 428–29 (1976). 45
In re Celine R., 1 Cal. Rptr. 3d 432 (2003). 12
In re Christopher B., 147 Cal. Rptr. 390 (Cal. 1978). 81
In re Christopher S., 2002 WL 31033062 (California, September 12, 2002;
    unpublished). 103
In re Complaint as to the Conduct of the Honorable Ronald D. Schenck, 870
    P. 2d 185 (Oregon 1994). 55
In re Complaint of Wesley Scott Bridges, 728 P. 2d 863 (Oregon 1986). 37
In re Conduct of Schenck, 870 P. 2d 185 (Oregon 1994). 55
In re Coughlan, 2003 WL 22136814 (Minnesota App. 2003). 104
In Re Crate, 273 P. 617 (1928), rv'd, 279 P. 131 (Cal. 1929). 156
In re Diane, 494 N.Y.S. 2d 881 (1985). 81
In re Hancock, 136 Cal. Rptr. 901 (1977). 57
In re Hendel, (Connecticut Judicial Review Counsel, March 6, 1989 [unreported
    memorandum of decision] (WestLaw JDDD database). 82
In re Hey, 425 S.E. 2d 221, 222–224 (W.Va., 1992). 82
In re Honorable James P. Dunleavy, 838 A. 2d 338 (Maine 2003). 162
In re Inquiry Concerning Harrell, 414 S.E. 2d 36 (1992). 58
In re Inquiry of Broadbelt, 683 A.2d 543, 546 (N.J., 1996). 82
In re Jeanette H., 275 Cal. Rptr. 9, 15 (1990). 163
In re Julian L., 78 Cal. Rptr. 2d 839 (1998). 59
In re Lavine, 41 P. 2d 161, 163 (Cal. 1935). 157
In re Linda O., 95 Misc. 2d 744, 408 N.Y.S. 2d 308 (Fam. Ct. 1978). 25
In re Lucero L., 96 Cal Rptr. 2d 56 (2000). 54
In re Marriage of Timothy E. Slayton, 103 Cal. Rptr. 2d 545, 549–550 (2001). 103
In re Michael R., 7 Cal. Rptr. 2d 139 (1992). 59
In re Padget, 678 P. 2d 870 (Wyo. 1984). 25
In re Paternity of Amber J.R., 557 N.W. 2d 84 (Wisc. 1996). 25
In re Paternity of Stephanie R. N. v. Wendy L. D., 541 N.W. 2d 838;
    1995 WL 56300, 56318 (Wisc. 1995; unpublished opinion). 95
In Re Paul L. Wood, 686 So. 2d 35, 36 (Louisiana 1997). 36
In re R.W.B., 241 N.W. 2d 546 (N.D. 1976). 25
In Re Randall B. Kopf, 767 S.W. 2d 20 (Missouri 1989). 36
In re Robert J. v. Leslie M., 59 Cal. Rptr. 2d 905 (1997). 25
In re Zeth S., 108 Cal. Rptr. 2d 527 (2001). 18
In the Interest of A.V., 554 N.W. 2d 461 (North Dakota 1996). 54
In the Interest of J. A. W. N., A., 94 S. W. 3d 119, 121 (Texas 2002). 106
In the Interests of David A., 1998 WL 910258 (Conn. Super Ct., Dec. 18, 1998). 11
In the Marriage of Hanks, 10 P. 3d 42, 47 (Kansas 2000). 103
In the Matter of Anonymous Member of the South Carolina Bar, 377 S. E. 2nd 572
    (South Carolina 1989). 36
In the Matter of Carl S. Black, 941 P. 2d 1380 (Kansas 1997), 114. . . . . 38, 42

In the Matter of D. Keith Jennings, 50 P. 3d 506, 506–508 (Kansas 2002). 107
In the Matter of Daniel L. Swagerty, 739 P. 2d 937 (Kansas 1987). 39
In the Matter of Disciplinary Proceedings Against Curt M. Weber, 579 N.W. 2d 229
 (Wisconsin 1998). 41
In the Matter of Disciplinary Proceedings Against Daniel R. McNamara, 421
 N. W. 2d 513, 367–370 (Wisconsin 1988). 57
In the Matter of Disciplinary Proceedings Against Frank X. Kinast, 530 N.W.
 2d 387 (Wisconsin 1995). 40
In the Matter of H. Children, 608 N.Y.S. 2d 784, 785 (New York 1994). 10
In the Matter of Kopinski (1994) 2 Cal. State Bar Ct. 716, 728. 159
In the Matter of Robert C. Yacavino, 494 A. 2d 801 (New Jersey 1985). 42
In the Matter of Rodney H. Roberts, 366 S. E. 2d 679, 680 (Georgia 1988). 36
In The Matter of Terri Stroh Tweedly, 20 P. 3d 1245, 1247 (Kansas 2001). 36
In The Matter of the Application for Disciplinary Action Against Shirley A. Dvorak,
 611 N.W. 2d 147 (North Dakota Supreme Court, May 18, 2000). 50
In the Matter of the Application for the Discipline Of Richard W. Curott, 375 N. W.
 2d 472, 473–474 (1985). 36
*In the Matter of the Proceeding Pursuant to Section 44, Subdivision 4, of the
 Judiciary Law in Relation to Louis Grossman, A Judge of the Civil Court of the
 City of New York and Acting Justice of the Supreme Court, First Judicial District,
 Commission on Judicial Conduct State of New York, November 20,
 1984* (1984 WL 262214). 53
Iowa Supreme Court Board of Professional Ethics and Conduct v. Donna Lesyshen,
 585 N. W. 2d 281 (Iowa 1998). 38
J. A. R. v. Dept. Health & Rehab. Servs., 419 So. 2d 780 (Fla. App. 1982). 81
Jenkins v. County of Orange, 260 Cal. Rptr. 645 (1989). 45
Jones v. Sieve, 281 P. 2d 898 (1986). 56
Joni B. v. State, 549 N. W. 2d 411, 413 (1996). 153
Kelm v. Kelm, 749 N.E. 2d 299, 225–226 (Ohio 2001). 102
Kentucky Bar Association v. L.M. Tipton Reed, 814 S. W. 2d 927 (Kentucky 1991). . . . 36
Kentucky Bar Association v. Ronald A. Newcomer, 977 S. W. 2d 20 (Kentucky 1998). . . 14
Klemm v. Superior Court, 142 Cal. Rptr. 509, 512 (1977). 21
Kniskern v. Kniskern, 80 P. 3d 939, 941 (Colorado 2003). 104
L. L. H. v. S. C. H., 2002 WL 1943659, at 3 (Alaska 2002; unpublished). 104
Lassiter v. Department of Social Services, 101 S. Ct. 2155 (1981). 44
Lassiter v. Department of Social Services, 452 U.S. 18 (1981). 51
Leaf v. Supreme Court of the State of Wisconsin, 979 F. 2d. 589, 592–593 (1992). 152
Legal Servs. Corp. v. Velazquez, 531 U.S. 533 (2001). 7
(*Lester v. Lennane*, 101 Cal. Rptr. 2d 86 (2000)), and sexual harassment
 (*In Re Gordon*, 53 Cal. Rptr. 2d 788 (1996)). 53
Lester v. State Bar, 131 Cal. Rptr. 225 (1976). 37
Littman v. Van Hoek, 789 A. 2d 280, 281–282 (Pennsylvania 2001). 103
Lone Wolf v. Lone Wolf, 741 P. 2d 1187, 1190 (Alaska 1987). 103
Los Angeles County Bar Association Professional Responsibility and Ethics
 Committee, Formal Ethics Opinion No. 504, May 15, 2000. 72
Los Angeles County Department of Children and Family Services v. Superior Court,
 59 Cal. Rptr. 613 (1997). 18
Los Angeles County Dept. Children's Services v. Superior Court, 7 Cal. 4th 525 (1996). . 16
Louisiana Attorney General Opinion, No. 00-446 (February 19, 2001). 20

Cases and Ethics Opinions 251

Mackey v. Mackey, 2001 WL 111267 (Alaska Civil Appeal 2001). 111
Marchal v. Craig, 681 N. E. 2d 1160, 1162 (Indiana 1997). 103, 112
Martin v. Martin, 734 So. 2d 1133, 1136 (1999). 103
75 Maryland Attorney General Opinion 76 (February 8, 1990). 73
Maryland Bar Association Ethics Opinion 89-53 (1989). 80
Maryland v. Craig, 110 S. Ct. 3157 (1990). 68
(Matter of Ross, 428 A.2d 858 (Maine 1981)). 53
McCartney v. Commission on Judicial Qualifications, 116 Cal. Rptr. 260, 268
   (1974). 53
McClure v. Thompson, 323 F. 3d 1233 (9th Cir. 2003). 78
McCullough v. Commission on Judicial Performance, 260 Cal. Rptr. *557* (1989). 59
Merco Construction Engineers, Inc. v. Municipal Court, 581 P. 2d 636 (Cal 1978). . . . 157
Merrill Lynch, Fenner & Smith, Inc. v. Benjamin, 766 N.Y.S. 2d 1 (2003). 104
Michigan Bar Opinion CI-970 (1983). 80
Michigan State Bar Standing Committee on Professional and Judicial Ethics,
   Opinion RI316 (December 13, 1999). 39
Miller v. Miller, 620 A. 2d 1161, 1165 (Pennsylvania 1993). 104
Milstein v. County of Los Angeles, 2001 DJDAR 7514, 7515 (2001). 45
Minnesota v. White, 536 U.S. 765 (2002). 84
Mississippi State Attorney General Opinion No. 94-0408 (August 17, 1994). 48
Moeller v. Superior Court (1997). 72
Montigny v. Montigny, 233 N. W. 2d 463, 467 (Wisconsin 1975). 60
Moore v. Moore, 809 P. 2d 261 (Wyo. 1991). 57
Nashid v. Andrawis, 847 A. 2d 1908, 1101–1102 (Connecticut 2004). 103
Nevada Standing Committee On Judicial Ethics And Election Practices, Opinion
   JE99-002, April 5, 1999. 84
New Jersey v. Clark, 735 A. 2d 1, 4-6 (N. J. 1999). 18
New Jersey v. T.L.O., 469 U.S. 325 (1985). 81
New York Advisory Committee on Judicial Ethics, Opinion 88-150, December 8,
   1988 (1988 WL 547000). 25
New York Advisory Committee on Judicial Ethics, Opinion 89-104 (September 12,
   1989). 24
New York Advisory Committee on Judicial Ethics, Opinion 96-34, April 25, 1996
   (1996 WL 940912). 23
New York Attorney General Informal Opinion No. 88-54 (August 17, 1988). 20
New York State Bar Association, Committee On Professional Ethics, Opinion 751
   (May 6, 2002). 49
North Carolina State Bar Opinion Number RPC 175. 75
North Carolina State Bar Opinion RPC 14 (October 24, 1986). 18
North Carolina State Bar Revised Opinion Number RPC 120 (July 17, 1992). 75
North Dakota Attorney General Opinion (December 9, 1999) [1999 WL 1939465]. . . . 17
Obrien v. Jones, 96 Cal. Rptr. 2d 205 (2000). 158
Office of the Attorney General of Kansas, Opinion No. 90-33 (March 19, 1990). 49
Oklahoma Attorney General Opinion No. 00-15 (February 23, 2000). 85
Oklahoma Bar Association v. Max M. Berry, 969 P. 2d 975 (Oklahoma 1998). 13
Oregon Attorney General Opinion Number OP-5543 (June 12, 1984) at 1–2
   [1984 WL 192140]. 17
Paige Kenal. B. v. Molepske, 580 N.W. 2d 289 (Wisconsin 1998). 81
Panzer v. Doyle, 680 N. W. 2d 666, 684–685 (2004). 151

People v. Aron, 962 P. 2d 261 (Colorado 1998). 37
People v. Baird, 772 P. 2d 110, 111 (Colorado 1989). 36
People v. Barbara J. Felker, 770 P. 2d 402, 404 (Colorado 1989). 35
People v. Chappell, 927 P. 2d 829 (Colorado 1996). 38
People v. Dowhan, 951 P. 2d 905, 905–907 (Colorado 1998). 38
People v. Finley, 519 N. E. 2d 898 (Illinois 1988). 162
People v. Mercer, 35 P. 3d 598 (Colorado 2001). 38
People v. Mucklow, No. 00PDJ010 (Colorado, December 16, 2000). 51
People v. Paulson, 930 P. 2d 582, 583 (Colorado 1997). 36
People v. Puttman, 61 P. 961, 962 (1902). 158
People v. Rolfe (Colorado Case No. 98SA114, August 10, 1998). 51
Riley v. Erie Lackawanna R. Company, 119 Misc. 2d 619, 463 N.Y.S. 2d 986
 (1983). 57
River West, Inc. v. Nickel, 234 Cal. Rptr. 33, 41 (1987). 22
Roberts v. Commission on Judicial Performance, 661 P. 2d 1064 (1983). 52
Rozmus v. Rozmus, 595 N.W. 2d *893* (Nebraska 1999). 49
Santa Clara County Counsel Attorneys Association v. Woodside, 7 Cal. 4th 525;
 28 Cal. Rptr. 2d 617 (1994). 157
Santosky v. Kramer, 102 S. Ct. 1388 (1982). 44
Santosky v. Kramer, 455 U.S. 745 (1982). 51
Scott v. County of Los Angeles, 32 Cal. Rptr. 643 (1994). 45
Shaftsbury v. Hannam, 23 English Reports 177, Ch. 1677. 101
Smith v. Organization of Foster Families, 431 U. S. 816, 834 (1977). 55
Smith v. Superior Court, 440 P. 2d 65, 73 (Cal. 1968). 5
Soliz v. Williams III, 88 Cal. Rptr. 2d 184, 195–196 (1999). 82
South Carolina Attorney General Informal Opinion, April 2, 1996 (1996 WL
 265508). 33
South Carolina Bar Ethics Advisory Committee Opinion 97-15 (December 1997). 40
South Carolina Bar Ethics Advisory Committee, Advisory Opinion 89-01 (1989),
 at 1-3. 19
South Carolina Bar Ethics Advisory Committee, Opinion 85-21 (1985). 75
State Bar of California Formal Op. 1984-84. 22
*State Bar of Michigan Standing Committee On Professional and Judicial Ethics,
 Opinion Number CI-427*. 85
*State Bar of Michigan Standing Committee On Professional and Judicial Ethics,
 Opinion Number JI-76* (December 9, 1993) (1993 WL 566228). 85
State ex. Rel. Fiedler v. Wisconsin Senate, 454 N. W. 2d 770, 773 (1990). 152
State v. Bayfield, 531 N. W. 2d 32, 34 (1995). 155
State v. Bolin, 922 S. W. 2d 870, 873 (Tenn. 1996). 54
State v. Horn, 594 N. W. 2nd 772 (1999). 154
State v. Simmons, 299 So. 2d 906 (Louisiana 1974). 54
Succession of Wallace, 574 So. 2d 348 (Louisiana 1991). 162
Tara M. v. City of Philadelphia, 145 F. 3d 625 (3rd Cir. 1998). 81
Tennenbaum v. New York City, 222 N.Y.L.J. 25, col. 3 (October 15, 1999). 87
Tennessee Attorney General Opinion No. 93-10 (February 3, 1993). 18
The Florida Bar v. Charles F. Wishart, 543 So. 2d 1250 (Florida 1989). 41
The Florida Bar v. Jeffrey Evan Cosnow, 797 So. 2d 1255 (Florida 2001). 16
The Florida Bar v. Susan K. Glant, 645 So. 2d 962 (Florida 1994). 76
The Florida Bar v. Walter Benton Dunagan, 731 So. 2d 1237 (1999). 14

Cases and Ethics Opinions 253

U. S. v. Gonzales, 765 F. 2d 1393 (9th Cir. 1985). 57
Utah Attorney General Opinion No. 77-027, October 14, 1977. 33
Utah Ethics Advisory Committee Informal Opinion 01-1, January 25, 2001. 84
Utah Ethics Advisory Committee Informal Opinion 97-4, August 28, 1997. 57
Utah Informal Ethics Opinion 99-6, September 23, 1999. 83
Utah Informal Opinion No. 88-2, April 15, 1988. 83
Utah State Bar Ethics Advisory Committee Opinion 97-12 (January 23, 1998). 77
Utah State Bar Ethics Opinion Number 95-06 (July 28, 1995). 70
Veasey v. Veasey, 560 P. 2d 382 (Alaska 1977). 57
Virginia Ethics Advisory Committee Opinion 00-3, March 27, 2000. 83
Virginia Judicial Ethics Advisory Committee in Opinion 99-7, November 17, 1999. . . . 84
Virginia Judicial Ethics Advisory Committee Opinion 00-4, May 8, 2000. 57
Virginia Judicial Ethics Advisory Committee Opinion 01-04, March 28, 2001. 83
Virginia State Bar Opinion 1076 (1988). 80
Vitakis-Valcine, 793 So. 2d 1094, 1099 (Florida 2001). 108
Vogt v. Vogt, 455 N. W. 2d 471, 474–475 (Minnesota 1990). 105
Wayno v. Wayno, 756 So. 2d 1024, 1025 (Florida 2000). 103
Wenger v. Commission on Judicial Performance, 175 Cal. Rptr. 420 (1981). 56
West Virginia Judicial Investigation Commission Opinion, November 25, 1997. 84
Wisconsin Judicial Conduct Advisory Committee in Opinion 99-3, April 14, 1999. 84
Wisconsin Judicial Conduct Advisory Committee Opinion 01-1, January 8, 2002. 83
Wisniewski v. Clary, 120 Cal. Rptr. 176, 179 (Cal. Ct. App. 1975). 160

Index

age, 2, 4, 8, 9, 30, 31, 87, 227
   competence to decide, 30, 31
alternative dispute resolution, 116, 117, 119, 145
   advantages, 93, 95, 100, 103
   bad faith, 110, 111
   bias, 97
   binary solutions, 92, 93
   binding arbitration, 102, 104
   confidentiality, 93, 105, 108, 110–117
   disadvantages, 95
   discretion to review, 103
   domestic violence, 96, 98, 99, 105
   duty of candor, 107–109
   evolution, 100
   family law cases, 89, 90. *See*
   formal training, 91
   good faith, 106, 107, 109, 110
   litigation critics, 92
   mediation, 50, 89, 90–100, 104–106, 109–119, 145
   neutrality, 93, 94, 97, 106, 110, 112, 117, 118, 125
   overloaded systems, 88
   prejudice, 97
   pressures to informally resolve, 89
   pro se, 89
   public trials, 100
   puffing, 107, 108
   self-determination, 118
   tribunal, 42, 46, 92, 107–109, 137, 139
   voluntary, 90, 94, 96, 98, 111, 117
   waiver, 50, 65, 66, 112, 115, 125–127, 135
appearance of impropriety, 20, 23, 24
attorney-client relationship, 14, 71, 72, 78

competence, 27, 37, 43, 49, 50, 81, 91, 124, 125, 127, 153, 159, 162, 163
conflicts of interest, 7–15, 18, 20, 22, 23, 74, 126, 135, 137
right to counsel, 61, 62, 65, 66, 89, 123, 136, 154

best interest, 8, 9, 11, 17–19, 29, 30, 33–35, 48, 52, 54, 59, 68, 72, 76, 81, 87, 91, 94, 95, 101–104, 118, 123, 128–130, 132, 133
burden of proof, 25

characteristics, 92
children
   attorney, 103, 106, 108, 109, 119, 121, 128–131, 133, 134, 159
   competence, 4, 30, 31
   confidentiality, 47, 68–70, 72–74, 77, 81, 82
   conflicts of interest, 2, 7, 9
   crime or bodily harm, 72, 147
   custody, 1–6, 8, 10, 11, 13–16, 19, 23, 25, 28–31, 33, 35–43, 50, 51, 53–55, 68, 73, 75–77, 88–90, 92–108, 111, 113, 114, 117–122, 124–127, 129, 140, 141, 147, 148, 151, 152, 158, 163
   dependency, 1, 2, 5–10, 12, 13, 16, 18–20, 23–26, 28, 29, 31, 33, 35, 37–40, 42–44, 46, 48–52, 54–56, 59–68, 74–76, 81, 82, 85–88, 90–96, 98–102, 106–108, 111, 114, 115, 117–132, 134–138, 140–143, 147, 148, 151–154, 156, 158, 159, 161–163
   due process, 44, 51, 59–61, 65, 77, 78, 81, 92, 93, 97, 100, 110, 115, 116, 121–123, 137

255

children (*cont.*)
  siblings, 2, 8–13, 87, 135
  standing, 4, 5, 13, 27, 39, 80, 94, 120, 123–125, 154, 161
competency, 4, 5, 27–32, 43, 49, 73, 74, 120, 124, 125, 127, 161, 163
  American Academy of Matrimonial Lawyers, 27, 31, 70
  Fordham Conference Report, 31, 32
  illegal conduct, 38
  inexperience, 37, 42
  Jean Koh Peters, 32
  parents' attorneys, 13, 35–38, 40, 42, 43, 74, 76
  separation of powers, 24, 25, 148, 151–154, 156–163
confidentiality, 2, 9, 10, 14, 17, 19, 33, 34, 47, 68–70, 72–74, 77, 81, 82, 93, 105, 108, 110–117, 127, 134, 135, 147
  death or substantial bodily harm, 69, 70
  dual role, 23–25, 33, 75, 133, 134
  Fifth Amendment, 25, 78, 79
  guardian ad litem, 2, 18, 19, 29, 30, 33, 39–41, 53, 57, 72–74, 76, 132, 133
  inadvertence, 80
  mandated child abuse reporters, 71, 75
  posttraumatic stress, 69
  privileged, 41, 79–81
conflicts of interest, 2, 7–16, 18, 20, 22–24, 74, 126, 134, 135, 137
  appearance of impropriety, 20, 23, 24
  caseworker, 21, 206
  child clients, 69, 74
  collateral proceedings, 14, 114
  continuance, 25, 52, 59
  disqualification of attorney, 22, 34
  dual role, 23, 24, 33, 75, 133, 134
  government attorney, 49
  immunity, 25, 45
  membership in organizations, 26
  multiple representation, 8, 9, 12
  parents' attorney, 13
  part-time, 23, 75, 76
  recuse, 24, 26, 56
  separate proceedings, 15
  siblings, 9–13, 87, 135, 177, 197
contempt, 28, 68, 78, 138, 146, 150, 159
counseling clients, 47, 117
cross-examination, 50

discovery, 40, 50, 51, 90, 93
  exculpatory information, 45, 47, 51, 52, 114, 115
  informal, 3, 40, 43, 51, 63, 90, 94
disqualification, 10, 22, 26, 34, 55

evidence, 3, 7, 24, 32, 38, 41, 44, 45, 47, 48, 51, 52, 54–56, 64, 70, 76–81, 87, 94, 97, 107, 112–116, 128–132, 134, 138, 141, 146, 150
  ex parte communications, 38, 57
  judges' fact investigation, 56

family law, 1, 2, 4, 26, 27, 49, 55, 88–90, 95, 121, 123
  custody, 25, 36, 39, 40, 41
  dispute resolution, 3, 50
fraud, 52, 105, 108, 109, 137
  alternative dispute resolution, 105
  confidential data, 8, 10, 14, 68, 69, 71, 78, 80
  confidential facts, 81
  duty to disclose, 47, 139
  silence as fraud, 22, 155
frivolous actions, 27, 130, 131, 140
future crimes/threats, 113
  harm to clients, 138, 147

government or department attorneys, 6, 49
  best interest of children, 2–4
  competence, 27, 31, 35
  counseling, 6
  criminal cases distinguished, 25, 54
  justice versus zealous advocate, 3, 6, 29, 33, 42, 48, 57, 137
government or department attorneys
  justice versus zealous advocate, 34
guardian ad litem, 18, 33, 39–41, 57, 72–74, 76, 132, 133, 141
  differences from attorneys, 2, 19, 29, 33, 40
  duties, 18, 29, 30, 33
  guardian ad litem, 40

incompetency, 30, 31, 35, 38, 61, 74, 125, 126, 138, 139
  children, 31, 126

judges, 6, 23–26, 28, 35, 52, 54, 56, 58–60, 74, 82, 83, 85–87, 92, 103, 107, 108, 117, 118, 136, 148, 150, 153, 154, 157–159
  appearance of impropriety, 23, 24
  bias, 55, 56
  disqualification, 26

Index

duty to educate the public, 6, 60
ex parte communications, 38, 57

legal Education, 85, 120, 146, 152, 153, 161, 163
loyalty, 2, 8–10, 14, 17, 34, 47, 73, 74, 77, 81, 127, 134, 135, 137, 139, 159, 163

right to counsel, 62, 89, 121, 123, 154
children, x
competence, 5, 35, 37, 43, 62, 81, 91
due process, 44, 51, 59–61, 65, 78, 81, 92, 93, 97, 100, 110, 115, 116, 121–123, 137
parents, 61, 62, 65, 66, 136, 154

separation of powers, 24, 25, 148, 151–154, 156–163
administrative agencies, 146, 151, 163
attorney-client relationship, 9, 22, 61, 62, 145, 146, 148, 158, 159, 162, 163
bar associations, 92, 146, 151
California Judicial Council, 127, 160
Catch-22, 5, 22, 63, 76, 130, 146, 159
comity, 149, 151, 152, 155, 156, 160, 161
competent counsel, 49, 61, 64, 122, 159, 161, 163
concurrent jurisdiction, 148–150, 156, 157, 159, 160
delegation of power, 151

executive, 2, 24, 25, 145, 146, 148, 150–152, 155, 156, 158, 163
fee schedule, 154, 155
history, 44, 65, 70, 148, 151, 152
inherent power, 101, 148, 151, 153–156, 159, 160
Megan's laws, 147
multivariate test, 153
Sarbanes-Oxley Act of 2002, 146
the public, 6, 8, 26, 28, 45, 60, 68, 75, 83, 85, 86, 117, 145, 146, 150, 153
wisconsin, 71, 95, 151–155

third Parties, 100, 102
counsel, 2–4, 6–8, 10, 12, 13, 15, 18–23, 28, 33, 36, 37, 39–41, 43, 44–49, 51, 53, 61–67, 78–80, 82, 83, 89, 99, 105, 106, 109, 120–142, 146, 150, 153–155, 157, 159, 161, 163

withdrawal of counsel, 14, 73, 76, 162
witnesses, 15, 23, 41, 48, 50, 52, 53, 89, 115, 127
access to, 41

zealousness, 27, 28, 33, 37, 43, 47, 81, 127, 134, 159, 163
children's attorneys, 7, 28–30, 35, 69, 72
civility, 42

For EU product safety concerns, contact us at Calle de José Abascal, 56–1°, 28003 Madrid, Spain or eugpsr@cambridge.org.

www.ingramcontent.com/pod-product-compliance
Ingram Content Group UK Ltd.
Pitfield, Milton Keynes, MK11 3LW, UK
UKHW010900060825
461487UK00012B/1250